SportCult

Cultural Politics

A series from the Social Text Collective

Aimed at a broad interdisciplinary audience, these volumes seek to intervene in debates about the political direction of current theory and practice by combining contemporary analysis with a more traditional sense of historical and socioeconomic evaluation.

Randy Martin

Toby Miller

editors

A Cultural

Politics Book

for the Social

Text Collective

SportCult

Cultural Politics / Volume 16

University of Minnesota Press

Minneapolis ▸ London

GV
706.5
.S73896
1999

Published by the University of Minnesota Press
111 Third Avenue South, Suite 290
Minneapolis, MN 55401-2520
http://www.upress.umn.edu

Printed in the United States of America on acid-free paper

Library of Congress Cataloging-in-Publication Data

SportCult / Randy Martin and Toby Miller, editors.
     p.   cm. — (Cultural politics ; v. 16)
     Portions previously appeared as a special issue of Social text, v. 50, spring 1997.
     Includes bibliographical references.
     ISBN 0-8166-3183-2 (hardcover). — ISBN 0-8166-3184-0 (pbk.)
     1. Sports—Social aspects. 2. Sports—Anthropological aspects. 3. Sports—Political aspects. 4. Sports—Economic aspects. I. Martin, Randy. II. Miller, Toby. III. Title:
Sport cult. IV. Series: Cultural politics (Minneapolis, Minn.) ; v. 16.
     GV706.5.S73896   1999
     306.4′83—dc21   98-45941

11 10 09 08 07 06 05 04 03 02 01 00 99   10 9 8 7 6 5 4 3 2 1

Contents

Part IV. Signifying Sport

Acknowledgments

This book got its start as a special issue of *Social Text* (volume 50, spring 1997), edited by Toby Miller with an assist by Randy Martin. Half of what appears here first appeared there. Our coeditors at the journal came through for us in myriad respects (as they always do). Anne McClintock put us through to Qadri Ismail, and Andrew Ross hooked us up with Grant Farred, while beyond *Social Text*, Fred Myers connected us to Heather Levi. All the contributors have our thanks for their work, their good cheer, and their aplomb at distance learning, from which we have gained much. Monica Marciczkiewicz, the managing editor of *Social Text*, is a wonder, and worked tirelessly to bring the issue together. Bruce Robbins guided the book into its berth in the Cultural Politics series with his usual agility.

At the University of Minnesota Press, Micah Kleit was a superb editor prior to his departure—intelligent, inspiring, and encouraging. Jennifer Moore was most cooperative in getting the manuscript ready for publication. The production staff has honed and refined what you see before you. Two anonymous readers gave acute commentary and helped us to see the project whole. To all, our deep appreciation.

Toby would like to give a nod to all those sadistic physical education teachers in high schools, whose best efforts were insufficient to make him hate all sport. Randy is likewise appreciative that the formative traumas of competitive tennis and swimming have not kept him deskbound in later life. As this book aims to bring together sport as work and play, it is worth raising a glass to the friendship that emerged out of this editorial collaboration.

Randy Martin   Toby Miller
Clinton Hill, Brooklyn   Greenwich Village, NYC

Fielding Sport:
A Preface to Politics?

Randy Martin and Toby Miller

For a long time now, studies of sport have run by the numbers, played by the books. We have come to believe that we know what we need to know about sport's popularity from its demographics. We have learned to assume that if we master the rules, we are already inside the practice. Yet a good bit of sport's appeal lies beyond the quantifiably rational and the visibly cognitive. A close encounter with the bodies at play and at work in athletic contests promises to help us rethink not only the parameters of sport itself, but the very conception of the practical and the popular as they have been understood in cultural studies more broadly.

The pervasiveness of sport, its dispersion throughout all manner of sites, may *describe* its popularity without offering much by way of *explanation*. More strongly from a conceptual vantage point, what allows sport to be so pervasive also affords a view of society set in motion. The places where sporting activity transpires are the consequence of a whole array of mobilizations that form our collective physique, by drawing bodies together and sorting them out. The very proliferation of sites needs to be explained in its own right, and cannot be taken as simply so many fixed receptacles of a series of events. Here, participation figures much more explicitly in what makes for practice. In the complex coordinations of doing and viewing (so much in evidence among accomplished athletes and fans), far more is getting done than can be represented in clear acts of decision. For every point made, far more has been gathered in training and concentration than could possibly be counted. As such, sport indicates that there is always something excessive in the practical accomplishment of goal-oriented tasks, and suggests what is strange in otherwise quotidian involvements. Enmeshed in all the standard means of accounting, paragon of the idea that the well-tempered self means business, sport appears to affirm a rigid distinction between fact and value, talent and reward, even as it belies this distinction in a promise of transcendence and the prospect of other avenues of social development. As a way into these various contributions, Toby Miller's introductory essay tracks the various guises under which sport appears and, by so doing, provides a guided tour through which we can begin to assemble all the moments and relations that constitute society-in-sport and appear throughout this volume.

The essays in "Building Nations," the first of the four sections that make up this collection, problematize the whole idea of development within a national frame. Against the notion that the path to progress has already been paved with respect to postcolonial nation building, the transnational traffic in sport combines unevenly with movements to direct social advance on national soil. May Joseph's look at the imagery of martial arts under Tanzanian socialism, Grant Farred's take on cricket after South African apartheid, and Qadri Ismail's refiguring of the violence of state making in Sri Lanka ask us to focus on collective practices through which notions of progress get enacted. If the nation can no longer be taken as a stable receptacle of society, the belief in a natural attachment of the self to the body is no more secure. The pieces on aerobics by Randy Martin and Michael Real and the explorations of bodybuilding and wrestling by Jon Stratton and Heather Levi, which constitute the second section, examine what kinds of selves get made when bodies are both the subject and the object of a whole menu of techniques. "Building Bodies" reveals the labor process that is part of culture, such that *working out* refers not only to these more specialized and restricted practices, but to a whole movement of the ethos of productivity into the domain of leisure.

The money made and the usefulness invented through games and their accoutrement have become a familiar business proposition. Yet when the work of making sport is considered more expansively, as the means through which the energies of a social body are gathered and set in motion, a more complex economy is suggested. Although much sporting stuff is of the standard sort of commodity, the activity itself sees the moment of production united with consumption—as soon as a play is made, it is rung up as a sale. Players can be inventoried, plays can be rewound and reviewed, broadcasts can be delayed and repeated, but because consumption is part of the participation that makes for the activity itself, the conventional separations in an economy of exchange do not consistently apply. Even the now familiar claim that popular culture is a simulacrum, an effusion of copies without an original, seems credibly reversed in sport. The copying, the endless mimicry of moves, replenishes the body with all the fullness of an originary moment.

The essays in "Buying and Selling Nations and Bodies," our third section, place the social representations of self and society offered by sport into the circuitry of a global capitalist economy. The media magnate as news maker discussed by David Rowe and Jim McKay, the diffusion of golf course design in Bradley Klein's study, and the effusion of basketball trash talk monitored by Gitanjali Maharaj are more than accounts of new forms of trade. These essays help us think about what capitalism has become of late, where not only what appears on the market, but the very means by which commodities move, defies the imagery of fixed components of exchange and is both dazzling and disorienting.

These novel modes of transit for money and meaning suggest the larger usefulness of sport for studying society on the run, or, more properly, one that runs from its own familiarities and stabilities in search of self-expansion. Bruce Robbins's reworking of the upward mobility narrative, Amanda Smith and her colleagues' dialogue on the difference women make to how sport is reported, and Rosemary Coombe's rejoining of body and sign in sports trademarks are all exercises in the innovative politics of representation that sport study makes available. These essays make up the final section, "Signifying Sport," which is equally to do with how signs are put into play, assembled, and reconstituted through the heavy breathing and sweat of sport in the world.

The confluence of movements among bodies, where production and consumption are inextricably connected, promises to give greater material weight to what has come to be loosely referred to as *cultural flow*, a phrase meant to suggest that meaning and value accrue to, and substantially form, signs as they move through space. Sport demetaphorizes global flows and actualizes affiliations and common fantasies that are too often treated only in their virtuality. What once may have seemed to be a movement only in one direction, from center to periphery, an image distributed simultaneously to so many local screens, can now provide a picture of more active response by sporting publics.

This does not mean that attending to sport is a sufficient condition for storming other political arenas. At the very least, however, when the practical and the popular are amalgamated in the way we have been suggesting, it becomes more difficult to cordon off dimensions of social life that are otherwise inseparable. Thus the moments of identity-in-difference (the vast diversity of modes of selfhood) and political economy (the power that issues from the ability to control production and distribution) can become reintegrated within the same problematic by following the travails of the social body. This may in turn offer a different way in to the relationship between the politics of recognition (how cultural differences are accorded value) and productionist paradigms (where what we make gets assessed for what it is worth). Because sport is so deeply implicated with cultural difference and social division, it is easier to begin with the intersection of political forces, rather than taking the mutual insinuation of race, class, gender, sex, and nation as somehow discrete origins that must be made to arrive at a common terminus. Although it is unlikely that sport as an activity is unique in being able to stage this conceptual reintegration, once we appreciate that these seemingly unconnected hands have been drawn from the same deck, we can begin to put other dealings back in touch.

The larger project joined by the essays that compose this volume entails a rethinking of our approach to sport that can enlarge the field of cultural politics. The scholars assembled hail from many disciplinary quarters and have in their past work displayed various proximities to the matter of sport. All told, the book draws on a certain eccentricity of expertise in an effort to decenter convention. Our aim is to contest the stories that can and do get told through sport, whether as a cultural frame of reference meant to explain the success (or failure) of individuals, the wealth (or poverty) of nations, or the urges to love and war. At the same time, it is important to remember that the domains of cultural, social, and political theory are themselves immersed in forms of competing allegory. We cannot take for granted the field of metaphors and dreams out of which we spin our critical explanations. Sporting metaphors have slid so readily into the annals of social life, and yet they have remained, for the most part, critically un-digested. Given that sport continues to rivet our attention, metaphorization may be irresistible. At the very least, critical analysis can give the beneficia-ries of cliché a run for their money. And that may be an allegory worth competing for.

Defining Sport

With great persistence, thinking about sport seems to overwhelm or at least to complicate the terms and categories we use to comprehend it. This prob-lem is evident in any attempt at definition, but does not relieve us of the responsibility to specify what we are talking about. Consider this as a can-didate: a competitive form of play organized according to a definite set of rules and determinate boundaries of time and space. Fair enough. Or is it? The competitive aspect of sport is perhaps the most freighted allegorically. Competition is so frequently treated as a first cause, an essential feature of either human nature or the real world, that it is difficult to trace its particu-lar effects and operation. Opponents face off in a Manichaean contest that will render one a victor and the other vanquished. Competition is both means and ends, an animating spirit that infests the body and compels excel-lence, and the just reward, the final judgment that affirms—with unrivaled clarity—the purpose of the event. The contestants meet on equal terrain, their fate is theirs alone to determine, and in the end both are the better for having revealed the truth of their character.

As with most tautology, this formulation conceals much, not the least of which is competition's presumed opposite principle, cooperation. It is not simply that a preoccupation with winning can distract one from the task at hand, nor is it a certainty that the desire to win gives one the means to do so. And although winning is definitive, like all other accumulations, its moment of realization is fragile, and yields to the demand to start all over again. When we move from the tabulation of results to a view of the game from the perspective of doing it, the competition itself requires closely articulated coordination—even if the sport is a solo affair.

In sport, the body is strategic, its intelligence operates in motion, and its ability to anticipate what the other may do—which lies at the heart of the effect called competition—already presupposes a deep dependence on those others in the contest, to make one's own participation possible. Yet what are marshaled as means in this body far outlive their ends. The pleasures of participation are carried as much by this successful incorporation of capacity to play as by the final destination of victory or defeat. Is this as true of gymnastics as it is of rugby? Of the javelin as of table tennis? In different forms perhaps, mediated through different techniques and protocols, but a leap, a throw, a kick or stroke is never free of what precedes or follows it. Whatever the biomechanics that could see through these gestures as so much exercise physiology, the difference lies in how they get reassembled, so that the game becomes whole, but also moves.

And what of the roaring fans, as Robert De Niro wants to remind Wesley Snipes in the baseball stalker film *The Fan* (1996)—a work that may have tried to generate its own audience around discontent at the prior season's players' strike? Are the fans not the final authority for which the player is obliged to perform? De Niro's character, a disemployed knife salesman, reaches across the curtain of anonymity that separates the many from the few to compel his $40 million hero to take the game as a matter of life and death. More prosaically, what of the vast interdependencies of transportation infrastructure, of promotion and telemarketing, that allow a public to assemble, or the teams of groundskeepers and office staff, ticket takers and trainers, to put the team on the field? Fandom may reveal more about present conditions of subsistence than can be gleaned from calorie counting. Identifications with teams, stars, and other cultural entities appear as necessities that also run high surpluses. The tax revenues that support new stadium construction, or the income that cable television companies receive, represent monies channeled within a larger economy that does not distinguish among sports followers and detractors. Perhaps this is starting to sound a bit like capitalism itself—mutual association of interdependent labor, rationalized techniques of production and consumption, privately mandated allocations of social wealth, all at an immense scale, that goes by the name of competitive individualism. If so, then it should be clear that the allegorical power of sport is right on the money.

But surely capitalism is not the mother of sportive invention. Competitive contests hail from many historical contexts and cultural climes. That these practices share the same ideological resonances of competition and individualism should in no way be assumed, nor should the very meaning of sport be taken as particularly stable (especially if—as among the Mayans or the Trobriand Islanders—it *is* a politics that formally articulates with the processes of governance, and not simply something political that can be appropriated by various constituencies). Yet perhaps one reason that sport can carry such allegorical baggage, across space and time, lies with its liberation from any obligation other than the pursuit of leisure. Conversely, the proliferation of sport in society is said to derive from exactly the same source. But now we are back to a bundle of arguments that are not specific to sport, but are said to describe modernity itself—functional differentiation of activities into separate spheres, where each summons its own purpose as a thing in itself. Sport is its own master, played for the fun of it. Now this vaunted domain of leisure was won for the many by means of a protracted struggle over the duration of the working day. Given that the shadows are lengthening over this glorious accomplishment in the form of longer workweeks and lower wages, it is far from certain that the future of an expanding allocation of leisure time is secure—although the outlook for sport may be a safer bet.

But aside from the tendency of available free time to rise or fall, there is a thornier problem with the idea of sport as leisure. Obviously, what is play for some is work for others. And what is pleasurable for all is thoroughly shot through with exchange value, whether in the form of purchasing spectatorial leisure time or of suiting oneself in the condiments of play. More difficult to sort out, however, are the ways in which sport is different from work. The self-disciplining of the body, the maximization of efficiency, the drive to succeed—all sound, even for the devoted amateur, like the continuation of a work ethos through other means. In terms of some phenomenology of a laboring kinesthetic, what compels exertion may ultimately succumb to release in moments of endorphin-driven euphoria. This is a promise of self-realization on which few jobs can deliver. On the other hand, for professional athletes, no matter what their salaries, the surpluses they generate are taken from them just as readily as from any assembly-line worker. This is complicated, no doubt, when megastars incorporate, circulating their name recognition and making their own share of investments. Players' associations lack the control over labor markets that an American Medical Association once enjoyed, and are far from the kinds of policy interventions that an American Federation of Labor might consider necessary to defend its members' interests.

True, in a pickup game of one sort or another, the boss is likely to be absent, and the spoils of labor are distributed among the participants. And yet as a fantasy structure, the narratives of upward mobility based on the very real movement that athletics demands remind us that work-driven ideals need not be fully repressed before they return. And speaking of tales of self-advancement, it should be apparent that these are not universal narratives. It could be said that the various sports themselves have become great sorting machines for the likes of racial, gendered, sexual, and national orientation. No doubt, we are generally informed that it is just the reverse, that "white men can't jump," or that in tennis, women play strategy to men's power. In a climate of ever-renewable xenophobia and homophobia, immigrants from Cuba or the Dominican Republic are somehow acceptable in the great American pastime, and diving can countenance stars like Greg Louganis, who happens to be gay. These stories stick for all their exceptions, and seem to affirm the notion that there is a natural playground for all of us, even if the very different work that play is doing for each of us somehow gets confused.

Part of what helps to naturalize sport is the presumed objectivity of the rules. This is law for the rest of us. On the streets, in the parks, players may provide their own counsel. In the big shows, they must be represented. Rules not only regulate peaceably, they can also run afoul of play or players. Sport is policed more actively/noticeably than daily life, its every move scrutinized for transgression, keeping alive the century-old anxiety that a crowd in motion is a threat to public order and must be constantly kept within bounds. It is also one location where the lawgivers can be directly contested by those subject to their authority. No doubt this can have its own consequences for the participants, and the rules themselves get preserved through the dispute, as if officiating were an instance of sheer hermeneutic willpower. More profoundly, the very tension between the normative, which rules typically enforce, and the exceptional, usually considered a form of normative breach, is vividly displayed in sport. The star player does not cheat so much as transcend normative constraint, and in this moment of transcendence, the rules themselves appear invisible or marginal—how *did* Utah Jazz forward Bryon Russell fall to the floor as Michael Jordan made the winning points of the 1998 NBA finals? And yet such beatification of the exalted draws upon an excluded ugliness; the rules and their expression are ultimately interdependent.

Yet there is much in sporting activity that eludes formal regulation. Boxing proscribes low blows but certainly sanctions violence. The homosociality that flies under a banner of athletics celebrates a bodily lust that avoids sexual energies in name only. This mixing of sex and violence is considered healthy in sport by those who would uphold the boundary between the two in other arenas of life—an exceptionalism that may suggest a much closer affinity between these two bodily drives than is typically accepted. For contact sports especially, this spectacle of normative violence not officially sanctioned by the state raises the question of whether such events exercise the legitimate use of violence that Max Weber claims is monopolized by the state. Where the materiality of the physical leaves off and the metaphorical picks up is not so clear here. The ultimate and extreme fighting contests, in which combatants shed real blood, do not come in a neatly removable jacket of metaphor. Nor is the bone-shattering violence done to prepubescent gymnasts lost on those who trade in teenage injury and salvation. The wounds these practices inflict are not describable as merely metaphorical suffering or cautionary tales.

To introduce metaphor where these bodies have been already affirms that sport slips out of its concrete location and bounded sites and operates in mythic as well as real time. Surely the mythos of sport is part of what engages participants in some collective quest. But the question of sport's occurrence is made more complex when we reflect on the *practice* of participation—what people bring with them, what they give, and what they get. When participation is examined more closely and critically, one casualty will be the notion of passive spectatorship, a generalized image of social life that sidelines people's agency as the parade passes by them. The idea that watching someone else doing something anesthetizes the mind and renders the eye a mere opening through which life pours in gained currency under the banner of a society of the spectacle. Accordingly, in a society saturated with mass media, pleasures would be taken visually and vicariously. More pointedly, the capacity to act in the world would be substituted for the action that passed before a person's field of vision. While this perspective was meant to signal the dystopic aspects of an otherwise triumphant constitution of mass publics, it also tended to fulfill its own prophecy by eliminating the prospect of critical engagement with social acts, reducing all communication to visual reception. It *is* important to be skeptical when public gatherings serve private ends, but it is also necessary to appreciate that spectatorship is a form of rhetoric. Watching frequently leads to argument, to bawdy enactment, and to other kinesthetic diversions. As a perspective on how publics get formed, participation corporealizes the disembodied spectator. In short, the active/passive opposition associated with the society of spectacle is confused in sport.

A similar flattening of critical participation can be seen in the theatrical model of catharsis. Based on conventions of Greek tragedy, this framework assumes that when a public gathers at an event, there is a transference of identification from the playing arena to those in attendance and back. The heroic figure striving for perfection is felled by (typically) his own flaw. A Ben Johnson fails a drug test, and is no longer the world's fastest human. A Mike Tyson is disqualified for improperly tearing at Evander Holyfield's flesh. Disgusted by the transgression, we are gratified that justice has prevailed. By this means, publics are supposedly cleansed of their impulses to deviate from the law, and they return to a docile state. The conditions for upward mobility are rudely reimposed, and things such as race relations, that might momentarily have promised a veritable transcendence of terms or positions, return to their place. The wholesale acceptance of such a fable as an adequate account of how people attend to these events sits uneasily with many sectors of a sporting public. The messages are seldom so clear, the lessons rarely so straightforwardly learned. Perhaps what allows other stories to get told and other inferences to be drawn is that there is more to attendance than the fixed targets of catharsis will allow. From Little Leagues to trading cards to tailgate parties, getting to a big-time sporting event is enriched by participation all along the way. The protocols of watching sport on television, or listening to a game on the radio at work, may or may not match other broadcasts for their terms of involvement. When set in motion by sporting publics, these codes and conventions cloud the presumed partitions between participation and spectatorship, as they do the boundaries between live events and their media dispersion. It is precisely because sport can operate simultaneously at various scales of space and time that it is able to operate so powerfully within society.

The Question of the Popular

All of this reflection on the meaning of sport does not suggest that it is undefinable. Rather, it should be analyzed as a problematic, not as a discrete item—a framework for understanding more than an already consolidated object of analysis. This interrogation of sport raises the question of how popular culture gets studied. The idea of studying the popular emerged as an antidote to a historiography of great men and events in which value derived from the claim that these persons and deeds were exemplary of all that transpired in an age. In this light, it appeared that very few kinds of representation qualified for serious study, and great confidence was placed in the belief that nothing of significance was being excluded. Hence the popular has come to be aligned more closely with the category "everyday life," where this refers not simply to the normal course of things, but also to what is fundamentally excluded from attention and evaluation.

Cultural studies itself has analyzed all manner of practices that lie beyond the canon, although, surprisingly, sport has received less attention than many hitherto neglected activities. At issue is not merely the rendering of those countless invisible acts into the register of tangible facts and figures, such as the calculation of attendance or audience share as a percentage of the total population. Sport already displays this irreducible tension between the stats and the plays, and surely much of theoretical interest can be gleaned from the study of cultural productions that directly touch relatively few people. On the other hand, popularity itself needs explanation, beyond the circularities of reason that there is money to be made in creating demand for legal monopolies of supply (athlete drafts, broadcast rights) or that people do what they know and therefore keep traditions alive. The big business of sport has come too late to account for its popularity in any simple causal fashion. So, too, the relationship of general kinesthetic desire to physical education in the school curriculum is complex, transected by myriad determinants of taste. Well-nigh universal exposure to sport has not meant that people are always doing or knowing the same thing.

Where sport may be most helpful to the general development of cultural studies is in moving beyond the conventional wisdom as to what constitutes the quotidian. It would seem that the point of studying daily life is not that it is routine or otherwise unremarkable, but that what is neglected or defiant of official registration is fundamental to how society itself is made and remade. Although sport is commonly practiced and part of the daily routines of many, it is, for those who attend to it, unceasingly remarkable. The repetition of a game never seems to dissolve what is excessive about it, which is, after all, what generates the desire to return to play. Quite the contrary, from the perspective of popular participation, sport points toward a very different use of social surplus, of involvement in collective activity that extends, surpasses, and renews its own conditions. Although sport is certainly suffused with commodity relations, it is not exhausted by them. In a realm so fully commodified, leisure is laced with a freedom to pursue other principles for a public to gather together. This production of the popular, here the work done together to make possible further association, affiliation, coordination, and expenditure, may be concentrated in sport, but it transcends those bounds. Pursuing this avenue of the popular may reveal what is dangerous in those masses who gather at local fields, at megastadia, or in private homes to partake of the sporting life.

Sports Axis: The National versus the Global-Local

Sport mobilizes the masses, but to what ends? It is a geography, but what does it map? The Soccer War between El Salvador and Honduras in 1969, in which the two national teams' rivalry in World Cup qualifications sparked a skirmish over borders, and the 1936 Berlin Olympics, which pitted race against nation, attest to the strong uses of sport in national mobilization during the twentieth century. The clarity of boundaries and the opposing sides on the playing field readily allegorize conflicts among nations. The national team is part of every portfolio of sovereignty, and the various world competitions recruit no end of affiliation to a country's code. Winning in these contests is less damaging but also less ambiguous than the spoils of war (which also does a great deal of spoiling, especially since Vietnam, when combat has perhaps delivered less direct political benefit than in earlier times). And yet a nation is clearly not the only club to which a sporting team can belong. Professional team sports rally urban allegiances that divide national territory into competing city-states. The niche markets constituted by cable sports channels assume still different spatial patterns of allegiance.

Affiliations to the street, neighborhood, school, or sport itself tug in different directions. The geography of sport is also made tangible by the migrations of touring athletes, who triangulate home and away with the various sites of their televised reception. To the extent that sport takes on its own authority because the pleasures of viewing are attached to particular athletes' performances, the secular powers of the sports hero can provide a cultural currency of identification no less potent than the extragovernmental powers of transnational corporations. Of course, truly global stars are, in themselves, transnational corporations, and the narratives of their achievements and the attachments to their trajectories of success may not necessarily support existing geopolitical arrangements. But because stars lack something like a state, it is less clear on behalf of what political project these attachments may be mobilized. Rather, they complicate any idea of the direct line said to run between citizen and state and open up reception to other channels of power.

Professional sports remind us that the politics of recognition and economy and the politics of identity and difference are located in the same field.

To follow one's favorite star is to watch the market in action, as much as it is to identify with moves and uses of the body that are not so easily measured or exchanged. And the market—because success depends on competition, not monopoly—shows us how necessary regulation is to the survival of capitalism: there is more left to play with if no one team has all the goods. Sport, therefore, also embodies the phantasmatic improbability of neoclassical dreaming. Talk about sport commingles what we see of value in a person's appearance with whether he or she is justly rewarded for what he or she does. To the extent that such talk is itself a feature of daily life (and with increasing participation of women in school and professional sports, this is less and less a male domain), identity and economy are interwoven, just as justice and value frequently take inchoate form in the popular imagination. Of course, there is no guarantee that racism, sexism, homophobia, or moneyed privilege will not compromise any conscious appreciation of the very links discussed here. In this regard, we can think of sport as a kind of prepolitical activity, an arena where needs, demands, and desires can take shape and receive sustenance before they are institutionally articulated as politics. If what are typically taken as disparate dimensions of social life are productively enmeshed in sportive participations, we may be able to begin our critical analyses with what we thought needed to be conceptually drawn together, namely, the interlaced problems of justice and identity, value and recognition.

The point of all this is that in sport, the national, global, local, and personal coexist through the same practice, although all of these spatial configurations may spin in different directions rather than support each other. The geography of sport is not calibrated on any single map, and the affiliations and attentions that point to powers not subsumed by the national take place on grounds that are at once local, national, and global. Similarly, although narrative is unavoidable in speaking of sport, not all of what constitutes sporting activity can be narrativized. There is much in the sheer physicality of the pleasures of sporting bodies that cannot be readily named, or doing so leaves out the energies marshaled to make the activity possible. It may be useful to speak of a sporting sublime, an urge to speak of what is lost to speech, when we talk so incessantly about what is already past. These complexities suggest that sport will not be conquered by a single method or analytic approach and that perhaps a palpable decentering of our habits of thinking about sport is necessary before we can understand it.

The essays collected here aim at a new perspective, and for the standard operations of sport (in the United States especially) there are some noticeable absences. Our intention is not to offer a reader that is representative of scholarly approaches to sport, but a critical intervention that highlights some lines of reciprocity between sport and cultural studies. Football, baseball, and hockey are nowhere represented—nor are dozens of other sports with less financial backing or cultural capital. And although many of the pieces discuss subject matter situated in the United States, others take their examples from beyond these shores. From this global space, they reflect on the dynamics of the national, and from within this nation-state, there is a definite turn away from canonicity. The result, we hope, will offer a different geometry for measuring the shape of sport's significance, one as impatient with the singularizing gaze levied upon the topic as with the resistance to theorizing its practical and political aspects. While acknowledging much intelligent commentary on the body of texts, we want to focus on the corporeality of fields—here, the different ones that we play upon for physical and mental exercise. Sport has the potential to carve an analytic terrain for cultural studies across the social sciences and humanities. Our aim is to focus this version of cultural studies on sport and, by so doing, produce a more focused transdiscipline.

Whether one is a player, a spectator, or a willing nonparticipant, sport is unavoidably part of collective physical education. Presumably, if all that we required for sport were to "just do it," at the very least, we would not need the injunction. If we are to think the world of sport, but also to imagine the world through sport, we begin to see that sport has more to teach us than can be learned from any single game. The field is vast, and its pleasures and travails need to be taken seriously. This, at least, is the project to which the present volume is devoted.

Competing Allegories

Toby Miller

How irritating and prevalent sport can be as a figure of speech. Of course, metaphor in general is unavoidable. The point is to evaluate its use in sport—mostly to valorize the market and chauvinism—and compete for that allegorical value. In place of bodily worth based on monetary exchange value or nationalistic sign value, we can look to more autotelic and collaborative ideas. But they can only follow a careful analysis of the history and currency of sport. To that end, this introductory chapter addresses four critical features: business, the body, the nation, and television. In each, sport needs to be confronted as a central component of world and local culture.

Business

Most histories of leisure argue for an epistemological break that occurs with European industrialization; prior to that point, it is thought, distinctions between work and its other are irrelevant. Capitalism is held responsible for this discontinuity because it transforms carnival, ceremony, and play into precisely delineated changes in production. That position is under challenge for reducing precapitalist ideas about sport to the utopia of festival. For example, British ruling-class dismay at the supposed drudgery of professional cricket venerates its heritage by finding fault with the here and now as cheapened by money. In fact, that domain was opened up through new labor markets to domination by working people in place of the bourgeoisie. Far from originating in organic connections to everyday working life, sport has in some ways been enriched by departing from an "old boys" logic to an inclusive commercialism. Rather than working-class leisure pastimes subjected to standardization and commodification following a brutal division of labor, sports are said to descend through social structures. The ball games of fourteenth-century Japan and seventeenth-century Florence were complex symbols of courtier diplomacy, and what we define as warfare was perceived in the Renaissance as a sporting art. Many linguistic antonyms to the concept of work were in use prior to capitalism: Latin opposes active and contemplative lives, whereas sixteenth-century Italian and French and fifteenth-century English include elaborate ideas about recreation. There are discourses everywhere about the problem of boredom and the need for distraction, especially among ruling elites (Burke 138–40, 142; Marqusee 28).

Internationally, the history of our global sports system sees most nations adopting games as imports from visitors or colonists that are taken up by ruling classes and then diffused through the society. There are few institutionalized organic pastimes. In Latin America, most of today's games were introduced by British sailors to port towns or capital cities across the nineteenth century. Where there was a substantial resident British presence, expatriates organized competitions that made their way down the social strata. Sometimes middle- and ruling-class locals returned from travel to Europe with sporting ideas and drives that were gradually democratized and professionalized. This is not to deny the continued value of indigenous games, such as Bolivian *tinku*. But they generally thrive among isolated peoples or romantic elites in search of a restored pastoral idyll, like the ruling-class Argentinians who have revived gauchoesque pato as an alternative to polo for showing off equestrian skill and social superiority (Mason 13; Arbena 106–9).

I am not arguing that such trade in culture is entirely welcome; for instance, once the international division of sporting labor began in earnest in the 1980s, the Dominican Republic, where baseball had become a popular domestic game, found its local leagues ripped apart by the attentions of U.S. scouts. But on the other hand, Dominican newspaper accounts of Major League games repatriate stars by focusing on the fortunes of local players to the virtual exclusion of their Major League clubs. In the mid-1970s, business interests decimated Canadian amateur hockey to revive the U.S. professional league. Radical critics called for community activism to reclaim hockey's supposed connection to the social world. This position understands sport as authentic self-expression that can be endangered by commodification from below (in a geographic sense). Such romantic organicism denies the partial view of nation and community provided by men's sport and forgets the financial base to Canadian hockey in focusing on new sources of funding to the neglect of local history (Klein "Sport" 81; Gruneau and Whitson 24–27).

How should we make sense of sporting capitalism, given that expenditure on sport fluctuates with macrohistorical events—in the United States, the Second World War and the Korean War reduced consumption—but not in terms of conventional business cycles? Attendance at events in the four major North American professional sports has grown through most recessions, and the gross national sport product is expected to be $121.1 billion by the end of the twentieth century. There are two key aspects to this success. First, sports themselves have corporate rules, governance, and legal personalities, in addition to company ownership of teams. Second, they offer advertising and goodwill to sponsors, which have been involved since the 1860s, increasingly via the media. Gillette paid $100,000 for radio rights to the 1939 World Series, with a tie-in that sent sales figures up 350 percent. Today, the company provides airline travelers with an in-flight TV-highlights magazine to the same end. In the 1980s, Macintosh sold $3.5 million in computers the day after a Super Bowl commercial, and $155 million over the next three months. Fox and Frito-Lay coordinated the 1995 football season such that TV segments cut from commentators on a play to commercials of them eating Wavy Lays, and each packet of the product came with a Fox National Football League schedule. This second aspect is a key to the unique nature of the first. The life world of sport is said to transcend commerce, conferring prestige on its associates and immunity from anticartel legislation. That is why, for many years, basic restraint of trade prevented basketball and football players from functioning as free labor. Now they have some ability to do so, but the owners have compensated by adding revenues from the media and free services from the state (Vogel 244–45; Sabo and Jansen 170; Cashmore *and* 143; Montemayor; Marshall and Cook 308, 311, 319–20).

The most dramatic case of recent commodification is the Olympics. When International Olympic Committee (IOC) president Avery Brundage saw an athlete's bag covered with an airline logo in 1972, he had it removed from the Munich Village. But whereas the 1976 Summer Olympiad in Montreal gained 81 percent of its funds from government sources, the equivalent figure for the 1984 Los Angeles Games was 5 percent. That year, the decision to sell the privilege of carrying the Olympic Torch for three thousand dollars per kilometer drew a Greek protest delegation, led by Culture Minister Melina Mercouri. But by 1988 in Seoul, even the Soviet Union had avowedly shifted its interest in sporting success away from nation building and socialist prestige and toward new markets. Sports had been corporatized, and expansion now relied on televisuality. U.S. rights to the Atlanta Games cost $715 million, compared with $401 million for 1992 in Barcelona. This is part of a major reconfiguration away from the idea of amateur sport as a public good provided by the state, to the state as an indirect servicer of private investment that then has a multiplier effect. Andrew Young said of preparations for the Atlanta Games: "We hope we have taken commercialism out of sport by taking commercialism for granted. With no financial problems, we can concentrate on Olympic ideals. If you are struggling for money, then you will probably struggle for ideals" (quoted in McKay and Kirk 10).

It's good to know Young has a materialist analysis that sees ideals flowing from monetary position. But Mercouri was on hand again to suggest the decision to award the event to the United States in place of Athens (where the centenary of the modern Olympics would logically have been held, since the 1896 Games had been there) showed the "Parthenon does not run the Olympics, Coca-Cola does" (Houlihan 156; Real "Postmodern" 14; MacAloon "Missing" 130).

The news is not all bad. Some corporations have seen the potential of supporting fringe actors and activities in sport, ameliorating the chauvinisms of traditional amateur games bodies. Adidas, for instance, realized long before the IOC that emerging sovereign states should be courted. The company dedicated resources in the 1970s to forwarding the claims of African and Central European sports federations, and drew consequent rewards when sporting attire was selected to outfit teams, in addition to free advertising. From the very first days of women's activism for access to marathons, in the 1960s, Avon tied its door-to-door globalization strategies to the struggle, funding races, hiring lobbyists, and connecting the sport to beauty and makeup. Many companies broke down the segregation of women from men in sport by supporting employee athletics as part of a drive toward productivity gains. Nike learned the lesson: a 1990s female-empowerment campaign sent sales to women up 40 percent. Avon sponsors the U.S. Olympic Team as part of its bizarre "Avon Salutes the Woman inside the Athlete" campaign. A double-page spread in *Vanity Fair*'s issue on the Atlanta Games invited readers to look at an image of an elderly woman in evening wear surrounded by four swimsuited men and "[g]uess which one's the Olympic gold medalist in springboard diving." The answer was Aileen Riggin Soule, who had won the event in 1920. She was described in bold type as "just another Avon lady." This support is contingent, of course: the company felt very differently about lesbian involvement in sport, and cut sponsorship of women's tennis after the 1981 palimony suit against Billie Jean King (Houlihan 164; Cooper 72–74; Brodeur 233; Lurie 123–24; Savan 225; Hall 56). Which brings us to the body.

Body

Despite its absence from much social and cultural theory, sport is a privileged site for kinesiologists measuring bodies in search of improved performance. Sport science is instrumental and apolitical yet committed to competition, with statistics providing Tayloristic evaluation and control. Analogies between the sporting body and the automobile are exemplified in BMW's 1996 range of cars. A company catalog describes these vehicles as "athletes of grace, power and championship performance" built in "the spirit of the Olympic Games." The sporting body is also a common topic in popular sociology, notably Christopher Lasch's lamentations over lost transcendence. Lasch sees contemporary American sport as a degraded version of what was once a beautiful "release from everyday life," the paradox of a heightened, very specific awareness that used to be attainable through intense concentration and a replication of childhood's singular obsessions. Applying intellect and force to such unproductive pastimes offended twentieth-century social reformers, who sought to harness this energy to nation building and economic productivity at the same time as capitalism was transforming sport into a practice of spectatorship. Lasch's position typifies the view of sport from a romantic left-right desire for what is always already lost, with the body shifting from free play to lax consumption (Lasch 181–82, 185; Hall 51; Loy, Andrews, and Rinehart 70).

Less poetically, social theorist Norbert Elias analyzes sport and social structure synchronically and diachronically, coining the term *figuration* to designate how people inhabit social positions. The figural keys to sport are exertion, contest, codification, and collective meaningfulness. Without these, its magic attractions—tension and catharsis—cannot be guaranteed. Elias asks why there is such fascination with rule-governed contests between individuals and teams, evident from a trend that fans out from the European ruling classes after the sixteenth century. Sentiment and behavior are codified, supplanting excess and self-laceration with temperant autocritique. The displacement of tension and the search for ordered leisure allocate to organized sport the task of controlling and training gentry, workers, and colonists alike. High tension blended with low risk promises both popular appeal and public safety in a utilitarian calculus of time and joy. Of course, this was subject to local customization and struggle. Henning Eichberg points to contradictory, nonlinear shifts in European sport between the thirteenth and nineteenth centuries, with enclosure and the open air in an ambiguous relationship. Sometimes, sealed-off spaces are deemed appropriate for ruling-class privacy, with fieldlike surroundings suitable for workers' exercise. But the spatial separation of sport from nature in late-nineteenth-century industrialization marks a trend. Bodies in motion are progressively contained, enraging hygiene movements but permitting surveillance, spectacle, and profit (Elias "Introduction" 19–21, 38–39; "Essay" 165, 173–74, 150–51, 155, 159).

Following Elias, Joseph Maguire typifies the sporting body as a model of discipline, a mirror, a site of domination, and a form of communication. The disciplined body is subject to allo- and autoregimentation, remodeled through dietetics and training to police performance. The mirroring body functions as a machine of desire, encouraging mimetic conduct via self-presentation as the desired other and the purchase of commodities associated with this other. The dominating body exercises power through physical force, both on the field and—potentially—off it. Finally, the communicative body is aestheticized as an expressive totality, balletic and beautiful. As Maguire points out, this taxonomy is neither exclusive nor hermetically distinct. Its categories bleed into one another, and can be internally conflictual or straightforwardly functional. They are the outcome of history, publicity, and privateness: human, commercial, and governmental practices that involve implicit negotiations to maintain boundaries. Maguire's four types clearly reference a century of science applied to masculinity/femininity. In the nineteenth century, it was thought that women could bear healthy children only if they exercised in moderation (picking up an anxiety dating back to sixteenth-century Europe that exercise could transform women into men) and that eating red meat generated large muscles. Today, three discourses articulate science with gender through sport. Categorization labels certain physical and behavioral norms as male or female that are substantiated in terms of nature or society. Activities coded as male are evaluated to see whether they "contaminate" women participants. Sex-role analysis accounts for differences in the uptake of sport by girls and boys through socialization. And androgyny studies "permit" intermingled behavior across gender. Against these social-psychology approaches, distributive critics emphasize inequalities of opportunity and power. A sociological model displaces a psychological one, but it remains a liberal position: as long as conditions are in place for equilibrium, whatever happens from that point is meant to be, with sport in need of equalization, not transformation. By contrast, the left problematizes the overall historical, social, economic, and cultural mythology of sport (Fiddes 176–77; Park 70; Hargreaves 48, 30–31; Dewar 151–57; Hall; Mitchell and Dyer 96–97).

Of course, the sporting body is always bracketed with sex. In the 1890s, Oskar Zoth ingested liquid extracts from a bull's testicles to improve his cycling and swimming. The last English Football Association Cup Final before the Second World War was allegedly won and lost on the strength of which team took monkey-gland tablets in training (the losers). Indian wrestling ascetics have long constrained the flow of semen to exercise power and authority: celibacy and the mat. Today, anabolic-androgenic steroids that provide testosterone are central to sport. Steroids are officially proscribed by all international sporting authorities. They are dangerous to the liver and may cause cardiac damage and sexual problems. (The mad weight lifter disease that reportedly sends users into "roid rage" is unconfirmed.) Pressures on performance have led to widespread use. The U.S. Department of Health reported a quarter of a million schoolboys were taking steroids in 1991, mostly in athletic programs (Alter; Klein "Life's"; Marshall and Cook 308; Moss, Panzak, and Tarter; Sabo 7; Lueschen 97).

The male body is sport's everyday currency. This makes it most unusual in societies where "man" stands for everyone and is rarely subject to specific inquiry. The boxer's or cyclist's photograph that cuts the body into tiny bits to measure and master it is more publicly and explicitly evaluative than any comparable site of display. As sports move away from violence toward inclusive audience strategies, the boxer is supplanted by/redefined as the centerfold. The displacement of speech by sight as the critical hermeneutic method that began in early-modern Europe at last moves onto men in the sexual way that it colonized women much earlier. Male pinups are common today in teen magazines and even British tabloid newspapers. It is now possible for the 1993 Miss Wintersun contest at Surfer's Paradise, the first step toward election as Miss Australia, to be won by a Damian Taylor (Dyer 104; Harari), and *Sports Illustrated*'s notorious swimsuit issue featured men in 1994.

Sam Fussell claims that muscles are "the latest props of the dandy" (577). And sport allows men to watch and dissect other men's bodies in fetishistic detail, a space for staring without homosexuality alleged or feared. The fetish of admiring body parts ("look at those triceps") gives a scientistic pleasure and alibi. A man weight lifting at close proximity gives off signs of pleasure-pain akin to facial correlatives of the male orgasm, a sight otherwise denied men defining themselves as straight. One lifter has said a good pump is "better than coming"; no wonder turning tricks is as common in such gyms as the disavowal of homosexuality (Morse 45; weight lifter quoted in Shilling 144; Klein "Life's").

The overtly gay sporting body is a complex signifier in a sphere rife with homophobia and hypocrisy. Women's college teams are regularly vilified in the media in sexualized language, and despite the significant number of lesbians in the old Women's Professional Basketball League, "out" players were harassed and fired. College coaches are known to begin the first practice of the year with the requirement that players not be "lesbian during the season," and the new pro leagues of the late 1990s were coy about marketing themselves to their large lesbian audience. Like Billie Jean King, Martina Navratilova lost major endorsements when her sexual practices became public, litigated knowledge. Out sports stars include former NFL running back David Kopay and offensive tackle Roy Simmons; Major League outfielder Glenn Burke; swimmer Bruce Hayes; the late English football striker Justin Fashanu; diver Greg Louganis; Australian Rugby League forward Ian Roberts;

bodybuilding world champion Bob Jackson-Paris; golfer Muffin Spencer-Devlin; skaters Matthew Hall, Rudy Galindo, and Doug Mattis; and decathlete Tom Waddell. Intense but denied connections between sex and sport make the terrain risky, as Louganis's rejection by NBC when he offered his services as a commentator for the Atlanta Games suggests. A member of the Canadian women's hockey team coaching the triumphant Mighty Dykes at the New York Gay Games was said to have dodged Canadian TV crews during the event. The moral panic about girls being made into lesbians through sport extends beyond education and into allegations of compulsory homosexuality. In 1993, cricketer Denise Annetts complained to the New South Wales Anti-Discrimination Board that she had been dropped from the Australian national team for being straight—a rare opportunity for the women's game to gain publicity in the mainstream press (Cahn 246, 266; Lenskyj; Pronger xi; Reed 24; Pener 28; Blinde and Taub).

Women were not admitted to track-and-field events at the Olympics until 1928. Inclusion came in response to a separatist Games in 1922. Just as male organizations co-opted women's sports in the 1920s, the 1980s saw a repeat. Title IX of the 1972 U.S. Educational Amendment Act barred discrimination by gender in federally assisted teaching institutions. The representation of women in intercollegiate sports rose from just 9 percent of total numbers in 1966–67 to 32 percent in 1985–86, while high school participation went up 500 percent. But college sports budgets for women have not developed as they should. What was designed to desegregate gender has seen men take over the senior administration and coaching of women's sports. Prior to Title IX, 90 percent of women's college sport coaches were women. Today, the proportion is below 50 percent. The National Collegiate Athletic Association (NCAA) failed when it sought to reverse Title IX, but did lure colleges away from the Association for Intercollegiate Athletics for Women with the promise of media exposure and money. Put another way, women have more opportunities to play, but drastically reduced access to power. At the same time, the mainstream press resumes women's power to heteronormativity. *Time* magazine's 1982 cover story "Coming on Strong, the New Ideal of Beauty" endorsed athletic femininity because "men may decide it is sexy for one basic reason: it can enhance sex" (Jarvie and Maguire 161; Bale 90; Nelson; Dewar 155; Cahn 260–61, 254–57; *Time* quoted in Ellsworth 47).

Nation

Sport is a crucible of nation, cognate to the rites of passage of war or revolution. There are clear connections between training soldiers and athletes and

21

the strategies of generals and coaches. Karl von Clausewitz described a trini-tarian form to war and the state: material enmity, military presence, and po-litical leadership. Sport's version would be a national divide, team competi-tion, and management. Pierre de Coubertin founded the modern Olympics to follow the example of British muscular Christianity and redeem French masculinity after the shocks of the Franco-Prussian War. The Mexican Revo-lution moved quickly to institutionalize sport in the 1910s as a sign and source of national unity. When the Argentine Olympic Committee was founded in 1922, it promised to work for "the perfection of the race and the glory of conquering what is noble, worthy, and beautiful." John F. Kennedy established the President's Council on Youth Fitness to counter a "growing softness, our increasing lack of physical fitness," which constituted "a threat to our security." The Peace Corps argued in *Sports Illustrated* in 1963 that sports were more productive terrain for its mission than teaching because they were "least vulnerable to charges of 'neo-colonialism' and 'cultural imperialism.'" Perhaps, but they can be serious business. The 1969 Central American Soccer War broke out when the Honduran government expelled all Salvadorans following a match between the two countries. The events of 1989 in Central and Eastern Europe were characterized by intense passions associated with this aspect of sport. Steaua military athletes shot at the secret police in Romania, Dinamo Club players defended their patrons, the Securitate, and the captain of the national rugby union side died in battle. In East Germany, Katarina Witt and fellow sports celebrities Roland Matthes and Kornelia Ender had their homes sacked. That reaction repeats the treatment of Astylus when he switched nationalities prior to the 480 B.C. Olympics: his old house was destroyed. From a very different angle, the Sandinistas abolished professional sport, focusing instead on nation building through a large-scale sport-for-all policy (Allison 92; Arbena 110–12; Shapiro 71, 74; Kennedy quoted in Lasch 183; Skillen 350; Peace Corps quoted in Kang 431).

These stories reference the utilitarian side of nations and sport. A healthier, fitter population reduces the cost of public health, guarantees a functioning workforce, and helps tourism. A recent Aotearoa/New Zealand minister of recreation and sport referred to his portfolio as a route to "social and economic prosperity" through the promotion of "active, physical life-styles." He identified an additional benefit: "being *into* sport" ensured being "*out of* court." This long-standing criminological obsession deems familially-based and formal sporting activities to be worthy, integrative norms, whereas informal leisure is demonized. Even the former Jamaican Socialist prime minister Michael Manley (also a distinguished historian of cricket) pushed such a line: male violence is a danger that can be pacified and redirected into an appropriate sphere—literally, national fitness. Just as schools have often used the gymnasium for discipline, so too the nation. Come on down, Matthew Arnold. But more than that, sport becomes inflected with an ethnocentric notion of correct behavior, associating delinquency with racial minorities and youthful muscularity. With diminished employment prospects in the latter half of this century, such moral panics are as much to do with governments preparing people for a leisure-defined poverty as with training them to work (minister quoted in Volkerling 8; Agnew and Petersen; McMurtry 422; Griffin 119; Scraton 169–71, 174).

Richard Gruneau has identified a nation-building "moral entrepreneurship" in sport that matches its commercial side. Amateurism and educational policy run alongside commodification. They have frequently been in dialogue and accommodated each other, but the outcome generally follows the money. Business borrows the language of ethical improvement and bodily perfection. These cultural rather than commercial technologies may be bound up with notions of fairness and intersubjectivity, but they are easily redisposed. Consider the official narrative of baseball. In 1905, Albert Spalding, a sporting goods manufacturer, was worried by the (correct) popular belief that baseball derived from British children's pastimes. Anxious that this diminished baseball's ability to be the national game, Spalding charged a six-person commission with identifying an individual who could be promoted as its inventor. Abner Doubleday was named, because the witness to the commission with the earliest memory of baseball saw Doubleday playing it in Cooperstown in the 1830s. Spalding publicized this as indicative of American exceptionalism: baseball was unlike the worn-out sports of the rest of the world. In the process, he no doubt expected to sell a good deal of equipment. Meanwhile, the so-called Progressive Era combined racism, the church, and temperance to police and, where possible, prohibit the boxing film, especially when it featured African American men displaying superior skill and power against white opponents (Gruneau 91–92; Arnold; Guttmann 71–72; Streibel).

We need to interrogate who stands for the nation in gender and racial terms. Consider efforts by U.S. colleges to recruit athletes who can heighten the institutions' standings as nationally prominent entities that do more than educate. "The latter-day scramble for Africa" in the 1970s was an unseemly search for African track-and-field stars that resembled nineteenth-century imperial powers seeking new territory. In 1960, U.S. colleges recruited 8 percent of their athletes from Africa. By 1980, the figure was 33 percent, following numerous Olympic successes by middle-distance runners. Once African student-athletes came to the United States, they were brutally overworked to service boosterism, leaving with devastated bodies that allowed no room for further success on behalf of their own countries. Approximately 75 percent of local and international black male athletes on sports scholarships do not gain degrees, and many NCAA schools never graduate the sports scholars who enter as freshmen. Black men and women have much greater chances of becoming doctors, lawyers, and dentists than professional athletes. Women of color occupy a particularly ambiguous position in American sport. Although the Olympic success of African American women sprinters since the 1960s has given them (quadrennial) national attention, they have suffered increasingly sexist and racist depictions in the media. Content analyses of *Sports Illustrated* demonstrate misogynist and white biases. The most widely read segment of newspapers, the sporting pages, routinely give greater attention to animals than to women. And women's sport and fitness magazines allocate the vast majority of their attention to white women. For all men and women, the prospects for upward mobility from sport vary between 0.004 percent and 0.007 percent, and there appears to be a shorter life span for African American professional baseball players than for whites, who are kept on longer after their prime. Major League Baseball stands as a public disgrace for its racist hiring and management (Bale 79, 74; Cahn 269–71; Leath and Lumpkin; Davis; McKay "Just" 194–95; Sabo and Jansen 170; Rowe and Brown 101; Lumpkin and Williams; Jiobu; Lapchick and Benedict).

And as both Andrew Tudor and Hugh O'Donnell have shown, national mythmaking through sport is common across continents. Stereotypes signify as ethical norms that argue for/train/generate new habits among the citizenry. Still, fissures do appear. In 1990, the *Los Angeles Times* ran what has become an infamous interview with British Tory politician Norman Tebbitt, who charged migration with endangering the "special relationship" between the United Kingdom and the United States. He also suggested Britain impose a "cricket test" on migrants: "Which side do they cheer for?" would sort out whether South Asians in England watching the local side play Pakistan or India had adequately assimilated. In the House of Commons itself, Tebbitt related this question to death threats against Salman Rushdie before warming to his real intention: keeping Hong Kong Chinese (British subjects) from migrating before 1997. After Hassiba Boulmerka won the women's fifteen hundred meters at the 1991 World Athletic Championships, she was feted by President Chadli Benjedid on return to Algeria. Boulmerka was denounced by segments of Islam, however, for displaying her legs on television, and subsequently moved to France, winning Olympic Gold in Barcelona under the pall of death threats (many countries have refused to include women on their

Olympic teams at all, for religious reasons) (Tebbitt quoted in Marqusee 137–38; Jarvie and Maguire 175; Guttmann 129; Vines 49). During the mid-summer 1994 World Cup, Iranian TV viewers were reportedly given a special montage: whenever U.S. cameras cut to shots of the crowd, programmers in Iran edited in footage of people in winter garb from other matches, hiding decadent Western attire from their fragile audience. Meanwhile, U.S. marketers continued to advertise the sport as more truly international than the World Series and the Super Bowl, which look pitifully intramural to outsiders. A problem at one site—difference and diaspora—is a virtue at another.

The uneasy meeting ground of nation, sport, and media can put significant political issues on the international public agenda, especially via the Olympics. Leni Riefenstahl's *Olympia* (1936–38), for example, sparked debate about Nazism. The entry of the Soviet Union into the Olympics in 1952 produced a medal-table rivalry along Cold War lines, nourished and analyzed by the press. The black scarves, socks, and saluting gloves worn by Tommie Smith and John Carlos after the two-hundred-meter sprint in the Mexico City Games captured the world spotlight for African American politics (if not the attention of the *New York Times*, which found room to report the event on page 59). There was minute-by-minute coverage of the Munich murders and political boycotts of sporting competitions by African nations, and the United States and the Soviet Union determinedly emphasized the conflictual intersection of cultural politics and international affairs. Sport opens up major ideological differences to global public view, frequently via transnational protocols that go beyond the chauvinisms of individual interests through international sports law. Our contemporary moment sees intra- and transnationalism via sporting organizations based on nations (the Olympic, Pan-American, World Student, European, and Commonwealth Games, and the World Cups of soccer, track and field, and swimming) with diasporic movements and First People dispositions gathering momentum as sources of political and/or sporting power through protests at international sporting events and the global trade in players. The most concentrated and powerful intersections of nation and sport take place at these media-saturated, time- and space-compressed, international competitions. The nation and TV have been crucial sites for both solidarity and an unwelcome othering (Given 47; Goldlust 118; Nafziger; Shapiro 78).

Television

In Germany, Britain, and the United States, sport and TV have been together since before World War II. In Japan, television coverage of American-style men's and women's wrestling is often associated with the growth in popularity of the new technology in the mid-1950s. But sport and television have a complicated history. The U.S. networks were initially cautious about Olympic coverage. Multisport events seemed a risky venture without proven North American spectator interest until Congress passed the Sports Broadcasting Act in 1961. This act orchestrated sport-TV relations as a cartel, permitting comprehensive collusion (as it would be termed and outlawed in any other industry) by professional sporting bodies in negotiation with the networks. That regularized the relationship for TV programmers. Then the dramatic success of the Soviet Union from the 1960s, followed by the emergence of the German Democratic Republic as a major sports power in 1972 (it had been excluded from the Olympics up to that time), provided a geocultural metaphor of high political moment—even if the Soviet Union led the medal count with remorseless regularity, much to the amusement of those skeptical that economic planning does not produce competition. The Munich Games produced two marketable stars: a white American male with unparalleled swimming success, Mark Spitz, and the Soviet Union's teenaged Olga Korbut, whose gymnastic achievements displaced the stereotypical image of state-socialist sporting machinery with a hyperfeminine one. And when Black September struck, the focus turned to more directly metaphorical ground, with the use of sport-as-religion to make a political point. In addition, the multisports appeal produced a different viewing demographic from conventional U.S. sports, as women and the well educated joined the audience. A price is paid for this financing: the Seoul Olympics became "the breakfast Games" for people in the Southern Hemisphere, including the competitors, so that New Yorkers could watch live action in prime time. The Calgary Winter Games were extended by four days purely to provide ABC with a third weekend of coverage, and NBC showed less than a third of events in Atlanta in real time: the "plausibly live" policy. Across the 1980s, the three principal U.S. networks and specialist cable channels increased annual sports coverage from 4,600 to 7,300 hours. The NFL operated at a profit without selling a solitary stadium seat, even before its U.S.$17 billion network contracts of 1998. Deals like the NCAA-CBS coverage of Final Four basketball up the ante on schedules, rules, recruiting, and training in a supposedly amateur activity. The extent of illegal payments to young athletes is as well-known as the actual rate of upward social mobility through sport is hidden (Thompson 65, 67; Houlihan 156–58; Vogel 244–45, 247; Sabo 4; Sack). Corporate globalization does not necessarily disintegrate nationalism from televised sport: for many people, the most memorable Super Bowl halftime of recent years was in 1991, when a child sang to U.S. troops home from the Persian Gulf and the sign "USA" was formed by bodies in the stadium.

TV sports talk normally has at least a residual referent in the (gendered) nation. Chauvinistic, discriminatory national stereotypes become not just aspects of verbal description, but influences on the wider discourse about the nation, both internally and overseas. Geoffrey Lawrence and David Rowe's account of televised cricket argues for "a substantial homology between the values articulated in televised sport and bourgeois values, such as disciplined labor and competitiveness. . . . it is integral to the capitalist mode of production." Commentary legitimates loyalty and industriousness, accepts commodity relations and masculine dominance, commends vigorous competitors who abide by the rules rather than overreacting to misfortune, claims the existence of a meritocracy, and directs viewers away from criticisms of life under capitalism (167, 169–76). Embellishing sport with drama is integral to the process (Bryant, Comisky, and Zillmann). Instructions to broadcasters such as the following are not uncommon: "Create a feeling that the competitors don't like each other. . . . Studies have shown that fans react better, and are more emotionally involved, if aggressive hostility is present. . . . Work the audience at the emotional level and get them involved in the game" (Hitchcock 75).

Most prime-time commercials on the networks target consumers through the ordinary, familial stuff of life, with equal amounts of romance and suburbanality. But sports programming focuses on fame. Competition and physique displace togetherness and similarity to associate merchandise with success. Conversely, some companies use sport on television to claim corporate citizenship. In 1988, DuPont announced it would no longer manufacture plutonium and was even thinking about putting an end to cholorofluorocarbons. The company wanted to look prosocial and altruistic. Its advertising agency devised a commercial about a disabled person who "lost both legs to a Vietcong rocket" but returned to basketball thanks to artificial limbs from DuPont plastics—a redemptive story demonstrating the chemical giant's public-spiritedness. And it promised to cut down those CFCs by the next millennium (Jhally 170–71; Savan 117–18).

It would be misleading, however, to assume that a left or right functionalism can adequately describe TV sport. Garry Whannel argues for a conflictual intersection of sport, media, and nation. Although television has generated a star system for sports, that intensely individuated genre of personhood conflicts with national values of unity and thrift. TV simultaneously draws upon verbal myths of collectivity and difference, via audio commentary that emphasizes the nation through its team representatives and visual coverage that concentrates on specific stars. Contradictions may open up. And conflict is part of heroism, because the qualities of the hero are logocentrically dependent on undesirable and, above all, different behavior. Plus the various media that describe a special event—newspapers, Internet discussion groups, television, radio, guidebooks on the competition, the Web, videotapes—in different genres (news, highlights, and live coverage) also scramble the unity of such moments.

Most popular culture asks its public to reconsider intranational social allegiances, to play with class, gender, or ethnic identification and be entertained. When viewers tune in to the Olympic Games, they are certainly addressed as biased observers who want to see representatives of their nation at work. But it is also assumed they want transcendent excellence, to be part of an ethic, however fractured, of international spirit. It may even be that this spirit is most clearly present in its televisual reality, rather than among competitors and officials. A study of the 1984 Olympics showed viewers across seventeen countries were angered by the cultural imperialism, nationalism, and chauvinism on display, which they registered through a comparison of TV texts with Olympic ideals. Regulators were deluged with complaints about Australian broadcasts of the 1988 Olympics because of repeated jokes about non-Anglo-Saxon names and women's bodies, and Korean Americans across the United States were appalled by NBC's coverage. We all know audiences are not as easily programmed as texts, and academic analysis of U.S. TV sports spectators shows that both women and men spend their time in front of the set talking about "work, friends, cheerleaders, horniness, pizza-eating habits, and current movies" (Hartley 111, 116; Real *Super* 233–34; Brummett and Duncan 235; McKay *No* 96, 115–16; MacAloon "Commentary" 183; Messner, Duncan, and Jensen; Miller and Miller; Disch and Kane).

What to Do?

Sport is compromised for the left by its associations with disciplinary pedagogy, official ideology, civilizing missions, sexism, and homophobia. Games are highly rationalized, with means-oriented rationality central to their place in education and commerce, through the very quantification that is so insidious for workers. Clearly, the new international division of cultural labor, combined with textual trade, means sports and athletes now move around the world in person and as signs in ways that open up race, gender, and nation through capitalist expansion. Arrangements such as the Olympic programs are essentially huge multinational sponsorship infrastructures that coordinate services to corporations, negotiate media coverage, and license intellectual property rights across the globe (Rowe *Popular* 10; Guttmann 2–3; Jarvie and Maguire 230-63; Rowe, Lawrence, Miller, and McKay; Nafziger 502). Can the commercial empire of sport move beyond these limitations, or does it simply displace vicious patriarchal nationalism with insidious commodity fetishism? And what should our response be?

There are good sides to sport. First, it offers secular transcendence as well as unwelcome domination. Second, it values equal access. Third, some of its bureaucracies are suggestive organizational buffers between the state and commerce (without the totalizing politics of the church). Companies and international organizations dominate transnational culture. Sport's global processes, although part of those developments, offer other models. Along with corporate and nationalistic aspects, they embody unique components of international civil society. Extragovernmental, not-for-profit secular associations are much more powerful in sport than in any other area: the Fédération Internationale de Football Association and the IOC, for example. These bodies are dominated by First World countries, white affluence, boosterish expansionism, masculinist preoccupations, and undemocratic processes, but they provide a third voice, and an ethically inflected one, against state and multinational power. The U.S. Olympic Committee may have successfully sued the Gay Games over ownership of the Olympic name in the Supreme Court in 1987 (it did not take such actions against the Police, Diaper, or Dog Olympics), but the resultant publicity spread information about the alternative games across the world, along with special-interest magazines such as *Cocksucking Jocks, Ass Eating Jocks,* and *Jock Loads* (Pronger 252).

Some international organizations do excellent work in the area, notably those that otherwise look geopolitically anachronistic. Although UNESCO's attempts to supplant the IOC in the 1970s foundered along with the non-aligned movement's calls from Colombo for a New International Sports Order, less overtly radical institutions have provided successful stages for change, and UNESCO itself continues to promulgate definitions of "inappropriate commercialization" and works with the IOC to eliminate discrimination by gender. We can see a discourse of cultural rights in such international organizations, via the Supreme Council for Sports in Africa, the 1976 European Sport for All Charter, and its 1992 successor, the European Sports Charter. They feed into liberal developments inside the state apparatus, such as the Canadian Sport Coalition, guaranteeing access to disabled people and safe viewing conditions to spectators at stadium events. The Olympic Charter's Fundamental Principles include "building a peaceful and better world by educating youth through sport practiced without discrimination of any kind and in the Olympic spirit, which requires mutual understanding with a spirit of friendship, solidarity and fair-play." Those words led a young Asian Australian to propose that the 1956 Games in Melbourne conclude with the obverse of the Opening Ceremony. In place of marches by teams, the Olympiad would close with a promiscuous intermingling across nations, a carnivalesque unsettling of codes. Combining such ideas with the more prosaic life of international law can expand cultural rights, as the International Gay Rodeo Association has done over the past twenty years through its mixture of conventional competition with heterodox dress and conduct. The 1994 Gay Games challenged its own norms. When Stephane Vachon of Edmonton announced his withdrawal from an ice-skating event because his partner had fallen ill, officials asked if anyone in the crowd knew the necessary dance pattern. Charles Sinek, a straight coach, borrowed skates, practiced "the lady's part"—which he had long taught—for a quarter of an hour, and skated with Vachon; the pair won. That Hollywood-style trope was repeated, again with signs made to resignify, when Bill Wasmer danced as Gene Kelly to "Singin' in the Rain," shifting gear to accompany "It's Raining Men." The Commonwealth of Nations, having gone through a series of welcome postcolonializing shifts in identity from British Empire to British Empire and Commonwealth onto its new title, is a promising model of small-state diplomacy, following the dramatic success of African nations in imposing a boycott on the old South Africa. A Working Party on Strengthening Commonwealth Sport has reformed the Commonwealth Games to increase representation of women and do more for underprivileged young people (Nafziger 500, 505, 491 n. 6; McMurtry 419, 421, 424; Marchese; Feder; Houlihan 85–86, 90–91, 147).

This background is suggestive for future political action. Of course, there needs to be a shift in media production protocols and their presentation of national sport and culture. Given the U.S. Treasury felt justified in denying ABC a license for unrestricted coverage of the 1991 Pan American Games in Havana, such reform seems some distance off. Intellectuals on the left should lobby the networks and college sporting departments to heed and exceed civil rights legislation, and participate themselves in the lives of student athletes, stressing the improbability of a professional sporting career. Further, we need to intervene in areas such as international organization and dispute resolution; the developing field of global sports law sees debate conducted in terms of cultural rights, where we can also contribute (Hargreaves 183–84; Nafziger 495, 490, 489).

We should also organize against racial discrimination and performance hypocrisy in sport. Stacking is a dual metaphor. It refers to the primary labor market in men's football, where only whites need apply for most head coaching and quarterback positions: African Americans constitute about 70 percent of the NFL population and 6 percent of playmakers, with major implications for salaries and endorsements. Quarterbacks—most of them white—routinely identify with management and are among the few football players whose income is guaranteed regardless of physical condition. In bodybuilding, stacking connotes heavy use of swallowed and injected steroids to counteract side effects and maximize short-term gains in performance. In a sport that inscribes fantasies of superhuman power in its titles—Messrs. World, Universe, and Olympia—Nietzschean excess is hardly surprising. Terry Gene Bollea (aka Hulk Hogan) has testified that steroids are mandatory in some wrestling competitions. Let's disarticulate this hypermasculinity from the question of drugs, however. Performance-enhancing substances should be permitted in sport if they are legal and have been safely prescribed. The hypocrisy that allows dietetics, dietary supplements, beta-blockers, training in chambers that simulate other climates, electronic medical treatment, new starting blocks, painkilling injections, the contraceptive pill (taken by some athletes to regulate menstruation), shoes, poles, spikes, and physiological monitoring, but not certain lawful drugs such as cold suppressants, is inexcusable, a throwback to fantasies of pure and perfect competition that is necessarily contradictory. Let a thousand flowers bloom on drugs. They are dangerous—as is sport, as are legal drugs of recreation and medicine, as is the overwhelming bodily strain that athletes are subjected to by coaches. Many more people die from car racing, running, horse riding, boxing, and playing squash than from taking performance-enhancing drugs. In some countries, injuries sustained while playing sport are comparable in cost to those from traffic accidents. By slotting drugs into an ethical no-zone, and leaving competitiveness and differential life chances out of the critique, sports authorities assault athletes. Drug-using athletes are symptoms, not criminals (Lapchick and Benedict 12; Gramm and Schnell 67; Klein "Life's" 107, 115; "Wrestling"; Cashmore "Run" 23; McKay No 144–45).

What about metaphor's role in sporting allegory? It reinforces patriotism, especially at times of great conflict or formal celebration (promotions for the 1991 rugby league series between New South Wales and Queensland referred to the players as "scuds" and "patriots"). Twenty years earlier, the process worked the other way: Secretary of Defense Melvin Laird euphemized the mining of Haiphong Harbor and increased bombing of North Vietnam as "an expansion ball club," the Nixon White House staff called itself "operation linebacker," and Tricky Dicky's own nickname was "quarterback." During his presidency, Reagan regularly cited the role he played as footballer George Gipp in the 1940 biopic of a Notre Dame football coach, *Knute Rockne, All American.* This was supposed to stand as a universal sign of Americanness. Reagan repeatedly quoted Gipp's dying words inspiring his side to new heights—"Win one for the Gipper": we heard this in his 1981 commencement address at the university commemorated in the film, when he opened the 1984 L.A. Olympics, as a rallying cry during the Nevada Senate race in 1986, and at George Bush's nomination two years later. His henchmen troped it during the shameless 1998 vote to make Washington, D.C.'s airport name live forever in infamy. Reagan also referred to Walter Mondale in 1984 as "Coach tax-hike" (Shapiro 80, 87; McKay "Sport" 256; Reagan quoted in Monnington). This metaphorization associates romantic male sacrifice with national glory through classic second-order meaning: the mythic last words of a historical character as portrayed in a film. Four decades later, the actor playing him redisposes the words for political purposes, cleaving to himself the persona of the original speaker. Enunciation loses historical specificity.

The dominant allegorization of sport cross-validates the market and the nation through myths of representativeness, justice, and upward mobility that idealize politics, economics, and the social. Part of Reagan's success derived from his ability to narrativize and telescope, to distort conflict and then redispose it. Forty years ago, Richard Hoggart identified these qualities as crucial to the appeal professional sport holds for working people: the capacity to make politics both personal and concrete. This is not about doctrines of healthy bodies and minds, but dash and skill combined with fealty. Umberto Eco describes the discursive body of sport, when games played become games described and commentary overdetermines activity. He calls this "sport squared," more talking than doing. The next phase, "sport cubed," finds the commentary part of a media apparatus. The process is taken to an infinite multiplication once the media text itself is cited and remade: "discourse on a discourse about watching others' sport as discourse." There is no reason this articulation should be the province of the right. We have the beginnings of a proverbial pragmatics in the work of Harvey Sacks. He explains how some precedents come to be rearticulated and others not: why the very clear meaning of sporting speech (hitting below the belt, stacking the deck, way out in left field) intricates spatial metaphors with fairness, drawing attention to events that otherwise might pass without comment by invoking a moralizing discourse (McKay *No*; Rowe "Players'"; Hoggart 108–9; Eco 161–62; Sacks 106–7; McHoul).

The complex double-declutching between the personal immediacy of sport and its collective symbolic power has to be evaluated for costs to those who comply with or refuse it. The left might draw on sport as an ethical, intertextual center, just as dominant discourse has done. To assist the process, we need work on sport that analyzes business, the body, the nation, and television, encompassing the principal discursive formations of the phenomenon. I think of these as concerned with sport qua entertainment, education, political symbol, and science in experienced, governed, and commercial forms. This requires a combination of political economy, textual analysis, and ethnography across the sports media, amateur and professional organizations, international agencies, and corporations, tracking the commodification and governmentalization of bodies. Such work could make for some reciprocity between sport and mainstream sociocultural theory. Developments in global capitalism toward the effacement of divisions between production and circulation enter the agenda, too. Sport shows how the body is an always already mediated object rearticulated with the supposed essence of the person via training and play. Sports stars instantiate the possibilities and limitations of life within formal and informal rules and expectations. The sport watcher's body, too, in its visceral reaction to events of great moment on TV or at a stadium, is a crucial site of public commitment and energy, frequently in destructive and violent ways. This key cultural technology can have its meanings changed if these iterative moves turn away from competition and hierarchy and toward collaboration and exchange (equally valued aspects of most sports).

Sporting spectatorship and participation have significant positive aspects. Yes, narcissism, a high component of commodification, intense sexist pressure about body image, and unpleasant associations with militarism and Tayloristic discipline are dominant. But there is also a physical pleasure and ecstasy that can come with the meld of individual and collaborative striving and watching in sport, a phenomenal form that merges the empirico-transcendental couplet. This has meant a certain reclamation of public and private health from a male-dominated medical establishment, criticisms of fast-food and cigarette capitalism, and the generation of new, noncompetitive sport alternatives that connect to environmental awareness and experience. So if we can't get away from sports metaphors, let's at least fight to control the allegorical ground.

Works Cited

Agnew, Robert, and David M. Petersen. 1989. "Leisure and Delinquency." *Social Problems* 36, no. 4: 332–50.

Allison, Lincoln. 1994. "The Olympic Movement and the End of the Cold War." *World Affairs* 157, no. 2: 92–97.

Alter, Joseph S. 1995. "The Celibate Wrestler: Sexual Chaos, Embodied Balance and Competitive Politics in North India." *Contributions to Indian Sociology* 29, nos. 1–2: 109–31.

Arbena, Joseph L. 1993. "Sport and Social Change in Latin America." In *Sport in Social Development: Traditions, Transitions, and Transformations*, ed. Alan G. Ingham and John W. Loy, 97–117. Champaign, Ill.: Human Kinetics.

Arnold, Peter J. 1994. "Sport and Moral Education." *Journal of Moral Education* 23, no. 1: 75–89.

Bale, John. 1991. *The Brawn Drain: Foreign Student-Athletes in American Universities.* Urbana: University of Illinois Press.

Blinde, Elaine M., and Diane E. Taub. 1992. "Women Athletes as Falsely Accused Deviants: Managing the Lesbian Stigma." *Sociological Quarterly* 33, no. 4: 521–33.

Brodeur, Pierre. 1988. "Employee Fitness: Doctrines and Issues." In *Not Just a Game: Essays in Canadian Sport Sociology*, ed. Jean Harvey and Hart Cantelon, 227–42. Ottawa: University of Ottawa Press.

Brummett, Barry, and Margaret Carlisle Duncan. 1992. "Toward a Discursive Ontology of Media." *Critical Studies in Mass Communication* 9, no. 3: 229–49.

Bryant, Jennings, Paul Comisky, and Dolf Zillmann. 1977. "Drama in Sports Commentary." *Journal of Communication* 26, no. 3: 140–49.

Burke, Peter. 1995. "Viewpoint: The Invention of Leisure in Early Modern Europe." *Past and Present* no. 146 (February): 136–50.

Cahn, Susan K. 1994. *Coming on Strong: Gender and Sexuality in Twentieth-Century Women's Sport.* Cambridge: Harvard University Press.

Cashmore, Ellis. 1994. *. . . and Then There Was Television.* London: Routledge.

———. "Run of the Pill." 1994. *New Statesman and Society* 7, no. 328: 23–24.

Cooper, Pamela. 1995. "Marathon Women and the Corporation." *Journal of Women's History* 7, no. 4: 62–81.

Davis, Laurel. 1997. *The Swimsuit Issue and Sport: Hegemonic Masculinity in Sports Illustrated.* Albany: State University of New York Press.

Dewar, Alison. 1993. "Sexual Oppression in Sport: Past, Present, and Future Alternatives." In *Sport in Social Development: Traditions, Transitions, and Transformations*, ed. Alan G. Ingham and John W. Loy, 147–65. Champaign, Ill.: Human Kinetics.

Disch, Lisa, and Mary Jo Kane. 1996. "When a Looker Is Really a Bitch: Lisa Olson, Sport, and the Heterosexual Matrix." *Signs: Journal of Women in Culture and Society* 21, no. 2: 278–308.

Dyer, Richard. 1992. *Only Entertainment.* London: Routledge.

Eco, Umberto. 1987. *Travels in Hyperreality: Essays* (trans. William Weaver). London: Picador.

Eichberg, Henning. 1986. "The Enclosure of the Body: On the Historical Relativity of 'Health,' 'Nature' and the Environment of Sport." *Journal of Contemporary History* 21, no. 1: 99–121.

Elias, Norbert. 1986. "An Essay on Sport and Violence." In *Quest for Excitement: Sport and Leisure in the Civilizing Process*, Norbert Elias and Eric Dunning, 150–74. Oxford: Basil Blackwell.

———. 1986. "Introduction." In *Quest for Excitement: Sport and Leisure in the Civilizing Process*, Norbert Elias and Eric Dunning, 19–62. Oxford: Basil Blackwell.

Ellsworth, Elizabeth. 1986. "Illicit Pleasures: Feminist Spectators and Personal Best." *Wide Angle* 8, no. 2: 45–56.

Feder, Abigail. 1994. "Kiss Me, Skate." *Village Voice*, 5 July, 140.

Fiddes, Nick. 1991. *Meat: A Natural Symbol*. London: Routledge.

Fussell, Sam. 1993. "Bodybuilder Americanus." *Michigan Quarterly Review* 32, no. 4: 577–96.

Given, Jock. 1995. "Red, Black, Gold to Australia: Cathy Freeman and the Flags." *Media Information Australia* no. 75 (February): 46–56.

Goldlust, John. 1987. *Playing for Keeps: Sport, the Media and Society*. Melbourne: Longman Cheshire.

Gramm, Cynthia L., and John F. Schnell. 1994. "Difficult Choices: Crossing the Picket Line during the 1987 National Football League Strike." *Journal of Labor Economics* 12, no. 1: 41–73.

Griffin, Christine. 1993. *Representations of Youth: The Study of Youth and Adolescence in Britain and America*. Cambridge: Polity.

Gruneau, Richard. 1993. "The Critique of Sport in Modernity: Theorizing Power, Culture, and the Politics of the Body." In *The Sports Process: A Comparative and Developmental Approach*, ed. Eric Dunning, Joseph A. Maguire, and Robert E. Pearton, 85–109. Champaign, Ill.: Human Kinetics.

Gruneau, Richard, and David Whitson. 1993. *Hockey Night in Canada: Sport, Identities and Cultural Politics*. Toronto: Garamond.

Guttmann, Allen. 1994. *Games and Empires: Modern Sports and Cultural Imperialism*. New York: Columbia University Press.

Hall, M. Ann. 1993. "Gender and Sport in the 1990s: Feminism, Culture, and Politics." *Sport Science Review* 2, no. 1: 48–68.

Harari, Fiona. 1993. "The New Face of Beauty." *Australian*, 18 June, 15.

Hargreaves, Jennifer. 1994. *Sporting Females: Critical Issues in the History and Sociology of Women's Sports*. London: Routledge.

Hartley, John. 1992. *Tele-ology: Studies in Television*. London: Routledge.

Hitchcock, John R. 1991. *Sportscasting*. Boston: Focal.

Hoggart, Richard. 1971. *The Uses of Literacy: Aspects of Working-Class Life with Special Reference to Publications and Entertainments*. Harmondsworth: Penguin.

Houlihan, Barrie. 1994. *Sport and International Politics*. London: Harvester Wheatsheaf.

Jarvie, Grant, and Joseph Maguire. 1994. *Sport and Leisure in Social Thought*. London: Routledge.

Jhally, Sut. 1990. *The Codes of Advertising: Fetishism and the Political Economy of Meaning in the Consumer Society*. New York: Routledge.

Jiobu, Robert M. 1988. "Racial Inequality in a Public Arena: The Case of Baseball." *Social Forces* 67, no. 2: 524–34.

Kang, Joon-Mann. 1988. "Sports, Media and Cultural Dependency." *Journal of Contemporary Asia* 18, no. 4: 430–43.

Klein, Alan M. 1991. "Sport and Culture as Contested Terrain: Americanization in the Caribbean." *Sociology of Sport Journal* 8, no. 1: 79–85.

———. 1995. "Life's Too Short to Die Small: Steroid Use among Male Bodybuilders." In *Men's Health and Illness: Gender, Power, and the Body*, ed. Donald Sabo and David Frederick Gordon, 105–20. Thousand Oaks, Calif.: Sage.

Lapchick, Richard E., and Jeffrey R. Benedict. 1993. "1993 Racial Report Card." *CSSS Digest* 5, no. 1: 1, 4–8, 12–13.

Lasch, Christopher. 1979. *The Culture of Narcissism: American Life in an Age of Diminishing Expectations*. New York: Warner.

Lawrence, Geoffrey, and David Rowe. 1986. "The Corporate Pitch: Televised Cricket under Capitalism." In *Power Play: Essays in the Sociology of Australian Sport*, ed. Geoffrey Lawrence and David Rowe, 166–78. Sydney: Hale & Ironmonger.

Leath, Virginia M., and Angela Lumpkin. 1992. "An Analysis of Sportswomen on the

Covers and in the Feature Articles of Women's Sports and Fitness Magazine, 1975–1989." *Journal of Sport & Social Issues* 16, no. 2: 121–26.

Lenskyj, Helen. 1991. "Combating Homophobia in Sport and Physical Education." *Sociology of Sport Journal* 8, no. 1: 61–69.

Loy, John, David L. Andrews, and Robert E. Rinehart. 1993. "The Body in Culture and Sport." *Sport Science Review* 2, no. 1: 69–91.

Lueschen, Guenther. 1993. "Doping in Sport: The Social Structure of a Deviant Subculture." *Sport Science Review* 2, no. 1: 92–106.

Lumpkin, Angela, and Linda D. Williams. 1991. "An Analysis of *Sports Illustrated* Feature Articles, 1954–1987." *Sociology of Sport Journal* 8, no. 1: 16–32.

Lurie, Rachel. 1994. "Martina and Me: A Trilogy." In *SportsDykes: Stories from On and Off the Field*, ed. Susan Fox Rogers, 120–29. New York: St. Martin's.

MacAloon, John. 1987. "Missing Stories: American Politics and Olympic Discourse." *Gannett Center Journal* 1, no. 2: 111–42.

———. 1989. "Commentary: Critical Data and Rhetorical Theory." *Critical Studies in Mass Communication* 6, no. 2: 183–94.

Maguire, Joseph. 1993. "Bodies, Sportscultures and Societies: A Critical Review of Some Theories in the Sociology of the Body." *International Review for the Sociology of Sport* 28, no. 1: 33–52.

Marchese, John. 1993. "Bustin' Stereotypes." *New York Times*, 26 September, 8v.

Marqusee, Mike. 1994. *Anyone But England: Cricket and the National Malaise*. London: Verso.

Marshall, D. W., and G. Cook. 1992. "The Corporate (Sports) Sponsor." *International Journal of Advertising* 11, no. 4: 307–24.

Mason, Tony. 1995. *Passion of the People? Football in South America*. London: Verso.

McHoul, Alec. 1997. "On Doing 'We's': Where Sport Leaks into Everyday Life." *Journal of Sport & Social Issues* 21, no. 3: 315–20.

McKay, Jim. 1991. *No Pain, No Gain? Sport and Australian Culture*. Sydney: Prentice Hall.

———. 1992. "Sport and the Social Construction of Gender." In *Society and Gender: An Introduction to Sociology*, ed. Gillian Lupton, Patricia M. Short, and Rosemary Whip, 245–65. Sydney: Macmillan.

———. 1995. "'Just Do It': Corporate Sports Slogans and the Political Economy of 'Enlightened Racism.'" *Discourse: Studies in the Cultural Politics of Education* 16, no. 2: 191–201.

McKay, Jim, and David Kirk. 1992. "Ronald McDonald Meets Baron de Coubertin: Prime Time Sport and Commodification." *ACHPER National Journal* no. 136 (winter): 10–13.

McMurtry, Roy. 1993. "Sport and the Commonwealth Heads of Government." *Round Table* no. 328: 419–26.

Messner, Michael A., Margaret Carlisle Duncan, and Kerry Jensen. 1993. "Separating the Men from the Girls: The Gendered Language of Televised Sports." *Gender & Society* 7, no. 1: 121–37.

Miller, Phyllis, and Randy Miller. 1995. "The Invisible Woman: Female Sports Journalists in the Workplace." *Journalism and Mass Communication Quarterly* 72, no. 4: 883–89.

Mitchell, Susan, and Ken Dyer. 1985. *Winning Women: Challenging the Norms in Australian Sport*. Ringwood: Penguin.

Monnington, Terry. 1993. "Politicians and Sport: Uses and Abuses." In *The Changing Politics of Sport*, ed. Lincoln Allison, 125–50. Manchester: Manchester University Press.

Montemayor, Gail. 1995. "Fox Sets New Marketing Goals for Football Season." *Marketing Society News* 6, no. 2: 5.

Morse, Margaret. 1983. "Sport on Television: Replay and Display." In *Regarding Television*, ed. E. Ann Kaplan, 44–66. Los Angeles: American Film Institute, 1983.

Moss, Howard B., George L. Panzak, and Ralph E. Tarter. 1993. "Sexual Functioning of Male Anabolic Steroid Users." *Archives of Sexual Behavior* 22, no. 1: 1–12.

Nafziger, James A. R. 1992. "International Sports Law: A Replay of Characteristics and Trends." *American Journal of International Law* 86, no. 3: 489–518.

Nelson, Mariah Burton. 1994. "Personal Focus." In *Gay Games IV Official Souvenir Program*, 1994, 34–35.

O'Donnell, Hugh. 1994. "Mapping the Mythical: A Geopolitics of National Sporting Stereotypes." *Discourse and Society* 5, no. 3: 345–80.

Park, Roberta J. 1994. "A Decade of the Body: Researching and Writing about the History of Health, Fitness, Exercise, and Sport, 1983–1993." *Journal of Sport History* 21, no. 1: 59–82.

Pener, Degen. 1994. "The Games Men Play." In *Gay Games IV Official Souvenir Program, 1994*, 26–30.

Pronger, Brian. 1990. *The Arena of Masculinity: Sports, Homosexuality, and the Meaning of Sex*. New York: St. Martin's.

Real, Michael R. 1989. *Super Media: A Cultural Studies Approach*. Newbury Park, Calif.: Sage.

———. 1996. "The Postmodern Olympics: Technology and the Commodification of the Olympic Movement." *Quest* 48, no. 1: 9–24.

Reed, Susan. 1994. "Unlevel Playing Fields." In *Gay Games IV Official Souvenir Program*, 1994, 20–24.

Rowe, David. 1991. "Players' Worktime: Sport and Leisure in Australia." *ACHPER National Journal* no. 131 (autumn): 4–10.

———. 1995. *Popular Cultures: Rock Music, Sport and the Politics of Pleasure*. London: Sage.

Rowe, David, and Peter Brown. 1994. "Promoting Women's Sport: Theory, Policy and Practice." *Leisure Studies* 13, no. 2: 97–110.

Rowe, David, Geoffrey Lawrence, Toby Miller, and Jim McKay. 1994. "Global Sport? Core Concern and Peripheral Vision." *Media, Culture & Society* 16, no. 4: 661–75.

Sabo, Donald. 1993. "Sociology of Sport and New World Disorder." *Sport Science Review* 2, no. 1: 1–9.

Sabo, Donald, and Sue Curry Jansen. 1992. "Images of Men in Sport Media: The Social Reproduction of Gender Order." In *Men, Masculinity, and the Media*, ed. Steve Craig, 169–84. Newbury Park, Calif.: Sage.

Sack, Allen L. 1991. "The Underground Economy of College Football." *Sociology of Sport Journal* 8, no. 1: 1–15.

Sacks, Harvey. 1995. *Lectures on Conversation* (ed. Gail Jefferson). Oxford: Basil Blackwell.

Savan, Leslie. 1994. *The Sponsored Life: Ads, TV, and American Culture*. Philadelphia: Temple University Press.

Scraton, Sheila. 1987. "'Boys Muscle in Where Angels Fear to Tread': Girls' Sub-cultures and Physical Activities." In *Sport, Leisure and Social Relations*, ed. John Horne, David Jary, and Alan Tomlinson, 160–86. London: Routledge & Kegan Paul.

Shapiro, Michael J. 1989. "Representing World Politics: The Sport/War Intertext." In *International/Intertextual Relations: Postmodern Readings of World Politics*, ed. James Der Derian and Michael J. Shapiro, 69–96. Lexington, Mass.: Lexington.

Shilling, Chris. 1994. Review of *Body Matters*. *Sociological Review* 42, no. 1: 143–45.

Skillen, Anthony. 1993. "Sport: An Historical Phenomenology." *Philosophy* 68, no. 265: 343–68.

Streibel, Dan. 1989. "A History of the Boxing Film, 1894–1915: Social Control and Social Reform in the Progressive Era." *Film History* 3, no. 3: 235–57.

Thompson, Lee Austin. 1986. "Professional Wrestling in Japan: Media and Message." *International Review for the Sociology of Sport* 21, no. 1: 65–82.

Tudor, Andrew. 1992. "Them and Us: Story and Stereotype in TV World Cup Coverage." *European Journal of Communication* 7, no. 3: 391–413.

Vines, Gail. 1988. "Is Sport Good for Children?" *New Scientist* 119, no. 1622: 46–51.

Vogel, Harold L. 1995. *Entertainment Industry Economics: A Guide for Financial Analysis* (3d ed.). Cambridge: Cambridge University Press.

Volkerling, Michael. 1994. "Death or Transfiguration: The Future for Cultural Policy in New Zealand." *Culture and Policy* 6, no. 1: 7–28.

Whannel, Garry. 1992. *Fields in Vision: Television Sport and Cultural Transformation.* London: Routledge.

"Wrestling Promoter's Trial on Steroids Charges Begins." 1994. *New York Times,* 7 July, B6.1A.

Part I ▶ Building Nations

Kung Fu Cinema, Frugality, and Tanzanian Asian Youth Culture: *Ujamaa* and Tanzanian Youth in the Seventies

May Joseph

In the opening scene of his performance piece "In Between Space," Shishir Kurup, a Los Angeles-based Asian American performance artist, narrates growing up in Mombasa, Kenya, in the 1970s:

> We live over here in Pandya House, a tenement building with shops and offices below. Over here is the Regal Cinema which exclusively plays American shoot-em-ups, Italian spaghetti-shoot-em-ups and Chinese Kung-Fu-em-ups. Sam Peckinpah, Sergio Leone, Run-Run Shaw, Raymond Chow. Tickets are two shillings and forty cents for rows A–J (which work out at about a quarter in American cash), 3/6 for rows K–Z and 4/8 for the balcony. In this theater Eastwood is badass, McQueen is cool, Bronson is tough and Bruce Lee can kick all their asses. Shane and Shaft and Super-Fly and Cleopatra Jones. We hear names like Thalmas Rasulala and Lee Van Cleef. Eli Wallach is the Ugly, Yul Brynner the King and I the kid with the open mouth stuffing popcorn down my throat. In the Indian film houses, Rajesh Khanna, "Shotgun" Sinha, Dharmendra, reign supreme. Amitabh Bhachan isn't quite the god he is soon to become and Zeenat Aman is the babe of all our nocturnal emissions.[1]

What Kurup invokes for Mombasa could be found elsewhere in the East Africa of this time. This seventies cinema had a transnational impact that intertwines broader ideological, nationalist, Pan-Africanist and anticolonialist sentiments in the local cultural politics of production and consumption. In the midst of Cold War tensions, nationalist fervor, state sovereignty, and a visible Pan-African solidarity, 1970s East African popular culture is a crucible of the competing international ideologies of socialism, communism, and capitalism across and within national borders. The simultaneous transnational figuration of these ideologies had an impact on local cultural politics within Third World socialisms.[2]

In Tanzania, for example, experiments in socialist democracy foregrounded education and cultural nationalism as primary tools for solidifying the fledgling state. Tanzanian youth were mobilized toward the broader goal of promoting a socialist youth culture. The harnessing of youth in the interest of national culture influenced the subjectivities, pleasures, and spectatorships possible. This in turn affected the styles and self-fashioning consumed and publicly exhibited by youth.

In this essay, I investigate some of the connections among diasporic South Asian youth culture, state socialism, and transnationalism by considering the immense appeal and wide circulation of Bruce Lee and kung fu cinema during the seventies in Tanzania. I examine the early years of nation building through the mobilization of youth from the subjective standpoint of my experiences as a Tanzanian Asian youth during the Africanization and nationalization measures of Dar es Salaam during the 1960s and 1970s.

The popular practices of *ujamaa*, Julius Nyerere's implementation of Tanzanian socialism, coalesce in interesting ways with the phenomenology of kung fu spectatorship. Juxtaposed, they generate a montage of urban Tanzanian youth culture around "the performance of frugality." The notion of a performance of frugality looks at the performed sites of anticonsumption, implied by *ujamaa*, or self-reliance. By suggesting here that ideologies are enacted, I dislodge the structural/functionalist approach to socialism and instead probe the phenomenological avenues of self-invention for youth within the discourses of the state. In this essay, I unpack the realms of imaginative self-fashioning that shape Tanzanian Asian youth culture under African socialist modernity.[3]

From 1962 to 1985, Tanzania developed a uniquely pedagogical approach to state formation that was known as *ujamaa*. *Ujamaa* was an approach to nation building based on village communalism. As Julius Nyerere, the Tanzanian head of state, declares in the controversial policy paper "*Ujamaa*: The Basis of African Socialism":

> *Ujamaa*, then, or "familyhood," describes our socialism. It is opposed to capitalism, which seeks to build a happy society on the basis of exploitation of man by man; and it is equally opposed to doctrinaire socialism which seeks to build its happy society on a philosophy of inevitable conflict between man and man. We in Africa have no more need of being "converted" to socialism than we have of being "taught" democracy. Both are rooted in our own past—in the traditional society that produced us. Modern African socialism can draw from its traditional heritage the recognition of "society" as an extension of the basic family unit.[4]

Ujamaa implemented "villagization," a system of rural development based on communal self-reliance.[5] This policy move asserted a number of ideological strategies aimed at decolonizing the state. By invoking traditionalism and "familyhood," Nyerere countered Western conceptions of the nuclear family by offering an African-derived conception of communalism, stemming from indigenous kinship systems that are extended. He proposed *ujamaa* as a community-based system of development that shares available wealth rather than accumulates it in the interest of the individual.

The *ujamaa* policy shifted the emphasis away from Soviet and European traditions of socialism toward indigenous traditions of socialism that shaped local practices of governance. *Ujamaa* villages were not to be created through the violent collectivism of Soviet communism. Rather, the paradigm of familyhood offered a different philosophical and epistemological tradition from its Western counterparts, and therein lay its possibility for local transformation.[6]

The philosophical underpinnings of *ujamaa,* or self-reliance, were grounded in a destabilization of Western theories of modernization. For Nyerere, the dilemmas afflicting recently decolonized and exploited African states demanded specific local strategies of development. Consequently, Western periodization narratives with the focus on urbanization imposed upon newly independent states such as Tanzania demanded critical reconsideration. This conscious effort to critique Western notions of modernity combined with a policy of nonalignment articulated by the Bandung conference and Afro-Asian nations generated alternative approaches toward African modernity such as *ujamaa.* As a radical measure to delink from the dependency relationships of Western aid sources in the long term, this policy privileged the rural over the urban. It attempted to redress class inequities urgently by emphasizing the majority constituencies of peasants and workers over the minority urban bourgeoisie.[7]

There were many levels at which *ujamaa* as a theoretical argument had implications for critiques of modernity. It consciously attempted to create a nonaligned African socialist theory of economic development that was organic and people centered. *Ujamaa* also operated as an ideological vehicle for Africanization, by drawing upon indigenous as well as international philosophies of social change in a uniquely Tanzanian model that privileged the agricultural majority. And it drew upon the idea of tradition as a corrective to the simple dichotomies of tradition and modernity prevalent in modernization theories of development, where tradition implies backwardness. Instead, Nyerere infused the idea of tradition as a contingent, shifting, and inseparable part of the modernization process, through the practice of villagization.

Criticisms from within the Tanzanian experiment dispelled the utopian hopes of finding ways of resisting Western notions of accumulation through the government creation of *ujamaa* villages. Instead of a pastoral communalism that was community oriented, democratic in spirit, and free from the ills of landlordism, a complex hierarchy of centralized power interrupted this vision. Women, children, and the urban and rural poor were marginalized in these socialist initiatives.[8] But during those heady early years, policies were still unfolding, the air was thick with change, and promise was on the ground.

Frugality and Tanzanian Asian Youth

Urban youth emerged ambivalently under the sign of *ujamaa*, as it emphasized rural development and the engagement of youth in economic self-reliance activities during these early years of socialism. On the one hand was the sense of vibrancy and rapid social change, with racial integration in the school systems, literacy programs, modernization of the school curriculum with introduction of new science and modern mathematics, Africanization of education through the introduction of Swahili as the medium of instruction, and the introduction of civics, which resulted in students trying to talk and behave like socialists. On the other hand was a distinct antiurban logic fueled by *ujamaa*'s principles. Teachers and pupils of primary and secondary schools in Dar es Salaam were obliged to practice socialist tenets through agricultural projects. The idea was to inculcate a sense of responsibility toward the larger community, which was presumed to be agricultural. The resulting tensions between youth and the antiurban policies of the state created new sites of antagonism and invention for urban youth.[9]

The performance of frugality is one such avenue of self-invention that emerges in the tension between urban youth and antiurban policies of early *ujamaa* implementation. Frugality in *ujamaa* is a structure of feeling between the logic of consumption and the practice of anticonsumption under policies of economic self-reliance. As theorized by Nyerere, frugality was a strategy for culturally delinking the youthful state.[10] It offered strategies of personhood drawing upon indigenous African socialism through the inculcation of a national consciousness of self-reliance. Sports, dance (*ngomas*), marching, farming, and national service were all aspects of this performance of frugality. These spheres of physical embodiment were practiced as state-implemented technologies of care for youth.

Rising anti-Asian and antiurban sentiments under intensive Africanizing measures connected the frugality of Tanzanian Asian youth culture to *ujamaa*. One site of this connection was the popularity of kung fu cinema during this time. The reception and translations of kung fu instantiate the struggles of frugality that shaped a non-African Tanzanian youth constituency under socialist modernity.

The early 1970s saw an influx of Hong Kong, Chinese, and American kung fu cinema into urban Tanzanian popular culture. As part of a larger international film market of Hindi films, Italian spaghetti westerns, Soviet exports, American westerns, and the very popular blaxploitation films, Bruce Lee's *Enter the Dragon* (1973) generated a passion for kung fu among urban South Asian Tanzanian youth. Popular song lyrics like "Everybody was kung fu fighting," posters of Bruce Lee on the streets of Dar es Salaam, the fetish for the nunchaku and black-cloth Maoist shoes, the speedy martial movements of beachside wrestling matches, side kicks, and one-finger push-ups were popular. The Mao suits worn by groups of railway technicians from China and North Korea brought to Tanzania during the seventies—and worn by Lee as well—held a certain chic for local Asian youth. The images of Jim Kelly, Fred Williamson, Tamara Dobson, Pam Grier, Grace Jones, and Richard Roundtree also circulated as representations of "America" or the "West."[11]

Tanzanian 1970s youth culture's heterogeneity was inflected by its inherited colonialist logic of residential segregation. The popular youth cultures of minorities such as the Asians were visible in the Asian parts of the city, such as Mosque Street and Upanga. Bollywood (Hindi) cinema played at downtown movie houses like the New Chox, Avalon, and the Odeon, as well as at the popular drive-in theater in Dar es Salaam. Amitabh Bhachan, Rajesh Khanna, and Zeenat Aman embodied a hip Indian diasporic popular sensibility, but the rise of Bruce Lee as a charismatic and diabolical Asian superhero operating between communist and capitalist economies broke the borders of an otherwise segregated urban Asian Tanzanian youth culture.

The popularity of Hong Kong and Chinese kung fu cinema, epitomized by Bruce Lee films, created a multiethnic spectatorship within the implicitly segregated city of Dar es Salaam. As an ambivalent sign of Maoist socialism and American self-invention, Bruce Lee's films opened up desire and pleasure within contradictory sites of cultural citizenship such as the movie houses, the rapidly integrating movie audiences, and American popular culture itself. Lee and the kung fu cinema he popularized shifted the binaries of the Black/white axis of race discourse in the reception of popular cinema in Tanzania by presenting a predominantly Asian visual field for a heterogeneous Tanzanian audience.

Tanzanian spectatorship in the 1970s drew upon new definitions of pleasure, social space, and emancipatory possibilities within an African-style socialism. It forged a realm of visual modernity through the rhetoric of frugality and a radically new technology of the self. The economy of kung fu movement echoed a local aesthetics of the frugal, unadorned but active socialist body, capable of serving the state. This empathy, combined with

Maoist-inflected rhetoric and the narrative of capitalist versus revolutionary, youth versus feudal lord, and decadence versus scarcity, resonated with the structure of Tanzanian socialist pedagogy.

Kung fu foregrounds an abhorrence of any technology other than the self as a means of juridical and revolutionary intervention, highlighting the importance of frugality as an everyday strategy. It does this through the striking absence of guns or bombs, a genre formula that is theatrically fastidious for its austere focus on the frugal body. By marking capitalism and decadence onto the body, socialist notions of self and spatiality emerge in Lee's films *Enter the Dragon, Fists of Fury* (or *The Big Boss*), *The Chinese Connection* (or *Fist of Fury*), and *Return of the Dragon*. In contrast to the deindividualized rhetoric of Tanzanian socialism, however, Lee valorizes the disenfranchised masses on whose behalf he fights, but foregrounds the individualistic self as problem solver.

The question of what kind of pleasure this contradiction produces for socialist youth longing links kung fu cinema to Tanzanian socialist technologies of self. Kung fu spectatorship brings together the disjunctures among the material frugality of the socialist state, the aesthetic frugality of unadorned martial bodies combating capitalist evil such as greedy landlords, and the excess of the spectator consuming Hong Kong and American cinema in a culture of anticonsumption. It performs the disjunctures between policies of structural delinking and the transnational flows of enjoyment and consumption. Watching kung fu cinema stages the tensions between a desire for transnational circulation of commodities under conditions of scarcity. It performs the ambivalence of frugality as it invites spectators to consume globalizing commodities such as Hong Kong cinema, structuring a transnationally linked sphere of enjoyment.

Struggling between the seductive machines of First World technologies of the body and everyday life under conditions of frugality within African socialism, youth consumed kung fu, with its contradictory play with gender, sexuality, and masculinity. These dimensions were otherwise silenced under the centralized one-party state of the Tanzanian African National Union, later the Chama Cha Mapinduzi, whose privileged forms of cultural citizenship were inflected by its proletarian and agrarian-based economic policies of socialist belonging.

Decolonization, Governmentality, and the Invention of Youth

The circulation of kung fu cinema in the seventies in Tanzania raises the particular methodological, ideological, and aesthetic dilemmas embedded in the category "youth" during the first decades of decolonization in an African socialist state. The dilemma of theorizing "youth" outside a European/U.S. framework lies in the epistemological assumptions of Anglo-American youth subcultural theory. This theory is predicated on the established sovereignty of the state, from within which forms of late-capitalist culture produce notions of self, education, leisure, location, community, hegemony, and antagonism in relation to the state. Consequently, much theorizing of youth studies of the 1970s and 1980s assumes certain institutional orthodoxies regarding the forms of state legitimation of cultural and legal citizenships, through which notions of youth culture as pathology and moral panic emerge in Britain and the United States.[12]

The work of the scholars of the Birmingham school of cultural studies has been crucial to laying the groundwork for such an analysis. This work addresses representations of white and Black working-class youth in Britain.[13] Although the theories of the Birmingham school offer approaches toward reading "youth," the particular contexts of socialist states such as Tanzania caution against the drawing of easy parallels between youth formations across national and political cultures. The heterogeneity of Tanzania's 120 ethnicities, for instance, complicates the theories of difference that Anglo-American youth discourse offers. A dialogue of homogeneity and hybridity, of authenticity and inauthenticity, has molded the dialogue on race as these heterogeneous communities emerged as a socialist majority that was cautiously if not explicitly ambivalent toward its commercially successful non-African communities, such as the Asians.

As opposed to the longer history of nation formation around which Anglo-American subcultural theory emerges, the recentness of postcolonial sovereignty creates the epistemological and historical bind of theorizing youth within a contingent modernity in formation. The early writings of Julius Nyerere, from 1952 to 1967, are useful here. They offer a continuous political analysis of the institutional, cultural, and representational practices of colonial bureaucracies that articulated "young people" in discrete and obvious ways in the interests of the colonial mother country.[14]

In an effort to counter the debilitating neglect of youth in the colonial era, Nyerere proposed a radical approach to educating youth. He initiated efforts to update and Africanize the curriculum, introduce African history, and implement Swahili as the medium of instruction. He critiqued the anthropological model of civilizing missionaries Christianizing indigenous populations, through which the colonial bureaucracy sought to perpetuate itself. Instead, he proposed postcolonial pedagogical strategies of Africanization for decolonizing youth culture. Such a syncretic modern approach to cultural delinking seeks to reverse colonial penetration rather than presume mono-cultural isolation.

For Nyerere, education was crucial for decolonizing the state and consolidating the socialist nation. With the implementation of Swahili as the lingua franca and language of education, a visibly socialist Swahili youth culture was forged as national culture. Schools were nationalized and generated a secular, nationalist, anticolonial youth culture. Under the secularity of nationalization, ethnically diverse schools coexisted, shaping varied conceptions of youth in relation to the state, to religions such as Islam, and to the intraethnic cultures within which youth existed in Dar es Salaam. Ex-colonial institutions such as Boy Scouts and Girl Guides; the technical institutes teaching needlework, cooking, and carpentry; the sports clubs; and the Christian youth groups, such as the YWCA and the YMCA, articulated Tanzanians as "youth." Youth emerged as a diverse, polylingual, multidenominational constituency.

State policies demanded that the socialist commitments of youth be affirmed through physical expressions of solidarity. These physical manifestations were performances of socialist commitment, consolidated around projects of self-reliance, mainly agricultural, where young socialists were trained in notions of communal responsibility. Under the overarching gaze of the state during the first decade of independence, youth negotiated the multiple forms of containment and coercion through which subcultural forms sprang outside the overdetermined space called national culture.[15]

For Tanzanians in the 1960s, a hegemonic "national" culture was still struggling to be articulated through delinking, nationalization, indigenization, vernacularization, and self-reliance.[16] "Youth" was a founding category for the radically socialist state. Consequently, emergent expressive youth cultures had to contend with either containment or co-optation by the state. The struggle to create a cohesive national youth culture in opposition to the existing colonial legacy of "Englishness" fabricated by the machines of schooling, church, jurisprudence, administration, and bureaucracy became a new orthodoxy against which subcultural forms emerged.[17]

In resonance with Lenin and Mao, Nyerere prioritized youth in his experiments with African socialism. He emphasized this by establishing new forms of education. This situated youth in a powerful relation to the emerging state.[18] The anti-imperial strategies of many African intellectuals and revolutionaries, such as Patrice Lumumba, Kwame Nkrumah, C. L. R. James, Walter Rodney, Frantz Fanon, Leopold Senghor, Samora Michel, Tom Mboya, and Ngugi Wa Thiongo, contributed to the theory of youth formulated by Nyerere. Youth was a pedagogy of nation formation for Nyerere. This contrasted with the colonial neglect of youth during the 1940s and 1950s. Under such contending ideological and cultural terrains of antagonism and desire, "youth" emerged as a new orthodoxy, a rhetoric of statehood that was conformist but radical in its larger political aim.[19]

Nyerere's self-conscious theorization and implementation of youth culture into Tanzanian public life was dialogically linked to the international public sphere. His pedagogy of youth—the mobilization of youth in the interests of the state—should be viewed in the context of the instrumental role played by the internationalist youth movements in the communist states of the Soviet sphere, China, and other Third World nations. His long-ranging hope was to forge alliances across African states to overcome the pressures of dependency economies that surfaced as the new face of imperialism: neocolonialism. Striving for a Pan-African post-nation-state federation, he deployed the language of radical social democracy on historically new terms: socialist, nationalist, and Pan-African. The resulting solidarities and contradictions among these three contending ideologies produced a locally vibrant African socialist youth modernity.[20]

Ujamaa emerged as a new anti-imperial and egalitarian logic of self-help. Its central figure was the nation's youth, upon whose shoulders lay the future of nation building. *Ujamaa* sought a self-reliant state that had decolonized ideologically, phantasmatically, and territorially. It was symbolized by school youth working in public spaces. Such work involved tending the *shambas* (state-owned vegetable gardens), marching practice, planting trees on the roads of the city, clearing public spaces, and sweeping and maintaining the school compounds, among other activities.[21]

Lenin-Mao-Nyerere: The Performance of Statehood

In *The Tasks of the Youth Leagues*, Lenin locates youth as the fundamental base of the production of statehood and lays out his prescription for a pedagogy of youth as citizens. Lenin states that "we must deal in detail with the question of what we should teach the youth and how the youth should learn if it really wants to justify the name of communist youth, and how it should be trained so as to be able to complete and consummate what we have started."[22] Nyerere's treatises on nation building follow closely Lenin's prescriptive pedagogical model about modern education. He formulates a specifically Tanzanian-based model for African socialism. Elaborating on what "proletarian" culture might signify for Tanzania, Nyerere's foremost project was the modernization of education through the mobilization of youth. Interpreting Lenin's prescription for educating the youth leagues by "learning, organizing, uniting and fighting," Nyerere introduced an array of activities to generate what Lenin calls the "shock group" of youth who can help "in every job . . . displaying initiative and enterprise."[23]

Suburban vegetable gardens were central to this project. Lenin elaborates on the vegetable garden as a means of abolishing disparities between classes, particularly the intelligentsia, by dissolving the division between the theory and practice of communism. "The members of the League should use every spare hour to improve the vegetable gardens, or to organize the education of young people in some mill or factory," Lenin writes, in order that they may view labor differently than they did in the past.[24] This idea became central to the category "youth" in Tanzanian socialism, as the policies of *ujamaa* approached the schooling of youth through the implementation of physical activities such as work in the *shambas* in the name of nation building. Young socialists had to participate in grassroots economic self-reliance activities, of which agricultural projects involving the tilling of the land were an important part.[25]

"Youth" emerged as a decolonizing postcolonial public sphere through which the newly independent nation-state became manifest. Parades, marches, and *ngomas* (folk dances); children waving flags by roadsides as Nyerere and other state functionaries drove by; compulsory large-scale youth drills with clubs, hand gestures, sticks, and guns; and mandatory summer camps linked the schooling of youth to the creation of good citizens. Learning how to wield a *jembe*, or hoe, to maintain a *shamba*, growing one's own vegetables, was a crucial part of the curriculum in many high schools. The implementation of the word *ndugu*, or comrade, for both genders alike, and the radical move to make Kiswahili the primary means of instruction at school and university, aided this project. The compulsory marching every day before or after school and the regime of students' sweeping and dusting their own school compounds followed Lenin's advocacy of youth organizing the cleaning of city blocks or villages; hence one could observe the primary students of Dar es Salaam walking to school with brooms and school boxes. This was an elaborate and pervasive instrumentalization of the category "youth" within the national fabric, and the shape of modernization under African socialism.[26]

Nyerere's visit to China in 1965, the establishment of the "Arusha Declaration" in 1967, and the nationalization of banks and industries in the public and private sectors earlier that year consolidated Nyerere's Leninist/ Maoist notions for a new African democracy forged and sustained by youth. The establishment of organizations such as the Tanzanian National Service and policies such as "Education for Self-Reliance" cohere with Maoist principles of producing the state through the training of youth as citizen-workers.

Along with the ideological hybridization came the influx of cultural com-
modities in the guise of North Korean table tennis coaches, Chinese books,
Chinese stationery, Soviet mathematicians and physics teachers, Chinese
shoes, Chinese railway engineers for the Tanzanian/Zambian railway project,
Soviet export cinema, and an influx of kung fu cinema à la Raymond Chow,
Lo Wei, Run Run Shaw, and Warner Bros.[27]

Technologies of Frugality: Kung Fu and the Ambivalence of Enjoyment

"Hong Kong invaded the U.S. film biz this weekend as 'Rumble in the Bronx,'
starring Jackie Chan, and 'Broken Arrow' directed by John Woo, scored a
one-two punch at the box office," wrote Andrew Hindes for *Variety* in late
February 1996.[28] *Rumble in the Bronx* soared to the top of the box office
with an estimated gross of $10 million, followed closely by the John Travolta
vehicle *Broken Arrow* at $8.3 million. The seventies are back in the retro
style, complete with bell bottoms and flared synthetics. Kung fu is making a
nineties return in New York, with tae kwon do, hapkido, kick boxing, karate,
aero-boxing, Thai boxing, and Brazilian capoeira providing a range of martial
arts-inflected styles of choreography. Christian Slater quotes Bruce Lee in
the opening sequence of *Broken Arrow*, and with *Rumble in the Bronx*,
Jackie Chan has come into his own in the United States, no longer a shadow
of Lee, though citationally invoking him. Observing this, I am reminded of
another time with plastic clothes, bell bottoms, platform shoes, Afros, and
Bruce Lee.

Bruce Lee's first big film was *Fists of Fury* (originally titled *The Big
Boss*; 1972), directed by Lo Wei and produced by Raymond Chow. This
anticapitalist/antifeudal propagandist film is closely linked to populist socialist rhetoric that privileges the worker or peasant, embodied most dramatically by Lee himself in his Chinese worker suits. Like the rest of his films,
The Big Boss presents a field of contested class and race relations to a public
of peasants and the proletariat. Social space in Lee's films demarcates narratives of good versus evil and urban versus rural. There is the evil boss of the
ice factory in *The Big Boss*, the drug lord/capitalist entrepreneur Mr. Han in
Enter the Dragon, and the Rome-based American Mafia ring in *Return of the
Dragon*.

The Big Boss did not attain great popularity in Tanzania until the success
of Lee's Warner Bros. venture *Enter the Dragon* (1973), directed by Robert
Clouse, produced by Weintraub and Heller in conjunction with Raymond
Chow, with music by Lalo Schifrin. The phenomenally successful *Enter the
Dragon* broke a predominantly Black/white cinematic field constructed by

the deluge of classical Hollywood narrative films in Dar es Salaam. The hegemony of Hollywood was interrupted only by a modest glut of Hindi films frequented by a largely Asian Tanzanian audience. Lee's international stardom problematized the narrow spectrum through which race was constituted in Tanzanian popular cinema. As both Mahmood Mamdani and Isaac Shivji point out, this was a time when anti-Asian sentiments were fermenting in the public sphere at large, exacerbated by legislative moves to nationalize Asian businesses. These developments had far-reaching repercussions for a cultural politics of race in Tanzania.[29]

Enter the Dragon was phenomenally successful, and ran to packed houses in Dar es Salaam during the early seventies. Its seductively racist narrative provides an exciting sense of internationalism that in retrospect is merely a Hollywood rendition of the starving exotic Oriental enclave much fetishized by the British and the Americans: Hong Kong as a colonial metropole. The aura of kung fu's internationalism in *Enter the Dragon* is a trans-Pacific fantasy—both Orientalist and pro-American, with chop-socking Asians, Shaolin temples, and chop-socking Westerners. The opening sequences of the film locate Hong Kong as a cosmopolitan fetish of the Pacific—for capitalists, secret agents, martial artists from both the East and the West, and drug lords. John Saxon, Bob Wall, and Jim Kelly provide the spectrum of Westernness through which Lee's own transnational identity is realized, both Asian American and Hong Kong Chinese at the same time. In the film, Lee is an agent of the British government working against Chinese criminals. With the arrival of the Anglo-American (John Saxon), the African American (Jim Kelly), and the Asian American (Bruce Lee), the narrative sets up an imperialistic relationship between travelers and natives, juxtaposing Vietnamese refugees in Hong Kong harbor with evil Chinese landlords, and martially trained youth against the cosmopolitan sportsmen/travelers from the West.

Enter the Dragon raises interesting questions about the visual and narrative ambiguity of spectatorial pleasure in a postcolonial context. The film's colonialist ideology of British and American hegemony in Hong Kong is barely concealed in the good Americans/bad Asians plot. The American trio's exploits in Hong Kong frame them as the good guys in opposition to evil feudal local landlords. This implicitly locates local audiences in states with a nonaligned foreign policy, like Tanzania, in contradictory relations to the idea of good being produced by the cinematic narrative—that of Americans coming to free Hong Kong natives by fighting local landlordism. This contradiction would have been heightened by the fact that the ideological confusion surrounding that good was in opposition to the tension in current local Tanzanian politics regarding landlordism and Africanizing measures. The mood was one of nationalization, and the issue of local land-lordism was one of the crucial rallying points of economic nationalism being mobilized at the time. Hence the visual pleasure of good reigning over the bad by restoring Western hegemony through the overthrow of local land-lordism conflicted in diametrically opposing ways with local issues of African sovereignty.

Another axis of spectatorial ambiguity is that posed by Jim Kelly, whose popularity as an African American actor provided a visual hook for Tanzanian spectatorship in more ways than one. Kelly flees police brutality and white supremacy in Los Angeles and belongs to a Black-power enclave in the form of a Black karate school. He embodies a notion of American "cool" that is in empathy with Tanzanian notions of Pan-African cool, as he wears red bell bottoms and an Afro and embodies a style politics in sync with Black nationalist sentiments in Dar during the seventies. Kelly complicates the politics of white and Asian American masculinities pitted against generic "Oriental" masculinity by introducing the violent race politics in Los Angeles, which has forced him to leave his city. He marks the Pan-African con-nections to Asia through ideological solidarities with Third World struggles, the martial arts, Asian religions, and the transnational exchange of socialist kitsch. But, as Kelly's death in the film reduces the complexity of his nar-rative presence to a prior, stereotyped racist representation, it produces a resistant reading that inflects the closure of the film. In a sequence remi-niscent of lynching scenes from the 1950s, Kelly's body is impaled on a hook with chains and lowered into a vat of acid. The stereotypical racist so-lution of Kelly's death scene negates the potentially imperialist fantasy tale of Westerners cleaning up the world of evil. Instead, the haunting of a his-tory from the imperial home, the United States, through the image of the dead Kelly interrupts the colonialist self-righteousness of "Americans" in the "Orient."

The politics of the body played out is linked to the gendering of the film. Whereas at first it replicates the misogynist and sexist logic of mainstream early kung fu cinema through the production of women's bodies as objects of pleasure, the figure of Angela Mao, a hapkido black belt, as Bruce Lee's sister, Su Li, offers a new kind of representation. Mao kung fus her way through a battalion of Han's men, preferring suicide with a piece of glass to the horror of rape at the hands of the evil American, played by Bob Wall.

Angela Mao embodies a new kind of socialism—an agent against patri-archy and traditional notions of femininity. She dismantles the coordinates of gender role-playing as she opens up other ways of socializing women's bodies. Mao's kung fu creates a transgendered space outside familiar representational forms, as she performs the martial, socialist body of the comrade, discarding the binarisms of gender by opening out its negotiable spaces, such as kung fu, as a site of social militancy. Blurring the distinction between genders rhetorically, Mao enacts both the promise of kung fu and its failure. She enacts its promise by demonstrating that she fights better than most men, with an indestructible sense of self. Her death, however, performs its failure by reiterating the reductive ways that gender and sexuality work to subject women's and other minority bodies to violence. Mao's socialist body echoes closely with the kinds of popular rhetoric transgendering the public through the calling of all persons—irrespective of gender—comrade or *ndugu*.

Tanzanian cultural politics of the early seventies were also tied to the rabidly nationalist anti-immigrant sentiments expressed in Lee's films. He is pro-Chinese peasant, anti-Japanese, anti-Soviet, and anti-Western in *The Chinese Connection* (1972), directed by Lo Wei. Consider the xenophobia expressed as Lee beats a Japanese Bushido boxer and an ex-Soviet champion boxer. Combined with the film's attempted critique of colonial Shanghai of the 1930s, this produces a confusing melange of critique and racist stereotyping. The Japanese occupation of Shanghai and the northern provinces in *The Chinese Connection* resonates with the strong anti-Asian sentiment perpetuated at the time in Tanzania, situating the immigrant petit-bourgeois entrepreneur in antagonistic relation to the interests of the nationalist masses.

In *Return of the Dragon* (1973), Lee plays a country bumpkin from Hong Kong who avenges the harassment meted out to his immigrant restaurateur relatives by an underworld ring peopled by immigrants from the United States and other countries. The climax, as in most of Lee's films, is structured around a choreographed fight sequence, in this case, his encounter with the American Chuck Norris in the Roman Coliseum. Lee asserts his anti-Western sentiments by destroying all threats to his relatives' future in Rome, epitomized by Norris, only to find out that there is no place outside capital itself, as his uncle turns out to be working for the criminals.

Lee died before completing *The Game of Death* (1974), which is set in Bangkok, but the structuring ethnocentrism in the film is nationalist in contradictory ways. Lee demonstrates the superiority of Chinese kung fu over other forms by decimating a Korean hapkido specialist, an escrima stylist, a Japanese samurai, and a Black boxer played by Kareem Abdul-Jabbar.[30] The jingoistic ideological content, the film's bare-bones through line, and its often atrocious production qualities do not detract from Bruce Lee's kung fu performance. Lee's choreography creates contradictory spaces for the participation of heterogeneous subjectivities that constitute the audience under the faceless charisma of statehood itself. The power of his films lies in his cultish persona and brilliance of movement, but the popularity of his films in Tanzania accrued a narrative depth that the plot and diegesis did not.

The tensions of race, gender, ethnicity, and masculinity raised in *Enter the Dragon* foreground the transcultural misreadings through which Bruce Lee gains his popularity internationally. The film highlights the complex ways in which Lee himself is situated as a hybrid Asian American, binationally affiliated—working in Hong Kong and California. Lee was an American citizen and had opened schools of jeet kune do in Seattle and Oakland. His multicultural clientele included such African Americans as karate champion Jim "Kung Fu" Kelly, Lew Alcindor (who later took the name Kareem Abdul-Jabbar), and the judoist Jesse Glover; Anglo-Americans such as Steve McQueen, James Coburn, and Stirling Silliphant; Asian Americans such as Japanese American judoist Taky Kimura and Filipino American escrimaist Dan Inosanto; and others, such as Roman Polanski.[31]

Lee was clearly the first transnationally situated Asian American actor working for very different markets in Hong Kong, Hollywood, and the Third World at the same time. His transnational interests created very different pressures on his status as a megastar across Asia, Africa, and other Third World countries. The international economies of kung fu filmmaking and its distribution also blurred the distinctions among ethnicities and national contexts. For Tanzanian Asian youth, there were few or no distinctions among Hong Kong cinema, mainland Chinese cinema, and Warner Bros. cinema. Films with kung fu were generically read as mainland Chinese or Maoist, and Chinese cinema was reduced to the kung fu genre.

Technologies of the Self: Foucault's *Askesis* and Nyerere's Frugality

A reading of kung fu enables one to revisit the informal avenues of enjoyment under East African seventies socialism. Bruce Lee's popularity as an *uchina* or Chinese hero at this particular juncture is interesting for many reasons, one being his privileging what I would delineate as a technology of frugality—the body as a weapon of frugality. Lee's technology of frugality was a philosophy of efficient and minimal action, whereby the opponents' weaknesses are utilized to fuel the self's power. For Lee, a little was enough. Frugality became a voluntary technology of plenty, an articulation of agency. Lee's cultivation of an aesthetics of frugality on-screen cohered with a philosophy of frugality laid out by Nyerere in 1965 in a speech to the nation:

> In February I went . . . to China, and there I learned one very important thing . . . they are a frugal people. . . . it would be very foolish of us . . . indi-

vidually or as a nation, to appear as rich as a country like America. Everyone knows that we are not rich. And the only way to defeat our present poverty is to accept the fact that it exists, to live as poor people, and to spend every cent that we have . . . on the things which will make us . . . more educated in the future.[32]

From the vantage point of the 1990s, such a reading of China seems simplistic and reductive, as contemporary forms of capital and exchange have permeated even the much-desired frugality of China. Still, such an aesthetics of frugality laid out by Nyerere has broad implications for a phenomenology of frugality through which youth forges avenues of enjoyment.

A phenomenology of frugality is structured around imaginative embodiments of little as enough, of anticonsumption, of which kung fu partakes. The choreography of kung fu trains the body as a weapon of vigilance. It hinges upon a technology of self otherwise relegated to the state through the police, the military, sports, national youth service, and other forms of regulative socialization. Kung fu valorizes an aesthetics of self-governance that is closely aligned to forms of control that produce and sustain state-saturated societies such as Tanzania.[33] In such societies, the individual, articulated as youth, is produced through various institutional regimes and practices as the vigilant and productive machine of the state. Youth becomes a technobody whose every action and enjoyment should be directed by a pedagogical practice of statehood.

One aspect of such an aesthetics of frugality is the ascetic and athletic care of the self. In his lectures on the technologies of the self, Michel Foucault discusses how the practice of *epimelesthai sautou*, '"to take care of yourself," "the concern with the self," "to be concerned, to take care of yourself," was a crucial philosophy for Greek cities in Hellenistic times.[34] Through a close reading of the Socratic dialogues, Foucault describes the following. He argues that Socrates considers his mission useful for the city, in fact "more useful than the Athenians' military victory at Olympia—because in teaching people to occupy themselves with themselves, he teaches them to occupy themselves with the city."[35] Foucault links the care of oneself and the city to forms of Christian asceticism eight centuries later and its edict to know oneself.[36]

As part of his meditation on the care of the self, Foucault elaborates one of the three Stoic techniques of self: *askesis*. Foucault describes *askesis* as a remembering, not a disclosure of the secret self. "It's the memory of what you've done and what you've had to do."[37] The two poles of this principle are *melete*, or meditation, and *gymnasia*, or "to train oneself." As Foucault points out, there is a spectrum of intermediate possibilities as well.[38] Bruce Lee's choreography occupies this intermediary possibility of the care of the self, which in extension becomes a care of the youthful body in the city, through a performance of gymnastic frugality, kung fu.

In Bruce Lee's kung fu films, the meditative self, physical training, and the juridical process work in mnemonic fashion to restore order to the chaotic youthful city. The striking presence of gangs of young men training in kung fu schools, whether Chinese or Japanese, the comparative absence of women as agents, and the movement in groups of youth across the city in search of justice link kung fu to notions of male sociality in the modern city in Lee's films. Lee's choreography reads as a performance of informal juridical practices of youth within the city. The fight sequences in his films emphasize an urban reclusiveness, enacted in the crowded street, in public spaces like the Coliseum or in the winding alleys of Macao, restoring order to the chaotic city. The economic theories of frugality put forth by Nyerere and Foucault's technologies of self related to asceticism merge in Bruce Lee's choreography of the self and the city.

Kung Fu, Radical Historical Subjects, and Feminist Imaginings

In a larger context, kung fu choreography embodies a viable technology of self for people of small frames, implicitly critiquing conventional masculinity. Though Lee's style of kung fu, wing chun fist, is popularly associated with male homosociality, its origins lie in a form developed by Yin Wing Chun, a Buddhist nun from mainland China. Wing Chun invented wing chun fist as self-defense for females and people with small frames. Hsuing-Ping Chiao suggests that it emphasizes speed as opposed to strength. Chiao states that Lee learned wing chun fist at age thirteen from Yip Man, the sixth-generation master of the wing chun fist school.[39] The privileging of speed over strength is an important factor in understanding the wing chun fist form in terms of a radical historical subject such as the martially trained Buddhist nun in thirteenth-century China who first developed it. This provides an explicit link between kung fu and feminism—it opens arenas for the negotiations of gender through movement and choreography within kung fu history and as a visual possibility for women to break boundaries within public space.

The connections between kung fu and feminist interpretations of martial movements are not evident in the visually gendered identities of early kung fu cinema. Much early kung fu cinema preserves the status quo of men as fighters and women as objects of pleasure. Seventies kung fu cinema maintains the dichotomy of docile women and warring men, but the occasional ruptures are startlingly uncompromising and even empowering. For instance, the emergence of new historic subjects such as Hong Kong hapkido black belt Angela Mao ("lady kung fu," mentioned above), Black kung fu expert Tamara Dobson, and other martial artists such as Chen Hsin, Chen Kuan-Tai, Meng Fei, Wang Tao, and Tanny dismantles orthodox notions of gender, valorizes androgyny, and creates transgendered choreographies, relieving the conventional framing of male martial bodies.[40] These brief choreographic ruptures of women martial artists are important because they pull apart stereotypes of women as weak, dependent, or victimlike. The women challenge those expectations by decimating dozens of young men through dexterity, intelligence, martial skill, and strength.

Hollywood's Tamara Dobson, along with Hong Kong cinema's Angela Mao and Tanny, popularized androgyny, muscular fighting bodies, martial movements, lesbian desire, and campy femininity. Before lipstick feminisms came platform feminists, giving patriarchy the karate chops it never expected. As a martial art for small frames, kung fu gained currency among teen feminists as self-defense and a technology of care from men.

The kung fu kicking special agent Cleopatra Jones (Tamara Dobson), six feet two inches tall with platform shoes, carrying a cosmopolitan "cool," demonstrates a connection between feminist critiques and a Black radicalism that is mobile and internationalist. Jones organizes antidrug maneuvers in Turkey with a group of agents in *Cleopatra Jones* (1973). She also fights drugs in her community back home in the United States. Jones's worldliness, her articulation of power and gender on visually new terms, makes possible other ways of being Black within capital.

In *Cleopatra Jones and the Casino of Gold* (1975), Jones's lesbian sexuality allows new lines of desire with the Hong Kong kung fu kicking, dart-throwing British super agent Mei Ling Fong (played by Tanny), a historically new alliance on-screen. In this film, power and desire are constructed along the axis of same-sex identification and antagonism among three women: Shelley Stevens, Tamara Dobson, and Tanny. The irreverently antipatriarchal undercurrent in the film's spectatorial field opened up alternative imaginings in seventies youth culture.

Kung Fu and the Emergence of New Historic Subjects

Another connection between kung fu and the emergence of new historic subjects is an iconoclastic multicultural dimension that Lee made popular on-screen. He shattered the hermetic secrecy of kung fu by teaching it to anyone who wanted to learn the form, raising interesting questions about kung fu and race. The links of Lee to African Americans like judoist Jesse Glover, Kareem Abdul-Jabbar, and Jim "Kung Fu" Kelly speak to the appeal, eclecticism, and malleability of the form transnationally, to all frames and cultures. The establishment of Black karate schools and other Black martial art schools in Los Angeles and elsewhere in California is noteworthy in this respect. The widespread popularity of kung fu among the blaxploitation films of the time links kung fu to Pan-Africanist and Black nationalist embodiments of the care of the self. The self becomes a tool of revolution, fighting drugs, white hegemony, injustice, and the state with kung fu. The films of Jim Kelly, Tamara Dobson, Pam Grier, Jim Brown, Richard Roundtree (*Shaft*, 1972), Ron O'Neal (*Superfly*, 1972), and Kareem Abdul-Jabbar are interesting in this respect. Jim Kelly's *Black Belt Jones* (1972) features a Black karate school with a picture of Bruce Lee hanging, shrinelike, in the background. In *Enter the Dragon*, Kelly is seen taking leave of his fellow martial artists at a Black martial arts school in Los Angeles before going to Hong Kong. The link between martial arts and the training of Black men to live in a hostile police state is foregrounded in Kelly's film.

The work of Michele Wallace, Gladstone Yearwood, bell hooks, Manthia Diawara, Mark Reid, and Ed Guerrero, among others, addresses the misogyny, sexism, and stereotyping of African Americans in blaxploitation cinema of the seventies while also marking the possibilities these films held for the development of Black cinema.[41] Building on the analyses of such authors, it becomes possible to read the cultural capital of blaxploitation cinema as it circulates, gets viewed, and translates in ways that exceed its reception in the United States.

Tamara Dobson, Pam Grier, Jim Kelly, Richard Roundtree, Ron O'Neal, and the early blaxploitation superheroes made possible a new kind of visual pleasure for Tanzanian Asian youth. The spectrum of martial art styles popularized by Bruce Lee's jeet kune do and other forms of karate and judo incorporated into kung fu films by actors/sportsmen like Kelly, Fred Williamson, Brown, Dobson, and Abdul-Jabbar presented a technology of self that was aesthetically in empathy with the conditions of frugality in Tanzanian popular culture. As a sophisticated choreography for a martially oriented militaristic dance, it suited the local emphasis on discipline and sport. This linking of kung fu to Black struggle in blaxploitation films rearticulated resistance and rehearsals of revolution across ideological lines. These Pan-African implications of Black struggle resonated with popular Tanzanian youth sentiments of the time. As such, kung fu cinema had an impact on Tanzanian popular culture, particularly in its practice of frugality as a style of movement. The body is the only machine of action; there are neither guns nor any other autonomous technologies, apart from the self.

The connection of kung fu cinema to a diasporic schlock consciousness in the seventies is complicated in its relations to race, gender, the Cold War, and the more transnational imaginings perpetuated through kung fu kitsch. Lee's films in particular are visually disorienting as the eclectic ethnicities of the actors and landscapes in the films blur the distinctions between context and period. The visual field is "Chinese," but the actors are of Thai, Malay, Japanese, and Chinese ethnicity; the landscapes are those of Hong Kong and Thailand, and, adding to the distantiation, the badly dubbed dialogue provides a Brechtian alienation effect through its asynchronous sound.

Still, kung fu's connections to Tanzanian socialism, Black nationalisms, Bollywood fight sequences, emergent feminisms, and a diasporic youth consciousness of seventies kitsch return today with a nineties twist. Spin-offs from kung fu cinema have been more important than the genre itself, with a nostalgic resonance in the saturated violence of contemporary Hollywood. Its embeddedness in an aesthetics of frugality inadvertently raises the question of how frugality travels across national and political cultures. The globalizing influences of Hong Kong cinema and its particular translations in Tanzanian popular culture as a mediating space between scarcity and excess, between "Asianness" and Tanzanian Asians, and between capitalist kitsch and socialist ideology opens up the intricate transnational linkages in the circulation of meaning generated through consuming movies.

Kung Fu and the Practice of Frugality

Tanzanian socialism took youth as central to its project. As Ishumi and Maliyamkono state, "This ideological conditioning was carried to its extreme in the teaching of civics, a school subject dubbed Political Education since 1967, which resulted in virtually all pupils trying to talk, act or behave like socialists. This was indeed an ideological success, even though, in retrospect, it may have been more deceptive and pretentious than real."[42] The particular embodiments, translations, and cultural capital of socialism were closely linked to the informal ways in which youth imbibed and made local forms of socialist desire, whether in antagonism or consent.

An important part of the mechanics of state formation was the performance of frugality, the emphasis on communal self-reliance as embodied in the practice of *ujamaa*. As I have shown in this essay, there is a formal parallel between the performance of frugality in youth mobilization and the staging of frugality in kung fu cinema that resonated with the youth culture of

1970s Tanzania. The gender ambiguity of the wing chun fist and the appeal of an explicit "technology of self" toward a consciousness of nation building offered a nascent transnational aesthetic of frugality for emerging expressive youth cultures.

With the state appointing itself as the home of youth through the rhetoric of family, and the head of state assuming the role of teacher or father of the nation, the paternalistic formulations of socialist practice become linked to state control. Whereas Nyerere's more stringent critics have dismissed his experiments in socialist pedagogy as authoritarian, I argue here for a more nuanced consideration of a critical and daring experiment in grassroots social transformation as it interfaces with globalizing popular culture. The philosophy of self-reliance articulated in *ujamaa* was farsighted and utopian, but doomed to be structured as failure by the West. Instead of dismissing forms of postcolonial citizenship in peripheral states as failure, we need a more capacious reading of the kinds of desire, longing, and imaginative reinventions that fill up the abstract spaces of state formation.

Notes

I would like to thank Randy Martin, Gitanjali Maharaj, and Radhika Subramanium, whose close readings and careful editorial comments were invaluable. Many thanks also to Manthia Diawara, Ngugi Wa Thiongo, and my esteemed colleagues at Performance Studies for the stimulating discussions and suggestions that fueled this essay. Most of all, I am indebted to Toby Miller, without whose encouragement and meticulous edits this essay would never have been realized.

1. Shishir Kurup, "In Between Spaces," in *Lets Get It On: The Politics of Black Performance*, ed. Catherine Ugwu (Seattle: Bay, 1995), 34.

2. Ali Mazrui, "Cultural Forces in African Politics," in *Africa and the West*, ed. Isaac James Mowoe and Richard Bjornson (Westport, Conn.: Greenwood, 1986). See also Mazrui, *Cultural Forces in World Politics* (Nairobi: Heinemann, 1990); and Mazrui, *The African Condition* (Cambridge: Cambridge University Press, 1980).

3. There were many spheres of youth practices, but my observations are inflected primarily by my experiences as a Tanzanian Asian youth schooled under *ujamaa* in Dar es Salaam and Arusha. The rhetoric of a classless and raceless society worked to conceal as well as to foreground the kinds of racisms and classisms that developed under the transforming structures of Tanzanian civil society.

4. Julius Nyerere, "*Ujamaa:* The Basis of African Socialism," in *Freedom and Unity/ Uhuru Na Umoja* (Dar es Salaam: Oxford University Press, 1966), 170.

5. Julius Nyerere, "The Arusha Declaration," in *Freedom and Socialism/Uhuru Na Ujamaa* (Dar es Salaam: Oxford University Press, 1968), 247.

6. Donatus Komba, "Contribution to Rural Development: Ujamaa and Villagisation," in *Mwalimu: The Influence of Nyerere*, ed. Colin Legum and Geoffrey Mmari (Trenton, N.J.: Africa World Press, 1995), 36.

7. See Joe Lugalla's excellent study of *ujamaa*'s effects on urbanization. Lugalla empha-sizes the neglect of urban restructuring through the ambivalent state policies toward urbanization during this time. Consequently, urban planning in Dar es Salaam per-petuated the colonial legacy of town planning, instead of benefiting the marginalized urban majority. Joe Lugalla, "The Post-Colonial State and the Urbanization Process: 1961–1993," in *Crisis, Urbanization, and Urban Poverty in Tanzania: A Study of Urban Poverty and Survival Politics* (Lanham, Md.: University Press of America, 1995), 37–39. See also Knud Erik Svendsen, "Development Strategy and Crisis Management," in *Mwalimu: The Influence of Nyerere*, ed. Colin Legum and Geoffrey Mmari (Trenton, N.J.: Africa World Press, 1995), 109.

8. John Iliffe, "Urban Poverty in Tropical Africa," in *The African Poor: A History* (Cambridge: Cambridge University Press, 1987). See also Joe Lugalla, *Crisis, Urbani-zation, and Urban Poverty in Tanzania: A Study of Urban Poverty and Survival Politics* (Lanham, Md.: University Press of America, 1995).

9. A. G. Ishumi and T. L. Maliyamkono, "Education for Self-Reliance," in *Mwalimu: The Influence of Nyerere*, ed. Colin Legum and Geoffrey Mmari (Trenton, N.J.: Africa World Press, 1995), 52, 53, 54.

10. Julius Nyerere, "Frugality: 26 April 1965," in *Freedom and Socialism/Uhuru Na Ujamaa* (Dar es Salaam: Oxford University Press, 1968), 332.

11. Geoffrey Mmari, "The Legacy of Nyerere," in *Mwalimu: The Influence of Nyerere*, ed. Colin Legum and Geoffrey Mmari (Trenton, N.J.: Africa World Press, 1995), 178. Mmari suggests that Nyerere's style in dress was considered a copy from China of Chairman Mao. These observations are based on my experiences as a kung fu fan and spectator at many a beach wrestling match performed at Kivukoni Beach. Kung fu also inflected styles of disco dancing in Dar at this time, where simulated kung fu arm and leg movements would be incorporated into the bumps, free-style, and disco dancing.

12. I am indebted to Gordon Tait's recent unpublished work on subcultural theory for lay-ing out the groundwork that enabled me to think through this issue.

13. Centre for Contemporary Cultural Studies, ed., *The Empire Strikes Back: Race and Racism in 70's Britain* (London: Centre for Contemporary Cultural Studies/Hutchinson Education, 1982); Stuart Hall and Tony Jefferson, eds., *Resistance through Rituals* (London: Centre for Contemporary Cultural Studies/Unwin Hyman, 1976).

14. Ishumi and Maliyamkono, "Education for Self-Reliance," 51–53.

15. Ibid., 47–49.

16. Julius Nyerere, *Freedom and Unity/Uhuru Na Umoja* (Dar es Salaam: Oxford Uni-versity Press, 1966), 162, 258, 316, 332.

17. Julius Nyerere, *Freedom and Socialism/Uhuru Na Ujamaa* (Dar es Salaam: Oxford University Press, 1968), 262, 337, 385.

18. Nyerere, *Freedom and Unity*, 159, 162, 323, 332.

19. Ibid. See also Ishumi and Maliyamkono, "Education for Self-Reliance," 47, 48. Ishumi and Maliyamkono point out the serious educational poverty afflicting Tanganyika on the eve of independence.

20. Dan Nabudere, "The Politics of East African Federation, 1958–1965," in *Imperialism in East Africa* (London: Zed, 1982), 111.

21. Nyerere, *Freedom and Socialism*, 256–57.

22. V. I. Lenin, *The Tasks of the Youth Leagues* (Peking: Foreign Language Press, 1975), 3.

23. Ibid., 19.

24. Ibid., 18–20.

25. Ishumi and Maliyamkono, "Education for Self-Reliance," 52.

26. Schools such as Forodhani Primary School and Azania Secondary School in Dar es Salaam, as well as the Arusha Secondary School, implemented some of these practices.

27. The Arusha Secondary School was an interesting site in terms of the transnational flow of Soviet and African American teachers.
28. Andrew Hindes, "Hong Kong Invasion at US Box Office (Feb 23–25)," *Variety*, 26 February 1996.
29. See Mahmood Mamdani, *Imperialism and Fascism in Uganda* (Trenton, N.J.: Africa World Press, 1984); Isaac Shivji, *Class Struggles in Tanzania* (New York: Monthly Review Press, 1976).
30. Hsiung-Ping Chiao, "Bruce Lee: His Influence on the Evolution of the Kung Fu Genre," *Journal of Popular Film and Television* 9 (spring 1981): 37–38.
31. Bruce Thomas, *Bruce Lee, Fighting Spirit* (Berkeley, Calif.: North Atlantic, 1994).
32. Julius Nyerere, "Frugality," in *Freedom and Unity/Uhuru Na Umoja* (Dar es Salaam: Oxford University Press, 1966), 332.
33. I take the phrase "state-saturated societies" from Samir Amin, who uses the term to describe states whose ideologies infuse every aspect of everyday life, and whose institutional pervasiveness determines the lives of their citizens. Former communist and socialist societies are obvious examples of societies where state socialisms shape all avenues of thought and experience. See Samir Amin, "The System in Crisis: A Critique of Sovietism, 1960–1990," in *Re-reading the Postwar Period* (New York: Monthly Review Press, 1994).
34. Michel Foucault, *Technologies of Self* (Amherst: University of Massachusetts Press, 1988), 19.
35. Ibid., 20.
36. Ibid., 20–21.
37. Ibid., 35.
38. Ibid., 37.
39. Chiao, "Bruce Lee," 33.
40. I use the term *new historic subjects* to imply both the new political subjects and the historically new conditions that create new subjectivities, as Ernesto Laclau and Chantal Mouffe have elaborated upon in *Hegemony and Socialist Strategy* (London: Verso, 1985).
41. See Ed Guerrero, *Framing Blackness: The African American Image in Film* (Philadelphia: Temple University Press, 1993); Manthia Diawara, ed., *Black American Cinema* (New York: Routledge, 1993); Mark Reid, *Redefining Black Film* (Berkeley: University of California Press, 1993).
42. Ishumi and Maliyamkono, "Education for Self-Reliance," 53.

The Nation in White:
Cricket in a Postapartheid South Africa

Grant Farred

What know they of cricket who only cricket know?
▸ C. L. R. *James,* Beyond a Boundary

It is historically appropriate that a black cricketer from the Caribbean should bring into proper view the way in which the overwhelmingly white South African team is regarded by the rest of the postcolonial world. More than in any other part of the globe, the Caribbean is a community where the sport's ideological import is treated with the utmost seriousness. The West Indies is a region where "knowing cricket" is indivisible from a consciousness of history, colonialism, race politics, and socioeconomic conditions. It was in this spirit that West Indies cricket recently delivered its stinging indictment of South Africa's white team. Caribbean cricket leveled its criticism in the person of Brian Lara, the game's most eloquent ambassador today. Brian Lara is the éminence grise of the contemporary game: batsman extraordinaire, holder of the world record in runs scored in an international match, and among the youngest players to captain his native Trinidad and Tobago. In the buildup to the World Cup quarter-final game between the West Indies and South Africa in March 1996, Lara showed that a critical awareness of the consequences of racism is as integral to Caribbean cricket as is brilliant stroke making and ferocious fast bowling.

Interviewed by the Delhi-based magazine *Outlook,* Lara used this exchange as an opportunity to distinguish between the impact of a surprising defeat by a black African team and the prospect of losing to a predominantly white African side. The ignominious defeat by Kenya, a country boasting only a small amateur league and without any real traditions in the sport, seriously damaged West Indian cricketing pride. South Africa, however, was another matter altogether. Congratulating the Kenyans in their locker room after the West Indies' embarrassing loss to the east African cricket minnows (in the preliminary rounds of the competition), the Trinidadian articulated a deep-seated ressentiment at the racial makeup of his forthcoming opponents. "It wasn't that bad losing to you guys [Kenyans]," he remarked. "Now, a team like South Africa is a different matter altogether. You know, this white thing comes into the picture. We can't stand losing to them."[1] Undoubtedly,

Lara's pronouncement bore more than a trace of rationalization for the West Indies' humbling loss to a nation of cricketing rookies. Nevertheless, it stands as a courageous and scathing attack on the enduring inequalities of apartheid. International cricketing icon and the West Indies captain-in-waiting, Brian Lara broke with cricket's renowned custom of civility—a set of practices so sacrosanct that, as C. L. R. James puts it in *Beyond a Boundary*, a player would "cut off a finger sooner than do anything contrary to the ethics of the game"[2]—and spoke directly against the abiding legacy of white South African privilege. The consequences of apartheid were evident to Lara, no matter that they were no longer underwritten by institutional racism. The South African squad the West Indies team was about to play was composed of thirteen whites and a teenage coloured prodigy named Paul Adams.

Lara's attack on the postapartheid team anoints him as the most recent heir to the legacy of Caribbean cricket radicalism, a tradition that is several generations old. Outstanding among the earliest proponents of cricket activism were, of course, Lara's fellow Trinidadians C. L. R. James and Learie Constantine. From the 1920s to the late 1950s, these Trinidadians were in the vanguard of the struggle against white administrative control of the game in the West Indies. (Although black players had been dominating the West Indies team for decades by the 1950s, they had always done so under tutelage of a white captain. Black Caribbean cricketers and fans bitterly opposed this final vestige of British colonialism.) James spearheaded the public campaign to appoint Frank Worrell as the first black captain of the West Indies team in 1959. In the words of former Jamaican Prime Minister Michael Manley, "C. L. R. James, his patriotic hackles no less than his sense of injustice aroused, led the assault."[3] More recently, James and Worrell's cudgels were taken up by the outspoken ex-West Indian skipper and Lara's batting predecessor, the Antiguan Viv Richards. In the wake of Nelson Mandela's 1990 release, the eloquent Richards cautioned that South Africa should not be (re)admitted to test cricket until all of the nation's people could compete equally for a place on the team. Unless a gradual approach to the country's international reintegration was followed, Richards suggested, the South African team would reflect the constitutional and structural inequalities of apartheid. Richards's views are especially instructive if one recalls the historical precedent of Zimbabwe, a nation with the same racial cricketing profile as South Africa.

Like South Africa, UDI (Unilateral Declaration of Independence) Rhodesia's national cricket team was exclusively white. For all intents and purposes, Rhodesia was an integral part of the South African cricketing structure; in the 1970s, Rhodesia's was one of five teams that used to participate in the local interprovincial competition known as the Currie Cup. Following the establishment of an independent Zimbabwe in 1980, the new state was not immediately admitted to full international competition by the governing body. Instead, the International Cricket Council (ICC) adopted a policy of piecemeal admission to the world game for a country that was for the first time developing a nonracial cricketing tradition; the country had to nurture its postindependence players outside the South African cricket context.[4] The Zimbabwe team, which was and still is mainly white, undertook and hosted second-tier tours designed to schedule matches against the second-string teams of countries such as England and Australia. One of the by-products of the ICC's ruling was that it facilitated the development of black and Asian players in Zimbabwe. After more than a decade, the southern African nation achieved full international cricketing status.

The ICC's response to the Zimbabwean situation is in sharp contrast to its historic protection of white South Africa. In both its current and its previous guise (in 1961 the Imperial Cricket Conference dropped the "imperial" in favor of "international" as the reality of postcolonial India, Pakistan, and the West Indies made itself increasingly manifest), the organization has defended the right of the apartheid team to be included in its ranks. South Africa's cause has traditionally been championed by the lily-white establishments of English and Australian cricket, countries whose administrative hierarchies bear a striking resemblance to that of the apartheid state—although, it should be said, England's on-field personnel have in the past fifteen years or so become more representative of a postcolonial metropolis. Because of England's status as founder nation of the world governing body and as "home of the game," the country has exerted a tremendous influence on the politics of cricket. Despite the protestations and objections of the "newer" postcolonial members (who today outnumber England, Australia, and South Africa, the "established" ICC nations) about the country's racist policies, the apartheid team was allowed to participate in international competition until 1970. Of course, the South African team was not invited to tour the Caribbean or the Indian subcontinent, nor did it extend invitations to those countries.

The apartheid side, which regularly played against England and Australia, demarcated the racial divide within the ICC. Supported by its ex-white colonies, postimperial England (which until very recently had veto rights within the organization) insisted upon the right of the apartheid team to enjoy a limited, but symbolically salient, role within the world body. England and Australia's position within the ICC is indicative of a particularly virulent racism because it had such scant respect for the domestic efforts of the nonracial cricket within South Africa. It seldom, despite concerted attempts by those in the nonracial fold, even paid lip service to the internal opposition; this strategic disregard explicitly established the white apartheid establishment as the guardians of the South African game. As objectionable as the stance was, it was one adopted and vigorously defended in the face of strong postcolonial opposition. Not even its own public embarrassment in what became known as the D'Oliveira Affair (when Basil D'Oliveira, a coloured cricketer from Cape Town who had obtained British citizenship and selection to the 1968 England team to tour South Africa, was rejected because of his race) initiated a rethinking in English cricket policy toward South Africa. It took the concerted efforts of England's former black colonies in the early 1970s, with the West Indies and India leading the charge, to isolate the apartheid team. And even then the success was greater on the cricket oval than in the boardrooms of Lords, the game's London headquarters. Because of South Africa's historic links to its traditional white rivals, it is thus not surprising that upon the eradication of legislative apartheid, the country was immediately welcomed back into the international cricketing fold. (The financial incentive of South African tours, to both "traditional" and the postcolonial venues, also played no small role in the country's rapid return to the international cricket stage.) Clearly, Zimbabwe was not going to be a blueprint for the (re)admission of its southern neighbors into the ICC.

However, the relative success of the Zimbabwean model, which Viv Richards may or may not have been invoking, only adds luster to the Antiguan's prophetic judgments on South African cricket. The inequities in the South African game have, six years after Mandela's release, become increasingly evident. On the eve of the 1996 competition, the former West Indian vice captain Conrad Hunte "warned that it was time" for South Africa "to prove its commitment to a multi-racial national team by selecting two non-whites for the forthcoming World Cup side."[5] Hunte's plea fell on deaf South African ears. In the fourteen-man squad, Paul Adams was the lone representative of the traditionally disenfranchised communities.

It was at this state of South African cricketing affairs that Brian Lara aimed his ire, a criticism that evoked substantial turmoil. Apologies were called for by the South Africans and delivered by the Trinidadian player and the Caribbean management. But in typically Lara fashion, the furor did not deter him from scoring a majestic 111 runs in the West Indies' triumph over the South Africans. His riposte to apartheid inequality was as decisive on the field as it had been groundbreaking off it. As expected, however, the anti-racism and opposition to historic structural inequality that motivated Lara's comments were not addressed, either in the international cricketing press or in the postapartheid society's media more generally.

But for all those invested in South African cricket, supporters and critics alike, the controversy generated by Lara's *Outlook* interview offers a rare opportunity to reflect seriously upon the game—and all other postapartheid sports codes. An evaluation of apartheid, how its residues have shaped the current condition of cricket, and the future of the game in South Africa is urgently required at this juncture in postapartheid society. Brian Lara provided the occasion for an intervention into South African cricket because he critiqued its racist formation. As important, he has inadvertently disrupted a narrative of emerging international sporting dominance that is developing in the newly democratized nation. South Africa is becoming a major power on the African continent in football (soccer) and an international force in cricket and rugby. An engagement with the complicated politics of South African sport could be no more timely and necessary than in this exceptional, euphoric, and nascent moment in the "new" country's cultural history.

Between May 1995 and March 1996, when the Lara-inspired West Indies eliminated South Africa from the World Cup, triumphs in sports arenas of all kinds flowed thick and fast for a nation just recently admitted to the international fold. Banned from the previous two Rugby World Cups because of apartheid, South Africa entered the competition for the first time with a bang. The country not only hosted the 1995 event, but Amabokoboko (as the rugby side is locally known) beat a highly talented New Zealand team to become the world champions. In January 1996, South Africa again served as the venue for an international competition, this time the continent's premier football competition—the Africa Nation's Cup. The South African football team, Bafana Bafana (a Xhosa term that means energetic and youthful but is colloquially translated as "the Boys"), is managed by whites—and was until mid-1997 captained by a white player as well—although it contains a representative mix of black, white, and coloured players.[6] This team triumphed over a young Tunisian squad in the 1996 Nation's Cup final—the team went on to make South Africa's debut at the 1998 World Cup in France. On both occasions President Mandela, draped alternately in the national rugby and football shirts, was in attendance at the stadiums and in the vanguard of the cheering. There was, quite literally, much flag-waving and dancing in the streets. The leafy avenues of the traditionally white suburbs and the rutted roads of the townships alike were home to fans inebriated with the joys of athletic conquest. The Nation's Cup football celebrations had barely subsided when the cricket team, skippered by the moderately talented Afrikaner Hansie Cronje, secured victory over England in the five-match test series. Played during December 1995 and January 1996, the first four matches ended in draws before South Africa manufactured a win in the fifth international at the Newlands ground in Cape Town. It was the cherry atop the new nation's rather resplendent sporting cake.

In the midst of the nation's procession of athletic victories, it is the cricket accomplishments that deserve special attention. Within South African culture, cricket has come to occupy a signal position. Located between football and rugby, respectively identified as the sports of the black majority and the old Afrikaner ruling elite, cricket is presented as a neutral ideological terrain, untainted by an association with the dominant political formations of the present or the past.[7] Portrayed as an arena of unqualified, but benign, white control, it is seen as white authority made palatable, exemplary even, by the concerted efforts of white administrators to recruit a new following among township residents. (The township dwellers are presumed to be primarily, but not exclusively, black. The game is more rooted within the coloured and indian communities, so they represent a very different kind of target.) Unlike Afrikaner-identified rugby, cricket has traditionally been the province of English-speaking white South Africans. The sport is therefore, however misguided and simplistic the perception, imbued with the liberal and progressive strains of that constituency. The pioneering status of post-apartheid cricket is captured in "Field of Dreams," a historically flawed—if evocatively titled—account by the *Times* of London:

> South Africa's cricket organizers took a leap ahead. The cricket hierarchy, under Dr Ali Bacher, began taking the sport to the black townships, establishing cricket clinics, training black schoolteachers to coach cricket. After the ANC returned from exile in 1990, a merger between the white and black cricket bodies allowed the sport to return to international competition in 1991. In November of that year, a South African cricket team visited India.[8]

All too quick to praise Ali Bacher as a cricket missionary to the townships, the *Times* disregards the long tradition of organized nonracial cricket—which it incorrectly refers to here as "black." Decades old, in one institutional formation or another, nonracial cricket was run by the South African Cricket Board (SACB) until the end of the apartheid era. (In an earlier incarnation this body was called SACBOC—the South African Cricket Board of Control.) Like all other codes that represented the coloured, black, and indian communities (and rare white individuals), the SACB functioned under the auspices of the South African Council on Sports (SACOS). Like their administrative colleagues in, inter alia, football, rugby, tennis, and swimming, the SACB was an underresourced organization charged with a dual social responsibility: it had to work diligently to keep alive the tradition of athletic excellence while simultaneously fostering and maintaining a culture of political resistance.

This was a struggle that SACOS conducted not only nationally but globally through its international arm, SANROC—the South African Non-Racial Olympic Committee. This nonracial sports organization was deeply committed to the principle that disenfranchised South Africans would never compete in sport with their enfranchised counterparts until a fully democratic society was achieved. Participation in SACOS was constructed as being in and of itself an act of political opposition. By foregrounding its nonracial principles and intervening wherever possible in the society's political debates, SACOS transformed the football field, the athletic track, the swimming pool, and training sites for field hockey, baseball, and tennis: these cultural spaces were all reinscribed as venues of ideological resistance. The politics of cultural opposition established SACOS as a crucial vehicle for challenging the hegemony of the National Party (NP) government.

In the mid-1970s the effectiveness of SACOS and SANROC was demonstrated internationally and consequently attacked by the NP at home. The government's reply, however, constitutes a rare instance of apartheid legislative subtlety. The years 1976 and 1977 marked a crucial cultural turning point for white South Africa. The apartheid state found itself on the defensive, responding to local and global events that combined to effect a massive upheaval in South African society. Almost without any warning, mid-1976 found white South Africa confronted by a potent two-pronged attack: increasing black political resistance internally and the prospect of growing cultural isolation internationally. The Soweto student-led revolt of 16 June 1976 revealed patently the angry depths of the nation's disenfranchised. Black youth had claimed the classroom as *the* center of antiapartheid struggle, an arena they would not relinquish for a decade and a half. About a month after the Soweto uprising, in faraway Quebec, Canada, the 1976 Montreal Olympics were marred by the specter of apartheid. Bitterly opposed to the tour that year by the New Zealand national rugby side (known, ironically enough, as the All Blacks) to apartheid South Africa, black African countries protested this visit by boycotting the Montreal Olympics. The marked African absence was so serious that Commonwealth countries, seeking to prevent a repeat of the Montreal boycott, convened to sign the Gleneagles Agreement. This agreement prohibited international teams from touring the apartheid republic. Individual competitors in sports such as golf and tennis were exempted from this ruling because it interfered with these sportspersons' livelihood; no matter, of course, that black South Africans would never have the opportunity to earn their living in this way.

The Nationalist Party government's response to the political tumult was both brutally swift and constitutionally tardy. The 1976 student revolt was quickly and violently crushed, but the spirit of opposition was by no means permanently quelled. Political disturbances in black high schools and universities became a regular feature of South African life, assuming a particular resilience throughout the 1980s. But it would take some fifteen years before the demands of the 1976 youth were met—it was only with Mandela's release in February 1990 that the country's black political leaders were freed and negotiations for a nonracial democracy commenced. The apartheid government's cultural rejoinder to the Gleneagles Agreement, however, was as rapid as that of its trigger-happy security forces of that era. In the middle of 1977 the Nationalist Party inaugurated a policy that Piet Koornhof, its minister of sport and recreation, euphemistically referred to as "normal sport." It was a policy named without any sense of historical paradox: if sport was being "normalized," then this very logic would surely render every other facet of apartheid existence "abnormal," not to mention immoral. It was an implicit, if unconscious, act of self-indictment. Rhetorically and ideologically, the phrase *normal sport* incriminated the entire edifice of apartheid. Recognizing this uncritical irony, SACOS picked up on the contradiction with a keen veracity. It replied promptly to the government's new legislation by coining a resonant slogan: "No Normal Sport in an Abnormal Society."

In truth, however, moral self-incrimination mattered less to the Nationalist government than the prospect of participating again in international sport. The policy of "normal sport" demonstrates white South Africans' obsession with sport and their hunger for international competition. It should be said, however, that a preoccupation with sport is by no means a province exclusive to whites, as was evidenced by the widespread enthusiasm generated by the city of Cape Town's unsuccessful bid to host the 2004 Olympics.[9] However, in the 1970s sport was a cultural imperative so powerful for whites that it compelled the apartheid regime to repeal laws that were decades old and important, if not central, to the ideology of racial separation. The introduction of this National Party policy marks an instance of creative apartheid legislation: it overturned the laws that forbade interracial athletic contests without endangering the basic tenets of apartheid. "Normal sport" allowed South Africans of all races to train and compete with and against each other, to belong to the same sports organizations, and to share sports and other facilities such as hotels and restaurants. However, apartheid circa 1977 was strictly a sporting democracy. This was a cosmetic attempt to appease the international sports community while maintaining the pillars of apartheid. "Normality" was clearly circumscribed; it did not extend beyond the cricket boundary or the football sidelines. The apartheid laws that forbade the equality of education, housing, and health and restricted personal relations remained untouched. Needless to say, the franchise was still exclusive to whites. All these elements were integral to SACOS's anti-"normal sport" platform, a position that was supported by all but a minority of sportspersons in the coloured and indian communities.

Despite its nonracial principles, one of the major critiques leveled against SACOS pertained to its racial composition. Like most other SACOS affiliates, the SACB drew the bulk of its membership and its leadership from the nation's coloured communities while remaining committed to making inroads into the black townships as well. SACOS's pronouncedly coloured profile was especially evident in the Western and Eastern Cape, where this community predominated; these two regions formed, not coincidentally, the SACOS base. In a province such as the Transvaal, the black majority's support for the organization was tepid, at best. (In Natal, another region with a preponderance of blacks, SACOS's main constituency was South Africans of South Asian extraction, colloquially known as indians.) The lack of black support for SACOS, especially in a sport such as football, requires a fuller explication than can be provided in this essay.[10] However, suffice it to say that there is an inverse proportionality between SACOS's administrative achievements in the black community and the popularity of the sport's code. The less popular a sport in the black community, the greater the nonracial body's success; the more popular the code, the less SACOS prospered. The nonracial organization enjoyed most success in sports such as cricket and rugby, codes without significant cachet in the black community. On the other hand, it failed to convince the majority of amateur and professional black footballers to forswear the lure of "normalcy." In a Gramscian word, SACOS was insufficiently rooted in the black community: its watchword, noncollaboration with the apartheid state in any form, was admirable, but the organization was neither ideologically nor racially organic to black South Africa. SACOS's signal achievement was its ability to isolate white South Africa internationally; its most notable failure was its inability to duplicate that success internally. Within the disenfranchised society itself, SACOS was always a principled but never a genuinely popular voice; SACOS could never substantively transcend its coloured roots.

SACOS's platform, however, did enable affiliates such as the South

African Cricket Board to take crucial political positions on sport. Those critiques, so innate to the SACB, are conspicuously lacking within the dominant narratives of contemporary South African cricket. The politics of cricket has been replaced by a trend toward restraint, so much so that commentators have become remarkably subdued about the root of the material disparities that distinguished the SACB from the overwhelmingly white South African Cricket Union (SACU). This cultivated silence encourages an omission of SACB history, quietly sanctioning a neglect of the SACB's tradition of resistance. In its stead, a piece such as "Field of Dreams" foregrounds a trajectory that is not only philanthropic and colonialist (Bacher "began taking the sport to the townships"), but one that is problematically singular in its reading of the disenfranchised's cricket traditions. It does not explore how cricket was deeply grounded within the coloured and indian communities and more sparsely and shallowly rooted among black South Africans. The coloured community's cricket culture is rich and filled with milestones. One of these is the achievement of Mohammed Idris Yusuf. In the 1936–37 season, Yusuf, playing for Government Indian Schools Cricket Club against Star Cricket Club in Bulawayo, Southern Rhodesia, scored an undefeated 412. Cricket's holy book, *Wisden* (which records all the first-class matches of every season), noted that this was the thirteenth highest score in the history of cricket at that time. Nonracial cricket's limitations aside (its ideology, its racial formation, or its material deprivations), the history of the SACB enunciates clearly that the disenfranchised's cricket is not a cultural practice in its genesis; contrary to perceptions that currently dominate, township cricket is not a sport that has no a priori history.

Without many resources, nonracial administrators such as Hassan Howa and Stan Abrahams worked diligently in the working-class black, coloured, and indian townships, the middle-class suburbs, and the schools to nurture a cricket culture commensurate with SACOS's political philosophy. The SACB ran cricket clinics in the coloured townships of the Cape Flats and initiated programs in the adjoining black areas. Today those SACB accomplishments are seldom acknowledged, Hassan Howa's political memory and Stan Abrahams's administrative astuteness are rarely invoked. This trend extends naturally to the cricket oval itself. The exploits of SACB players such as the mercurial spin bowler (a slow bowler who makes the ball spin in both predictable and unexpected ways) "Lefty" Adams, the fast bowlers (or speed merchants, as they are sometimes known in the game) Vincent Barnes and Jeff Frans, the exciting Majiet brothers, Rushdie and Saait, both high-caliber all-rounders (players who bat and bowl with equal skill), and brilliant batsmen such as Ivan Dagnin, Khaya Majola, and Michael Doman are seldom remembered. (Vincent Barnes, at the end of his career when apartheid ended, made a brief appearance for his provincial team. A forty-two-year-old Majola still plays local club cricket in the Transvaal, the captain of the all-black Soweto team that recently toured England.)

The achievements of these players and the traditions of their various clubs and provinces demonstrate that nonracial cricket is of an old vintage. The cricketing culture that produced the talented Paul Adams is not the result of a sporting message brought by well-meaning white administrators such as Ali Bacher. It is a culture that was carefully administered by the likes of Howa and honed in the cricket nets and on the playing fields by Lefty Adams, Vincent Barnes, and Saait Majiet. Paul Adams traces his cricket roots to an independent and, indeed, oppositional tradition to that of Bacher, now executive director of the United Cricket Board of South Africa (UCBSA). Lest we forget, when the Bacher-like philanthropists came, they brought with them more than shining red balls and carefully oiled bats. They were missionaries of apartheid acquiescence and unabashed advocates of "normal sport."

There is, of course, one cricketer from the nonracial fold who has achieved a prominence that has interrupted the dominant narrative for almost thirty years. His position is truly exceptional, his skills so tremendous that apartheid law could exile him but never thwart his ability. His accomplishments have assumed such legendary status that his name has been indelibly etched into the annals of apartheid history: Basil D'Oliveira, or Dolly, as he is more commonly known on the hardy cricket fields of the Cape Flats and the manicured ovals of England. More than any other single individual, Basil D'Oliveira was responsible for South Africa's sporting isolation. A coloured player who came up through the ranks of St. Augustine's of Cape Town, one of nonracial cricket's most established clubs (which also produced Paul Adams), D'Oliveira was sponsored by his community to try his hand at the mid-level professional game in England. Dolly worked his way through the professional ranks in England, making his debut for the county of Worcestershire in 1960 before being selected to represent his adopted country in 1966. Largely presumed to be an automatic choice for the 1968 England team to South Africa, Dolly was initially omitted from the squad by a pusillanimous selection committee who knew that the tour would be jeopardized by the inclusion of the coloured immigrant from Cape Town. A great controversy erupted in English cricket following Dolly's exclusion, but he was picked at the very last minute as a replacement for the injured Tom Cartwright. The South African prime minister, B. J. Vorster, refused to admit an English team that he described as the "team of the anti-apartheid movement." The 1968 tour was called off and South Africa's cricketing wilderness was only two summers off. Bill Lawry's 1970 Australians were the last official visitors until the 1990s.

Basil D'Oliveira returned to South Africa in January 1996 to watch the fifth test at Newlands, in which the country of his birth beat the country he has called home for more than thirty years. During the match, the UCBSA arranged a luncheon to honor Dolly. Bacher, who would have played against him had the 1968 series taken place, was characteristically full of hubris during the proceedings. He hailed the ex-England all-rounder as "one of the most famous people in South Africa's non-racial society" and thanked him for "transforming" the apartheid state.[11] Always a man of few words, and flanked by the irrepressible Archbishop Tutu and Bacher, D'Oliveira was too moved to reply. Had he been able to respond, however, one wonders whether he might have recalled the coloured poet Arthur Nortje's "Song for a Passport." Like much of Nortje's poetry, "Song for a Passport" ruminates on the condition of exile from South Africa. However, this poem possesses a poignance that is striking because it is overwritten by the determination to remain permanently outside the experience of apartheid South Africa:

> Now interviews and checks are in the offing:
> O ask me all but do not ask allegiance![12]

These final lines from "Song for a Passport" provide an especially apt metaphor for D'Oliveira, an exile whose "allegiance" to his adopted country has remained constant despite the postapartheid South African cricketing establishment's recent attempts at reclamation. At the UCBSA luncheon Bacher enthused, "Deep down we will always regard you as a South African."

The D'Oliveirian moment is instructive within postapartheid cricket for a variety of reasons, not least of which is the way Dolly's reclamation has been so different from the reintegration of a white player. The reinscription of D'Oliveira has been a national project, one that provides a sharp contrast to the unproblematic ways in which an exiled white cricketer quietly assumed a leading role on the postapartheid playing field. An Afrikaner from the heartland city of Bloemfontein, Kepler Wessels was a talented left-handed batsman who moved to Cape Town to play for Western Province before leaving to represent the English county of Sussex; his career in England lasted from the mid-1970s through the early 1980s. Frustrated with South Africa's isolation, he decided to look elsewhere for a national home. Migrating to Australia and marrying a woman from Down Under, he qualified for his new country's national team. In the course of making his new home in

Australia, the Bloemfontein native pledged, expediently as it turned out, undying allegiance to his adopted country. Wessels's career in the Australian team lasted about half a decade—he failed primarily because he was unable to play West Indian fast bowling—after which he promptly returned to the land of his birth. Because of his subsequent disloyalty to Australia, Wessels's notoriety Down Under has taken on a markedly (un)popular aspect. A subplot of the recent Australian movie *Muriel's Wedding* parodies the Wessels scenario. It depicts a white South African swimmer so desperate for international competition that he offers to pay an Australian woman to marry him so that he can participate in the next Olympics. Physically and ideologically, the swimmer is a dead ringer for the dour-faced Wessels.

However, Wessels was only one of a number of white South Africans who tried to overcome apartheid-inspired isolation by becoming athletic mercenaries. Their talents blunted by a lack of competition, enfranchised South African sportspersons introduced a whole new commercial dimension to international athletics. They traded their talent for new passports, if not new national identities; countries such as Britain were all too willing to barter. Most famous among these South African sporting "expatriates" is the middle-distance runner Zola Budd. A Bloemfontein native like Wessels, the barefoot wunderkind with the pronounced Afrikaner accent assumed British citizenship in order to compete in the Los Angeles Olympics. Americans remember Budd only too well. In her (unsuccessful) effort to win a medal for Britain, she literally (if inadvertently) pushed the Olympic favorite Mary Decker Slaney right out of the race. When Wessels made his debut for Australia in the 1982–83 series against England, his opponents included his old Western Province batting partner Allan Lamb, an Englishman of very recent standing.

Wessels's decision to quit the Australian team turned out to be a most timely departure, as political changes would have it. He was barely back in South Africa when the postapartheid era arrived and he was appointed captain of a team sorely lacking in international experience. Wessels's South Africanness, his loyalty—to the country of his birth, anyway—was always already presumed. His brief stint as "Australian" represented only a hiatus enforced by the international ban on competition with the apartheid state; Wessels's true national status was as valid in an apartheid South Africa as it was in a postapartheid society. D'Oliveira's South Africanness, no matter how liminal or nostalgic, required a greater effort to reconstruct. More strikingly, the white South African's expedience was never scrutinized, nor were the different motivations for Dolly and Wessels's "foreign" cricketing experiences explored.

Unlike Wessels, the old St. Augustine's cricketer resists easy reinterpellation into postapartheid history for a complex of reasons that range from the political to the personal. The least important of these is his renowned reticence. The most significant reason is that his 1968 selection put a firm end to the notion that racist politics could be kept out of South African sport. Constitutionally denied the right to represent his country, he was exiled by apartheid; in his turn, his selection by England exiled South Africa. Today white South Africans can praise Dolly fulsomely, but they cannot bury the painful memory of the isolation their sport endured because of his selection. Apartheid society's refusal to acknowledge the legitimacy of his new national identity and his status as an English cricketer propelled it into the international sports wilderness. Notwithstanding the glossy efforts of postapartheid cricket's administrators to reappropriate this (once rejected) native son, Basil D'Oliveira remains a silent rebuke to the injustice of apartheid sport. Much of the tacit admonishment that D'Oliveira represents derives from his historic standing: he is a reluctant symbol of the talent and the skills that flourished in nonracial cricket. Because he is the exceptional cricketer who escaped apartheid oppression and thrived outside it, he is simultaneously a reminder of the cost of white racism.

The symbolic Basil D'Oliveira has been reclaimed in toto, transformed from metaphor and metonym of nonracial cricket into icon of an egalitarian postapartheid sport. D'Oliveira has had to assume the burden of overrepresentation, the exceptional cricketer who stands in place of and replaces the entire disenfranchised community. Overrepresentation functions here like the Derridean concept of *erasure*—for everything said, a great many things are left unspoken—in that the sign *Dolly* marks an attempt to prevent a series of pointed political inquiries. The elevation and celebration of the old St. Augustine's all-rounder represent a crucial instance of postapartheid cricket's effort to orchestrate amnesia about its own racist past. The UCBSA does not want to engage the following questions: How many other Dollies did nonracial cricket produce? What would the status of nonracial cricket have been had more players achieved his success? How is apartheid's culpability for the waste of nonracial talent to be measured? How different in racial composition would the South African cricket team be today if the SACB had not been so structurally underresourced? How many more Paul Adamses would there be in the current squad? These issues have to be taken up by reconstructing the D'Oliveira-Adams genealogy. Paul Adams is Dolly's heir, as the media are quick to claim, but a removed one. The lineage from Dolly to Adams extends through Lefty Adams, Ivan Dagnin, the Majiet brothers, and Michael Doman. The teenage spinner is the England player's great-grandson; the two St. Augustine's cricketers bookend the unheralded SACB generations who came in between.

The complex repercussions of D'Oliveira's exile, his inability to return as an English cricketer, and his ambiguous status today (local hero and insistent Englishman) demonstrate the burden of postapartheid nation building through sport. (Cricket's responsibility is especially onerous because rugby and football have no Dolly who has to be accommodated.) Assuming this task, the South African cricket community has attempted to produce a complicated and layered discourse that can address the demands of this historic conjuncture. Administrators, players, and the media are forging a discourse derived from the sometimes contradictory and occasionally complementary vocabularies of rationalization, apology, deferral, silence, and naturalization. In D'Oliveira's case the language of apology and an all-too-spirited attempt at (re)naturalization are at work. But Dolly is, as I have noted, the unusual case. His historic status demands a self-consciousness about the effects of apartheid. In general there is no such attention paid to the consequences, past and present, of racist sport.

In the process of negotiating between apartheid and postapartheid, the transformation of the antagonistic SACB and SACU into the UCBSA, the nation's cricketing community is clearly privileging only one version of the past. The history of whites in the game has assumed, through the absence of a sustained counternarrative, *the* status of South African cricket. The conflicts that marked SACB and SACU relations are not so much ignored as they are hegemonically rendered. History is, as they say, written by the victors—SACU claims the honors on that score. This particular formation of the UCBSA is in itself a telling commentary on postapartheid cricket and on South African society as a whole. As the UCBSA is currently constituted, in control of the sport's resources, editing and censoring its past, and selectively writing its traditions, there is no possibility for challenging the cricket accounts it presents. Therein lies an instructive cultural tale.

A counternarrative depends on the willingness, the historical capacity, and the resources with which to provide an alternative history. The unification of the two ideologically opposed cricketing bodies, in a climate of national reconciliation, did not lend itself to the remembering, celebrating, or enshrining of the ideological imperatives of SACOS's resistance. (The "United" in UCBSA reflects the ideological tenor of the times, the spirit of political reconciliation without a commitment to equity.) The "United" Cricket Board's first priority was international competition, not a comprehension of historic differences. The SACB never possessed the means to challenge the white cricket establishment publicly, to offer playing or train-

ing facilities comparable to those of the SACU. Nonracial cricket administered a moderately successful interprovincial competition, but it could not
organize international tours; it should be said, however, that SACB did not
include in its brief the development of an international cricket program.
Nonracial sport's main asset was its awareness of racism and injustice: politically principled, SACOS believed it had (postcolonial) History on its side.
In the "new" South African society, where national unity is the dominant
narrative of the day (although recently that account appears to be showing
the first signs of coming under public pressure), it is no longer possible to
invoke the high moralism of antiapartheid to combat the reductive and inac-
curate accounts of township cricket currently in vogue. The ANC government's commitment to national reconciliation, at considerable cultural and
political costs to the black community, renders unlikely the possibility—at
this too-late stage—of a Zimbabwe-like period of probation. The moment
for inaugurating such a policy is, sadly, past. At this juncture the best that
can be achieved is the reappropriation and refashioning of the SACB platform, tailored to suit the contemporary terrain. Unless such an intervention
is made, the disenfranchised's history will be distorted and disfigured beyond political recognition. It is already but a minimal heave from the scrap-
heap of (anti)apartheid history.

The SACU hegemony within the UCBSA was achieved through a dual
strategy: the evacuation of SACB history and, more strategically, the absorption of nonracial players and administrators, sans traditions. Nonracial players and clubs have had to accommodate themselves to new cricket infrastructures that bear no evidence of their struggles, their customs, or their
past. Administrators have simply been assimilated, for the most part nomi-
nally, into the official structures of the SACU, in the guise of the UCBSA.
Hassan Howa's successor as SACOS chief, Krish Mackerudj, is currently the
president of the UCBSA, an office with more ceremony than clout. Khaya
Majola and Rushdie Majiet, outstanding SACB players and administrators,
are among the few nonracial cricketers to have been appointed to full-time
positions in the new structure.

The story of disproportionate resources has to be retold.[13] It is the main
reason there are routinely ten white players on the national team. In the pre-
Paul Adams era, just a few short months ago, all eleven were white. (Depending on the condition of the pitch, whether or not the management
thinks it will be conducive to his type of bowling, Adams is sometimes omitted.)[14] But like D'Oliveira, Adams should not have to bear the burden of
overrepresentation. He should be one of several black—in the broadest sense
of the term—players on the team; he is not because apartheid inequities

militated against the disenfranchised community. The schools lacked facilities, if not committed teachers; the townships and the suburbs suffered from a lack of playing fields. If the national team is to assume any semblance of the society's racial composition, then the SACB platform has to be recovered. It is because of apartheid ideology that the SACU training facilities and their grounds—Newlands in Cape Town, Kingsmead in Durban, and the Wanderers in Johannesburg, to mention but three—dominate the South African cricket landscape. They now host the international contests, monuments to superior white capital—a currency that easily converted into white cricketing dominance. In and of themselves, these plush stadiums boldly attest to the triumph of SACU. At no point did the SACB possess comparable capital. Consequently, there are no memorials to the struggles of nonracial cricket, no SACB archives, no acknowledgment or incorporation of its struggles.[15] Moralism seldom converts into hard currency. It does, however, provide a ready counter to fictitious renderings of history.

One such attempt to reconstruct history is the SACU rendering of the "rebel tours" it organized from the mid-1980s to the very beginning of the 1990s. Frustrated by its international isolation, the SACU decided to embark upon a new strategy. It put together its own series of tours by attracting groups of players from other countries who were prepared to contravene the Gleneagles Agreement. Using funds secured from the government and South African Breweries, Ali Bacher was the SACU point man in these operations. Luring players with exorbitant amounts of money (by cricket standards, anyway), Bacher put together squads of renegade English, Sri Lankan, West Indian, and Australian players. These cricketers were either just past their prime or a little too young to have yet made their mark upon, say, the Australian or Sri Lankan game. These rebel tourists competed against the cream of white South Africa's talent.[16] (The West Indies and the Sri Lankan authorities banned their "rebel" players for life; the other two nations imposed bans that did not exceed three years.) The SACB and SACOS spearheaded the opposition to these visits, a resistance that was shared by a significant segment of the disenfranchised population.

Yet in October 1995 Bacher had the temerity to suggest that he did not grasp the depth of black resentment: "If we knew then what we know now about the bitterness those rebel tours were going to cause, we would have thought twice. This may sound a bit naive but the fact is that in those days the blacks were not allowed to demonstrate and it simply did not occur to us how strongly they felt."[17] Bacher, of course, has long since proved himself too shrewd an administrator to be ideologically "naive"; he simply has a cynically selective political memory. Moreover, he is in a position of cultural authority from which he can insert massive silences into black South African history. Whether or not blacks were "allowed to demonstrate," they had been doing so for centuries and with a particular intensity for more than a decade and a half by the time the "rebel tours" came around. The Soweto protest of 1976 was certainly not sanctioned by the National Party, nor were the insurrections of the mid-1980s.

The public conception and the re-presentation of the game, however, are most disturbing. The disproportionate racial representation, the retention of the team's (nick)name, and, most important, the ease with which a continuum between the apartheid side of 1970 and the postapartheid one of the mid-1990s has been established demonstrate how little has actually changed. But surely this cannot be the case. Have the political conditions not changed so dramatically as to call for a major reconceptualization of the national cricket team? Isn't there, after all, a huge difference between the government of Nelson Mandela and the apartheid regime of B. J. Vorster? However, the public discourse, for which the white press is mainly but not exclusively responsible, is one of insistent continuity. Black and white journalists, radio and TV commentators such as Heinrich Marnitz, Omar Henry, and Trevor Quirk consistently invoke the skills and accomplishments of the apartheid era's renowned players. The media recall Barlow, Mike Procter, the Pollock brothers, Graeme and Peter (the latter is currently chairman of the national selectors), and Barry Richards—some of the finest cricketers in the world at that time. Hansie Cronje, who captains a team in which he cannot properly command a place on individual merit, leads a side that is regularly measured against that of its "predecessors," the 1970 Springboks— skippered, incidentally, by one Ali Bacher.

In terms of pure cricketing talent, of course, there is no real comparison. Bacher's team boasted, as I mentioned, several world-class players. Richards and Graeme Pollock were among the best batsmen of their generation, and Barlow was an inspirational opening bat and a medium-pace bowler of ingenuity and verve. Procter and Peter Pollock were menacing quick bowlers, and the former was no slouch with the bat either. Of the current squad, only the all-rounder Brian McMillan and the fast bowler Allan Donald are recognized as players of international stature. In terms of racial composition, however, the parallel is apt. The South African cricketing universe circa 1998 is not markedly different from that of two generations ago. There are now thirteen white players in the national squad as opposed to fourteen. Only the unexpected rise of Paul Adams, the eighteen-year-old spin-bowling prodigy from the coloured lower middle class, distinguishes Cronje's team from Bacher's. The pivotal aspect of the comparison between the 1970 and the

1990s sides, however, is that it reconfigures white South African cricket history: it eliminates the twenty-year hiatus between the apartheid society's enforced isolation and the postapartheid state's readmission to world cricket. The "lost years" of the 1970s and the 1980s, alleviated only in part by "rebel tours," cannot be recovered, but they can be written out through an imaginary continuity.

Now that the postapartheid nation's (white) men have taken to the field again, resplendent in crisp white flannels, shirts, and pullovers and topped with the green-and-gold hat of the old apartheid team, the blow of two decades in the cricket wilderness has been ameliorated; at worst, it has been rendered a vague memory. It is entirely apropos that Wessels's and Cronje's teams should, like Bacher's and Peter van der Merwe's before them, take the traditional apartheid nickname of the Springboks. For verily, the Springboks have returned to international competition. Which of course begs the pivotal question: Is the postapartheid team *returning* to international competition or is the nation competing for the first time? If the postapartheid society is indeed a new and democratic one, then 1991 should mark South Africa's *entrance* into the international cricket arena. The all-white teams that competed prior to that moment should be acknowledged as cricketing footnotes, a testament to a racist past that should be neither hastily recalled nor too easily invoked. There are, after all, significant differences between the two epochs. During the apartheid era, black countries in the ICC, led by the West Indies and India, refused to play against white South African teams. Today the West Indies, India, Pakistan, and Sri Lanka are part of the South African cricket schedule. When the Springboks played against Australia in Cape Town or Durban in 1970, the grounds were strictly segregated, coloureds and blacks occupying the worst seats in the stadium. These seating arrangements have, interestingly enough, survived the demise of apartheid. At Newlands in Cape Town, coloured spectators still flock to their old places under the famous (if reconstructed) "Willows," named after the tall willow trees that provide shade from the summer sun in this corner of the grounds. Although largely replaced by a new stand now, the "Willows" are still favored in part because of economics, but largely because of a tradition that goes back decades. Much like the "Hill" in Sydney, Australia, the fans in the coloured section are full of witticisms and easy banter. The legacy of physical separation is stronger than the fledgling reality of postapartheid structural changes.

Both locally and internationally, however, the dominant designation of South Africa's postapartheid participation in international cricket is written as the country's readmission into the world fold. In and of itself the use of terms such as *readmission* and *return* are tantamount to legitimating the apartheid past; it implicitly authorizes white postapartheid hegemony. It invalidates the SACOS struggle, obliterates the history of nonracial cricket, and anoints the achievements of white players. Furthermore, such a conception of postapartheid cricket situates the likes of Basil D'Oliveira as the exceptional, dare one say token, black cricketer of merit and repute. There is as much at stake in the language of "return" as there is political significance embedded in the name Springbok.

It is not surprising that halfhearted efforts to rename the national team the Proteas, after a rare South African flower indigenous to the Western Cape, have fallen on deaf ears.[18] A renaming of the national cricket side is dependent upon a major ideological refashioning. It is a substantial project, one that requires a rethinking of a society's past, the ways in which its cultural signifiers function, and the ways in which political histories (of oppression and resistance) are inscribed within those signs. To rename is to appraise the past critically: it necessitates a realignment of political forces, the replacement of offensive old symbols with ones that are new and in ideologically good repair. South Africans, restricted as they are by the ANC government's policy of reconciliation, do not have such an option at their disposal. They trek into the postapartheid future emblazoned with the symbols of the apartheid past.

The issue of naming assumed considerable ideological salience during the selection of Paul Adams. Selected as the youngest and the newest member of the national team in December 1995, the media displayed a disconcerting lack of irony and self-reflexivity when they uncritically took to dubbing the coloured Adams the "SpinBok." He is certainly a spinner, a slow bowler with the ability to make the ball move in surprising ways. But a Springbok? As a coloured he is surely excluded by the apartheid-derived definition that links McMillan to Barlow. How is his lineage akin to that which connects Allan Donald to Peter Pollock? And how can the history of the Springboks be made to accommodate Adams? How does he reconfigure, or configure, Springbok history? Does he simply disrupt it, or can his selection be deployed more strategically?

In the initial media coverage of his selection, Adams's cricketing style provided an easy answer. He was exceptional, not so much in terms of race or talent, but by virtue of his unorthodox bowling action. Adams's style of bowling is indeed unconventional, to say the least. In a sport where smooth physical action and unadorned athleticism are prerequisites, Adams breaks all the rules. His delivery of the cricket ball is full of awkward contortions, so eye-catching that commentators such as Eddie Barlow have likened its ungainliness to a "frog in a blender." Journalist Jon Swift was equally imaginative, describing the delivery as the "strangled action of capsized terrapin." The animal imagery persists among Adams's cricket friends from the Cape Flats. Lapsing into the colloquial, they labeled him "Gogga," an unflattering but affectionate term for an insect.[19]

When attention did switch from Adams's style to his race (without ever relinquishing the former as spectacle), the trope of exceptionality intensified. Despite being the youngest player ever to be selected to play for apartheid or postapartheid South Africa ("Paul Adams became the youngest player to wear cricket's green and gold at 18 years and 340 days"),[20] that fact was overshadowed by his racial status. In one of the more considered pieces on Adams's race and his background, cricket columnist Peter Johnson wrote, "He is what was once dismissively known as a Cape Coloured, brought up in an area where . . . equality is a word they are just beginning to understand."[21] It is paradoxical, but telling, that Adams was at once touted as a symbol of postapartheid cricketing hope and as a vision of the society's cricketing future—reporter Mark Nicholas claimed him as a "torch for the new South Africa"[22]—while being interpellated into the hegemonic structures of old.

South Africa is a country that is psychically torn: the memories of inequality and injustice are deeply ingrained and yet the experience of democracy is novel and invigorating. There is a predictable commensurability between the psychic ambivalence and the immense importance that accrues so quickly to new symbols such as Adams. South African rugby has produced its second generation of this phenomenon in the coloured winger Chester Williams, quite literally (and expediently) the poster boy for the 1995 World Cup. The winger, and before him Errol Tobias, a scintillating coloured flyhalf who played "normal sport" (and currently mayor of his hometown of Caledon), has been fulfilling for the past few years the same role that Adams is in cricket. Cricket, in fact, has long been looking for its own "Chester Williams," a camera-friendly black body that bears testament to the bona fides of white-dominated sports codes and their administrators, the lone, alien(ated) black representative whose highly publicized presence reflects the "successful" transition of all aspects of postapartheid society, not just sport or culture. Both Adams and Williams are young coloured athletes who bear the burden of overrepresentation. The traditionally disenfranchised communities' national standing in cricket and rugby is contingent upon the every performance of their single representative. Sporting success translates all too easily, understandably so, into communal achievement; failure by Williams or Adams is inconceivable. This is an unfair burden, but one enforced by a status that is multiple in its contradictions: the historic condition of being a black athletic minority in a white-dominated sport in a black-majority society.

Overrepresentation has transformed Adams from gifted cricketer into a loaded sociopolitical symbol. He has become a figure worthy of emulation for the society's traditionally disenfranchised communities, a lodestar for the country's cricketing future. Paul Adams is a metaphor of possibility and transition. The young cricketer is a sign of potentiality, representing the hope that a society with a racist past can overcome its discriminatory history and meld into a nonracial and egalitarian society. Ideally, of course, the "equality" that his community has just acquired constitutionally will not be only a rhetorical but a transformative material experience. In that respect he becomes a figure of transition, the exceptional player through whom the future becomes racially distinct from the past. The next generation of South African cricketers, as prefigured in Adams, will look less like Hansie Cronje and more like the coloured spinner. The nation will still be clad in white, but those flannels will adorn black and coloured and indian bodies, as well as white ones: the nation re-presented. But in reality, Adams's selection inaugurates only a tentative new era, one that negotiates with the old edifices of representation and organizational dominance from a position of symbolic promise but structural disadvantage.

It is for this reason that Adams can be so effectively interpellated as the "youngest player to wear cricket's green and gold." In this rhetorical sleight of hand, he is both naturalized as national cricketer and subsumed under the sign of the Springbok. By designating Adams a Springbok, he is appropriated by being written into and against a history of oppression that is antagonistic to the teenage spinner. Apartheid is solely responsible for his lack of racial predecessors. Adams is being asked to make history bereft of basic resources such as cultural memory or the ideological traditions of his embattled community. He is expected to be a cricketing pioneer without a political past. Adams is deprived of his own community's history and unable to acknowledge how apartheid laws denied him a lineage such as the one that is a matter of rote to his teammates McMillan and Donald.

The teenage spinner is, like D'Oliveira, a bad fit with white traditions, yet the postapartheid nation in white flannels is symbolically dependent upon him for the maintenance of its racial dominance. Adams functions as a figure of possibility and as a marker of limitation. He affirms black potential while simultaneously confirming white hegemony. Through D'Oliveira's postapartheid reinscription and Adams's inclusion in the Springbok team, white South Africa is symbolically absolving itself of its racist history without having to relinquish the privileges it has accrued via apartheid. The nation in cricketing whites is a powerful metaphor for white South Africa's post-apartheid sporting dominance, an authority no longer fettered by the prospect of international or local cultural sanctions. The South African cricket team is an emblem of a rare postcolonial victory, a triumph untempered by an ICC probation, a radical disruption of the apartheid structures, or the memory of oppression. The major achievement of the nation in white is, appropriately, that it has won widespread postapartheid approval without being considered offensive. Except, of course, among those for whom the game signifies a great deal more than just cricket.

Notes

This essay is dedicated to the memory of the late Mr. Henry Dirks and the eleven other players on the Lansur United A.F.C. team of 1985. Lansur United (1983–1993) was a township football institution that embodied the spirit of nonracial sport.

This essay benefited from a series of conversations with Toby Miller and Kenneth Surin, cricket buffs both. I am indebted to Toby for his keen insights about cricket and his suggestions about Australian popular culture. Ken's vast knowledge of cricket was, as always, invaluable. I am grateful to Ken for his encouragement and for the historical background he provided. Finally, my thanks to Cynthia Young who read the piece with a sharp editorial eye and asked the kind of questions about the culture of cricket that I would have otherwise overlooked.

1. Quoted in "Lara Sorry for His Slip-Up," *Daily Mail*, 9 March 1996.
2. C. L. R. James, *Beyond a Boundary* (New York: Pantheon, 1983), 248. Brian Lara has recently succeeded Courtney Walsh of Jamaica as captain of the West Indies.
3. Michael Manley, *A History of West Indies Cricket*, rev. ed. (Kingston: West Indies Publishing, 1995), 148. See also James's *Beyond a Boundary* for a fuller account of the movement to appoint Worrell captain.
4. In the South African context, nonracial sport—a sociopolitical practice premised upon the shared humanity of all sportspersons—functioned as a sharp critique of the apartheid state's insistence on extending its doctrine of white racial supremacy into the arena of athletic competition. "Nonracial" sports bodies opposed their apartheid counterparts, which abided by the policy of institutional social separation on strongly moral and ideological grounds, but foremost among their motivations was the refusal to give any epistemological credence to the concept of race at all. Nonracial sports administrators and players regarded race as, at best, a superficial marker of physiognomical difference or, at worst, a tool of ideological expedience.
5. "Hunte Speaks Out," *Daily Telegraph*, 18 October 1985.
6. In South Africa, *black* denotes people of African descent, and *coloured* describes persons of mixed racial heritage; South Africans of South Asian origin are colloquially known as *indian*.
7. In his autobiography, white South African cricketer Jimmy Cook reveals the prevalence of this kind of thinking in traditionally enfranchised environs. Blinkered by their historical privilege, white cricketers such as Cook show themselves to be not only dis-

missive of political dimensions attendant to sport but also all too ready to absolve themselves of any responsibility for the inequitable state of cricket affairs: "Like so many South Africans, I wanted the day to come when both the legal and the social discrimination would end. I hold political views, but my thoughts here are as a sportsman, and as such I can only repeat what has so often been said in the past—cricket had moved with the times; our administrators had eliminated all elements of racism from the game. A few years before my time players had, during a game in Cape Town, staged a token walk-off in protest against discrimination. We had a clear conscience when it came to our approach to this serious and complex issue." Cook is so without a sense of historical accountability that he cannot see the irony of claiming a "clear conscience" and the "elimination of racism" from cricket on the basis of a single "token protest." Not even a recognition of the superficiality of this "walk-off" enables a white cricketer to understand the nonsense, and the arrogance, of his assertion. For Cook, and for most of the white cricket establishment (a constituency that all the while held fast to the notion that apartheid politics should be kept out of sport), actions such as these indicated the largesse and the progressive tendencies—"cricket had moved with the times"—of the white-dominated South African Cricket Union. See Jimmy Cook (with Frederick Cleary), *The Jimmy Cook Story: A Career at the Crease* (London: Pelman, 1993), 14.

8. "Field of Dreams," *Times* (London), 20 May 1995.

9. In the past couple of years a local anti-Olympic movement has been developing in Cape Town. A grassroots organization linked to left political groupings has been spearheading this drive because its members believe that there are more urgent issues to be confronted in South African society. Graffiti such as "Why spend R1,8 billion on the Olympics? Build Houses!" have become a feature of life on the predominantly coloured Cape Flats. There was presumed to be a fair measure of (tacit) support for the anti-Olympic movement as the entire South African sporting and political community watched these ideological antagonists do battle over sport—a battle, of course, only technically won by the barely recognized anti-Olympic group by virtue of the 2004 Games' being awarded to Athens instead of Cape Town.

10. The relationship between SACOS and the black community was so complex that it could not be accounted for by any single factor. SACOS's lack of resources prevented it from making significant inroads into the community, its ideological and political roots lay outside of the ANC (the organization with the greatest purchase in the black community), and SACOS's principles could not accommodate the cultural-real politics schism that characterized black sporting life in the "normal sports" era. The black community was able to reconcile the privileges its players accrued from participating in "normal sport" with the ability to oppose politically the very National Party government that oversaw this cultural practice. It was a contradiction that SACOS could address, an expediency beyond its ideological ken. These are some of the issues that have to be engaged as a crucial part of the cultural history of disenfranchised South Africa.

11. Quoted in "D'Oliveira Remains on England's Side," *Times* (London), 3 January 1996.

12. Arthur Nortje, "Song for a Passport," in *Dead Roots* (London: Heinemann, 1973), 30.

13. The 7 February 1996 issue of *Sports Illustrated* carefully and precisely documented this phenomenon. Touring the townships of South Africa, the magazine captured the continuing material deprivations that prevent black youth from competing on a level playing field with their white counterparts.

14. In recent months Adams has been joined by two fast bowlers, the coloured Roger Telemachus and the young speedster Makhaya Ntini, as the black representatives in the squad.

15. In the past two or three years a community-inspired movement, the "District Six

Museum," has been established. This organization, as part of an ongoing process, intends to document the history of deracination in Cape Town. The museum has been open for a short while now, and on 31 August 1996 it hosted a program titled "(Dis) Playing the Game: A Celebration of More than a Century of Sport," a testament to the history of nonracial sports organizations with their roots in the community of District Six. My thanks to Mr. Leslie Van Breda for this information.

16. Omar Henry, one of a small minority of coloured players who participated in normal sport, represented South Africa in a few of these "rebel" tests.

17. Quoted in "England's Trip of Hope," *Mail on Sunday*, 22 October 1995.

18. The name Proteas is, however, itself a name sullied by the apartheid past. During the early days of the "normal sport" era, the rugby team that represented the coloured community was known by this name; the black team was called the Leopards, and the white team was called, predictably, the Springboks. Errol Tobias, as I note below, is among the best-known rugby players to come up through the ranks of the Proteas. It should be noted, however, that the emblem on the national cricket cap bears an image of both the springbok and the protea; the latter, however, is almost never invoked as a national symbol.

19. All these commentators revived an old colonialist trope in their depiction of the young bowler. At the height of nineteenth-century British colonial rule in the Indian subcontinent, talented local cricketers were groomed for incorporation into the racist structure. Indian cricketers such as the great batsman Ranjitsinhji, his nephew Duleepsinhji, and the first Nawab of Pataudi were manicured by a certain kind of Orientalist discourse for English consumption in those days. They were presented as honorary Englishmen, so gifted as cricketers they were elevated to a level that exceeded that of ordinary colonial subjects. On this basis they were selected to play for the imperial state. Ranjitsinhji, who played during the era C. L. R. James labels the Golden Age of Cricket, ranks among the most accomplished batsmen ever. During this epoch, Indian spin bowlers were frequently described as "wizards," cricketers whose performances conjured up visions, as Ken Surin put it in a recent conversation, of "snake charming and rope tricks in a Kiplingesque bazaar." All because of the inscrutable and unpredictable ball movement these bowlers could induce. In the 1920s and 1930s, the aborigine fast bowler Eddie Gilbert was called for throwing, and some twenty years later the Barbados speed merchant Charlie Griffith was similarly accused.

20. "Breathing New Life into an Old Game," *Mail and Guardian*, 5 January 1996.

21. Peter Johnson, "Weird Magic of a Boy with a Sting in His Wrist," *Daily Mail*, 26 December 1995.

22. Mark Nicholas, "Whirling Adams Carries Cape's Good Hopes into Port Elizabeth's Lion's Den," *Daily Telegraph*, 23 December 1995. In much the same vein, Eddie Barlow ebulliently pronounced that the young spinner would "change the face of South African cricket"; quoted in *Jerusalem Post*, 26 December 1996.

Batting against the Break: On Cricket, Nationalism, and the Swashbuckling Sri Lankans

Qadri Ismail

To score, he had to get the leg-break away through two short-legs and force the off-break through two gulleys. Against the break all the time. . . .There are new roads for batsmen to explore.
▸ C. L. R. James, Beyond a Boundary

'Twas the eve of the vernal equinox, well before the southwesterly monsoon rains of 1996. Sri Lanka, naturally, was hot. The kind of heat that, as Michael Ondaatje puts it, walks around "hugging everybody"; an omnipresent, omni-pressing, suffocating heat. Things were a little cooler in Lahore, where the Sri Lankan team had made the final of the World Cup cricket tournament. In previous competitions, dating back to 1975, the team had lost no fewer than twenty of the twenty-four matches it had played.[1] This time, it sought to end the drought. This time, the little island nation was to beat all comers, including Australia (a continent), in the championship game.

A frame already exists for viewing "international" matches in South Asia, one inspired by C. L. R. James. In this reading, cricket is nationalism;[2] its spectators, nationalist. My argument against such a reduction is twofold. First, cricket and its spectators cannot be covered thus. Nationalism endeav-ors to fence the game in and exhaust its meaning; just as it tries, in Partha Chatterjee's phrase, to "seduce, apprehend and imprison" all phenomena within its grasp. But cricket runs out. In this brief space, a careful examina-tion is possible of just one such attempt to catch the game: Sinhala national-ism's hegemonic move to produce a seamless Sri Lankan nation out of (those who applauded) the cricket team's success at the World Cup. The examina-tion will, I hope, be adequate illustration of this frame's being out of joint, of the bind between cricket and nationalism not being natural, or inevitable, but produced—by the latter. I argue, therefore, that the meaning of cricket cannot be exhausted by nationalism and that the current discourse on cricket in South Asia needs revision. The second, consequent, and perhaps more im-portant thrust of this argument is the identification, if not construction, of a space for the spectator unmarred by nationalism, for the spectator who would cheer the team but not the nation. The existence of and necessity for such a space is not recognized in or allowed by South Asian cricket discourse.

Indeed, even making the claim for such a site is hazardous, given nationalism's omnipresence; and I am not entirely convinced that this essay successfully produces such a space. But the attempt, the commitment, is necessary—if not imperative—not just in the interests of cricket, but as a part of the critique of nationalism. Without such moves, however risky they may be, South Asian politics cannot be taken beyond the suffocating grasp of nationalism.

This essay, therefore, is written contra the Jamesian representation of cricket as nationalism (one enabled, in part, by the very Leninist understanding of nationalism found in James's work). It is also, crucially, written with the Jamesian: with a love for, and intellectual and aesthetic pleasure in observing, the game. Chatterjee has stated, on another occasion, that "interpretation [in these circumstances] acquires the undertones of a polemic" (52); what follows is analogous to a cheeky single.[3]

Thinking Cricket

Roy Dias, a former Sri Lankan cricket star, wrote in the *Indian Express* on the Sri Lankan World Cup performance: "At last we have found voice on an international stage." These sentiments were echoed and amplified in the Colombo *Observer* by Tissa Jayatilaka, who played at a parochial level: "It was not a terrorist bomb. Neither was it a natural disaster nor a political scandal of epic proportions. And yet, Sri Lanka had made the world headlines. The island nation won the cricket World Cup."[4] In these assertions, cricket is not about the skill and fortunes of the eleven men who actually play, but about the self-respect and pride—if not the vindication—of an entire, albeit small, nation.[5]

The illustrious predecessor of—and in some respects sanction for—this postcolonialist take on cricket is, of course, the work of Cyril Lionel Robert James. His magisterial, impeccably crafted, and moving quasi-autobiography *Beyond a Boundary*, first published in 1963, discusses the question, "What do they know of cricket who only cricket know?" In so doing, James transformed our comprehension of the game, took it out of the sports pages. He asserted that "social passions" used "cricket as a medium of expression" (60); that, in Victorian England, the great W. G. Grace helped incorporate cricket "into the life of the nation" (169); and that, in the West Indies, an emergent, anticolonial nationalism found voice most powerfully not through organized political groups, but at international cricket matches. It found voice both in the players' performances and in its commemoration by the massive crowds in attendance at these games. James's text is written in and with this voice; it is a powerful, defiant, celebratory instance of anticolonial West Indian nationalism.

But we must remember that *Beyond a Boundary* is the product of a very different conjuncture from ours, one that could be emblematized by the publication of Fanon's *The Wretched of the Earth* just two years before. It was possible then to be sanguine about the liberatory potential of nationalism, though even Fanon's faith n nation and national liberation was qualified. We, on the other hand, inhabit a conjuncture wherein we know that the nation, as an idea/l of community, is untenable; we know it to be inherently oppressive of its nonbourgeois classes, its women, its homosexuals, its "ethnic minorities." In contemporary South Asia we know that the present moment demands, at the very minimum, suspicion of the claims of the nation[6]— and therefore, for the purposes of this essay, of its exclusivist claims upon cricket.

In a recent essay, Arjun Appadurai poses the problem pivotal to any discussion of the relation between the two phenomena: "How [did] the idea of the *Indian nation* emerge . . . as a salient *cricketing* entity?" This question in particular, and Appadurai's provocative theses in general, animate my essay. His own answer to the question is part sociological and part ideological, found in "the dialectic between team spirit and national sentiment, which is inherent in the sport" (24). What follows is largely an attempt to investigate the implications of that statement, which is of the same discursive universe as James. For, as I argue, to make an analogy between team and nation is to place both entities outside a field of power, which is how nationalism represents the field of play.

We, however, must be wary of the ubiquitous and authoritative presence of nationalism. Reminiscent of Ondaatje's heat, nationalism tends to encompass everything, appear everywhere, affect the meaning even of phenomena apparently unrelated to it. Take, for instance, the fifth sentence of my opening paragraph: "In previous competitions, dating back to 1975, the side had lost no fewer than twenty of the twenty-four matches it had played." At first glance, this is an innocuous, descriptive, nonideological statement, one that Foucault might have called "tranquil" (25)—serene, self-evident, hiding nothing. But, surely, only within a nationalist frame, only if one assumes them to be representing the nation, can one presume a continuity between the cricketers who wore the lion cap at the first World Cup, in 1975, and those who did in 1996.

I do not base this assertion merely on the fact that the players who made up both sides are different. More important, the two teams were classed and gendered differently.[7] In the 1970s, the Sri Lankan side was composed almost entirely of upper-middle-class, Sinhala, male products of two exclusivist Colombo schools—who were not paid to play. In the 1980s, after test status, these "amateurs" gradually stopped making the team.[8] Today, it comprises rural and urban, working- and middle-class, men from a variety of schools in the Sinhala-dominated parts of the island; the new players are, to a man, professional. Hanif Markar has written of the transition: "The 'gentlemanly' cricketer has disappeared from sight. It [now] matters not how you play the game but whether you win or lose" (120). Thus the contention that the masculinity staged—and perhaps at stake— in these two periods is radically different. Up to the 1970s, it was bound to what Appadurai terms the "capability to mimic Victorian elite values" of sportsmanship: never disputing an umpire's decision, treating both imposters—victory and defeat—the same, and such like. This stiff-lipped masculine ethic was helped by the structure of the game: though played over five days, every test did not necessarily end in a decision. At the risk of sounding cynical, one could argue that it is relatively easy for those who do not have to contemplate losing, both face and money, to maintain a stiff upper lip. In the limited-overs variety, one team wins at the end of every day—and is rewarded very well for so doing. It quite literally pays to win, be aggressive, take risks. The pace of the game is no longer leisurely, or "preindustrial," as James puts it; now it releases much adrenalin and anxiety, in sportsman and spectator. The masculinity performed, being tough in the 1990s, bears no relation to the Kiplingesque. This is the age of an in-your-face masculinity.[9]

The two teams, therefore, share nothing—except being selected by representatives of the Sri Lankan cricket Board of Control, which is not the nation. Still, nationalism produces a continuity *and* insists upon an analogy between team and nation, one predicated on both being represented as groups or communities of homogeneous equals. To investigate the analogy, nationalism must first be interrogated—if very briefly—and its community, nation, situated in relation to power (before the same is done with team). Nation must also be seen in relation to country: the two are distinct categories. For instance, one can speak of *one country*, Sri Lanka, being inhabited by two competing nationalisms, the Tamil and the Sinhala, which in turn presume *two distinct nations*. Country, here, is a geographic and juridical category (schematically put = territory + state): its subjects, citizens, have, at least on paper, certain rights and privileges (for instance, passports) and are to be distinguished from the nation's subjects (nationals, in my usage) without rights, only obligations.[10]

Rethinking Nation

To an alarming degree, our current understanding of nationalism is informed by a single work by Benedict Anderson. As every cultural critic and his or her second cousins know, Anderson defines the nation as an "imagined community."[11] He deserves credit for insisting that we (re)think the nation as construct, though not necessarily for the reasons he insists upon, as a close reading of this text will show. This is one of the passages where he clarifies his definition:

> It is imagined as a *community*, because, regardless of the actual inequality and exploitation . . . in each, the nation is always conceived as a deep, horizontal comradeship. Ultimately it is this fraternity that makes it possible . . . for so many millions of people, not so much to kill, as willingly to die for such limited imaginings.(7)

Two quick questions arise from this. Can something be deep and horizontal simultaneously? Is it necessary to mention the autobiography of Robert Graves, or news reports of the Vietnam War, to inquire whether those who died "for England" or the United States—who ostensibly died "for" their "nations"—did so willingly?

The more important point to note about this passage is that it contradicts Anderson's thesis: it states that the nation is both *real* (a site of inequality and exploitation) and *imagined/conceived* (represented as fraternity)—a most intriguing hypothesis, but one that isn't explored further. For it to be held, a theory of ideology is required; otherwise, one cannot explain how inequality—to stick with Anderson's terms—is represented, *successfully*, as comradeship. This theory must also situate ideology in relation to hegemony; otherwise, the only possible explanation of how the exploited get persuaded *and* coerced into feeling a comradeship with their exploiters would be false consciousness.[12] Such a theory is available, of course, in Althusser, whose arguments could be crudely summarized thus: no hegemony without ideology; or, among the functions of ideology is the enabling of hegemony.

For foregrounding the question of "inequality," for bringing the cardinal issue of hegemony back into the study of nationalism, one must thank the collective effort of *Subaltern Studies*; most notably, the work of Partha Chatterjee and Ranajit Guha. Chatterjee has demonstrated the nation as an idea to be unthinkable without a notion of hegemony. Guha, in a fundamental and breathtaking rearticulation of Gramsci—who spoke often of the state as "coercion plus hegemony"—demonstrates hegemony to be a relation of dominance; that the element of "persuasion" cultural critics are so enamored of is not innocent of force; that, even if persuasion "outweighs" coercion in this equation, it does not negate the latter; that *persuasion is buttressed by, impossible without, coercion.* Read together, Guha and Chatterjee show that, insofar as the subaltern classes could be said to do anything for the nation, it is not tenable to hold that they do so "willingly";[13] subordinated groups are, if anything, "appropriated" for the nation. It is nationalism as ideology that represents this appropriation as a relation of consent.

These arguments are, of course, not unfamiliar to those acquainted with the history of Marxism;[14] they resonate strongly with Luxemburg's critique of the Leninist position on the "right" of nations to self-determination. Consequent to Lenin's yoking of the national with the colonial question, and Stalin's definition of the nation as an "integer" with positively identifiable attributes, interrogating the notion of nation as a seamless entity lost priority within the Marxist tradition. Thus, to return for a moment to the conjuncture of James and Fanon, making it easier for them, committed Marxists both, to oppose colonialism with the idea of *national* liberation. As indicated before, the present South Asian conjuncture requires revisiting the "loser" of the famous debate, Rosa Luxemburg.

Luxemburg was not, of course, the first Marxist to point out that the notion of "rights" is foreign to Marxism, or that nationalism and socialism should be considered incompatible; she was the first to do so systematically. A single longish quotation will have to take the place of a reading:

> A homogeneous . . . concept of the "nation" is one of those categories of bourgeois ideology which Marxist theory submitted to a radical revision. . . . *In a class society, "the nation" as a homogeneous socio-political entity does not exist. Rather, there exist within each nation, classes with antagonistic interests and "rights."* . . . There can be no talk of a collective and uniform will, of the self-determination of the "nation" in a society formed in such a manner. . . . Who has the authority and the "right" to speak for the nation and express its will? How can we find out what the "nation" actually wants? (135–41; emphasis added)

One would, today, identify nation as split along more lines—gender, "ethnicity," region, religion, sexuality, and so on—all expressing unequal relations of power between social groups.[15] Nationalism as ideology must—and does—deny all these power lines. Luxemburg, though in a different vocabulary, relentlessly foregrounds the same concerns: the nation as "antagonism."[16]

Thus my amazement at Anderson's blithe proclamation that nationalism was an "anomaly" for Marxism, or that it elided the topic. What requires investigation, rather, is how Marxism elided Luxemburg.

But, to move from one group of supposed equals, nation, to another, team, her work demands this query of Appadurai's Jamesian reading of a cricket team: who has the authority to speak for the Sri Lankan side? During the World Cup, the appropriately named Board of Control for Cricket in Sri Lanka allowed one person to address the media—the captain. The rest of the team signed contracts—were persuaded, no doubt—agreeing not to do so. This happening reinforces my contention that a team should not be seen as a group of free and equal (male) individuals, or a fraternity with common cause.[17] It is, at best, a fragile unit(y), composed of a captain, a vice captain, and nine other members; of superstars, role-players, and reserves. A team, any team, is not an assembly of homogeneous equals, but an entity enmeshed in power, marked in various ways. Like nation, it is no integer.

We can now scrutinize Sinhala nationalism's attempt to appropriate the cricket team, for its own ends, during and after the World Cup final. This analysis is dependent upon the following understanding of Sinhala nationalism: that, as political process, it sought to hegemonize the non-Sinhala social groups in postcolonial Sri Lanka and refused to accommodate itself to the demands of, most particularly, Tamil nationalism—preferring, instead, to oppose the latter, politically and militarily. As ideology, Sinhala nationalism acts often in the name of the country, Sri Lanka, and tries to pass for Sri Lankan nationalism. Through this process and ideology, it attempts to produce a Sri Lankan nation under Sinhala nationalist hegemony; and, as implied earlier, it makes use of every opportunity to do so, tries to appropriate, if not apprehend, every happening, including cricket, for its purposes.

The Missing Sri Lankan Nation

Michael Roberts has asserted that "at all international matches played in Sri Lanka . . . the identity evoked among onlookers has been that of 'Ceylonese' or 'Sri Lankan.' This overarching identity transcends internal divisions and encompasses Tamils, Sinhalese, Moors, Burghers, and Malays within one category" (411). How this "overarching identity" is produced by or at the cricket is not spelled out, and no evidence is presented to back up the pronouncement; presumably, the game somehow "evokes" a transcendental Sri Lankanness. At play here is the specifically Sri Lankan version of the South Asian discourse on cricket as nationalism: like the team, the nation "transcends internal divisions." Roberts, in other words, purports to take postcolonial Sri Lankan history into account: that even if the nation has been divided, even if its "ethnic groups" have been fighting each other, the nation somehow comes together during international matches. This can only be characterized as an incredible position. If cricket indeed unites Sri Lankans, then the national or ethnic problem could be solved very simply, by having the cricket team play 365 days of the year (resting, perhaps, on religious holidays—the number of which may consequently have to be reduced). But Roberts's position actually coincides with the Sinhala nationalist claim upon cricket: that international games make the country and nation coincide, that they make possible a Sri Lankan nation. As we shall see, Tamil nationalism disrupts this.

Roberts, of course, is not alone in buying the Sinhala nationalist story. Sri Lanka during the World Cup final was portrayed thus by the local correspondent of the *Indian Express:* "Life in the island . . . [came] to a complete standstill"; "All the beer was sold out in Colombo"; "Residents in north-central Anuradhapura even cancelled weddings to watch the match."[18] There was, in short, no higher priority on this day for any Sri Lankan, rural or urban, alchoholic or teetotaler, unmarried, married, or about to be, than cheering the team. This phenomenon cut across gender: "Women finished their cooking for the day early in the morning, so that they could watch the match." At moments like this, however, the production of a utopic, single-minded community around cricket begins to fracture: women, we are told, had to change their plans, their routine, in order to participate in this "community"; the cricket match does not allow them, even temporarily, to abandon the kitchen. In fact, in this account, it inconveniences them even further: they will watch the game, but only after doing their duty by the male viewers. In other words, the ideology of the nation, its representation of itself as consisting of equal nationals, unburdened by gender, cannot sustain itself. Women, here, are represented as playing one of the (supporting) roles nationalism persuades them to fulfill—being nurturers of the (masculine) nation.[19] Interestingly enough, the game apparently did not inconvenience even its male Sri Lankan spectators at war. The *Express* story made it a point to note that the Sri Lankan military, officers and troops, in barracks and battlefield, were busy not safeguarding the nation from the LTTE, but following the game on television.

The most remarkable feature of this news report is its self-evident tone: it does not explain the much ado over a cricket match. Given the discursive conditions of its production, it assumed no need to. Not only was there no other or higher priority, there couldn't have been any, for Sri Lankans on 17 March. As observed before, cricket in this argument is nationalism; and, more crucially, *nationalism on that day is cricket*. So, all Sri Lankans—including soldiers—will put on hold whatever else they are doing to sit, stand, stagger, or shiver in front of the television set and cheer. All Sri Lankans will cathect the team, uniformly and universally, regardless of ethnicity, class, or gender. The "dialectic" is at play; the united nation comes into being.

The Colombo *Sunday Times* editorial after the Sri Lankan team's victory shares these discursive norms:

> Little Sri Lanka's spectacular emergence as World Champions in cricket, has brought about positive factors that go far beyond the scoreboard. . . . Almost everybody in Sri Lanka started smiling again from last Sunday night and there was a happy feeling in the heart, despite all the crises facing us. Sri Lanka's revolution in World Cricket also brought about deep unity among people of all races and religions here. We hope the unity rebuilt on the playing fields will grow into other areas.

While echoing Roberts, this statement is also the product of a very different moment and politics—thus its pathos. What anchors it is not celebration or joy, as might be expected, but nostalgia, a profound sense of loss: it is assumed here that there once was a time when Sri Lankans smiled and were happy *because* they were without crisis. This pathos is of a piece with that of Dias and Jayatilaka, and requires attention, for the seamless Sri Lankan nation produced—if transitorily—in the passage cannot be understood without it.

From the early 1980s, Sinhala nationalism's military attempts to defeat the Tamil nationalist militancy had failed. In the fall of 1994, a new president was elected, on an antiwar platform. Chandrika Kumaratunga negotiated with the LTTE and, for four brief months in 1995, there was no combat, until the LTTE unilaterally broke off the cease-fire and resumed, among other things, its bombing campaign against the Sri Lankan state. The most spectacular target attacked in this new round of fighting was the Central Bank building, in the heart of Colombo's financial district, in January 1996. Saying they feared for their lives, the Australian and West Indian teams then refused to play scheduled World Cup games in Sri Lanka. At the beginning of the World Cup, therefore, Sinhala nationalism had nothing to rejoice about—no ethnic peace in sight, though once promised, just endless, seemingly unwinnable, war; not even a transitory salve in the form of a boost from successfully hosting the tournament.

With victory in the final, a new claim could be made: that, "at last," this little island—once reputed internationally for persecuting its minorities and thus made to feel even littler—"had made the world headlines," or "found voice" for positive reasons. The rest of the world had realized, acknowledged, that Sri Lankans (read Sinhalese) were capable of positive achievements, and, perhaps most important, that the country was united. Only for a moment—thus the pathos—but a moment that made Sinhala nationalism optimistic about its future. Now it felt it could, despite the continuing war, "hope the unity rebuilt on the playing fields will grow"; that its hegemonic project may yet be successful.

The war, the LTTE, would interrupt this happy story. But it must first be noted that the argument of Dias, Jayatilaka, and the *Times* is enabled by two slips: from team to nation, and from Sinhala (nation) to Sri Lanka (country). It is assumed, merely because the eleven players wore lion caps, that they represented the nation, whereas they could have been representing the country—or just themselves; they could have been representing nothing—just playing for the money, or status, or for pleasure.[20] Only within a nationalist frame can this slip appear natural. Second slip: again because of the symbols on the caps, and consequent to the first, it is assumed that because the nation was being represented on the field, those watching did so as Sri Lankans. But those cheering may not have done so as (ethnically unmarked) Sri Lankans— though, no doubt, some must have; they may not even have watched as "ethnics"—though some, perhaps many, would have; indeed, it is entirely possible that some watched as cricket fans—fans of the team of the country they were socialized in. But, for cricket to be nationalism, Sinhala nationalism must represent all those watching as Sri Lankan, as cheering not so much their team as themselves; in other words, make nationals out of citizens. It must, to use Guha's term, produce the nation "as an integer" (1992, 97); it must reassure its constituency that what was "lost" wasn't lost permanently; that the unified nation could be "rebuilt"; and it must deny all other meaning and imprison cricket, naturalize the nexus between team and nation.

With regard to a very different politics and conjuncture, anticolonial Gandhian India, Guha has argued, echoing Chatterjee and Marx:

> Gandhi had a use for the masses. It was of fundamental importance for the philosophy as well as the practice of his politics that the people should be appropriated for and their energies and numbers "harnessed" to a nationalism which would allow the bourgeoisie to speak for its own interests in such a way as to illustrate the illusion of speaking for all of society. (1992, 109)

It is beyond my brief to examine here the class, or elite-subaltern, "antagonisms" within Sri Lankan nationalism. My particular concern is with the "ethnic" contradiction, to which Guha's argument also speaks, because his essay fundamentally addresses the issue of antagonisms as such, relations of power, that nationalism must flatten. Nationalism claims to speak for the seamless whole; it will use every opportunity to do so; therein lies its pervasive, omnipressing power. Thus one might say, to paraphrase Guha, that Sinhala nationalism—of which the *Sunday Times* editorial is an instance—had a use for those citizens who watched the cricket final: they could be represented as Sri Lankan nationals (because the team wore caps marked Sri Lanka); and they were. In other words, nationalism, here, tries to apprehend cricket. But every cricket fan is not so easily seduced; for some of them the game will have other meanings; some of them will run out of nationalism's suffocating clasp.

For interpellation to work, the interpellated subject must, in Althusser's phrase, make a "one-hundred-and-eighty-degree physical conversion" (174) acknowledging the hailing. In this instance, every spectator must acquiesce to Sri Lankanness, *must cheer as Sri Lankan nationals.* For Sinhala nationalism to hegemonize Sri Lanka successfully, for the ethnic "antagonism" to be erased, the Muslim and the Burgher must join the Sinhalese in being Sri Lankan. Most important, the Tamil must do so, but Tamil nationalism disrupts the Sinhala nationalist story and hegemonic move.

On the eve of the final, Reuters interviewed the Paris-based spokesperson of the LTTE, Lawrence Thilakar. I would, given the war, not have expected him to give a damn about the outcome of the game, at least officially. But Thilakar had something to say: "All Tamils in the North and East love cricket. It's a part of their lives in school. All the schoolchildren love cricket and football. . . . I cannot wish Australia to win. At the same time, it's difficult to wish Sri Lanka to win." Though perhaps "spontaneous," this is not a *careless* response. Even the ranks of the LTTE, it would seem, could scarce forbear to cheer the Sri Lankan team. The nuance, however slight, must be noted: while Thilakar "cannot" (the language expresses certainty) desire an Australian victory, he merely found it "difficult" (not impossible, just difficult) to desire a Sri Lankan one. There is a pathos here, too, for this statement could be read as expressing a yearning to take politics, the politics of nationalism, out of cricket, so that the LTTE—still *citizens* of Sri Lanka—could cheer the Sri Lankan *team* without embarrassment or treachery, without being complicitous with Sinhala nationalism. The *Times* editorial, in contrast, would take a politics from cricket, if not *make* a politics from cricket.

But the *Times*'s is a politics that fails. Thilakar—who can never be both Lawrence Thilakar, Sri Lankan cricket fan, and Lawrence Thilakar, LTTE spokesperson—could not publicly acquiesce to Sri Lankanness under any circumstances. He will not publicly support the Sri Lankan side, even if he might want to—even if, as I suspect, he actually did in front of his television. In other words, this statement indicates that Thilakar's nationalness was in contradiction with his citizenship; or, more generally, that even if non-nationalist Tamils supported the Sri Lankan team, an ethnically unmarked Sri Lankan nation could not be and was not produced on this occasion. The (Sri Lankan) nation is not united in cheering the team. Sinhala nationalism might say so, attempt to produce such a nation, impose such subject positions on the spectators, but, at least with Tamil nationals, it cannot escape its own history.

My contention is that Sinhala nationalism can never do so. Markar argues that when the Indian cricket team toured Sri Lanka in 1985, a time when Sinhala nationalism appeared unlikely to compromise on its hegemonic claims on Sri Lanka, and when the Indian state was not so covertly backing the Tamil nationalist resistance,

> the [cricket] battle was between the Sinhalese (not Sri Lanka) and India (acting in the minds of some Sinhalese as a proxy for the Tamils) . . . very few Tamils wanted "their country" to win. . . . [And] during the recent series with Pakistan, many Sri Lankan Muslims had their sympathies with the Muslim country, some going even to the extent of lighting crackers when Pakistan won. (119)

What this implies of Sinhala nationalism need not detain us here. Markar's statement contests Roberts's claim that international cricket matches produce an "overarching" Sri Lankanness.[21]

Remarkably enough, Roberts's text itself is prompted by an instance of Sinhala nationalism actually preventing the assertion of Sri Lankanness at a cricket match. During a Sri Lanka versus Australia one-day game in 1981, a Burgher ("indigenous inhabitant of European descent") and, more important, Burgher-"looking" (405) spectator, Laddie, doubted the patriotism of another Sri Lankan, Sinha, who was, says Roberts, excessively friendly to an Australian player. This was, one might recall, at the time when the "gentlemanly" ethos was beginning to fade. Thus, even if the ethic of sportsman-(sic)ship demanded courtesy to the opponent, Laddie could be read as representing both the nascent professional ethos and the possibility of Sri Lankanness when he accosted Sinha. An irritated Sinha "wrapped up the issue," says Roberts, with a simple riposte: "I am a Sinhalese" (405). Roberts makes the important point that, if addressed to a Tamil or Muslim, an occupant of either of those subject positions, "could not conceivably have resolved the conflict in his favor by announcing that he was a Tamil [or Muslim]. Such a riposte would not even have occurred to him . . . because it could not have carried the same import" (418). Such a riposte is possible only from a powerful, if not hegemonic, subject position, the Sinhala nationalist—which will, as long as its project is hegemonic, always disrupt the possibility of Sri Lankanness. But, despite the only evidence he produces contradicting his argument, Roberts sticks to his faith in this being an extraordinary moment: "In the world of cricket this antagonism is normally submerged" (412). My argument is that these antagonisms are not, cannot be, submerged by international cricket matches; that Sri Lankan national community is not produced at these events. Sinhala nationalism's hegemonic move to produce a seamless Sri Lankan nation always fails.

Fabricating the Space

Yet the questions remain: Why did Thilakar have something to say about the game? Why did he not disdain its outcome? What was at stake in his feeling obliged to say that not just he, but "all Tamils in the North and East"—in LTTE-dominated Sri Lanka—"love" cricket? The answer will take us to that tenuous space I read as unmarred by nationalism; to get there, a detour via Ondaatje and a return to James are required.

Michael Ondaatje's *Running in the Family* is a hyper-Orientalized story of an elite Sri Lankan brood. In this Sri Lanka, the fantastic is the everyday and Ondaatje's family, his father in particular, get away with the most outrageous exploits, including a drunken disruption of the Sri Lankan railway during the war in 1943. It is, of course, class that allowed the father this privilege—something that doesn't occur to Ondaatje. In *Running in the Family*, Sri Lanka sounds like a classless paradise, without even servants—until the subaltern classes interrupt the smooth flow of the narrative. Once, they came looking for guns—and stayed to play cricket (a "quaintly decadent" sport, as Lazarus reminds us, to the North American audience addressed by this text).

On the eve of the insurrection of the Janatha Vimukthi Peramuna (the JVP—the National Liberation Front) against the Sri Lankan state in April 1971, the JVP appropriated as many weapons as possible from the general populace.[22] This included a shotgun that belonged to Ondaatje's stepmother, living then in Kegalle, a town in northwestern Sri Lanka. Ondaatje represents the JVP as consisting of "essentially the young . . . a strange mix of innocence and determination and anarchy" (100). Typically, he never once says what these "insurgents" were rebelling against; does not discuss their class or caste composition, or the social circumstances from which the JVP emerged; finds

101

the fact that the group consisted exclusively of Sinhalese unremarkable; is not interested in their own depiction of their ideology, as mixture of the Maoist and "Che" Guevarist—by no means anarchist. He sees no need, in short, to comment upon its project of revolutionizing the Sinhala nation. After securing the family shotgun, we are told, "the insurgents . . . put down their huge collection of weapons, collected from all over Kegalle, and persuaded my younger sister Susan to provide a bat and a tennis ball. Asking her to join them, they proceeded to play a game of cricket on the front lawn . . . for most of the afternoon" (101). Thilakar would enjoy this story. Because, unconstrained by the cricket-is-nationalism discourse, produced as he is by a different relation to both, Ondaatje produces a game that is a part of the Sri Lankan everyday.

Growing up in Kegalle, the young Ondaatjes would have their "hair cut on the front lawn by a travelling barber. And daily arguments over Monopoly, cricket, or marital issues" (145). Monopoly—a game that can be played only by those to whom property isn't a presumption or to be appropriated, but a self-evident possibility—would not be a part of the JVP everyday. Cricket, on the other hand, is; so much so, that it enables the subaltern and Susan Ondaatje to meet. It is easy to read this meeting as cricket producing community—across, in this instance, the power-lines of class and gender. But the circumstances of the meeting are not so sanguine: the gun owner also possessed the bat and ball, and, even if the latter have no exchange value, and are personal not private property, they are property nevertheless. Property that enabled a game only when Susan Ondaatje was "persuaded"— a choice of term Guha would no doubt approve—to provide the implements and to join in. Put differently, this game would not have taken place if the power relation between subaltern and elite had not been altered—if only for a while. Cricket, then, does not produce easy community, even at the quotidian level. The import of this story lies elsewhere.

It lies in the instant that the weapons—instrumental in and therefore metonym for the political project of redefining the nation—were put aside, momentarily, for the game; for pleasure, a pleasure produced by cricket. What Ondaatje offers, in an admittedly fantastic story, is a way of thinking and talking cricket (literally) outside the ambit of nationalism. (It is instructive of the reach of nationalism that one can find such a story only in a text like *Running in the Family*, which does its best to keep politics beyond its boundary.) This way of thinking cricket, the space thus fabricated, is by no means idyllic; it is not one unmarked by power, but it is outside the tentacles of (hegemonic Sinhala) nationalism. Which is why Thilakar would enjoy Ondaatje's story. As would James, despite his own nationalism, who says toward the beginning of *Beyond a Boundary*:

E. W. Stanton has written in the *Daily Telegraph* that in the West Indies the cricket ethic has shaped not only the cricketers but social life as a whole. It is an understatement. There is a whole generation of us, and perhaps two generations, who have been formed by it not only in social attitudes but in our most intimate personal lives. (49)

James is describing a process of socialization: cricket is a part of the masculine West Indian everyday—as it is the Sri Lankan. Because of this, a certain combine of routine and pleasure learned and internalized early in life, the JVP "insurgents" will put their guns aside and play; Thilakar would yearn to put his militancy aside and watch. This socialization, this playing every day, during the interval at school and in somebody's garden or on the street after school, produces the spectator of international games. Insofar as school and cricket are part of the ideological state apparatus, and the state is nationalist, so the spectator thus produced will be nationalist, too. But, as Althusser allows, interpellation doesn't always succeed.[23] If it did, we would be doomed always to be suffocated by nationalism. If it did, one could not have spectators who may be in profound contradiction with the nation—as were Ondaatje's JVPers, as are Thilakar and, at another remove, myself-as-spectator. Those successfully interpellated and/or hegemonized by nationalism might enjoy the game as nationals. Our pleasure—as citizens, fans of the team, who grew up loving cricket—is of another kind.

It is, therefore, with pleasure that a Sri Lankan passport holder writes the concluding section of this piece, on the championship game itself, presenting himself as a spectator:[24] someone who enjoyed watching the World Cup final; someone socialized into cricket in the country Sri Lanka, who cheered the team ardently while watching the final on a big screen in Chicago; but, perhaps most important in this context, someone who, when a group of nationals sang the (Sinhala) anthem upon the victory, pointedly sat down. I am not arguing that this spectator did not share community with these Sri Lankans—not to mention other, mostly South Asian, spectators supporting Sri Lanka—while the game was in progress; of course he did. An important component of the pleasure of such spectatorship is communal. But it is a community defined by purpose, not essence or allegiance to nation; one not exhausted by citizenship; a community, in Jean-Luc Nancy's terms, that is "exposed," whose bases must be articulated, and are not pregiven. Community, in other words, that is finite in both ambition and time; that, unlike nation, does not aim to reach indefinitely forward (or project itself as reaching infinitely back); a community that coalesced, on this occasion, to cheer the team (even if some, or most, of those present were simultaneously cheering the nation);[25] a purely occasional community, one without essence. However, this spectator did not share the *meaning* imposed on the game by other spectators, as an *achievement of the nation;* rather, he saw the victory as an achievement of the team—which, as stated earlier, is not seen as a bunch of homogeneous equals. He also did not share the "instinctive" production of a nexus between team and nation. In short, he refused to be interpellated by Sri Lankan nationalism (although, not being Tamil nationalist, for reasons different from Thilakar's).[26]

What follows, my account of the game, is not posed as a description but as a reading, as an interested intervention from someone who supported the team, but not the nation; from someone who insists upon this possibility. What follows is offered as an instance of this possibility, of that tenuous, slender, precarious space unmarred by nationalism. It is a product of my experience of Sri Lanka, nationalism, cricket—and politics; with "experience" understood, in Joan Scott's excellent rearticulation, as that "which we seek to explain" (26), and not as some truth that only I have access to because I was there when it happened. What follows, then, from this spectator, is also an intervention between Thilakar and hegemonic Sinhala nationalism, for Thilakar, too, occupies a space marred by nationalism—not to mention the particular horrors of LTTE nationalism.[27]

The Game Itself

One of the adjectives most often used by the foreign media to describe the Sri Lankan team is *swashbuckling.* This is meant to be endearing, but like Ondaatje's insurgents, or a pirate, might be: brave, romantic, yet somehow illicit. The Sri Lankan performance, this word suggests, was peculiar; the team did something it was not supposed to do. A subsequent editorial in the Madras *Hindu,* on what it termed Sri Lanka's "epochal" victory, is symptomatic of this attitude:

> The team that played the most impressive brand of cricket and played it consistently won the competition. In the event, it may even be a touch patronising, if not patently unfair, to describe Sri Lanka's historic victory as a miracle. . . . After Lanka's comprehensive defeat of Australia, arguably the best and the most thoroughly professional team in contemporary cricket, one can say that the gutsy bunch of cricketers from the emerald island have certainly proved their point.

What exactly was the point the Sri Lankans proved? They played the "most impressive" cricket, and did so "consistently," but that does not qualify them to be labeled the best team—or to be called even a tad professional. That honor must be reserved for the "thoroughly" professional Australians. There is a term for this kind of thinking and it is not "patronising"—although, coming from an Indian publication with a history of putting Sri Lanka in its place, the word would not be inappropriate; the term is *racist*.

I will argue here that the Sri Lankans were the most talented *and* the most professional team. The team won every match it played because it had outstanding batsmen in a version of the game that emphasizes batting,[28] and, most of all, because it had a plan, which was executed to perfection. The plan consisted, when bowling, of keeping every ball tight, no matter what happened with the previous delivery; when fielding, of hustling to save every possible run and making innovative placements, like a man wide of deep-mid-wicket; and, when batting, of scoring hugely in the first fifteen overs, when new rule changes regarding fielding restrictions make boundaries easy. (Traditional one-day wisdom demands hitting out only in the last few overs, when, ostensibly, there is nothing to lose. Teams adopting this routine against Sri Lanka discovered, too late, that by then the game was lost. Since the championship, many teams have changed their strategies, with the English doing so explicitly. If this does not work, the rules will perhaps be changed again.) In game after game, led by their unheralded—soon to be called swashbuckling—openers, the Sri Lankans raced to mammoth scores, mostly made in those first fifteen overs. This required not just talent but endless practice and intelligence—knowing how and where to hit the ball, not only the ability to do so. After every game, Arjuna Ranatunga, the Sri Lankan captain, was asked if he had a plan. After the third victory, it should have been obvious to even a cub reporter that there was strategy at work, that there probably was a Plan B as well. The questions, therefore, bespoke a different anxiety: swashbucklers were supposed to go out there, hit hard, and pray—South Asia, after all, boasts a zillion gods—not carefully execute a strategy; swashbucklers were not even supposed to have a strategy, that being the province of the professional.

The mental discipline that went into the Sri Lankan effort can be illustrated at length. I will discuss just one over in the final. It has, in Sri Lankan cricket discourse, a history: in the winter of 1995, the Sri Lankan team toured Australia and was defeated in both the test and one-day series. During the tour, the team was accused of a variety of unfair practices, including ball tampering and chucking; in turn, the team accused the Australian umpires of many bad decisions. The Sri Lankan press portrayed the Australians, including the umpires, as cheating in order to win at any cost, and as having insulted an entire nation (the dialectic at work, again). Later, when World Cup tickets went on sale in Colombo, those for the Australia game sold out first, within hours of being available. As I have mentioned before, the Australians refused to play the scheduled game in Sri Lanka, afraid of becoming collateral damage. This despite the Sri Lankan president's offering security at the same level as her own and a statement from Thilakar saying the LTTE did not and would not target cricketers. The Sri Lankan press now portrayed the Australians as fearing defeat if they played with "neutral" (third country) umpires. In a widely reported remark, Shane Warne, Australia's best-known bowler, justified the refusal: "Imagine you're looking in the shops and there's a drive-by bombing." Desperate to persuade the Australians to play, and to prevent further bad international publicity, the Sri Lankan foreign minister, Lakshman Kadirgamar, himself responded to this with a comment designed to dare the Australians to change their minds by challenging their virility: "Shopping," he said, "is for sissies." The tactic did not work; preserving life, in this situation, was presumably more important than asserting manliness.

Thus the Sri Lankan press portrayed the final, against Australia, as a grudge game. On its eve, Ranatunga was asked how his team would play Warne, who was having a superb tournament; some called him the world's best bowler. In a response as considered as Thilakar's, Ranatunga called Warne "overrated"; there were, he said, other equally good bowlers. He was, deliberately, setting the stage for a confrontation. As James has observed, in these situations, "the antagonisms and differences appeared . . . in the actual cricket, the strokes . . . [and so on]" (60). Ranatunga, as captain, had to put his bat where his mouth was. He did.

He won the toss and, because his side preferred chasing a target, asked the Australians to bat. No team batting second had ever won the championship; no matter. Chasing was part of the plan. Australia made 106 for just one wicket at the end of their first 25 overs and a large total seemed probable. But the Sri Lankans did not lose concentration or commitment, and kept the bowling tight and the fielding crisp; kept the pressure on. Consequently, the Aussies finished with just 241/7, a respectable but not necessarily winning score.

When Sri Lanka batted, its reliable, swashbuckling openers both got out with just 23 runs on the board. Then, unflinching at the sight of trouble, Aravinda de Silva, the team's best batsman and vice captain, and Asanka Gurusinghe, another veteran, batted very carefully. De Silva, often called swashbuckling in the past, played with great tenacity and purpose: he only went after the loose balls—which he sent scurrying to the boundary. Gurusinghe, on the other hand, was dropped twice. Indeed, the Australian fielding was most untidy, very unprofessional; they played, as a friend suggested, as if they knew they were guilty (of cheating in the past). The score was 148 when Gurusinghe got out to a weak stroke. Ranatunga walked in to join de Silva, and the fate of the game was still uncertain; given their performance, first in the field and now at bat, given a de Silva "on the go," as James might have said, it did not look like the Sri Lankans would lose. Still, you never knew. The skipper and his deputy, again batting without being in the slightest hurry or taking the slightest risk—after all, they could not disappoint the women who had cooked early, or the men with all that beer to drink, in that magnitudinally challenged island—advanced the score to 212 at the end of the forty-third over. Balls left: 42; runs left: 30; even the foolhardy would have thought twice about betting against a Sri Lankan victory.

On the fourth ball of the next over, Ranatunga faced Warne. He hit it back so hard the ball seared through the bowler's fingers for four. The skipper had waited patiently for this moment. It was easy to call Warne overrated; he also had to demonstrate it. He had to hit Warne—but only at the right stage of the game. If he had got out then, if Warne had made the catch, Sri Lanka was still likely to win; there was enough batting left. It was the right instant to make his point: a thoroughly professional, unswashbuckling, point. On the next ball, Ranatunga stepped up, took it on the full and lofted it to mid-wicket for six. Fireworks were heard in the little island. A quiet two runs were made off the last delivery. A Sri Lankan win was certain. Ranatunga, if you like, had displayed a rubbing-it-in-your-face masculinity.

I enjoyed that moment. Shane Warne had not been hit like this by anyone else in the tournament. Here was superbly skilled and masterfully intelligent batting; here, too, was a racist being put in his place. For, as dozens of people inquired (rhetorically) at the beginning of the World Cup, why did the Australians not refuse to play in England, or Warne make similar remarks, fearing an Irish Republican Army bombing? There was, of course, more than antiracism at play in those questions, in that over. The nation felt itself vindicated—otherwise, fireworks would not have been lit. So, one must ask: Is it possible not to be complicitous with nationalism (at its most masculinist) at that moment, especially if one enjoyed Ranatunga's hitting? I want to leave open the possibility that, at least with hindsight, the assertion of a distance is possible; otherwise, as I have said before, one would never be able to escape the grip of nationalism. Otherwise, the kind of space and spectator I am trying to construct cannot be.

So I would rather see my pleasure as akin to that at an analogous put-down in another sport I enjoy watching. Danny Ainge, providing expert commentary of the Knicks-Bulls play-off series in May 1996, referred repeatedly to the large print used in Dennis Rodman's autobiography, released just a few days before the game; this was necessitated, said Ainge, by the outspoken Bulls defender's many "illiterate readers"—presumably a reference to Rodman's large following in the "inner cities." After the game, Ainge asked Rodman himself about the font size; without batting an eye, the redhead replied, "Yes, Danny, I did it for you."

To get back to the cricket. Fourteen balls after the demolition of Warne, the captain, appropriately enough, nudged a delivery to third man and the game was over. Whereupon, wrote *Asiaweek*, "fans in Sri Lanka abandoned their TV sets and poured into the streets to celebrate." In Lahore, de Silva, who ended with 107 masterfully stroked runs, the first century in a final since 1979, was asked about his performance. Given his knock and the victory, he could take the risk of speaking, of defying his contract; the deeds of "the boys," he said, referring to the lesser-known players, had brought the team to the final; on this, the most important occasion, the "senior players" (men?)—the skipper and the deputy—had to and "did their duty." Even triumph could not erase distinctions between the players; relations of power could not but surface. The victory may have belonged to the team, but not all performances contributed equally to it.

Not surprisingly, the ultimate leader of the team/nation also staked a claim to the deed. President Kumaratunga declared (in a by now predictable statement), "We have shown that even a small nation can achieve great heights." The dialectic, again—"*we* have shown"—team and nation are one. But we can see now that this is nationalism at work, that there is no inherent dialectic between the two. That the answer to the pivotal question is: cricket is cathected because it is there. Sociological factors do contribute to its being a suitable object, to cricket's being a very popular sport in the country, but although there is no doubt something in cricket that makes it so popular, there is nothing inherent in it to make it especially attractive to nationalism. Nationalism appropriates and engulfs cricket because it uses every opportunity to further enhance its reach; because it seeks to impose everything possible with its own meaning; because it must be omnipresent; because, otherwise, it cannot be.

A few days after the great victory, the question of power surfaced in an entirely different sense. The Sri Lankan Electricity Board announced countrywide power cuts. 'Twas the vernal equinox. The little island, which generated most of its electricity through hydropower, had been experiencing a drought for months; the water level in its reservoirs was drastically low—a condition worsened by the consumption of an unprecedented quantum of electricity during the previous two weeks, culminating on 17 March. The country's power lines, like its tanks, were almost dry. The Electricity Board had wanted the cuts earlier, but the president considered it impolitic to authorize blackouts during the World Cup: yet another instance of nationalism overriding the country's priorities. So the reservoirs were allowed to lose more water than advisable. And the monsoon, as implied before, was at the tail end of the batting order.

Notes

This essay could not have been written without the generosity of Rob Nixon and a conversation I had in Chicago, two days before the World Cup final, with Mala de Alwis, Pradeep Jeganathan, Kanchana Ruwanpura, and David Scott. Pradeep kept insisting that night, though we did not follow, that it must be possible to cheer the Sri Lankan team without being complicitous with or implicated by Sri Lankan nationalism. I seek here to continue that conversation. Other conversations, comments, and criticisms also contributed considerably to the making of this essay: my heartfelt thanks to Tony Anghie, Sanjay Krishnan, Fenella Macfarlane, Toby Miller, Sonali Perera, Bruce Robbins, Radhika Subramanium, Milind Wakankar, and Tim Watson.

I would like to dedicate this article to Richard de Zoysa, with whom I have talked cricket at a match or two. He would have found much to smile about while reading it—if he were around to do so.

1. Extensive information on Sri Lankan cricket is available on the World Wide Web. See, for instance, Gihan Wickramanayake's cricket page (http://www.cs.cf.ac.uk/user/gihan.wikramanayake/cricket/sri_lanka).

2. Ashis Nandy, alone, resists this reading and rails against the appropriation of cricket by the nationalist masses. I cannot be sympathetic to such a position because Nandy resists from a peculiarly elitist, antimodern "Indian" space he finds analogous to the "authentic," original, leisurely/timeless (anti-)Victorian spirit of cricket, which, he says—drawing upon, but not altogether acknowledging, James—was also antimodern and antiindustrial. Upon inspection, this Indian space turns out to be Hindu (and Brahmin). Consequently, Nandy reads the Pakistani superstar, Imran Khan, as a "lapsed" Indian (47), blithely dismissing, in a single stroke, the history of (H)Indian nationalism that produced partition and Pakistan. My desire to respond vehemently at this point is tempered only by the possibility that Nandy's text is an elaborate joke. (Yes, Alan Sokal haunts this essay.) For, apart from the ironic tone in which his judgments are delivered, Nandy consistently flouts the protocols of conventional argumentation (though he could be employing an indigenous Indian logic that I, being Sri Lankan, have no access to): he flitters often from point to point without any effort to connect them; and, oftener, makes grand assertions without backing them up with anything remotely resembling evidence. For instance: "Indians, Pakistanis and Sri Lankans, who have a greater cultural respect for fate, have also . . . shown a greater tolerance for draws" (21). Nandy's text, in other words, demands assent, not engagement. Thus I cannot converse with it.

3. Neil Lazarus finds it futile to write about cricket in these United States, because the game is "unintelligible to most Americans . . . [and] popularly represented as . . . alien . . . aimless, quaintly decadent, and, as a sport, unassimilable" (92). He forgets that many U.S.-based cultural critics are the products of more than one culture. I request that those who are ignorant of cricket but don't think it "unassimilable" read this as another attempt in the promotion of transcultural literacy; and I apologize for not explaining all the nuances of the game, or my metaphors.

4. It is perhaps necessary to recall here the war in Sri Lanka, between the state and the Liberation Tigers of Tamil Eelam (LTTE). The best brief account of the country's "ethnic conflict" is by A. Sivanandan.

5. The representation of Sri Lanka as magnitudinally challenged will recur, and makes me wonder if Sri Lankan nationalism stages its nation as "small" when not triumphant.

6. This argument is expanded upon in the introduction to *Unmaking the Nation* (Jeganathan and Ismail). Similar arguments with respect to contemporary India, which the Hindutva movement seeks to hegemonize, are plentiful; Nivedita Menon puts it admirably: "terms such as . . . 'nation' no longer offer themselves to us in a form we recognize" (67).

7. This point owes much to Judith Butler's remarkable—and by now deservedly part of our received wisdom—reading of gender as a performative, not a constative category; as "not always [being] constituted coherently or consistently in different historical contexts" (3); and as not being determined by "sex." It follows, therefore, that there cannot be just two genders.

8. A "test" lasts five days and is played exclusively between countries granted full membership in the International Cricket Conference (ICC), in which the English and Australian cricketing authorities enjoy veto power. The Board of Control for Cricket in Sri Lanka was allowed such membership, after many applications, only in 1982. Test cricket was the dominant form of the game until the 1980s, when the one-day variety overtook it in popularity and as a profit-making venture (the two processes being, of course, connected).

9. Such a masculinity is paralleled in and heightened by corresponding changes in apparel. In test matches, players on both sides dress in white—as they have done for decades. In one-dayers, including the world championship, players wear distinctive colored uniforms, which further emphasizes the differences between them and intensifies the competitive aspect of this version.

10. The above is drawn from an argument that I expand upon in "Nation, Country, Community," where I advance a reading of nationalism as both ideology and political process and interrogate the idea/l of community—"nation"—promised by nationalism to its subjects ("nationals"). I also argue that, as ideology and political practice, the principal project of nationalism, the task that it sets for itself, is nothing more—or less—than conserving the nation. Thus nationalism seizes upon cricket, as it does other appropriate phenomena, to advance this endeavor.

11. Partha Chatterjee has convincingly argued that Anderson "seals up his theme with a sociological determinism" (21); that he does not convincingly demonstrate, *theoretically*, the nation to be a construct; that he does not interrogate the status of the real in his text. Chatterjee's brilliant *Nationalist Thought and the Colonial World* is an extended critique of *Imagined Communities;* however, I have yet to see a reference to Chatterjee's book in a discussion of *Imagined Communities.*

12. Anderson digs his own grave, as it were, because he explicitly refuses to see nationalism as ideology; it is, to him, an anthropological phenomenon.

13. For specific illustrations of this, see Chatterjee's chapter on Gandhi and Guha (1992). For an excellent (ethnographic) illustration, in relation to Sinhala nationalism, see

Pradeep Jeganathan; his essay minutely delineates a moment of such hegemony, enables one to understand that subaltern admission into the nation, or subject-position "national," is always conditional, conjunctural, impermanent, and to be negotiated—on bourgeois terms.

14. Anderson, interestingly enough, represents his position as a supplement to Marxism, which is perhaps why his text contains just one reference to Marx: "Nationalism has proved an uncomfortable *anomaly* for Marxist theory and, precisely for that reason, has been largely elided. . . . How else to explain Marx's failure to explicate the crucial adjective . . . : 'The proletariat of each country must, of course, first of all settle matters with *its own* bourgeoisie'" (4). This is an astoundingly arrogant and ignorant formulation. The only evidence Anderson marshals to damn all of Marxism is a single passage from *The Communist Manifesto*—a call to action, not a theoretical work. In any event, Marx in that passage speaks of the proletariat having a "country," not a "nation"—two terms he uses quite distinctly.

15. A similar lack is to be noticed, of course, in *Subaltern Studies* as well; as a collective project, it has not adequately addressed the question of the Muslim ("minority") or gender. What it has demonstrated—what makes the comparison with Luxemburg apt—is the nation as idea/l of community to be theoretically untenable. Unlike the position enunciated by Lenin and accepted as an article of faith by a certain tendency within contemporary Indian Marxism, *Subaltern Studies* has demonstrated, as did Luxemburg before, that it is theoretically unacceptable to take the position that each and every nationalism must be judged individually, with a view to measuring their "reactionary" or "progressive" content. The latter, incidentally, requires a merely empiricist response to nationalisms; it denies the possibility of a generalized understanding of nationalism, situating the phenomenon not in, but outside, theory.

16. One would today, following Althusser, prefer the term *contradiction*.

17. Nevertheless, as Rob Nixon has pointed out, the ideology of the team is of crucial service to nationalism, which uses it to "stage the suppression of self-interest for the collective good" (135). Nixon also argues that the profoundly masculinist thrust of the nationalist project is to be noticed in the fact that only male teams are so deployed. In other words, although the figure of woman is often invoked to represent the nation metaphorically—"motherland," "Singapore girl" and so on—*women* will not be allowed to represent the nation.

18. Remember the weather: it was hot. Because beer consumption increases toward harvest time, the stock was depleted in Anuradhapura, too (personal communication, chairperson, McCallum Breweries, Colombo).

19. For more on the general relation of women to nation, see Anthias and Yuval-Davis; for an account of the Sri Lankan Tamil instance, see Maunaguru.

20. As Janaka Biyanwila reminds us, "Professional cricket is about a money economy where the players are financially remunerated for their labor . . . [and devote] their lives to it because it's their livelihood" (22). This is something often forgotten in the nationalist rush to deprive the game of any profane meaning.

21. It follows, therefore, that when Appadurai calls "cricket matches between India and Pakistan . . . thinly disguised national wars" (43), this begs the question of how the Indian nation is cathected at these moments. It assumes that, during these games, all Indian citizens are Indian nationals. However, the relation of Indian Muslims to Indian (and Pakistani) nationalisms at such moments—in other words, whether they have been successfully hegemonized, and whether hegemony is a permanent "victory"—cannot be deemed transparent, but requires investigation.

22. The JVP rebellion was confined to southern, Sinhala-dominated parts of the country,

and was crushed ruthlessly; see, for instance, Jayawardena. Tamil militancy in Sri Lanka has a different history.

23. Althusser states: "Experience [!] shows that the practical telecommunication of hailings is such that they hardly ever miss their man" (174). In other words, sometimes hailing does not work; but Althusser does not explore the full implications of this. It is "misrecognition," hailing the wrong person, that concerns him, not the consequences of the right person refusing to make that "physical conversion." This lack is symptomatic: to explore the consequences of the failure of interpellation would be to incorporate an explanation of change into a theory, structuralist Marxism, notoriously resistant to explaining change.

24. However, it is written without a theory of pleasure, which must be incorporated into a fuller version of this argument, as must Appadurai's suggestion that the spectator's pleasure is brought about by agency in nationalism.

25. One could contend that, in cheering the Sri Lankan team, I too was being nationalist—if not in the same way as those who sang the anthem. The argument here is that one is always within nationalism. This essay, however, is also written against such intellectual and political pessimism. The more important point to note in this connection is that, whereas the nationalist would support the team no matter what, the kind of spectator I have constructed here would not—if, for instance, the selection of the team was "ethnically" discriminatory.

26. As I noted earlier, structuralist Marxism allows for, but does not explain, this possibility—thus leaving my assertion above open to the charge of voluntarism. I offer, as a somewhat shaky alibi, Madhava Prasad's reading of two categories of Raymond Williams and Edward Said (in the course of that excellent exegesis of Fredric Jameson and Aijaz Ahmad): "To be part of an existing constituency, whether it is race, nation, gender or a left formation, is not to be *committed* at all but *affiliated*. On the other hand, any of these [Saidian] affiliations, when historicized and retheorized, would give us, in Williams' sense, the basis for a commitment. The difference lies in the historicizing break that the intellectual has to make with natural affiliations" (76; emphasis added). The break is not just different; it is difficult to move from a naturalized affiliation to a commitment, especially at a moment when, like the current Sri Lankan, the emancipatory project offered (though not exhausted) by organized Marxism has, quite literally, been killed by organized (Sinhala and Tamil) nationalism (the JVP and LTTE, respectively). My spectator, then, can also be read as a lament for this lack—a lack, of course, that cannot be amended just by watching cricket.

27. For sustained critiques of LTTE politics, see Hoole, Thiranagama, and Sritharan, and Manikkalingam.

28. This is not a silly point: against the Kenyan team, these batsmen left no swash unbuckled, scoring a one-day record 397 runs.

Works Cited

Althusser, Louis. 1971. "Ideology and Ideological State Apparatuses." In *Lenin and Philosophy and Other Essays*. New York: Monthly Review Press.

Anderson, Benedict. 1991. *Imagined Communities: Reflections on the Origin and Spread of Nationalism*. New York: Verso.

Anthias, Floya, and Nira Yuval-Davis. 1989. "Introduction." In *Woman-Nation-State*. London: Macmillan.

Appadurai, Arjun. 1995. "Playing with Modernity: The Decolonization of Indian Cricket." In *Consuming Modernity: Public Culture in a South Asian World,* ed. Carol Breckenridge. Minneapolis: University of Minnesota Press.

Biyanwila, Janaka. 1996. "Cricket Mania, Men and Politics." *Pravada* 4, no. 7.

Butler, Judith. 1990. *Gender Trouble: Feminism and the Subversion of Identity.* New York: Routledge.

Chatterjee, Partha. 1993. *Nationalist Thought and the Colonial World: A Derivative Discourse?* Minneapolis: University of Minnesota Press.

Dias, Roy. 1996. [Article]. *Indian Express* (New Delhi), 14–18 March.

"Editorial." 1996. *Hindu* (Madras), 19 March.

"Editorial." 1996. *Sunday Times* (Colombo), 24 March.

Fanon, Frantz. 1961. *The Wretched of the Earth.* New York: Grove.

Foucault, Michel. 1972. *The Archaeology of Knowledge.* New York: Pantheon.

Guha, Ranajit. 1989. "Dominance without Hegemony and Its Historiography." In *Subaltern Studies VI,* ed. Ranajit Guha. New Delhi: Oxford University Press.

———. 1992. "Discipline and Mobilize." In *Subaltern Studies VII,* ed. Partha Chatterjee and Gyanendra-Pandey. New Delhi: Oxford University Press.

Hoole, Rajan, Rajini Thiranagama, and K. Sritharan. 1990. *The Broken Palmyrah: The Tamil Crisis in Sri Lanka—An Inside Account.* Claremont, Calif.: Sri Lanka Studies Institute.

Ismail, Qadri. Forthcoming. "Nation, Country, Community." In *Community, Gender, Violence: Reflections on the Subaltern Condition,* ed. Partha Chatterjee and Pradeep Jeganathan. New Delhi: Oxford University Press.

James, C. L. R. 1969. *Beyond a Boundary.* London: Hutchinson.

Jayatilaka, Tissa. 1996. [Article]. *Sunday Observer* (Colombo, Sri Lanka), 24 March.

Jayawardena, Kumari. 1985. *Ethnic and Class Conflicts in Sri Lanka.* Colombo, Sri Lanka: Centre for Social Analysis.

Jeganathan, Pradeep. Forthcoming. "All the Lord's Men: Ethnicity and Inequality in the Space of a Riot." In *Collective Identities, Nationalisms and Protest in Modern Sri Lanka* (2d ed., vol. 2), ed. Michael Roberts. Colombo, Sri Lanka: Marga.

Jeganathan, Pradeep, and Qadri Ismail, eds. 1995. *Unmaking the Nation: The Politics of Identity and History in Modern Sri Lanka.* Colombo, Sri Lanka: Social Scientists' Association.

Lazarus, Neil. 1992. "Cricket and National Culture in the Writings of C. L. R. James." In *C. L. R. James's Caribbean,* ed. Paget Henry and Paul Buhle. Durham, N.C.: Duke University Press.

Luxemburg, Rosa. 1976. *The National Question: Selected Writings.* New York: Monthly Review Press.

Manikkalingam, Ram. 1995. *Tigerism and Other Essays.* Colombo, Sri Lanka: Ethnic Studies Group.

Markar, Hanif. 1985. "The Games They Play." *Frontline,* 14 December.

Maunaguru, Sitralega. 1995. "Gendering Tamil Nationalism: The Construction of 'Woman' in Projects of Protest and Control." In *Unmaking the Nation: The Politics of Identity and History in Modern Sri Lanka,* ed. Pradeep Jeganathan and Qadri Ismael. Colombo, Sri Lanka: Social Scientists' Association.

Menon, Nivedita. 1993. "Orientalism and After." *Public Culture* 6, no. 1.

Nancy, Jean-Luc. 1991. *The Inoperative Community.* Minneapolis: University of Minnesota Press.

Nandy, Ashis. 1989. *The Tao of Cricket: On Games of Destiny and the Destiny of Games.* New Delhi: Penguin.

Nixon, Rob. 1994. "Apartheid on the Run." In *Homelands, Harlem, and Hollywood: South African Culture and the World Beyond.* New York: Routledge.

Ondaatje, Michael. 1984. *Running in the Family.* London: Picador.

Prasad, Madhava. 1992. "On the Question of a Theory of (Third World) Literature." *Social Text* nos. 31–32.

Roberts, Michael. 1985. "Ethnicity in Riposte at a Cricket Match: The Past for the Present." *Comparative Studies in Society and History* 27, no. 3.

Scott, Joan W. 1992. "Experience." In *Feminists Theorize the Political,* ed. Judith Butler and Joan W. Scott. New York: Routledge.

Sivanandan, A. 1984. "Sri Lanka: Racism and the Politics of Underdevelopment." *Race and Class* 26, no. 1.

Part II ▸ Building Bodies

The Composite Body:
Hip-Hop Aerobics and the Multicultural Nation

Randy Martin

"Why waste your time, you know you're gonna be mine." The nation calling? Or just the music to a fitness warm-up? As the tune changes, the assumed shapes matter. In what follows, I want to explore whether some of the linkages between nationalism and multiculturalism that would transform the prevailing usages of those terms can be exposed through a very specific cultural practice—hip-hop moves in an aerobics class at a fitness club. Although the politics of rap are far from unproblematic, and have been subjected to some very incisive and instructive criticism (Baker, 1993; Decker, 1993; Dyson, 1993, 1996; Rose, 1994), I will entertain, through the embodied promise of hip-hop, a certain "structure of feeling" that is generative of national difference; specifically, a departure from the prevailing ways of identifying with the authority of the existing polity.[1] This search for an emergent *societal* sensibility, couched in nationalist terms, is significant precisely at this moment of a hegemonic reconfiguration in the ideology and political economy, not simply of the United States as a nation, but of the entire global framework of nation-states.

The articulation between nationalism and the global framework of nation states, posed by the ideological confluence of foreign and domestic policy, will serve as the point of reference here to join two questions concerning the conceptualization of nationalism. First, if nations are historical and not natural phenomena that must constantly reconstruct their basis for existence as human communities, what principle of societal association gets asserted in the process? Second, what are the practical means for communicating and insinuating this historically bounded assertion of societal order as nation, in the everyday lives of the populace? The first question assumes that nationalism is ideological without specifying the content of that ideology. The second suggests that ideological form must be realized through some material communicative practice and technology. That neither the specificity nor relation of ideological form and content can be assumed from the fact of any given nationalism opens up possibilities from which politics spring. In the case of rap and hip-hop, the analysis of form and content (to the extent these terms remain conceptually distinct) of a particular expression may produce diverse images of nationalist politics.

One could say that multiculturalism of a certain sort is at least as old as nation-states, particularly if the exclusion of some cultural difference that resides on national ground but is considered alien to it is taken as a founding moment for a national polity. Yet the present manifestation of multiculturalism represents a recognition by the state itself of a certain discrepancy between the fictitious unity proclaimed by the nation-state and the multiplicity of identity that the state must now contain if it is to retain its legitimacy as the warden of a national entity. In this regard, multiculturalism marks and divides a double relationship. From the perspective of the state attempting to police a national monoculture, it is the refusal of any given identity to be contained within the center, to abide by the institutional boundaries by which the state allots recognition (a predicament to which social movements themselves are by no means immune, insofar as recognition and other material resources are mutually constitutive). From the perspective of those multiple identities, it is the insistence upon the unruly polyvocality of difference that hints at what is formative, not of nations, but of society. Between these two perspectives lies the politics of recognition—the state seeking to determine the form of what gets recognized versus the multicultural forces that are themselves agencies of self-recognition.

In the present context, multiculturalism is not only the name given to cultural diversity, but the terrain where opposing ideologies of culture are in contention. When multiculturalism is deployed as a negative point of reference (a bad other, or ontological threat) to consolidate the new order, it is as a discourse and as a political economy of racialization. This political economy wields race in word and deed as a principal means for dividing society, and seeks legitimation in no small part by treating the divisions within society as natural consequences of the differences among cultural groups. By means of these racial divides, those who are as authentically domestic as any others are linked to the foreign, both in terms of their origins and therefore fidelity to the national way of life and in terms of some putative cultural association to whatever ails peoples in less resource-full parts of the world.

Bodily Composition

To reimagine nation along more fully multicultural lines, I propose a conception of body not as a stable presence already available for appropriation, but as a composite entity mediated across a conflicted space of the imaginary (literally the representational domain where images appear) and the performative (the practical means through which imaginary forms are enacted). Dance both appears in the conjuncture of imaginary and performative spaces and puts the constitutive features of a composite body on display, for dance is both a bodily practice that figures an imagined world and a momentary materialization through performance of social principles that otherwise remain implicit. In particular, hip-hop moves are constituted across very different kinds of space laminated together to configure a composite body. Whereas the electronic media provide a mapped virtual space in which bodies can circulate, these composite bodies always seem to be getting away, disappearing in the moment of reception only to reappear in altered form in that virtuality.

The idea of a composite body may invoke associations with the bionic synthesis of flesh and machine or the cybernetic hybrid that rejects the dualism of nature and culture (Haraway, 1991). Whatever its debts to these notions, the image of a composite body operates on a slightly altered conceptual terrain that seeks to grasp the very motion of cultural processes that emanate from different sources and never fully come to rest. It is a body that is not one, but multiple; not a being, but a principle of association that refuses the neat divide of self and society, of the personal and the mediated, of presence and absence. The composite body is less an empirical type than a heuristic for thinking the physical constitution of complex social relations. Although all dancing bodies come to us live and already mediated, these two dimensions of bodily composition are quite vividly on display in a practice such as hip-hop. Here, the debts to both immediate enactment and the images from distant airwaves are more difficult to deny than they may be with those arts of dance that are sometimes said to spring directly from a singular body of origin. For multiculturalism as a critical perspective rather than a government policy, the composite body allows us to focus on how difference is associated among those assembled in the nation, rather than being forced to sort out one body from another.

This essay examines a moment in the larger process of production of this composite body, in a seemingly discrete site of reception for hip-hop, an Orange County, California, fitness club aerobics class that I attended twice weekly for some five months in 1993. This site is juxtaposed to the conventional means through which an image of the monocultural nation is constructed, namely, the nightly television news broadcast that relies heavily on racial representations, particularly of crime, that are set off against other segments such as sport and entertainment. Hopefully, elements of a nationalism and multiculturalism that efface the power of this nation-state's racist imaginary may begin to emerge from the transracial reception to an internally differentiated hip-hop culture.

My purpose here is not to take the aerobics class as typical of how the

119

nonblack population relates to hip-hop culture, or to graph the effects of the former on the latter, for I shall suggest that the relations of racial appropriation are more complex than any simple model of cultural translation would allow. Rather, my aim is to specify how instances of popular culture are situated in and figurative of a certain multicultural and national context, a context that mediates their relationship but one in which, for the most part, persons who attach to practical instances (songs, videos, dance or fitness clubs) never actually meet except in the present scene of writing, where I attempt to imagine their connection. This, then, is a reflection on how impersonal or mediated forces—those that never meet face-to-face—produce concrete effects. The understanding of mediated relations, irrespective of the medium through which they pass, is crucial if the idea of society is to have any purchase.

For myself, I am tracing the contours of my own composite body through this one mediating link, because the study of culture in capitalist society is precisely the study of such mediations. The spirit of this inquiry is to take my own suspicions about the demonization of nationalism (which as an internationalist of a certain stripe I am susceptible to) and multiculturalism (of which I am a partisan in search of practical affiliation) to see what may be repressed in them. By reflecting upon my own process of incorporation into the body politic, I am mapping the scene of what mobilizes my own affinities and affiliations within the multicultural nation.

Here, the Beat

If disco opened the pop kinesthetic in the late 1970s to a live encounter with the vinyl surfaces that would get torn asunder with the development of hip-hop, aerobics made those bodies come clean a decade later. At its most sanitized, the circulating sexuality of the disco was transferred to a phone-sex 900 number. The proliferation of fitness clubs in the 1980s indicated a transfiguration of bodily publicity that encased each body in a machine or subjected it to the rigors of the workout.

As a countermove, we might see in the aerobics class a distant cousin of the jook, what Hazzard-Gordon (1990, 155) calls the "dance arena" that provided a space where differences within the African American community were negotiated. The eighties were not the only time to see popular dance move from indoors to the streets and back inside again in the form of the house party. Hazzard-Gordon reminds us that during the 1940s, in a move that anticipated the civil rights movement, black dance left the jook joint for the streets, where gangs filtered through block parties. Today's fitness club certainly lacks the economic supports of mutual aid the jooks provided and offers little respite from discriminating effects elsewhere. The images of the perfectible body emanate from beyond the pulleys and weights where the work-to-fit body is manufactured. The unrelenting music that accompanies each stroke of the fitness regimen attains its greatest functionality on the dance floor of the aerobics class. The making of bodies uninterrupted by other kinds of social division constitutes the club's tacit kinesthetic democracy, a place where efforts at participation are rewarded in kind, but one that, like the jooks of old, still awaits its civil rights movement.

Although I grew up amid sport, and sought many venues for dancing, I had always resisted this move into the aerobic until, in what seemed a safely temporary stay in the Southern California of my youth, I found myself a member of the Irvine Family Fitness Center. In addition to the various instruments of corporal adjustment, the center has a full complement of aerobics classes and their derivations. Among them was one called funk but inflected with hip-hop. At my first class, well over a hundred Anglo- and Asian American, predominantly female, bodies obediently followed the steps of the instructor—usually the lone African American in the room. The image of this face-off fits neatly within the visual rhetoric of race that has come to dominate the airwaves, where the nonblack masses attend to their own pleasures by watching their black idols at play (despite the highly problematic recruitment of Asian Americans into the mythos of assimilation).[2] These particular demographics seemed consistent with the notion that aerobics is already gendered as a scene of bodily transformation under the regimen of the gaze. That such a setting would be a site for the reception of hip-hop, with its nationalist associations, introduces certain confounding prospects into the construction of nation that are themselves generally absented from political discourse.

The teacher, it turned out, despite assuring us that she assembled all the combinations herself, also traveled to Los Angeles to take hip-hop classes with those who were *really* down. There, by her account, her own teachers' bodies could all be found somewhere on MTV, but her fellow students, clad in baggy pants and oversized jackets, were all drawn from the 'hood. Such sheathings of course would never do in the fitness club setting, where shiny skins that look like they are newly molted are de rigueur. There also seemed to be little doubt in the teacher's mind that transforming the flesh took precedence over reflecting on the broadest possible contours of hip-hop's national kinesthetic. Surely, this most bland of assimilative processes was no more radical than adding fruit to frozen yogurt. Like fruit, steps can travel. But it is interesting to reflect on the shape those aerobicizers were getting

121

into. This unexpected site of reception for hip-hop could be placed somewhere between the privatized space in front of the television screen, where the demands on the body are difficult to discern by way of its response, and the space of the mythological 'hood itself, where the presumed identification with the representation of hip-hop may get in the way of noting its effects. Let's see what I learned.

Just-in-Time Production

The faithful gather on the sidelines of the long, mirrored hall. They await the completion of the class before theirs. There is a moment of congestion as the two waves of bodies filter through each other. The earliness is intended to secure the class taker the most desirable placement in the room. Some come early so that they are assured a place in the front center; others arrive beforehand to secure a spot in the back corner. Based on conversations and greetings, each person seems to know only a few others in the room. For the class as a whole, corporeal knowledge is assembled in anonymity. Given the width of the room, it is difficult to see everyone, so that even at this scale the community must be imagined. The reference for this imagination is the instructor, Teri Kotinek, who in the interval of five to ten minutes between classes scheduled in the same studio allows for an anticipation of her arrival not entirely unlike that found at a rock concert. She comes in with a handheld microphone and greets the class in the larger-than-life tones of an entertainer (her credits include a stint on *Soul Train*). Buffeted by the driving music that she slips into the tape machine, this quotes the excitement of the concert (or more precisely, a live television show) as much as it references an aerobics class.

She builds on this sense that something is about to happen that people can get swept up in while she offers a process of enlistment in the mutually created event that will follow. Invariably, she surveys those in attendance to ascertain who is there for the first time. She offers a mixed message, enticing frenzied output while admonishing people to "go at their own pace." Beyond juridical considerations of torn bodies, this last phrase, which she will often couple with an exhortation to fuller expenditure, signals the impossible but ongoing conjuncture of the demands that this community fulfill its imaginary with the constant slippage or pacing of a particular body through it. Against the enveloping tide of synchronous movement and stereochronic music, going at one's own pace as a common strategy for taking the class hints at the differentiation generated by this socializing process. Despite the common commands, bodies may come out moving more differently from one another than when they went into the class, for difference of a certain sort lies amid what they learn.

The initial synchronizing gesture erupts out of the alignment of spatial polarities, the face-off between teacher and students, desire and mirrored demand. The initial rocking side to side with arms punching the air is simple enough to accustom one to getting the movement without having to see it. This sideward rocking calibrates what will become the central fact of dance and music and establishes the strong lateral emplacement in the space that aligns bodies with the structures of dancing. The architecture of the room is such that visual depth based on frontal reflection in the mirror (some four bodies deep) is more superficial than the invisible linear pull of thirty bodies across. The choreography adheres in its Cartesian precision to these two forces of visuality and viscerality.

At least several times during the class, Teri will interfere with this opposition by selecting those who can't be seen to demonstrate a phrase of movement or routine. She is clear about her didactic principles in this. "I selected these people because they all do it differently. She does it hip-hop. This one does it with technique. And this one just does it." She also plays with hierarchy in the course of her teaching, offering different variations for "new" and "advanced" (which I sometimes hear as "dance") people. Having introduced this distinction, she then makes fun of those who would adopt it as their own. "Now look at these people laughing like they think they're advanced people. No, just kidding." Whenever she disses someone, whether that person is inside the class or outside, she will add "just kidding" to put the point in play. This relation of inside and outside is itself interesting, for all her references to popular figures, which she places in the familiar (e.g., Michael for the young Jackson brother), name the anonymous forces that place demands on the body. By refamiliarizing such influences and melding her cultural and pedagogical authority, she offers them in miniature within the space of the local. These references also help break up her own discourse as composed intertextually of the authority of techniques for the perfectible body with the pleasures of popular culture. These two texts are also structurally related in the organization of the class.

The first half hour is represented as the "warm-up," a movement phrase that accumulates out of a series of moves that she shows through constant repetition and that remains basically the same each class. In the second half hour, she teaches a "routine" whose newness to all is intended to level differences in familiarity and aptitudes for movement and allow the focus of the class to slide from getting in shape to getting into hip-hop. Yet, from the very beginning of class, she herself offers hip-hop as the means to a style rather than simply an ends to fitness, by opposing her authority as teacher to that of performer when she invariably takes liberties with the movement she has presented. Hip-hop proceeds as the very movement away from its pedagogical conditions toward its performative promise. Rather than speaking a language of performance as that which is other to technique, she offers something else to compensate for the urge to follow her technical imperatives too closely.

To modulate any fixation on getting the steps right, Teri provides commentary on the context that has brought people to the fitness club that draws out and upon the contradictions of the situation. One evening, before offering us a special extra segment of the class to work on "abs" (the sculpting away of the body's center as an offering to beauty), she delivered a testimonial on the vagaries of anorexia and a homily on the beauties of a size twelve. Another evening, in a pitch for a benefit for a community organization in Long Beach ("Orange County seems to have enough") that assists persons with AIDS, she asked the room what they "had done for AIDS" in the last year. Here she made the connection between the (re)construction and the ravishment of the body that was presumed to divide the class from its outside. The curious syntax of doing something "for" AIDS, like multiculturalism itself, introduced the class into a field where difference became the figure that made the imagination of community possible.

Thus far, this account has been a teacher-centered one, assuming that Teri was the medium for introducing hip-hop where it would have been presumed absent. Even a casual glance around the room reveals a range of affinities with hip-hop, from professional associates of the teacher who occasionally take the class, to those evidently knowledgeable of the music, to those who clearly hip-hop on their own, to the interested neophytes and novices.

Dancing together, this diversity is assembled. In the last minutes of the class, difference is put on display. The dense packing of bodies in rows and columns that affords the immediate supports of emplacement is loosened a bit. The group is divided in two and performance is given the status of a mutual offering common to many practices of black dancing, including hip-hop—half of the group performs while the other watches and then applauds. These last moments signal the end of restraint that comes from the problem of pacing through an aerobic situation.

The faucets of sweat have already opened and closed several times and the heartbeat raced and settled. The aerobicized body has been made pliant to the point where it need no longer attend to its own aerobic situation. In these last minutes, when the phrase is learned (such as it will be) and available in its entirety as an activity, the roomful of people is suddenly in a position to draw upon its own local history. The same process of vamping that initiates the class now serves as a kind of gating device out of which the dance will spring. The accumulated phrase generally occupies something in the vicinity of a minute's worth of dancing, enough to provide the thrill of navigating one's way through its landscape.

For me, the experience of dancing hip-hop is that of a process of rhythmic self-containerization that, at the moment it has put its fourth wall into place in the endless obligation of 4/4 time, provides a way out into another space in the making. Part of this has to do with the process of assembly of bits of movement that are one measure long. But part seems to lie in the pleasure of hip-hop's own syntax, which establishes the patterned expectation of breaking with itself, a desire for indeterminacy of outcome that rests on an initial move toward repetition. If break dancing formed in the spaces the DJs opened up in the records for instrumental passages, hip-hop's own increasingly dense layerings disseminate these spaces throughout the music. In these classes, unlike earlier forms of hip-hop movement, such as electric boogie, we never touch. Rather, contact is made available in those moments (offered in practically every measure of the music) where the body breaks out of its recently acquired predicament in the direction of what lies outside it. That outside then becomes the anchoring point for the next constituting move. It is this ready availability of exteriority that joins the dancing bodies.

Against the rather diffuse openness is the persistent linearity of how the dance moves in space. Viewed from above, it could be said to be confined within a screen not unlike a television. Viewed from within, the composite body dimensionalizes effects not available on a screen. Beats are taken in that are never seen. The fissures of rhythm in the composite body allow it to break in several directions at once. Finally, there is the question of the movement itself, its deceptive simplicity. Rarely is there more to the choreography than steps with alternating feet in the horizontal dimension and jumps in the vertical. There may be more demanding coordinations, like a hitch kick (a movement that requires sequentially placing both legs in the air), but this is the exception within the vocabulary. The demands of the steps themselves come in the speed with which they pass, the precision with which their reorientations are executed, and, most elusively, whether the body in question looks like it is dancing them.

Dancing the News Away

This account, along with the teacher, has already anticipated the unmeetable demand to look anything like her. But in this impossibility, a fairly wide space is opened up between the correct sequencing of the steps and the sense of dancing them. This is where dancing itself touches upon its imaginary, for it is only from the perspective of the entire dance edifice (here what fills up both time and space with motion) that it is possible to assess whether one is getting it. This "it," what we could call style, is what joins langue and parole, lexicon and syntax, presence and absence—in short, the totalizing frameworks for the imagination of community with instances of performing the danced connections that would make the composite embodiment of community possible. Because this community is made in motion, it resists containment to any single site where bodies congress. Because the body in question emerges from beyond the mirror, in the electronic reflections and splicings that hip-hop moves circulate through, the irreducibly composite affiliations take their place on the aerobic dance floor as well.

No doubt, style comes late in this game, but the notion that hip-hop is the key to these folks' bodily salvation approaches something of Williams's (1977) structure of feeling, bringing an embodied desire for racial difference in through the back door of a county constructed (under the ancien régime of spatial apartheid in Southern California) in order to be free of racial difference. That is not to say that the desire for blackness, long activated in the white imagination, that takes the former as a transgressive rapture that always returns to its place is not also in operation, but simply that other forces are at play.[3] Put another way, one could ask whether in the appropriation of otherness that has been profitable in myriad forms over centuries of capital, you ever really get it for free. Here, dance insinuates a difference from what the body had been to now enlarge its capacity for being. It inserts into that model of sameness contained in the obsessive gaze in the classroom mirror, an other truth of body's ideality, one that never quite fits and helps to break up the authority of the ideal. Style contends somewhat uneasily with perfection, in that getting the style down makes it appear as if you are looking at someone else in the mirror. No doubt, the constitution of a gaze always bears such complications, only now the divide between body and image is converted back into a difference to which dancing itself is the negotiation.

There is also another sense in which dancing negotiates the mirror—namely, that in the very industrialization of fitness that packing more than a hundred bodies into a room displays, getting "the routine" is not routinized behavior for most. People must glance at one another not simply to make hostile comparisons but to try to get it right. Value returns in the use people find to make of one another. Hence the authority of perfection is used at least partially to subvert itself. Those bodies may go out into the Orange

County night with a wedge of complicity with the culture they are normally called upon to oppose before turning on the evening news.

For all of its limitations, the most comprehensive figuration of nation in the media is the evening news. It could be said that the limitations of the news belie its principles of operation. The very redundancy of the news, its repetition of formula, its marking of the day's end, provides a stability of representation that constitutes a field from which being called or interpellated into the nation becomes possible. The problem that this interpellation poses is above all that of scale. How can the enormous expanse of nation be reconciled with the privatizing limits of the citizen body? Insofar as it is a technology of national ideology, the news functions to invert the order of that national scale by reversing the spatial values of the globe with the internal temporality of programming. In effect, the smaller the scale, the longer the coverage. Twenty minutes of "local" news, two minutes of national, one minute of world, and the separate voices that mark the time of sports and weather typify the ratios of coverage in a half hour punctuated by the different spaces of advertising.

Taken together, the broadcast could be said to provide viewers with a map of their own emplacement in the world that also reduces that world in and to a single stroke. Sports reporting also narrates what are projected as local affiliations in the field of the national, and weather literally maps the process whereby an eye is placed on the national space as it converges on one's own backyard. The content of those twenty minutes of local stories, the unspeakable crimes brought to you live, are perpetrated by entities frequently described as savage, wild, or tribal.[4] The civilizing voice of the news anchors one at home by effectively racializing the space of the private, so that irrespective of one's own racial identification, the domain beyond the private is a space of terror for all to fear.

This space of terror is of course the public sphere, where no demands can be made (we can only seek protection from it) and therefore no politics is possible. Although the news is putatively local, the spatial hierarchies of affiliation, the very conformities of the genre across locality and network, establish it as a technology of nationalism. Negatively, by the spaces it sanctions, as much as positively, by the security offered through a placement in a virtual space, news locates the citizen body in the national field. The crime story, rather than being an account of what the economy is doing to the country, becomes the most abiding figure for narrating the nation. Indeed, between 1991 and 1993, when I was taking these aerobics classes, coverage of crime on the major networks tripled, so that by the latter year, "crime was the leading story on the network news" (Donziger, 1996, 69). Given the rapacity of racist narratives broadcast on any given night, checking the facile absorption of the savaging tales may require a bit of a running start, a leg up to which the aerobics class makes a modest contribution.

Toward the Postracial

The bodies leave the fitness club not only aerated with multiple racial inflections, but with a complication of the gaze that is less likely to look into a mirror (or television screen) and see a simple other. This body of one coupled with another is put into circulation through the social kinesthetic without passing through the impossible first step of consensus. As part of a structure of feeling that supports a disposition to politics prior to the experience of a shared predicament that might incite people to action, consensus in the newly imagined multicultural nation is not necessarily a prerequisite of mobilization.

Perhaps even so mediated a transfusion of another corporeality could offer a counterweight to that fragile unanimity within the body politic. This prospect could be joined with the problematic status of my own political and cultural authority of representation. I speak now of the risks entailed in speaking for others. Whiteness is possessive, but it is not a possession; it calls but does not offer an already consolidated response. Although whiteness as a call to singularity and exclusion may emit a persistent drone, it may also encounter a busy signal.

If dancing can momentarily silence that me whose ascribed situation has historically been deployed in the effacement of difference, with the commands of an other, then those very noises become complicit in interfering with my own privilege to speak the world. This is an interference that would well serve the discourse of nation, for all of its aspirations to assert the monologic voice of the patriae against the possibilities of all others taken together. The only globally realized capitalist nation-state insists that it be heard as an already consolidated and singular voice. Against this consolidation of order, it is possible to introduce a certain silencing of those standard representations of self (in terms of gender, race, and sexuality as well as the class and national privileges of global capital) that are affiliated with dominance.

Paradoxically, the silencing of those particular voicings affiliated with dominance through other means of identification among those who have but a partial stake in the whole apparatus of domination may go far in permitting the mobilization of practices of difference to emerge. For this reaffiliation to blossom into a different kind of national kinesthetic, one that is properly multicultural, the desire to be the other must transgress the partition that is said to divide the cultural from the political.

What has been registered here is but a moment in the imaginary and performative from which the composite of what I call my body is emitted. That I would dwell on the time shifts of all those aerobic steps could in no way stand as an inventory of where any body has been. Nor can it suggest a project of aligning a national sign with its embodied referent. The challenge for grasping the distances among these disparate locations is not in how to identify the body that they typify, but how to map the national landscape they imagine—that is, to conceive a kinesthetic context where what is different between the production of a black nationalism and a national fitness craze might be joined. The violence done to a body to make it fit into a putative national ideal is itself made crazy, or split by that very body's desire to be an other. The subjection to this order of difference is typical of what and how contemporary bodies are composed within the diversity of spatially engaging practices we all inhabit. This topos is a multicultural landscape without fixed boundaries whose referents must be constantly and sentiently mobilized.

The multiple affinities to racial and other identities that are drawn to hip-hop are precisely what compose a heterodox national body. In actuality as opposed to virtuality, the nation too is composed of countless such tenuous connections. Against the confidence that all these weak linkages might be held together by a solitary narrative of nation, such as that proposed by the evening news, this diffuseness of the composite body can introduce some very productive doubt. Between that desire to cast oneself against the flickering screen and the desire to emerge from the other side of the aerobic mirror is a bodily space that admits of an unconsolidated diversity that I would here champion as properly multicultural.

Multiculturalism can also name the aspiration for a postracial constitution of difference. By *postracial*, I mean simply that the structures of institutional division by race would yield to a societal context for identification in which associations formed by people through all manner of activities would be mutual and self-constituting. A postracial politics does not preclude an ongoing cultural or historical significance for racial or other categories of identification. Rather, it acts against the history that made racial classification such a fundamental aspect of colonialism. Further, it is implicitly internationalist in that the attainment of national sovereignty as a defense against divisive and appropriative incursions to which a population or territory is subjected would no longer be necessary for the articulation of any people's process of identification and differentiation.

The lines of contention are drawn by the different meanings of multiculturalism. The imaginary proposed by the news posts a nonnavigable divide between bodies of innocents and criminals, who are treated as essentially different from one another. Here multiculturalism is disguised as the threat of an alien nation to the monoculture. The surfaces of hip-hop emit an identity that hints at a different principle of bodily composition, one that circulates across national media borders and reconfigures the terrain of cultural difference itself.

Whether or not I ever moved to those pictures on the myriad screens and mirrors in this cultural landscape, there is no risk that I could become one with them or fuse into any one of them. The beats that fuel this desiring machine mark a structure of feeling that has no purchase on singularity. These images make no claim to be *the* news. But to begin to recognize those disparate spaces where I am not structured in dominance, I must do other than listen for the sound of the monolith. I must be moved myself through the nations (and not simply the notions) of others. Silencing that autonarrative that claims such omnipotence, the walk that separates my hip-hop encounters stretches on to alloy itself with the desires of others whose pulses I can just begin to feel. The heartbeat of America? No. These are the rhythms of a body that dances to a different composition.

Notes

1. The term *structure of feeling* is developed by Williams (1977, 128–35) to discuss the historically emergent or "preemergent" "inalienably physical" "changes of presence" in a given social formation.
2. The projection of an assimilationist myth that elides Asian identity has been effectively taken to task by such writers as E. San Juan Jr. (1992), whose book *Racial Formations/Critical Transformations* also contains an excellent overview of the political economy of racialization and its effects in the United States. I mention this here because a significant number of those who regularly attended the aerobics class were Asian Americans, a commitment that disturbs the presumptions of this group's cultural antipathy toward African Americans.
3. Lott's (1993) finely complex study of minstrelsy in the antebellum United States is particularly instructive here in elaborating how a particular performance idiom mapped the contradictory relations of race, class, and gender on the eve of their dramatic reinscription. Yet I wonder if the present conjuncture doesn't offer some reconfiguration of these racialized relations of spectacle and performance. Although white repugnance of blackness is still constructed through the spectacle of watching it (now on television, rather than in the theater), the desire for blackness is complicated by displacing what was an audience for certain spectacles into performative practices, from street basketball to the aerobics class discussed here.
4. The role of the racialized savage as fundamental to the constitution of the West is articulated by Trouillot (1991).

Works Cited

Baker, Houston, Jr. 1993. *Black Studies, Rap, and the Academy.* Chicago: University of Chicago Press.

Decker, Jeffrey Louis. 1993. "The State of Rap: Time and Place in Hip Hop Nationalism." *Social Text* 34: 53–84.

Donziger, Steven R. 1996. *The Real War on Crime: The Report of the National Criminal Justice Commission.* New York: HarperCollins.

Dyson, Michael Eric. 1993. *Reflecting Black: African American Cultural Criticism.* Minneapolis: University of Minnesota Press.

———. 1996. *Between God and Gangsta' Rap: Bearing Witness to Black Culture.* New York: Oxford University Press.

Haraway, Donna J. 1991. "A Cyborg Manifesto: Science, Technology, and Socialist-Feminism in the Late Twentieth Century." In *Simians, Cyborgs and Women: The Reinvention of Nature,* 149–82. New York: Routledge.

Hazzard-Gordon, Katrina. 1990. *Jookin': The Rise of Social Dance Formations in African American Culture.* Philadelphia: Temple University Press.

Lott, Eric. 1993. *Love and Theft: Blackface Minstrelsy and the American Working Class.* New York: Oxford University Press.

Rose, Tricia. 1994. *Black Noise: Rap Music and Black Culture in Contemporary America.* Hanover, Conn.: Wesleyan University Press.

San Juan, E., Jr. 1992. *Racial Formations/Critical Transformations.* Atlantic Highlands, N.J.: Humanities Press.

Trouillot, Michel-Rolph. 1991. "Anthropology and the Savage Slot: The Poetics and Politics of Otherness." In *Recapturing Anthropology: Working in the Present,* ed. Richard G. Fox, 17–44. Santa Fe, N.M.: School of American Research Press.

Williams, Raymond. 1977. *Marxism and Literature.* New York: Oxford University Press.

Aerobics and Feminism:
Self-Determination or Patriarchal Hegemony?

Michael Real

Many young women today do not realize that exercise for women as a widely available and socially acceptable endeavor represents a recent victory in women's struggle for equality with men.

I want to look at women's exercise, bearing in mind its narrowly defined constituency, but realizing at the same time that middle-class white America defines the model and the look of consumer capitalism. I also want to maintain a sense of all the positive features that exercise for women generates, including the development of independence and the opportunity for bonding between women; but I want particularly to scrutinize the way exercise has evolved in a commodified society so as to contain or limit these positive features.

▸ *Susan Willis*, A Primer for Daily Life

Sport and exercise is one of the more heavily contested terrains today in the struggle by women for self-determination. What do inherited gender-based attitudes and practices do to female efforts to develop and work out "the body"? Susan Willis and other feminist critics disagree in assessing the emancipatory and regressive aspects of women's exercise, particularly widely popular aerobics classes.

Willis charges that recuperative pressure takes "women's positive desires for strength, agility, and the physical affirmation of self and transforms these into competition over style and rivalry for a particular body look and performance" (70). Cheryl Cole (1994) and Jennifer Hargreaves (1994) echo Willis's charge that aerobics' motivation to please the male gaze has eviscerated its potential. Mary Duffy and Maura Rhodes (1993) claim the reverse: "The aesthetic payoffs took a back seat to the pragmatic . . . away from the emphasis on how we look to how we feel" (17). Susan Bordo (1993), Sandra Bartky (1990), and Hilary Radner (1995) find confusing progress in the process that works from the "dominated" body to the "resistant" body through aerobics and women's exercise. A recurring question is, Are women in aerobics classes motivated by an internal self-actualizing drive for fitness or by a search for pleasing "the male gaze" by achieving the external patriarchal standard of "the look"?

This study explores exercise and culture today by combining an examination of gender issues in sport and fitness with an ethnographic description of aerobic workouts. The ethnography is based on numerous brief interviews with aerobic instructors and students and some 350 to 400 hours of participant observation spread over seven years. It includes observations and comments from many clubs, but is centered on one particular facility, the 24 Hour Fitness Center in the University Town Center shopping mall in La Jolla, California.[1] Here is a brief scenario identifying our subject.

> Drive up to the gym, one of more than one hundred 24 Hour Fitness centers scattered across the United States. Park the car, grab your workout towel, join in the fast-walking parade into the club. At the counter, have your barcoded membership card electronically beeped. Select an activity. Mostly males in the free weight area. Mixed groups working the Nautilus machines. Mostly females in the aerobics room. As Four Non-Blonds ask over the sound system spread throughout the facility, "What's Going On?"

Workout routines, fitness clubs, and a new generation of exercise styles, many of them intended for women, have evolved in the second half of the twentieth century, particularly among the more privileged in affluent urban and suburban areas. On television this emerged with Jack La Lanne and Richard Simmons. On video the trend came in the form of workout tapes by Jane Fonda and, it seems, every celebrity short of Orson Welles. By 1985, an estimated twenty-two million people were participating in aerobic dance exercise. The once generic "gym shoes" became a high-tech commodity with infinite variations: running, tennis, walking, basketball, soccer, cross-training, specializations for every leisure activity except bingo. Running became a status symbol as much as golf remained a business bonding routine. New workout clubs emerged as privatized heirs to the YMCA, public parks, and school recreation facilities. Higher status than the working-class boxing gym but lower status than the private country club, with its leisurely golf, swimming, tennis, and social life, fitness clubs have become a haven especially for upwardly mobile, fitness-freak yuppies.

Aerobic Exercise Classes: "With Every Beat of My Heart"

What do we find in a detailed analysis of a fitness activity dominated by women, namely, aerobic exercise classes? In a cultural sense, what is the typical experience and meaning to those who participate in aerobic workouts? In developing a "thick description" in the form of an ethnography that seeks out the terminology and interpretations of the participants rather than a

133

priori analytic categories of the researcher, this analysis attempts to "pitch our tent with the natives" (Christians and Carey, 1989), "interpret the interpretations" (Geertz, 1973), and avoid deductive overgeneralizations about participants by "reading the text of the culture over their shoulders" (Geertz 1973).

The subjects of most ethnographies, members of pretechnological societies, would be amazed to observe a modern workout club. Physical effort is expended at intense levels for no external result. A traditional labor-intensive society would build bridges, buildings, or roads with the kind of physical effort expended in a health club. A poor society would rig up the exercycles and other machines to produce electricity or some other outcome from all the muscle force exerted. But the contemporary health club uses physical effort only for internal, personal benefit, not for external accomplishments. In the framework of human evolution, workout clubs seem to occupy a compensation niche for populations engaged in work that is mentally but not physically demanding and that is surrounded by labor-saving, creature-comfort devices that eliminate physical exertion.

The international growth and structure of fitness clubs and aerobics now extends throughout the developed world and into parts of the developing world. The structure is reflected in the development of the International Dance Exercise Association (IDEA), active in fifty countries and attracting more than five thousand instructors to its conventions. Likewise, the American Council on Exercise (ACE) International certifies organizations in different countries and has certified more than nineteen thousand instructors internationally. The American Aerobics Association International (AAAI) has eighty thousand members and has provided conferences and certification for instructors in Argentina, Colombia, Brazil, India, and numerous other locations around the world. Likewise, the Aerobics and Fitness Association of America (AFAA), founded in 1983, has more than eighty thousand members in seventy-three countries and more than seventy thousand certified instructors and claims to be "the world's largest fitness educator." Such organizations offer certification in primary aerobic instruction, step instruction, fitness practitioner training, personal training, fitness counseling, weightroom/ resistance training, and first aid and emergency response, as well as specialty workshops, extension programs, continuing education, home study courses, educational publications, and national and international special events. The World Wide Web offers further evidence of the globalization of aerobics with home pages and news groups from many sources in many countries.

The aerobics classes at the 24 Hour Fitness Center studied here are typical of those around the world in style and services. The club was founded in the early 1980s as one of sixty-six Family Fitness Centers in a chain created by Ray Wilson in Southern California with a total of some two hundred thousand members. In the mid-1990s the Family Fitness Centers were bought out and merged with almost ninety other clubs of the 24 Hour Nautilus chain and a few Gold's Gyms and World Gyms. The result is a system of some 155 gyms scattered across the United States and called 24 Hour Fitness. They are open twenty-four hours a day, seven days a week.

Specifically, in the La Jolla gym studied, there are forty-four aerobics classes scheduled each week, plus eight yoga classes, one "kidz danz" class, one "cardio karate" class, and two "aero kick" classes. The schedule is almost identical to that of other clubs around the world, such as the Club Montmartrois in Paris, which offers forty-seven classes per week in categories similar to those of the La Jolla club, though with more labeling by muscle groups—abs, glutes, and so on. Clubs of this type exist in major cities in many countries.

At the La Jolla 24 Hour Fitness Center, the typical aerobics class has perhaps thirty participants, ranging from late teens to active elderly but with a majority in their twenties and thirties. Asian, Latino, and Black participants constitute typically 20 percent, overrepresenting Asians from the general population and underrepresenting the other two groups. Classes are generally 80 to 90 percent female, as are the instructors. Members of the club typically pay $100 to $150 to join, depending on various membership packages, and $10 to $15 in a monthly fee, depending on length of membership. Although the club was remodeled only a few years ago and is in an upscale shopping mall, the rich have finer clubs available and the poor are not represented.

Many activities are aerobic—that is, high oxygen consuming—but the "aerobics exercise class" in general is a group activity in which an instructor leads a group of a few or a hundred in rapid, organized full-body movement accompanied by music, usually in a one-hour time block, for the purposes of conditioning and cardiovascular improvement. The leader calls out the moves, rather choppily in 4/4 cadence, devoid of the verbal stylizations of folk parallels such as square dance calling, and illustrates the moves as well. Members of the group, spaced in rows around the room, follow the instructions and copy the moves of the leader. It is a thoroughly centralized activity in which the leader has total control over the music, the sequence of moves and routines, and the manner in which movements are performed. Leadership can be passed around during a class, but this happens less than 3 percent of the time. Aerobics classes are authoritarian in style within a context of voluntary participation.

The sound system is operated by the instructor and feeds fourteen speakers planted in the ceiling. The music is normally pop, anything with a very strong, repetitious beat. The volume is typically loud but not over-whelming (because of a folk art museum upstairs that "feels" overly loud music despite the baffling insulation in the ceiling). The musical style may be technopop or mainstream rock or Motown funk or rap or salsa or even heavy metal or country and western. The sine qua non of the music is a strong, consistent rhythm. Lyric content is clearly nonessential, as is obvious if one notes the words: "Work that body, work that body, work that body"; "Push it, push it real good"; "You take me up the mountain"; "Get up, get up, get moving." In the past, instructors prepared and traded their own compilation tapes of pop songs, but they are prevented by copyright law, enforced by ASCAP and BMI, from that practice today. Instead, legally licensed compilations are continuously available from more than a dozen companies. Warm-up in the beginning is often to songs with a moderate but brisk beat, then stronger, more aggressive music carries the middle or peak workout, and slower songs, even ballads, lower the exercise heart rate during the ending cool-down period.

Like other exercise and self-improvement programs, aerobic activities are carefully graded for ability level, age, and personal preferences. Aerobics instructors excel in particular categories and are identified on the wall schedule by their first names: "Michelle, 8 a.m., Beginning Step"; "Norm, 5:30 p.m., High Impact." The low-impact class works participants through physiologically vigorous routines but with diminished impact on the muscular-skeletal structure. "Fat burner" classes offer low impact but with more ex-acting form, concentration, and attention to tightening specific muscle groups. High-impact instructors resemble dance ensemble leaders and may show the effects of formal training in jazz dance, ballet, or gymnastics. Step aero-bics classes also may be low impact, fat burner, or high impact but are often classified as simply advanced or basic step, or are broken into levels of step one, two, or three. Instructors compete in creating catchy titles: Step It Up, Killa' Step, Step Frenzy, Drop Dead Step, StepSation, Steptacular, and Step 'N Sanity.

Advanced aerobics classes, especially advanced step classes, are not only demanding and rapid but feature complex routines. Whereas basic classes often repeat movements to counts of four or eight with many repetitions at each number, the advanced step instructor may have the class doing combi-nations that extend into two-, four-, or eight-part sequences, with each se-quence including four- and eight-count sub-routines. A single sequence may move from basic step to alternating knee lifts to a T movement off the front and end of the step and then require moving across the board to repeat all those movements in a mirror pattern on the other side of the step board. Such complex patterns hold the concentration of advanced students and drive away the yet unpolished who quickly become hopelessly lost and, in a crowded room, may fear crashing into others.

The ability to concentrate and lead such intricate, complex patterns counters the bubblehead stereotype. The most rigorous advanced instructors are not only superbly conditioned athletes but also rigorously self-disciplined and intelligent goal achievers. The instructors at the La Jolla 24 Hour Fitness Center include an accountant, a flower shop owner, college students, a waitress, a makeup professional, and others. A not atypical instructor at this gym is Michelle Mazzoni. A native of Minnesota, Michelle earned her Ph.D. in bioengineering with a 4.0 GPA and works as a research scientist; in addition she leads aerobic classes each day of the week at varying levels. A few years ago, Family Fitness Centers paid only minimum wage to aerobics instructors, but now with certification by ACE and others it may pay instructors up to $15 for a one-hour class. Pay in gyms for aerobics instructors hovers not far above minimum wage, but top instructors at upscale clubs can make $30 an hour or more. Of course, one cannot teach aerobics classes for eight hours a day—the realistic healthy maximum is probably two a day because of the vigorous movement required—so the income from teaching aerobics is a salary supplement for these instructors and not a self-sufficient income.

The entire environment of the workout gym is systematic, technological, industrial, methodical. Nautilus machines isolate muscle groups and require methodical repetitions in sets, as do free weights. Working on the machines, which Willis (1991) calls "the symbol of male dominated industrial capitalism" (73), may even suggest the illusion of being part of a real physical labor force. In any case, members tend to appear serious and intent, breathing deeply and exerting, as they move through their personal routines. There may be only three or four small conversations in rooms of forty and fifty people. Males may gaze around the room from time to time, but the concentration in general is "internal" as members focus on effort, feel, and completeness. Some members appear to succumb to excesses of narcissism and self-preoccupation in the gym and beyond, but for others the all-surrounding, unforgiving mirrors are little more than a nasty reminder of imperfection, to be ignored if possible but to be used as motivation by guilt as needed.

Aerobic means "in the presence of oxygen," as opposed to *anaerobic,* which means "in the absence of oxygen." Aerobic fitness results from minimal training in such endurance activities as distance running, cycling, exercise walking, distance swimming, and aerobic dance. The one-hour class is a classic aerobic activity, with exercise heart rate periodically measured during several pauses in each class.

What are the health benefits? McDonald and Hodgdon (1991) have summarized the results of numerous empirical studies of the effects of aerobic fitness. They report that successful aerobic exercise programs protect against coronary heart disease, increase oxygen capacity, reduce total body mass and fat weight, decrease blood pressure, improve carbohydrate metabolism, improve bone density in females, improve slow-wave sleep, create higher levels of energy for longer periods, improve digestion, control constipation, improve intellectual capacity and productivity, and, at least temporarily, modify other health habits such as diet intake (17, 25). In addition, ninety studies of psychological effects of aerobic exercise have found that it is effective in combating, in decreasing order of impact, depression, anxiety, low self-esteem, and social maladjustment (182–86). Effects were similar for males and females except that females showed slightly less effect for certain forms of depression and anxiety. Results were virtually identical for young adults (under thirty years old) and middle-aged adults (thirty to sixty) and were similar but less complete for older adults (those over sixty).

Gender and Aerobic Exercise: Is It Empowering or Regressive?

Are aerobics classes that are shaped for female use entirely self-determined by independent female concerns, or do patriarchal influences distort the motivation and participation into something else? Women outnumber men by a ratio of nine or ten to one in the demanding participation of aerobic workout classes in the club studied here. Against the traditional exclusion and stereotyping of women in the sports world (see Bordo, 1993; Bryson, 1994; Creedon, 1994; Guttmann, 1991; Messner, 1994; Messner and Sabo, 1990; Nelson, 1994), aerobics is one area of exercise that women have in many respects carved out for themselves.

Overt and covert female orientations in aerobics contrast with male sports activities. Unlike traditional male bodybuilding gyms, clubs catering to women often include nurseries for young children as well as greater attention to brighter colors, lighting, and acoustics. The La Jolla club has a large, enclosed nursery room near the entrance. The large aerobics room is carpeted and features neon decoration over pastel walls. There are in aerobics no scorekeeping and no winners and losers, common ingredients of competitive masculine sports. Aerobics classes are designed for participation. There is little value in a spectator relationship to aerobics; it is something to *do*, not to watch, despite loiterers (most commonly male) occasionally hanging around the entranceways to the aerobics room or passively watching aerobics on television.

A female interest may also be reflected in introductory explanations by aerobics instructors. They convey concern for *trimming* specific body areas—abdomen, referred to as "abs" or "tummy tucking"; gluteus maximus, called "glutes" or "buns," as in Tammilee Webb's *Buns of Steel* (1992); quads, hips, shoulders, arms, and so on. In contrast, more masculine-dominated weight training tends to "bulk up" muscles. There are specific aerobic activities that women verbalize against—the announcement of push-ups may bring groans and complaints. Upper-body strength building is generally not emphasized in aerobics, except for occasional hand-weight classes or body-sculpting classes. There are other aerobic moves that men find awkward—hip flexors and wide-legged floor stretches in which even male aerobics instructors do not excel. The men tend to have more trouble with the stretching rather than the strengthening movements.

That men and women incorporate exercise differently in their lives has been borne out by studies conducted in Great Britain (Hargreaves, 1994, 24). Women were found to be less likely than men to engage in regular exercise, despite organized programs to increase their numbers. In 1986, 56.9 percent of men participated and 37.2 percent of women were involved, ten million men and seven million women. Twice as many men took their sport seriously (39 percent to 17 percent), and almost twice as many women never took part in sport (33 percent to 17 percent). More men than women played golf and tennis, as well as the traditional male sports of rugby and football. Swimming was slightly more popular among women than among men, but only aerobics appealed almost exclusively to women.

Iris Marion Young, in *Throwing Like a Girl* (1990), summarizes the effect of differential physical expression patterns for males and females: "Women in sexist society are handicapped. Insofar as we learn to live out our existence in accordance with the definitions that patriarchal culture assigns to us, we are physically inhibited, confined, positioned, and objectified" (153).

Susan Willis (1991) puts such trends in perspective by noting how different the context for women was as recently as 1971, when the Boston Women's Health Collective published its historic resource book for women, *Our Bodies, Ourselves*. Recently rereading that work, Willis writes: "I was amazed by the book's comparatively mild chapter on exercise. It urges women to get into exercise, investigate a YMCA program, or consider taking up a sport such as swimming, tennis, perhaps jogging. How tame these suggestions seem by comparison to the exercise standards many women set for themselves today" (65). Sixty-minute aerobic workouts four or five times a week or jogging twenty-five miles a week have replaced the simple exercise ideal for women at the Y.

For Willis, it is important that those older community recreation programs often promoted bonding among women, conversation, and a sense of community that cut across generations and socioeconomic classes; participants reported "they most appreciate getting to know, and to laugh and sweat with other women" (70). For Willis, those social benefits are lost when the experience becomes individualized, privatized, and commodified by being reduced to a workout tape on television or a typically silent attendance at a commercial health club, which may even include wearing the privatizing earplugs of a Walkman-style music system. Instead of the earlier conviviality, Willis sees emerging in women's workouts a "body rivalry" that has long been a feature of men's exercise. Willis perceives a trend that converts positive desires for physical affirmation of the self into negative struggles for superior body appearance.

Examining this question of socializing and conviviality within aerobics classes, one finds rivalry and competition are vaguely evident within the workout itself, even in the absence of competitive scorekeeping. One can observe an elevated social status among those who can perform at or near the front of an aerobics class without making mistakes or wearing down. One aerobics respondent explained how nervous she gets on the way to a class because she is afraid of not doing well. She suspects other women are noticing whether she is as good as she should be. In contrast, another respondent finds aerobics relaxing because she is doing it for herself and honestly does not care how she looks to anyone else as she does it. Unlike the above competitor, this relaxer stays toward the back of the aerobics room. When asked what aerobics means to her, one instructor responded, typically: "It gets the heart pumped up. Fun. A cardiovascular workout. I like teaching better than taking it. At least I know the music's good." The social environment of the aerobics class seems to inspire energetic performance, but only limited overt competition and rivalry.

Respondents at the gym often admit to something they would like to improve about their bodies if they could. Janet Wolff (1991) writes: "The female body is seen as psychically and socially produced and inscribed. At the same time, it is experienced by women—primarily as lacking or incomplete" (133). Four of the five in-depth interviews conducted by Kendall Morgan (1996) at a San Diego women's workout club found respondents dissatisfied with their own bodies. The exception was a woman who was surviving a twenty-year struggle against cancer. One interviewee reported she woke up one morning and noticed fat connective tissue on her thighs; she took a big garbage bag and threw away sixty dollars worth of food from her refrigerator and started going to the gym regularly. Another is motivated by what the scales read ("I'd like to lose at least ten more pounds"), what the charts recommend ("For my height and bone structure, I'm at the high end of my ideal"), and what she looked like at eighteen ("I remember how my body was before I gained weight my senior year"). Even a trim instructor, proud of her workout body, admitted jokingly, "I mean you always want bigger boobs, but I would never go out and get surgery."

Willis (1991) finds in such concerns an excess of exaggerated female sexuality. She is particularly concerned with the "gendered look" the workout produces: "long Barbie-doll legs, strikingly accentuated by iridescent hot pink tights, offset by a pair of not too floppy purple legwarmers . . . and finally a color coordinated headband (or wristbands)" (72). Makeup and jewelry are often included. That workout look of the 1980s has been replaced by de rigueur attire of crop tops and biking shorts or thong bikinis worn over leotards or various layered and color-coordinated combinations in quieter shades. When women wear these workout outfits while doing errands to and from the gym, Willis finds, their implied liberatory statement about seizing control over the making and shaping of the body instead becomes a defensive overgendering of the female. Thus, the gendered look of successful workouts for women contains the contradiction of asserting control and self-definition while conforming to cultural image norms defined primarily by the male gaze. The healthy utopian dimensions of realizing an ideal as defined by and for oneself and as experienced internally fight in dialectical tension with the stereotype of perfection driven home in the body types of health spa ads and commodity advertising in general. Bartky (1990) warns that the male gaze can be "internalized" in the way women evaluate other women's bodies and their own.

Cheryl Cole and Jennifer Hargreaves echo Willis's feminist critiques of aerobics. Cole (1994) repeats and supports Willis's charges that privatized workouts in commercial clubs and on video isolate women from one another and promote rivalry based on "the look." Hargreaves (1994) also echoes Willis:

> Although there are aerobics classes, for example, that take place in community facilities rather than commercial venues, and cater for women who are more interested in the enjoyment of exercise and the social interaction with other women than with the ideal of a beautiful body, they are in the minority.

Aerobics has been successfully packaged to persuade women, specifically, to participate in order to lose weight and improve their sex-appeal, rather than for reasons of fitness and enjoyment or for competition. . . . The focus of publicity is on appearance (the athletic-looking body), fashion (the trendy-looking image) and physique (the sexy-looking shape); rather than on movement (the active-looking woman). The idea of exercise is blurred with sexuality. (160)

The last point about publicity and media coverage is certainly true. Horne and Bentley (1989, 4) argue that "fitness chic" magazines promise fitness but are really built around "the look" (cited in Hargreaves, 1994, 161, 310). Even the publicity for the 24 Hour Fitness Centers studied here often presents visuals of attractive young males and females who look far more like professional models than athletes.

The *televised* forms of aerobics raise particular problems. Margaret MacNeill (1994) has studied in detail the presentation of aerobics in the popular Canadian program *20 Minute Workout* and compares this with presentation of a women's bodybuilding competition. She is specifically concerned with how television presentations have hegemonic effects. According to MacNeill, "The everyday practice of sending young girls to figure-skating lessons while their brothers go to the arenas to play hockey is an example of hegemonic relations" (274). For aerobic participation, MacNeill notes that the camera aimed directly at the instructor with a full-body shot is ideal as a standard frame for the active viewer. However, the *20 Minute Workout* used this view for only 36.63 percent of the shots. Another 18.28 percent of the shots were aerial shots, accentuating "'cleavage' shots of the women, in their low-cut leotards, exercising on a rotating stage" (276). The largest proportion of shots, 47.08 percent, were from an upwardly tilting angle, usually when participants were bent over from the waist. In addition, 62.57 percent of all shots were close-ups and medium shots rather than full-body shots. Predominantly, the hips, thighs, and buttocks were centered on. Also, 32.79 percent of all shots zoomed in or out. The rotating stage and camera angles and movement thus "titillated by the constant visual caressing of the female body" (278).

Evaluating this aerobic television coverage, MacNeill acknowledges that aerobics is "counterhegemonic to the notion that intense physical activity for women is harmful" and symbolizes "the increased opportunities for physical activity which are opening to women," but this occurs "in a form that stresses a preoccupation with beauty, glamour, and sex appeal as status symbols" (281). As a consequence, aerobics on television "caters to the voyeur through the sexualization of the images," and the objectification of body parts "tends to fabricate pornographic and erotic myths" (284). The presentational mode then of aerobics on television aligns it with dominant hegemonic relations and recuperates its liberating potential back into conformity with patriarchal culture.

Qualifying the Feminist Critique

But what of aerobics classes themselves in a feminist context? There are reasons to question the double charge that commercialized facilities create motives that isolate women from each other and that have to do only with appearance rather than fitness. Some feminist criticisms may be based on an earlier, less mature generation of aerobics. A report by Mary Duffy and Maura Rhodes in *Women's Health and Fitness* (1993) is more consistent with our ethnographic observations and reports than are some of the charges by Willis, Cole, and Hargreaves. Duffy and Rhodes report:

> Ten years ago, many women donned form-fitting leotards and pranced and puffed their way through an hour-long aerobics class for the *express purpose of looking good* in said garment. Spurred by vanity and a diehard crash-dieting mentality, dance exercisers faced the music and the mirror in hopes of sweating off—fast—what flab they couldn't diet off. (17; emphasis added)

In contrast, Duffy and Rhodes report that more recently "the aesthetic payoffs took a back seat to the pragmatic" (17). Aerobics participants found they felt better between workouts and had more stamina for workdays and chore-packed weekends. They find this important switch in motive has contributed to a slow but sure switch in the mode and mood of aerobics classes. A fourteen-year veteran of teaching aerobics, Molly Fox, told Duffy and Rhodes, "It's been a gradual evolution of awareness away from the emphasis on how we look to how we feel" (17). The health benefits documented above, a longer experience with the rigors and effects of aerobics, learning from injuries, and a practical desire to maximize the payoff in quality of life have made current aerobics instructors and students wiser than the first generation. Instructor certification may contribute to bureaucratization and overrationalization, but it also contributes to better motivation and healthful practices among instructors and participants in aerobics. Familiarity with exercise physiology and biomechanics has greatly increased. Duffy and Rhodes report: "What it all boils down to is a more holistic approach to exercise. The concern is not just how strong, toned, and well-

143

developed certain muscles are, but how well all the major muscle groups work together as a team" (18).

This sophistication, which one also finds frequently in random comments of participants, conflicts with the implication that aerobics has been irrevocably "recuperated" by male hegemony and patriarchal culture. Women still predominate in aerobics, and there is little hard evidence that all of them, or even most of them, are driven by the goal of the sexualized image of "the look" to please others. Aerobics participants are happy to look good, but many express motivations well beyond that. When asked why participants take or teach aerobics classes, responses cluster around "I enjoy it," "It makes me feel good," "I'm healthier," "It gives me energy," and so on. They may also add, "It keeps me looking better," but even that may reflect a concern for visible healthiness as much as sexual attractiveness. In fact, one participant who admitted she was trying to achieve a "look" emphasized that this look was itself a source of power for her and not victimization in relation to males. Radner (1995) notes that tending to her physical identity as feminine in this manner "accords agency and accomplishments to the subject that produces the 'looks'" (157).

When asked whether her motivation was more for appearance or fitness, one instructor responded, "Actually, for me it's more *mental*. It keeps my head cleared. It's like brushing your teeth. You need to do it. Sometimes I'm just enjoying myself, but sometimes you do it because you have to. When I do aerobics, I can deal with the rest of life better." Another instructor also mentioned the mental and emotional benefits that she considers beyond the level of either physical fitness or looking good. She also observed that many participants start doing aerobics because they want to change their appearance. They ask, "How long will it take me to lose X pounds?" She knows they want her to tell them that in a couple of weeks they'll be all trimmed up. Instead she says, "It may take a year, but you'll be able to keep the weight off then, and you'll be so much better off in many other ways."

Based on our unstructured interviews with participants, and until there is ethnographic evidence to the contrary, there seems little reason to generalize broadly that aerobics participants are motivated principally by the hegemonic demands of "the look." Such motivation may be more common to new participants, but many longer-term participants can tick off a range of motivations and benefits that go well beyond attempting to measure up to a single measure of appearance.

The conflict between internal and external motivation, however, is very real and continuing. The exercise industry appears to be slowly moving away from the external emphasis on "the look," but the vast majority of persons attracted for the first time to aerobics may well be motivated by the look. To these individuals, instructors cite the limits of aerobics and warn, for example, that one cannot change body fat in particular spots through aerobics, but they find participants wanting to do just that. Aging and extended experience of the aerobics participants tend to be associated with a shift from external motives to more internal, health-oriented goals. The baby-boom generation that jumped into high-impact classes in their twenties turned toward lower impact in their thirties, and now are shifting toward yoga and more internally directed, functional goals in exercise. This shift is not consistent across the board, however, and does meet resistance.

The other charge that aerobics in commercial clubs isolates women from each other and prevents the solidarity that is alleged in the older community centers and YMCAs is also a charge that requires further documentation. Participants in the classes studied often hustled into and out of the club and classes without speaking with others, but the overriding impression is that they want their workout to be "efficient," with maximum benefits and minimum time. Their social lives are clearly elsewhere. Often following classes, brief conversations arise, particularly around the instructor. These are about as much social interaction as takes place anywhere in these clubs among males or females. Two-person conversations between persons working on stationary machines sometimes take place, and conversations are slightly more common in the male-dominated free weights area than around the Nautilus machines, but participation at the gym, like the machines spread throughout, is generally individual, not interactive.

It is quite evident that the lifestyle of the vast majority of members of the 24 Hour Fitness Center includes the gym for physical fitness and not for other affective concerns. This may, however, be less true in some other aerobic settings, where the search for friends and affective relationships combines with the search for health and fitness. Less yuppie-dominated clubs sometimes feature large groups of women participants moving to a health bar to chat for an hour following exercise. But even a respondent from the all-women's gym mentioned previously emphasized the nonsocial nature of her motivation: "For me this is part of my workday, so I see it as an integral part of my workday, not as an opportunity for social relationships. . . . I notice that other women are very business-like also. It is like something they have to do like driving their kids to school" (Morgan, 1996, 9).

It appears that the actual participation in aerobics for most participants retains a liberating, self-actualizing female potential originally ascribed to it, without being completely victimized by the recuperative forces that exercise great influence over the mediated presentations of these activities on television and in magazines. Participants compare doing aerobics to brushing their teeth or driving their kids to school or taking ballet, and not to preparing for the senior prom or impressing a boyfriend.

Sport and Utopian Potential

At the same time, it should be acknowledged that the utopian potential is greatly reduced for this female activity in the current practice, in contrast to the male bonding and ideology generated around traditional male sports activities. The centuries-old, established male sport culture serves a wide range of psychological, sociological, and hegemonic male functions that bind men in an aggressive, interactive solidarity. A ball game becomes a utopian realization of idealized male solidarity and a utopian promise that collective life can be immensely rewarding in other areas outside the ball game. It is an idealized moment within a larger socially approved and supported set of public structures. There is no female sports equivalent to that in aerobics or elsewhere. The culture of female bonding receives less public endorsement and is built around less physically active recreational pursuits.

But if Morley (1994), Gray (1992), Moores (1993), Lull (1988), and other ethnographers of media experience are correct, there is no reason to think that women are not active, critical readers of the culture, including the recuperated aspects of aerobics. If Mary Ellen Brown (1994) can rightly find so much "reactive pleasure" available to women in talk around soap operas, then aerobics and fitness activities will certainly continue to be seized and used effectively by and for women. "Feminist ethnographic work has dealt with resistive pleasure—Radway's (1984) study of romance novels, Ang's (1985) analysis of *Dallas* viewers, Walkerdine's (1986) observation of family television viewing, or McRobbie's (1984) theorization of the resistive position of dance for young women" (Brown, 1994, 182–83). There is no reason to assume that aerobics lacks the resistive potential of what Brown calls "emancipation through the constant awareness of contradiction and the struggle to secure a space for the voice of the female spectator who speaks as well as sees" (182).

Beyond such resistive pleasures, aerobics offers genuine utopian possibilities as it combines exercise, fitness, solidarity, and dance art forms. It is an activity that can suggest and express meaningful aesthetic experience, experience that both suggests and inchoately realizes higher meanings and possibilities. Like any demanding activity, it can make possible reaching "the zone," as elite athletes refer to the experience of peak performance, or "the flow," as Mihaly Csikszentmihalyi calls that higher state. The aerobic utopian experience includes the experience of achieving personal goals as part of a communitarian activity. It is an extreme expression of what Henry Jenkins (1992) calls "participatory culture." The person and the group become a danced unity, an experience that may or may not spill over beyond that moment. The musical beat is working on participants, the instructor has everyone involved and challenged, and visual feedback from the mirrors cues and displays the unity. When everything is clicking for a participant who relishes aerobics or similar fitness and sports activities, it is a "natural high." The endorphins are pumping through the system, stimulated by exertion and an elevated exercise heart rate, and this is shared. There are numerous testimonies that subjects move beyond participating in aerobics initially as a laborious task performed in order to achieve health benefits and improved appearance; over time they begin to enjoy "the pleasure of the text" of aerobics for its own sake and for its integral part in a healthy life.

Summary: The Balance Sheet on Aerobics

Sport and exercise tend all too often to replicate the patriarchy and aggression of the dominant culture. They are Foucauldian vehicles of dominance and subordination. As Bordo (1993) notes, in "the organization and regulation of time, space and movements of our daily lives, our bodies are trained, shaped, and impressed with the stamp of prevailing historical forms of selfhood, desire, masculinity, femininity" (14). In the case of aerobics, the healthy exercise workout can be motivated by "other-directed" dreams of "the look" and can lead to a gendered commodification and objectifying of the participating subject. These are antidemocratic pressures in which self-determination is taken away from subjects and placed in control of others. These pressures can reduce a collective experience of feminine solidarity to a competitive and individualistic regression into the dysfunctional modes of late capitalism. Commodification, advertising imagery, patriarchal hegemony, and the commercializing drive of capitalism exert constant pressure to recuperate all the expressive forms of contemporary culture.

Yet the actual experience of aerobics participants in a live class shows considerable evidence that all is not lost. Bordo (1993), Radner (1995), and Bartky (1990) have written of the gym's potential for women to become not more masculine or more androgynous but more "feminine" as a cultivated ideal. Exercise for Radner (1995) is not just about good health but is "a central discourse of feminine culture" (145). The emancipatory potential of aerobics may be limited but not eliminated by the patriarchal commodity culture within which it exists. Participants find considerable positive benefits, both as women and as embodied humans. They experience satisfaction and self-determination in aerobics, even as the effects of commodification and privatization cannot be denied.

The structures of meaning in all human encoding and decoding activities are developed within the larger society's contextual frameworks of knowledge, relations of production, and technical infrastructure (Hall, 1973/1980, 1994; Van Zoonen, 1994). In this context, underlying structures and power relations around gender, race, ideology, and political economy shape both the encoding process within exercise organizations and the decoding process within individual and group aerobic participants. As these contextual structural factors exert more influence—for example, when aerobics become televised—recuperative and regressive forces take their toll. But as participants struggle to maintain and restore healthy balance in the actual doing of aerobics, this activity remains one of the more interesting and positive dimensions of the sports-gender-media nexus.

Notes

1. The observations and interviews from the La Jolla 24 Hour Fitness Center are supplemented with observations and interviews at the Balboa and the Encinitas 24 Hour Fitness Centers in the San Diego area as well as those of an unpublished similar study by Kendall Morgan (1996) of an all-women's fitness club in San Diego. In addition, Lorna Francis, Ph.D., and Jurnine Smithson, both widely experienced aerobics instructors and trainers, clarified and supplemented the information gathered at the clubs.

Works Cited

Ang, Ien. 1985. *Watching "Dallas": Soap Opera and the Melodramatic Imagination* (trans. Della Couling). London: Methuen.

Bartky, Sandra L. 1990. *Femininity and Domination: Studies in the Phenomenology of Oppression*. New York: Routledge.

Bordo, Susan. 1993. *Unbearable Weight: Feminism, Western Culture, and the Body*. Berkeley: University of California Press.

Brown, Mary Ellen. 1994. *Soap Opera and Women's Talk: The Pleasure of Resistance*. Thousand Oaks, Calif.: Sage.

Bryson, Lois. 1994. "Sport and the Maintenance of Masculine Hegemony." In *Women, Sport, and Culture*, ed. Susan Birrell and Cheryl L. Cole, 47–64. Champaign, Ill.: Human Kinetics.

Christians, Clifford G., and James W. Carey. 1989. "The Logic and Aims of Qualitative Research." In *Research Methods in Mass Communication* (2d ed.), ed. Guido Stempel and Bruce Westley, 354–74. Englewood Cliffs, N.J.: Prentice Hall.

Cole, Cheryl L. 1994. "Resisting the Canon: Feminist Cultural Studies, Sport, and Technologies of the Body." In *Women, Sport, and Culture*, ed. Susan Birrell and Cheryl L. Cole, 5–30. Champaign, Ill.: Human Kinetics.

Creedon, Pamela J., ed. 1994. *Women, Media, and Sport: Challenging Gender Values.* Thousand Oaks, Calif.: Sage.

Duffy, Mary, and Maura Rhodes. 1993. "Aerobics gets real." *Women's Health and Fitness,* December, 17–18.

Geertz, Clifford. 1973. *The Interpretation of Cultures.* New York: Basic Books.

Gray, Ann. 1992. *Video Playtime: The Gendering of a Leisure Technology.* New York: Routledge.

Guttmann, Allen. 1991. *Women's Sports: A History.* New York: Columbia University Press.

Hall, Stuart. 1980. Encoding and decoding. In *Culture, Media, Language,* ed. Stuart Hall. London: Hutchinson. (Originally published in 1973 as *Encoding and Decoding the TV Message,* CCCS Stencilled Paper. Birmingham: CCCS.)

———. 1994. "Reflections upon the encoding/decoding model: An interview with Stuart Hall." In *Viewing, Reading, Listening: Audiences and Cultural Reception,* ed. Jon Cruz and Justin Lewis, 253–74. Boulder, Colo.: Westview.

Hargreaves, Jennifer. 1994. *Sporting Females: Critical Issues in the History and Sociology of Women's Sports.* New York: Routledge.

Horne, J., and C. Bentley. 1989. "'Fitness Chic' and the Construction of Lifestyles." Paper presented at the LSA Conference on Leisure, Health and Well-Being.

Jenkins, Henry. 1992. *Textual Poachers: Television Fans and Participatory Culture.* New York: Routledge.

Lull, James, ed. 1988. *World Families Watch Television.* Newbury Park, Calif.: Sage.

MacNeill, Margaret. 1994. "Active Women, Media Representations, and Ideology." In *Women, Sport, and Culture,* ed. Susan Birrell and Cheryl L. Cole, 273–88. Champaign, Ill.: Human Kinetics.

McDonald, David G., and James A. Hodgdon. 1991. *The Psychological Effects of Aerobic Fitness Training: Research and Theory.* New York: Springer-Verlag.

McRobbie, Angela. 1984. "Dance and Social Fantasy." In *Gender and Generation,* ed. Angela McRobbie and Mica Nava, 130–62. New York: Macmillan.

Messner, Michael A. 1994. "Sports and Male Domination: The Female Athlete as Contested Ideological Terrain." In *Women, Sport, and Culture,* ed. Susan Birrell and Cheryl L. Cole, 65–80. Champaign, Ill.: Human Kinetics.

Messner, Michael A., and Donald F. Sabo, eds. 1990. *Sport, Men, and the Gender Order: Critical Feminist Perspectives.* Champaign, Ill.: Human Kinetics.

Moores, Shaun. 1993. *Interpreting Audiences: The Ethnography of Media Consumption.* London: Sage.

Morgan, Kendall. 1996. "Claiming No Innocence: Working Out the Experience of Change in an All Women's Gym." Unpublished manuscript, San Diego State University, San Diego, Calif.

Morley, David. 1994. "Between the Public and the Private: The Domestic Uses of Information and Communications Technologies." In *Viewing, Reading, Listening: Audiences and Cultural Reception,* ed. Jon Cruz and Justin Lewis, 101–23. Boulder, Colo.: Westview.

Nelson, Mariah Burton. 1994. *The Stronger Women Get, the More Men Love Football: Sexism and the American Culture of Sports.* New York: Harcourt Brace.

Radner, Hilary. 1995. *Shopping Around: Feminine Culture and the Pursuit of Pleasure.* New York: Routledge.

Radway, Janice. 1984. *Reading the Romance: Women, Patriarchy and Popular Literature.* Chapel Hill: University of North Carolina Press.

Van Zoonen, Lisbet. 1994. *Feminist Media Studies*. Thousand Oaks, Calif.: Sage.

Walkerdine, V. 1986. "Video Replay: Families, Films and Fantasy." In *Formations of Fantasy*, ed. V. Burgin, J. Donald, and C. Kaplan, 167–99. London: Methuen.

Webb, Tammilee, prod. 1992. *Buns of Steel* (exercise video). Del Mar, Calif.: Webb International.

Willis, Susan. 1991. *A Primer for Daily Life*. London: Routledge.

Wolff, Janet. 1995. *Resident Alien: Feminist Cultural Criticism*. New Haven, Conn.: Yale University Press.

Young, Iris Marion. 1990. *Throwing Like a Girl and Other Essays in Feminist Philosophy and Social Theory*. Bloomington: Indiana University Press.

Building a Better Body:
Male Bodybuilding, Spectacle, and Consumption

Jon Stratton

Bodybuilding and Commodity Spectacle

In 1893, Chicago held the World's Columbian Exposition. As an idea it was by no means original. The first of the expositions designed to celebrate the commodities that were the consequence of the new mass-production techniques was the Great Exhibition held at Crystal Palace in London in 1851. Here, the guiding purpose had been to revere the new production technologies and machines. As Thomas Richards tells it, the Great Exhibition "assembled the dominant institutions and vested interests of mid-Victorian England to pay homage to the way commodities were produced." Prince Albert had envisaged the exhibition as a lesson in the production of things. However, "the planning commission wanted to divide finished articles into departments for the sake of presenting them to consumers in the most convenient way possible." The consequence of the planning commission's victory was that "the Crystal Palace was a monument to consumption, the first of its kind, a place where the combined mythologies of consumerism appeared in concentrated form." The general public flocked to view the displays. For Richards, what is so striking about the Great Exhibition was "the use of the commodity as a semiotic medium—as icon, commemorative, utopia, language, phenomenology, annunciation; in a word, as spectacle."[1]

A year after the Great Exhibition, the first department store was opened in Paris. Rosalind Williams sums up the environment of department stores as "places where consumers are an audience to be entertained by commodities, where selling is mingled with amusement, where arousal of free-floating desire is as important as immediate purchase of particular items." In 1855 the first Paris exposition was held. Here, unlike at the Great Exhibition, price tags were placed on the displayed commodities. By the Paris exposition of 1900, Williams argues, "consumer goods, rather than other facets of culture, [had become] focal points for desire."[2] Three strands were interwoven in the establishment of twentieth-century Western commodity culture: desire, fantasy, and spectacle.

The 1900 Paris exposition's emphasis on the commodity as a spectacle set into fantasy played out what Karl Marx has theorized more generally as commodity fetishism. Marx's starting point in *Capital* is to ask why it is that

151

consumers experience a commodity as a thing in its own right, having no history of production. As Marx puts it, the commodity is "a mysterious thing simply because in it the social character of men's labour appears to them as an objective character stamped upon the product of that labour."[3] It is the understanding of the commodity as having a sui generis existence that Marx describes as commodity fetishism.[4] He argues that this understanding is a general result of capitalist exchange. The commodity bought from a shop does not show the history of its production. The worker may spend her or his workweek laboring in a factory to produce commodities, but when she or he goes to a shop to buy something the commodity being bought does not remind the worker of her or his labor and does not seem to have an origin outside of the shop. The consequence is that social relations in capitalist society are mediated by commodities rather than thought of as the consequence of the organization of labor in capitalism. In short, the commodity is naturalized.

It was not only manufactured products that got caught up in the new consumerist system. Writing specifically about the American experience, Mark Seltzer argues, "If turn-of-the-century American culture is alternatively described as naturalist, as machine culture, and as the culture of consumption, what binds together these apparently alternative descriptions is the notion *that bodies and persons are things that can be made.*"[5] What Seltzer is describing here is the generalization of the ethos of manufacturing. Even bodies began to be thought of as things that could be made, as, in short, products, and these products were subjected to the same spectacularizing processes as other consumer products.

At the Chicago's World Columbian Exposition two events took place that, retrospectively, may be understood as important moments in the quite different histories of the spectacularization of the female and male bodies.[6] One was the first performance of belly dancing in the United States. This took place as a part of the Egyptian, Persian, and Algerian exhibits.[7] Americans rapidly identified belly dancing as a form of sexual exhibitionism and, Americanized as "cooch dancing," it immediately became a standard feature of burlesque. In Robert C. Allen's words, "The cooch dance linked the sexual display of the female performer and the scopic desire of the male patron in a more direct and intimate fashion than any previous feature of burlesque."[8] In this, cooch dancing marked an important step in the development of the striptease, which, in its American history, was established around 1917.[9]

Cooch dancing and striptease provided a focus for the more general eroticization of the female body that was taking place in tandem with the spectacularization of commodities throughout the second half of the nineteenth century. However, it is the other event that is most important for this essay. As Kenneth Dutton tells the story:

> In 1893, the young Florenz Ziegfeld Jr. was desperately seeking original stage acts for the opening of his father's new Trocadero Theater in Chicago, which was to be one of the main venues of the World's Columbian Exposition. Having scoured Europe without much success, Ziegfeld found himself in the Casino Theater in New York where the musical farce *Adonis* was playing. At the end of each performance the curtain would be lowered on the principal actor who stood on a pedestal posed as a statue, then raised again to reveal that the actor had been replaced by . . . Eugen Sandow.[10]

Sandow had been born Friedrich Müller in Königsberg, East Prussia, in 1867. Starting out as a circus acrobat, he became an assistant to the stage strongman Professor Louis Attila. In 1887, at the Royal Aquarium in London, Müller defeated the stage strongman "Cyclops" (Frank Bienkowski of Poland), who described himself as "The Strongest Man in the World," in a test of strength.[11] When Ziegfeld saw him, he reacted at once "not merely to Sandow's performance, but to the enthusiastic response of the female members of the audience."[12] Clearly, the connections among the display of the male muscled body, male beauty, and female desire were already being made. Ziegfeld signed Sandow up to appear at the Trocadero.

It is at this historical moment that we find a new interest in the display of the male body. Ziegfeld promoted Sandow "not as the world's strongest, but as the world's *best-developed* man," in this way exploiting "the new fascination of audiences with the public display of an outstanding physique."[13] Sandow's act now hardly involved any feats of strength. Rather, it consisted of a series of poses. Following his success at the Trocadero, Sandow signed a four-year contract with Ziegfeld, who toured him through both the United States and England. The tremendous popularity of Sandow's show can be gauged by the fact that Ziegfeld himself made a quarter of a million dollars from the enterprise, and Sandow much more.[14] Ziegfeld went on to start the Ziegfeld Follies in 1907 on the model of the Folies Bergère, in this way capitalizing on and reinforcing the combination of fantasy, desire, and spectacle around the female body, but that is a part of the other story.[15]

Sandow parted company with Ziegfeld in 1896. In the same year, Sandow was featured in short films for both the Biograph Studios and Vitascope, and Sandow himself began to use a film of himself in his act. He continued to tour Britain and the United States until 1902. Subsequently, he visited Australia and New Zealand. In 1904, Sandow toured South Africa. In 1897, he opened his first Institute of Physical Culture in London. Then, as David Chapman remarks, "at the height of its popularity, there were twenty Sandow Institutes all over the British Isles, six of them in London alone."[16] In 1899, Sandow even pioneered mail-order physical culture with his *Half-Crown Postal Course*. Sandow died in London in 1925.

There are two periods in the history of bodybuilding as a spectacle. The first dates to around the beginning of the twentieth century and originates in the career of Sandow. However, Sandow was not the first bodybuilder. Alan Klein recounts this history:

> The earliest and most successful protagonist of bodybuilding was George Winship. His is an oft-told story in bodybuilding. Entering Harvard University in 1853, Winship was allegedly the puniest member of his class, easily bullied by others. Determined to stop his victimization he took on weight training, becoming known locally as the "Roxbury Hercules."[17]

This story has a mythic quality to it: the topos of the bullied weakling who rebuilds his body to turn the tables on his tormentors was also the centerpiece of Charles Atlas's later advertising campaigns. Regardless of its facticity, the story does suggest a prehistory to bodybuilding. Klein remarks that "the groundwork [for bodybuilding] was first laid in the fusion of the look of robust muscularity with ideological religious purity."[18] What was added to bodybuilding around the time of Sandow was the importance of display. What was subtracted was the connection with religious purity. It was this display, in the mirror, for an audience, and, later, on film, that was a central component in the renovation of bodybuilding as a spectacle in parallel with the establishment of the manufactured commodity as a spectacle.

Display was central to the new world of commodity spectacle. Integral to this transformation was the changing role of advertising. As Richards puts it, "Just ten years after the Great Exhibition closed its doors, the aim of advertising was no longer exposure but exposition." Advertising took on the role of allying commodities to fantasy and desire through its mode of display. In doing this it picked up and generalized what the Great Exhibition, and the later expositions, had started. Noting the Victorian liking for spectacle, Richards argues that "display, extravagance, and excess survived—but less for the sake of those who staged the spectacle than for the sake of the spectacle itself."[19] This new spectacle was the commodity spectacle expressed through advertising. Although not, in a direct way, linked to advertising, present-day bodybuilding expresses the same spectacular concerns. Klein begins his ethnography of bodybuilding, *Little Big Men*, with this thumbnail sketch:

Bodybuilding is a subculture of hyperbole. In its headlong rush to acquire flesh, everything about this subculture exploits grandiosity and excess. Not only are the bodies in this world large, but even the descriptions of them are extravagant. The goals of competitive bodybuilders are not simply to be champions but to become Mr. Olympias and Mr. Universes. There is no room for understatement in bodybuilding, no room for depth where surface rules. It is as if bodybuilding took as its modus operandi the advertising slogan mouthed by tennis star Andre Agassi, "Image is everything."[20]

Here we have a reading of bodybuilding that identifies precisely those elements of display, extravagance, and excess that are so central to the world of commodity spectacle. Moreover, Klein's simile makes the connection with advertising, and certainly advertising provides a historical context for the centrality of display in modern bodybuilding. Klein's description is of male bodybuilding in the late 1980s, but it applies to bodybuilding from the 1890s onward. While the female body in general was becoming eroticized as the site of male desire from around that time, a myth of the male body as a product and as a spectacular commodity was developing a limited circulation.

The second period in the history of bodybuilding as a spectacle began in the 1970s. Klein argues: "Dating to the award-winning film *Pumping Iron* in the mid-1970s, the subculture started to gain wide visibility. It has only been within the past decade that bodybuilding has been popularized through its milder variation, fitness training."[21] *Pumping Iron* was released in 1977. In order to understand the success of the film, we must look at the context in which it was released. Although display had been central to bodybuilding since the days of Sandow, in mainstream everyday life, including advertising, the male body was hidden. Women were targeted as the consumers of personal commodities and women's bodies, eroticized in the male gaze since the mid-nineteenth century, were used to sell commodities to men. Whereas women were thought of as having a "passive" desire, which meant that they could gaze on other women's bodies without getting aroused, "active" male desire meant that the male gaze on male bodies was thought to be problematic. There is no room here to discuss this history other than to signal the complicated association of bodybuilding as a spectacle with homosexual desire and with claims about the homosexuality of bodybuilders. The important point, for my purposes here, is that, from the late 1960s and early 1970s on, the expanding consumer industries started targeting men to be consumers of personal commodities and the advertising industry began to display seminaked and naked male bodies.[22] The popularity of *Pumping Iron* needs to be understood in the context of this new visibility of the male body,

155

as does the generalized acceptance of bodybuilding by men as a part of fitness regimes. As it entered the world of commodity spectacle more directly through personal consumer goods aimed at men and through the use of male bodies in advertising, so the male body got caught up in the extravagance and excess, and image, that mark the spectacle and that are acted out in the practice of bodybuilding. So generalized was this phenomenon that *Life* magazine could claim that bodybuilding had become the sport of the 1980s.[23]

The key to the spectacle of Sandow, and to twentieth-century male bodybuilding generally, lies in the promotional description of Sandow as the world's best-developed man. As we have seen, Richards argues that the spectacularization of the commodity lay in its use as a semiotic medium. The same is true of the body. For the male viewer, the meanings articulated with the ostensibly not eroticized, seminaked bodybuilt male body and the eroticized, seminaked female body have been quite different from each other. Where the female body was associated with male desire and consumption, and women were thought of ideologically as consumers, the male body was associated with productive labor, men being thought of ideologically as workers. The spectacle of the bodybuilt male body condensed and narrativized a story that involves labor, the natural, the manufactured, and the commodity and that may be understood through both Marx's theory of commodity fetishism and the importance of desire and fantasy in the construction of spectacle. In the first place, however, we have the notion of bodily "development." In modern Western thought, development has a utopian ring to it. It connects with the ideas of progress, of modernization brought about by building or rebuilding and, ultimately, with the idea of "developed countries."

The commodified world is thought of as fundamentally unnatural in the sense that it is composed of manufactured commodities. The satisfaction brought by these commodities is a consequence of their connection to a regime of fantasy allied to desire. For the satisfaction to be realized, the desire must be naturalized, which means that the fantasy must, itself, take on a natural quality. Here, of course, lies the paradox, for a fantasy does not remain a fantasy if it is realized. In this context we can understand the bodybuilt body as mythically attempting to combine the natural and the unnatural. The body was indisputably natural in the modern discourse of nature. However, the developed body, the bodybuilt body, is manufactured, worked on by labor. It is, in this sense, unnatural, a manufactured product—as a spectacle it can also be a commodity that, in Sandow's case as in the later cases of Arnold Schwarzenegger and Sylvester Stallone in a more indirect way, people pay to gaze upon.

In the first place, then, the bodybuilt body seeks to resolve the unnatural, in the sense of the manufactured, into the natural. In this mythic resolution the commodity would no longer be a fetish, in Marx's sense, because it would really be sui generis, and therefore natural. At the same time, the bodybuilt body also celebrates its builtness. It is the *developed* body, the body that has been worked over by labor. In this aspect, it asserts its productness, offering itself, like a commodity, as a spectacle to be desired; not necessarily to be "acquired," by way of emulation, by the one, either male or female, doing the desiring or, for that matter, to be "had" sexually—though this is one theme in *The Rocky Horror Picture Show* (1975)—but to be consumed *as* a spectacular creation of labor. Here, then, we have a narrative about labor. In Western capitalist society the traditional ideology is that men labor while women look after the home. It is no wonder, then, that it was the male body that was spectacularized as the bodybuilt body. In capitalist society, Marx tells us, labor is alienated from the product of labor, the commodity, by the cash nexus. In the bodybuilt body, the body that labors is also the body that is built. It is a closed circuit: the body is transformed by its own labor into the manufactured body, which is, at the same time, both natural and unnatural, simply a body but also a spectacle and a commodity.

In the first place, the myth of the bodybuilt body is premised on the idea that bodies can be (re)made. In order to appreciate the profound shift involved here, we can briefly compare two texts, Mary Shelley's *Frankenstein*, published in 1818, and the film *The Rocky Horror Picture Show*, which reworks the Frankenstein story, among others. When Mary Shelley's Dr. Frankenstein puts together a human body from parts taken from other bodies, what he produces is something monstrous to behold. As Frankenstein himself exclaims, "Oh! no mortal could support the horror of that countenance."[24] It is not equivalent to the "natural" bodies of the people with whom the human yet not-human creature comes in contact. Made by a human being from parts taken from other human beings, the creature cannot, itself, be human. Dr. Frankenstein has made life in the sense of making, and giving physical functioning, to a new creature made of human parts that has its own mind. However, the creature cannot be human because it has been manufactured by a (male) human being. Its visually monstrous body expresses its "unnaturalness" as a product.

In *The Rocky Horror Picture Show*, Dr. Frank N. Furter, who describes himself as a transsexual transvestite from the planet Transylvania, makes a man who is the object of his desire. Unlike Dr. Frankenstein's unnamed "monster," which remains excluded from the cultural world created by human language, Dr. Frank N. Furter's man is called Rocky. Interestingly, this precedes Sylvester Stallone's film *Rocky* by a year, but now, in the ahistorical world of uninformed intertextuality, provides an intertextual allusion. Being given a name, Rocky is incorporated into the human world. Dr. Frankenstein's "monster" is usually depicted in film versions as scarred and deformed from its composition out of body parts. Rocky, however, is blond, tanned, and muscled. We do not know how Rocky was made, but his coming out of the tank in which he was given life swathed in bandages suggests that he, too, was made of body parts. Unlike those of Frankenstein's creation, Rocky's parts have melded perfectly and, although he tends to walk a little stiffly, you cannot see the joins. Indeed, he appears intended to be a paragon of late-twentieth-century Western male physical beauty. Certainly Frank thinks so. In *Rocky Horror* the structure of desire has shifted fundamentally from *Frankenstein.* In Shelley's novel, after rejecting its creator, the monster vows, "I will be with you on your wedding night." What this means becomes apparent when the monster murders Frankenstein's fiancée, Elizabeth, after the wedding ceremony but before the marriage can be consummated. In *Rocky Horror*, having manufactured the object of his desire, Frank takes him to the bridal suite for the night to the strains of the Wedding March. Here, the desire of the male manufacturer is linked with a conventional claim about male bodybuilding, something that springs from a combination of the importance of self-regard and the importance of display, in a structure of homosexual desire.

The Body as a Machine

Underlying the development of bodybuilding as a spectacle is the conceptual history of the body as a machine. Since the sixteenth century, the dominant metaphor for the body has been that of a machine. Although he was not the first to use the image, Descartes's *Traité de l'homme*, written in 1632 but published posthumously in 1664, helped enormously to popularize it. Whereas Descartes claimed only to be comparing the body to a machine, La Mettrie in *L'Homme machine* (1746) provided a description of the body in terms of a clockwork machine. The use of, and naturalization of, the metaphor needs to be understood in the broader context of the early-modern putting into place of the ideology of individualism, the gradual secularization of science, and the new importance of mechanism, especially as a means of timekeeping. In turn, this last paved the way for the pervasive spread of new machinery during the Industrial Revolution, which helped to reinforce the naturalization of the metaphor of the body as a machine. During the nineteenth century the machinic understanding of the body was modified to that of a productive engine, like a steam engine, which produced, conserved, and used up energy. Through this whole period the machine became the dominant metaphor for describing "nature."[25] In this machine metaphor the natural machine was thought of as a given, often as God-given, with God as (for example, in the case of Newton's defender, Samuel Clarke), the great watchmaker.[26] Thus the body could be thought of as simultaneously machinic and natural.

Toward the end of the nineteenth century the body began to be thought of as a machinic product rather than as a machine of production. Today, retaining the ideology philosophically legitimated in Cartesian dualism, the most popular metaphor is of the body as a car driven by the mind. Anthony Synnott, noting that the first Model T Fords were produced in 1907, argues that "the automobile transformed thinking about the body."[27] However, this gets the relation the wrong way around. The car provided an ideal metaphor for the body, thought of as machine, but now being thought of also as a product/commodity.

Synnott notes how John B. Watson, the founder of behaviorist psychology, who had always thought of the body as a machine, had, by 1966, come to rethink that machine as a car. As Synnott quotes Watson: "Let us try to think of man as an assembled organic machine ready to run. We mean nothing very difficult by this. Take four wheels with tires, axles, differentials, gas engine, body; put them together and we have an automobile of a sort."[28] That cars are described as having "bodies" suggests a thinking about the car in terms of a human being or other animal. The metaphor then reinforces the machinic understanding of the human body. Commenting on the popularity of the metaphor of body maintenance, Mike Featherstone points out that "the term 'body maintenance' indicates the popularity of the machine metaphor for the body. Like cars and other consumer goods, bodies require servicing, regular care and attention to preserve maximum efficacy."[29]

The prominence of the car metaphor for the body springs from the centrality of the car as a product to the organization of Fordist mass production. Henry Ford introduced the assembly-line process, which broke down production into a series of specific tasks, at his Highland Park factory in 1914 in response to the huge demand for the Model T. From this time on, the car became the metonym for the mass-produced consumer product.

A new invention in the late nineteenth century, the car was rapidly spectacularized: "Beginning in 1898 an annual Salon de l'Automobile was held in Paris to introduce the latest models to the public."[30] The opening of the 1904 Salon "was attended by 40,000 people (compared to 10,000 who went to the opening of the annual painting salon), and 30,000 came each day for the first week."[31] Williams sums up Salon, writing that "[electric] lights transformed the automobiles themselves into glittering objects of fantasy."[32] The car had already become a very powerful spectacle.

A key aspect of the manufacture of the car is that it is made up from other mass-produced parts to complete the finished product. Cars are mass-produced and specific types of cars all look more or less the same, in the same way it is sometimes claimed that within the "races" of human beings all members of a "race" look more or less alike. The metaphor can easily be stretched. Cars are a means of transport, likewise bodies transport the person—that is, the mind, the privileged portion in the Cartesian dyad—through their lives. Like the parts of cars, parts of bodies go wrong and wear out. Usually car parts can be repaired, just as when a part of the human body is sick it can be made healthy again.

Sometimes car parts can be replaced. Since the 1950s, parts of human bodies have become replaceable too. The first successful kidney transplant took place at the Peter Bent Brigham Hospital in Boston, Massachusetts, in 1954. Dr. Christiaan Barnard performed the first human heart transplant on 3 December 1967 in Cape Town, South Africa. One aspect of Shelley's nightmare about a man made from parts of other men was being realized, but in the context of the discourse of production rather than of God and a given nature. Not surprisingly, perhaps, Barnard himself made use of the car metaphor in his book *The Body Machine*, published in 1981. Here he has a chapter called "The Chassis" and sections titled "On the Road," "Body Maintenance," and "In the Workshop."[33] Coming back to the idea of body maintenance, finally it becomes no longer reasonable or possible to continue to keep up the maintenance; inverting the metaphor, we anthropomorphize cars, saying that they die on us, like our bodies.

The metaphor of the body as a car has two main components: first, the idea of the body as a machinic product; second, the new recognition that the body, like the car, is made out of parts that can be replaced. Although the metaphor may have been used earlier, it seems that the new understanding of the body as made of interchangeable parts is what gave the metaphor a general currency during the 1960s.

Bodybuilding and the Body as Product

From the start, bodybuilding was a male activity. The *Oxford English Dictionary* gives as its earliest usage of the term *bodybuilder* a quotation from the *Boston Herald* of 21 December 1890. Two of the books published under Sandow's name have titles—*Body-Building, or Man in the Making* (1905) and *The Construction and Reconstruction of the Human Body* (1907)—that signal the new understanding of the body as something that is fabricated and can be remade.[34] In his 1979 autobiography, Arnold Schwarzenegger describes his attitude toward building his body: "You work on your body the way a sculptor would work on a piece of clay or wood or steel. You rough it out—the more carefully, the more thoroughly, the better—then you start to cut and define. You work it down gradually until it's ready to be rubbed and polished."[35] Here Schwarzenegger thinks of his body as an artistic product rather than a commercial product—that is to say, something outside of the capitalist exchange system—but the dominant metaphor remains the same.

In fact, the connection with art was not new. When Sandow appeared in *Adonis*, the New York newspapers described him as "having the beauty of a work of art," with "such knots and bunches and layers of muscle [as the audience] had never before seen other than on the statue of an Achilles, a Discobolus, or the Fighting Gladiator."[36] One of Klein's respondents, clearly a professional bodybuilder, made the further connection with display explicit: "I consider myself a performer first and a bodybuilder second. Because I'm on that stage to exhibit my art, I feel a little body makeup is in order. People pay money to see a show, and I want to give them something to remember that's quality."[37] The claim that the bodybuilt body is a work of art legitimates its development for the purpose of display. Unlike art, commodities are expected to be functional, to have a purpose beyond that of spectacular display. The same is true of competitive sport, in which bodies are put into active engagement where display is secondary to the sporting activity itself. It is precisely the primacy of this element of display, which is the end product of the competitive bodybuilder's labor, that has led to the immense problems bodybuilding has had in being accepted as a sport.

The *Encyclopaedia Britannica* notes that "the modern competitive form [of bodybuilding] grew largely out of European strong-man theatrical and circus acts of the 19th century."[38] Indeed, Sandow himself "was famous for piling nineteen people (including a fat man, a minstrel, and a clown) and a dog onto a board on his back and hoisting them all in the air before an audience."[39] As we have seen, Sandow stands astride the shift from exhibitions of extraordinary strength to the new acceptance of the idea that bodies, and here in particular male bodies, could be remade. Jane Stern and Michael Stern describe Bernarr Macfadden (1868–1955) as "the father of body building as we know it."[40] Macfadden almost single-handedly popularized physical culture in the United States. Born in 1868 in the Ozarks, Macfadden had an itinerant childhood, working for his keep, after his parents separated in 1873. He was a sickly boy who, in his early teens, decided that physical fitness was the way to health. Advice on his fitness regime came from William Blaikie's 1879 book *How to Get Strong and How to Stay So*. In 1898 he started the magazine *Physical Development*. Its massive increase in circulation over its first year demonstrates not only the novel popularity of physical fitness but also the changed attitude toward the body that enabled the idea of transforming the body to catch on. From printing 25,000 copies of the January 1900 issue, Macfadden printed 40,000 of the April issue and, estimating five readers for every copy, claimed to have 550,000 readers by December.[41] In 1897 Macfadden sailed to England, where he toured to promote his fitness system; he returned again in 1912, and met there the woman who would become his third wife.

Also in 1898, Sandow started a magazine titled *Physical Culture*. In his first editorial Sandow described the ultimate aim of physical culture as "to raise the average standard of the race as a whole." The following year, *Physical Culture* was renamed *Sandow's Magazine of Physical Culture*. *Physical Development* and *Physical Culture* were preceded by a French weekly journal called *L'Athlète*, founded by Professor Edmond Desbonnet, author of, as Chapman puts it, "a seminal history of physical culture" titled *Les Rois de la Force* (1911), in 1896.[42] The proliferation of such magazines suggests that bodybuilding became a popular activity among men in the 1890s.

Physical Development was a mouthpiece of the natural health movement and, subtitled *The Personal Problem Magazine*, "tackled everything from piles and sagging chins to inferiority complexes, recommending a combination of whole-grain diet, sunlight and exercise to cure all ailments."[43] In Macfadden's eyes a male body that was fit had to have some degree of visible musculature. To put it differently, the secular connotation of physical health supplanted the religious connotation of purity. The change in orientation signaled in the title of Blaikie's book and that of Macfadden's magazine marks an important turning point. The strongman's body had not been of interest in its own right, but as the source of his ability to perform exceptional feats. Strongmen were themselves exceptions. In contrast, the physical culturists asserted that everybody should be fit and, starting with Macfadden, mounted demonstrations of fit, bodybuilt bodies to show what could be achieved. Shifting from exhibitions as such, in 1903 Macfadden staged the first American physique contest as a way of promoting his magazine. The winner was named "the most perfectly developed man in America," a title that echoes Ziegfeld's promotional description of Sandow ten years earlier.[44]

Around the beginning of the twentieth century, there was "an efflorescence of periodicals often copiously illustrated with physique photographs including in most cases those of the magazine's owner."[45] It must be assumed that these magazines, with their photos of almost naked muscled men, were not being bought and read only by physical culture participants. In these photos we have the first displays of the male body with a legitimating excuse. In 1901, predating Macfadden's contest by two years, Sandow held a physique competition at the Royal Albert Hall in London. Here, "some 15,000 spectators assembled to watch the 60 finalists chosen by Sandow from various regional trials throughout Britain as they were judged on the balance and tone of their muscular development, general health and skin condition."[46] Clearly, physique competitions were as popular as the earlier staged displays of Sandow's own body.

We can date an American interest in competitive male bodybuilding from Macfadden's 1903 contest. The first Mr. America contest was held in 1939, sponsored by the American Athletic Union "in an attempt to organize what was becoming the widespread grass-roots phenomenon of physical culture exhibitions."[47] Then, "by 1947, thanks to the organisational flair of Joe Weider's brother Ben, Canada and the USA had joined to form the International Federation of Bodybuilders (IFBB)."[48] With the increasing internationalization of the IFBB, the Mr America contest was renamed the Mr. Universe contest in the 1960s. In the late 1960s, "the new international title of 'Mr Olympia' had been created to bring together the world's top professional bodybuilders including 'Mr Universe' winners."[49] These developments illustrate the spread of bodybuilding through, in particular, the Western world and its increasing popularity as a competitive sport.

Male bodybuilding also spread as a noncompetitive activity from around the 1930s. Its most important popularizer was Charles Atlas (1893–1972). Atlas, born Angelo Siciliano, won Macfadden's "America's Most Developed Man" contest in 1922 and, in 1929, he "and a young advertising man, [Charles P.] Roman, decided to incorporate and build up a business of Atlas home-study programs of isotonic exercises and nutrition tips."[50] Atlas's course used a system known as dynamic tension. According to Robert Ernst in his biography of Macfadden, the system had originally been put forward by Macfadden himself in *Physical Culture*.[51] It was marketed to young men and in many advertisements used a story the basis of which Atlas claimed was true and had happened to him. This involved a ninety-seven-pound weakling having sand kicked in his face on the beach, being humiliated, and having his girlfriend leave him for the bully who did it. Atlas claimed that taking his dynamic tension course would allow a man to be sure that something like this would never happen again. This narrative of shame, thwarted desire, and machismo associated bodybuilding with the earlier ideology of

163

strength, as well as with a claim to the desirability of the displayed male bodybuilt body.

In another of Atlas's advertisements, the copy reads: "Let me make you a new man in just 15 minutes a day. Yes, Sir, *That's my job!* I 'RE-BUILD' skinny run-down weaklings—fellows so embarrassed by their condition that they always hang back, let others walk off with the best jobs, the prettiest girls, the most fun and popularity." *The Rocky Horror Picture Show* picks up on the semantic ambiguities of "mak[ing] you a new man" in a song in which Dr. Frank N. Furter associates himself with both Charles Atlas and God, announcing: "In just seven days I can make you a man." Although Frankenstein's and Frank N. Furter's projects are more fundamental than Atlas's, the comparison is a good one. Atlas's advertising and the popularity of his course, which was advertised until well into the 1960s, showed the extent to which male bodybuilding, the idea that the male body was malleable and could be improved to give greater strength and health but also to look better, was becoming accepted among the general population.

Although the dominant concern in bodybuilding is with the overall image of the body, nevertheless this image is achieved through a concentration on body parts. Although the body's parts, as the bodybuilder thinks of the body, are not to be exchanged like those of a car, the body is nevertheless divided up into parts that can be worked on, improved as car engines can be worked on to give them more power. As Alan Mansfield and Barbara McGinn write:

> Body building is about developing individual body parts into a symmetrical, well-balanced whole, but it is important to note that although symmetry and proportion, that is, the way muscles and muscle groupings relate to each other, are crucial things for the bodybuilder's body, the discourse of bodybuilding produces a structure of fragmentation and objectification of the body. Basic and isolation exercises allow the bodybuilder to experience individual muscles and groups of muscles.[52]

These built body parts can be narcissistically fetishized by their owners. Mansfield and McGinn quote Carol Mock, a top American female body builder: "I loved training my arms. Watching my biceps and triceps literally explode, really turned me on."[53] However, perhaps the most well-known example comes from Arnold Schwarzenegger himself, who, in *Pumping Iron*, describes his experience of the pump like this: "Your muscles get a really tight feeling, like your skin is going to explode any minute, you know, it's really tight . . . it feels fantastic. It's as satisfying to me as, uh, coming is. You know, as ah, having sex with a woman and coming."

What I am arguing here is that the fragmentation of the body into parts is a consequence of the understanding of the body as a machine and is reinforced by the body-as-product being thought of in the analogy with a car. The metaphoric interchangeability of the car body and the human body allows for puns such as the one used in the title of a General Motors promotional and informational film called *The Bodybuilders*. The film's subtitle explains that it is about *The People from Fisher Body Who Help Bring a Modern Automobile "Up from the Clay."*[54] In addition to its description of how car bodies are modeled there is, here, a biblical connotation of godly creation that mystifies the labor process of (car) body production.

Seltzer suggests that "these technologies of regeneration, of man in the making, make visible the rewriting of the natural and of the natural body in the idiom of scientific management, systems of measurement and standardization, and the disciplines of the machine process."[55] The making of the body-as-product is described using the rhetorics that were developing around the increasingly automated mass-production practices. Scientific management, popularized in Frederick Winslow Taylor's *The Principles of Scientific Management* (1911), which disciplined the bodies of the workers in the cause of increased efficiency, became a strategy in the remaking of the body itself.[56] Harvey Green has noted how the idea of the body as a machine intersected with the new concern with efficiency:

> Among health advocates and reformers, efficient management of the body entailed avoiding waste of energy: the "efficient life" was as important as the "strenuous life." But views about the best way to achieve efficiency varied. Roosevelt, Sargent, Macfadden, and others argued that exercise—preferably in the outdoors, and especially in the wilds—built strength and supplemented the body's store of energy, or at least made it possible to realize the body's full potential.[57]

Here, the idea of the efficient body is played out through the metaphor of the body as a productive engine.

Stuart Ewen has described how the practices of scientific management have been reapplied to the process of (re)making the body. He outlines the daily gym routine in the mid-1980s of Raymond H-, a thirty-four-year-old middle-management employee of a large New York City investment firm. Ewen sums up the body Raymond H- wants as lean and hard: "The goal he seeks is more about *looking* than *touching*."[58] In order to acquire the desired look, Raymond H- uses rational management techniques:

> To achieve his goal, he approaches his body piece by piece; with each [gym] machine he performs a discrete task. Along the way he also assumes the job of inspector, surveying the results of each task in the mirrors that surround him. The division of labor, the fragmentation of the work process, and the regulating function of continual measurement and observation—all fundamental to the principles of "scientific management"—are intrinsic to this form of recreation.[59]

Ewen goes on to note that Raymond H-'s body ideal is "an aestheticized tribute to the broken-down work processes of the assembly line."[60] Here, assembly-line practices are used to rebuild the body bit by bit. We should remember that the assembly line was first successfully developed by Henry Ford to build cars, which, as we have seen, in turn became the metaphor for the body as a machinic product.

In this regime of scientific management, Raymond H- takes on the job of the inspector himself—something made possible by the presence of the mirrors.[61] In *Scientific American*'s three-volume encyclopedic publication from 1915, *The Book of Progress*, there is a description of the "Gilbreth Chronometer," invented by the management expert Frank Gilbreth. This was, essentially, a camera linked to a clock designed for time-motion studies on industrial workers: "Any workman may, for a time, deceive an inexperienced efficiency engineer . . . but the camera cannot be deceived. . . . The film records faithfully every movement made, and subsequent analysis and study reveals exactly how many of these movements were necessary and how many were purposely slow or useless."[62] If the mirrored walls of the gym allow self-inspection, film enables others to inspect. Here it is the labor process itself that is inspected; in other contexts it was the bodybuilt body that was coming under scrutiny as a spectacle. From the 1970s, film was the medium that catered to a new general interest in inspecting male bodybuilt bodies. As this body was displayed and became the object of a general gaze, so its laborious building mysteriously disappeared.

The Mainstreaming of the Bodybuilding Film

Through the 1970s, the spectacle of the male bodybuilt body became normalized at the same time that gym work was becoming generally acceptable as a part of the male fitness regime. As I have remarked, both these developments need to be set in the context of the new concentration on the male body in advertising as part of the extension of the sale of personal consumer goods from women to men. Film was where this normalization was most obvious. There was an extensive prehistory of male bodybuilt bodies in film, but, at least in the English-speaking world, muscle-man films were of limited cult interest. Sandow himself appeared in a film in 1894. Perhaps the most well-known of the pre-1970s film-star bodybuilders was Steve Reeves, whose cult films are mentioned in one of Dr. Frank N. Furter's songs in *The Rocky Horror Picture Show*. Reeves was a former Mr. Universe. His first film performance was in Ed Wood Jr.'s *Jail Bait* (1954). After this he went to Italy, where there was a long tradition of muscled bodies in film, dating back to Giovanni Pastrone's *Cabiria* (1914).[63] Reeves's first, and best-known, Italian film was *Hercules* (1959). The sequel, *Hercules Unchained*, was released in 1960. However, it was Arnold Schwarzenegger, and subsequently Sylvester Stallone, who rode to fame on the new acceptance of the spectacle of the bodybuilt body.

Schwarzenegger's first film, in which he used the stage name Arnold Strong, was the comedy *Hercules Goes to New York* (1970), in which he paid homage to Steve Reeves's most celebrated film role. In the film, Schwarzenegger plays Hercules, who, bored with life on Mount Olympus, disobeys Zeus's wishes and visits New York. Here he gets into a variety of scrapes, including losing a strongman competition when Juno takes away his divinely given powers. This film functions within the cult film genre of bodybuilder films. The first generally accepted celebration of the built male body as spectacle was the film *Pumping Iron*, released in 1977. Schwarzenegger had already starred in an earlier, and less well-known, film in which bodybuilding was the backdrop, *Stay Hungry* (1976). In a prescient moment in that film there is a remarkable chase scene in which the bodybuilders burst out of their competition hall and run down the city streets. As they realize that they are the subjects of fascinated stares, they begin to stop and pose.

Pumping Iron followed in the wake of the success of a 1974 photo-essay book of the same name that also starred Schwarzenegger. As Stern and Stern put it: "By the time [Schwarzenegger] retired as six-times-undefeated Mr. Olympia in 1975, body building was out of the closet."[64] As Schwarzenegger makes clear in his autobiography, his primary concern was with size. The bigger he could build his muscles, the more impressive his body would be. Although size was not everything—for example, both cut and symmetry are important—it was Schwarzenegger's hugeness that marked his body as a limit case for the male body as it became generally accepted as a spectacle on film. In competitive bodybuilding, judging was always based on appearance, so the generalized spectacularization of the bodybuilder's body was an extension of this gaze. Schwarzenegger had won his first major bodybuilding competition—Junior Mr. Europe—in 1965. In 1969, when he had won the National Amateur Bodybuilding Association's Mr. Universe title in London, Schwarzenegger was contacted by Joe Weider, publisher of *Muscle Builder* and *Mr. America* magazines and an entrepreneur in the bodybuilding world following in the footsteps of Bernarr Macfadden. Weider wanted Schwarzenegger to go to Florida and compete in the IFBB Mr. Universe competition. Schwarzenegger came in second, but stayed in the United States and won the competition the following year.

Pumping Iron was the record of a Mr. Universe bodybuilding contest and, as such, occupied a halfway house between the older, specialized world of competitive bodybuilding and the new experience of the public spectacle of the male body. In an important way, the film successes of Schwarzenegger, and Sylvester Stallone, were not prefigured by the 1930s and 1940s Hollywood success of Johnny Weissmuller. Weissmuller played Tarzan in twelve films, from *Tarzan, the Ape Man* (1932) to *Tarzan and the Mermaids* (1948). However, Weissmuller was generically quite different from Schwarzenegger. Weissmuller was an athlete, not a bodybuilder. He had been a freestyle swimming champion and won three gold medals in the 1924 Olympics and two in the 1928 Olympics. Although his success prefigured that of Schwarzenegger, and prefigured the spectacularization of the male body, Weissmuller's "look" was much more of the fit and healthy male body—the body of physical culture—rather than the built male body per se. Edward Said has described Weissmuller's Tarzan like this: "Unlike any of the other movie Tarzans who followed him, . . . he was not at all muscle-bound; until he got older and fatter his swimmer's physique blended perfectly with the general mystery of his origins and the source of his power. Everything about Weissmuller was flowing, harmonious and natural."[65]

Weissmuller's Tarzan was an exemplification of the supremely fit but still "natural" male body (in this way being a part of the older, physical culture-oriented, discursive order), whereas many of Schwarzenegger's roles perform limit cases of the spectacularized built male body, from the myth of the relation between strength and power in *Conan the Barbarian* (1982) to the reworking of the post-sixteenth-century myth of the body as machine in *The Terminator* (1984) and *Terminator 2: Judgment Day* (1991). The last two films have been written about often by authors analyzing the cyborgian qualities of the terminator. Although this is a relevant insight, the Schwarzenegger/terminator figure also plays with questions about the limits of bodybuilt bodyness and the ways in which the manufactured body, the body-as-product, already bears the signification of a machine.

In the late 1980s, Schwarzenegger moved away from playing roles designed around his bodybuilt body. The more banal of these films in their use of the bodybuilt body are *Commando* (1985) and *Predator* (1987). What is most surprising about *Twins* (1988) and *Kindergarten Cop* (1990) is how "normal" he looks. Much of this normalization has to do with the acceptance of the bodybuilt male body as a part of everyday life. Certainly Schwarzenegger is still massively developed physically in these films, but the general acceptance of the muscled male body means that Schwarzenegger's body—and those of Stallone and the other male bodybuilt film stars—is now only relatively exceptional in a world where recreational weights work is a standard aspect of the male fitness regime.

Conclusion

Dutton argues that the interest in the developed body in the twentieth century has been primarily an effect of the new technology of photography: "A new concern with supposed 'realism' coming in the wake of the camera has combined with the growing social expectations of the twentieth century to 'democratise' the developed body and make it an accessible object of mass culture and consumerism."[66] However, this does not adequately recognize the profound cultural changes involved in the establishment of consumerism. It is these that I have discussed in this essay in terms of spectacle. From the early years of the twentieth century, the interest in the spectacle of the male body, from both men and women—and I have not had room here to delineate the complexities involved in desire and the gaze around the bodybuilt body—was in the display of the muscled, "developed" body. Photography and film greatly aided the general availability of this display.

The new understanding of the body—in particular the male body—as a product, rather than simply the producer of products, was fundamental to the development of bodybuilding. From the 1890s, the bodybuilt male was being thought of as a spectacle and, in this way, was allied to the development of a culture of consumption promoted through commodity spectacle. With the new emphasis on the male body as a site of consumption in the late 1960s, the acceptance of the spectacle of the male bodybuilt body started to be generalized, something exemplified in the popularity of films starring male bodybuilders from the mid-1970s.

The bodybuilt body is alienated from the self, a product that can be worked on and examined in a mirror or in photographs or on film. As Klein sums it up: "Alienation is, in [bodybuilding], brought to new heights. The self is distinguished from the body, the body is beaten into submission."[67] At this point, the developed body was caught within the modern dichotomy of natural and unnatural. Richard Dyer puts it like this:

> The point is that muscles are biological, hence "natural," and we persist in habits of thought, especially in the area of sexuality and gender, whereby what can be shown to be natural must be accepted as given and inevitable. . . . However developed muscularity—muscles that show—is not in truth natural at all, but is rather achieved.[68]

The naturalization of the male bodybuilt body in the twentieth-century West operates in the context of the naturalization of consumerism and of the commodities that are consumed. In this process the labor power that manufactures the product is mystified. The traditional gendering of the bodybuilt body as male is, among other things, a function of the ideological claim that commercial labor is a male domain. Building one's own body is, at one and the same time, the epitome of unalienated labor in that it does not involve the cash nexus directly and the most profoundly alienating experience in that the body is treated as a product. As Dyer writes, "The muscleman is the end-product of his own activity of muscle-building."[69] Like the consumer who hopes that the purchase of a commodity will improve her or his life, the bodybuilder hopes that his labor will improve his body as he develops it. Here, the distinction between production and consumption is elided as the bodybuilder acquires his rebuilt body. Its display, as Charles Atlas implied to his great success, will bring the best jobs, the prettiest girls, and the most fun and popularity.

Notes

1. Thomas Richards, *The Commodity Culture of Victorian England: Advertising and Spectacle 1851–1914* (London: Verso, 1991), 3, 32, 66.
2. Rosalind Williams, *Dream Worlds: Mass Consumption in Late-Nineteenth-Century France* (Berkeley: University of California Press, 1981), 67, 66.
3. Karl Marx, *Capital*, vol. 1 (London: Lawrence & Wishart, 1970), 77.
4. A good recent discussion of commodity fetishism can be found in Sut Jhally, *The Codes of Advertising: Fetishism and the Political Economy of Meaning in Consumer Society* (New York: Routledge, 1990).
5. Mark Seltzer, *Bodies and Machines* (New York: Routledge, 1992), 152.

6. I discuss both these histories in Jon Stratton, *The Desirable Body: Cultural Fetishism and the Erotics of Consumption* (Manchester: Manchester University Press, 1996).

7. On this history, see Robert C. Allen, *Horrible Prettiness: Burlesque and American Culture* (Chapel Hill: University of North Carolina Press, 1991): 225–32.

8. Ibid., 231.

9. Ibid., 246–49.

10. Kenneth R. Dutton, *The Perfectible Body: The Western Ideal of Male Physical Development* (St. Leonards: Allen & Unwin, 1995), 121.

11. Ibid., 105.

12. Ibid., 121.

13. Ibid.

14. Ibid.

15. On the Ziegfeld Follies, see Allen, *Horrible Prettiness*, 243–46.

16. David Chapman, *Sandow the Magnificent: Eugen Sandow and the Beginnings of Bodybuilding* (Urbana: University of Illinois Press, 1994), 103. All of the information in this paragraph comes from this important biography of Sandow.

17. Alan Klein, *Little Big Men: Bodybuilding Subculture and Gender Construction* (Albany: State University of New York Press, 1993), 34.

18. Ibid.

19. Richards, *The Commodity Culture*, 70, 55–56.

20. Klein, *Little Big Men*, 3.

21. Ibid., 18.

22. On these issues, see Stratton, *The Desirable Body*, chap. 6.

23. Klein, *Little Big Men*, 38.

24. Mary Shelley, *Frankenstein* (Oxford: Oxford University Press, 1980 [1818]), 58.

25. On this history, see Francois Jacob, *The Logic of Life: A History of Heredity* (New York: Pantheon, 1974). See also Georges Canguilhem, "Machine and Organism," in *Incorporations*, ed. Jonathan Crary and Sanford Kwinter (New York: Urzone, 1992), 45–69.

26. On the argument from design, see Samuel Macey, *Clocks and the Cosmos: The Time in Western Life and Thought* (Hamden, Conn.: Archon, 1980).

27. Anthony Synnott, *The Body Social: Symbolism, Self and Society* (London: Routledge, 1993), 28.

28. Quoted in ibid.

29. Mike Featherstone, "The Body in Consumer Culture," in *The Body: Social Process and Cultural Theory*, ed. Mike Featherstone, Mike Hepworth, and Bryan S. Turner (London: Sage, 1991), 182.

30. Williams, *Dream Worlds*, 87.

31. Ibid.

32. Ibid.

33. Barnard's book cited in Synnott, *The Body Social*, 30.

34. Chapman, in *Sandow the Magnificent*, presents a list of works by Sandow (219).

35. Arnold Schwarzenegger (with Douglas Ken Hall), *Arnold: The Education of a Bodybuilder* (London: Sphere, 1979), 23.

36. Quoted in Dutton, *The Perfectible Body*, 121.

37. Quoted in Klein, *Little Big Men*, 44.

38. "Body Building," in *Encyclopaedia Britannica Micropaedia: Ready Reference*, vol. 2. (Chicago: Encyclopaedia Britannica, 1995), 317.

39. Jane Stern and Michael Stern, *The Encyclopedia of Bad Taste* (New York: HarperCollins, 1990), 46.

40. Ibid.

41. These figures are from Robert Ernst, *Weakness Is a Crime: The Life of Bernarr Macfadden* (Syracuse, N.Y.: Syracuse University Press, 1991), 24. This is a better biography of Macfadden than William Hunt's *Body Love: The Amazing Career of Bernarr Macfadden* (Bowling Green, Ohio: Bowling Green State University Popular Press, 1989).

42. Chapman, *Sandow the Magnificent*, 11. The other details here are from pp. 108–10.

43. Stern and Stern, *The Encyclopedia of Bad Taste*, 46.

44. Quoted without attribution in "Body Building," 317.

45. Dutton, *The Perfectible Body*, 125.

46. Ibid., 128.

47. Stern and Stern, *The Encyclopedia of Bad Taste*, 47.

48. Dutton, *The Perfectible Body*, 141.

49. Ibid.

50. "Charles Atlas," in *Encyclopaedia Britannica Micropaedia: Ready Reference*, vol. 1 (Chicago: Encyclopaedia Britanicca, 1995), 674. Dutton claims that Siciliano won Macfadden's competition in 1921; *The Perfectible Body*, 129.

51. Ernst, *Weakness Is a Crime*, 114. This was another Macfadden magazine that had the same title as Sandow's.

52. Alan Mansfield and Barbara McGinn, "Pumping Irony: The Muscular and the Feminine," in *Body Matters: Essays on the Sociology of the Body*, ed. Sue Scott and David Morgan (London: Falmer, 1993), 53–54.

53. Quoted in ibid., 54.

54. The video is by General Motors Corporation, Fisher Body Division (undated).

55. Seltzer, *Bodies and Machines*, 154.

56. On scientific management, see Harry Braverman, *Labor and Monopoly Capital: The Degradation of the Work in the Twentieth Century* (New York: Monthly Review Press, 1974). On contemporaneous Continental developments, see Martha Braun, *Picturing Time: The Work of Etienne-Jules Marey (1830–1904)* (Chicago: University of Chicago Press, 1992).

57. Harvey Green, *Fit for America: Health, Fitness, Sport and American Society* (New York: Pantheon, 1986).

58. Stuart Ewen, *All Consuming Images: The Politics of Style in Contemporary Culture* (New York: Basic Books, 1988), 188, 189.

59. Ibid., 189–190.

60. Ibid., 190.

61. The connection between bodybuilding and scientific management can be usefully thought about in terms of Michel Foucault's idea of the disciplinary gaze. A start in applying Foucault's thought to bodybuilding can be found in Alan Aycock, "The Confession of the Flesh: Disciplinary Gaze in Casual Bodybuilding," *Play and Culture* 5, no. 4 (1992): 338–57.

62. This information and this quote from *The Book of Progress*, comes from Stuart Ewen and Elizabeth Ewen, *Channels of Desire: Mass Images and the Shaping of American Consciousness* (Minneapolis: University of Minnesota Press, 1992), 36.

63. This tradition is discussed in Dutton, *The Perfectible Body*, 160–61.

64. Stern and Stern, *The Encyclopedia of Bad Taste*, 49.

65. Edward Said, "Jungle Calling," *Interview* 19, no. 6 (1989): 64.

66. Dutton, *The Perfectible Body*, 14.

67. Klein, *Little Big Men*, 245.

68. Richard Dyer, *Only Entertainment* (London: Routledge, 1992), 115–16. Dyer makes this point in the context of the way male power and domination are naturalized.

69. Ibid., 116.

On Mexican Pro Wrestling:
Sport as Melodrama

Heather Levi

In the months before I left to do fieldwork on professional wrestling in Mexico, whenever I told people what I was going to work on someone would respond by asking me, "Is it totally corrupt there like it is here?" I always found the question a bit strange. What does it mean to call professional wrestling corrupt? What it means, I believe, is that professional wrestling violates certain of their expectations surrounding the category of "sport." The question refers, first and foremost, to the widespread conviction that the outcome of each match is decided in advance. At base it is a reaction that simultaneously foregrounds and misrecognizes some of the central features of this performance genre. Mexican *lucha libre* (literally "free struggle" or "free wrestling") is a variant of the entertainment genre known in the Anglophone world as professional, all-in, or all-star wrestling. It is a transnational genre, performed in Europe, Asia, the Americas, and the Anglophone South Pacific, but it has been the object of greatest elaboration in the United States, Japan, and Mexico. In all cases it follows a certain set of conventions: it is a struggle between two or more wrestlers, in which a wide range of tactics are considered legitimate. Wrestlers compete not as themselves, but as characters that they (or their promoters) invent. The characters are morally coded, so that normally each match features one good guy (or team of good guys) and one bad guy (or team of bad guys). A wrestler enacting the role of bad guy cheats, uses unnecessary roughness, and displays cowardice and trickery. There are referees who, out of corruption and/or incompetence, are unwilling or unable to enforce the rules against the bad guys. To call such wrestling corrupt indicates a fundamental misunderstanding of the genre. It is not corrupt, but can be (among other things) a drama *about* corruption. As such, its relationship to other kinds of sport is unsettling.

The ambiguous relationship of all-star wrestling to other sports has inspired scholars in several national settings to take up the question of why fans enjoy watching presumably fixed contests. For the most part, these analysts have accepted the premise that it is important to categorize wrestling either as sport or as theater. My contention, however, is that the fundamental difference between professional wrestling and, say, soccer is not that one is drama and the other sport, but that as sports they represent different types of drama. Whether the contests are fixed or not, professional wrestling represents sport in the mode of melodrama.

The first analyst to treat professional wrestling as a social phenomenon was Roland Barthes, in his foundational 1957 essay "The World of Wrestling," which is included in his 1972 volume *Mythologies* (15–25). In the introduction to *Mythologies*, Barthes identifies his agenda: that of "treating 'collective representations' as sign systems [by which] one might hope to go further than the pious show of unmasking them and account in detail for the mystification which transforms petite-bourgeois culture into a universal nature" (9). In this context, Barthes considers professional wrestling as a demystified cultural form. He suggests that appreciation or understanding of the genre requires recognition of its contrivance. In contrast to Olympic or Greco-Roman wrestling, which Barthes characterizes as "a false wrestling, in which participants go to extraordinary lengths to make a show of a fair fight" (15), he celebrates all-in wrestling as the "true" form. The (assumed) fact of its staging, he argues, is irrelevant to its reception by the public and necessary to its value as a system of gestural signification. "The public is uninterested in whether or not it is rigged because it abandons itself to the primary virtue of the spectacle—what matters is not what one thinks, but what one sees" (15). It differs from boxing, for example, not because the latter is "real" and the former "fake," but because a boxing match constitutes a narrative that moves toward an intelligible outcome. In wrestling each moment is intelligible, and this intelligibility is predicated on the excessive clarity of every gesture. The roles of the wrestlers are written in their physiques; holds and pins are used not to elicit conventional signs of defeat, but to dramatize suffering and abasement of the vanquished. Rules exist to be exploited. Each sign in wrestling must be absolutely clear, because wrestling portrays "an ideal understanding of things," and corresponds, Barthes argues, not to other sports, but to Greek drama.

The central dramatic tension, in Barthes's estimation, is the development of the character of the villain in order to display villainy as a pure essence. In this system, the "fair fight," although possible, is not an ideal but a genre, a kind of novelty act. Fakery, rather than debasing wrestling as a sport, elevates it as a genre of theater. Stripped of the conceits of fairness and order, it does not do the work of conventional sports of naturalizing social relations under capitalism.

Most subsequent treatments of wrestling have utilized Barthes's paradigm in one form or another, raising questions about professional wrestling along two axes. First, who is responsible for the production of meaning in wrestling? Is it a collaboration between the wrestlers and the spectators (and thus social drama, in Victor Turner's sense), or is the meaning located in the narrative content of the matches themselves (and thus theatrical drama with social content and effects)? The second question, related to the first, is: What political ends does professional wrestling serve?

Irene Webley (1986), for example, argues that in Australia, New Zealand, and the United States the meaning of wrestling lies not in the wrestlers' performance alone, but in the relationship between the wrestlers and the "crowd." The spectacle as a whole is constituted by this relationship, and the wrestling match itself is only its motor. But in a departure from Barthes, Webley locates the central dramatic tension not in the idealization of villainy, but in the intersection of moral and *ethnic* coding of the wrestlers. She asserts that the meaning of the spectacle is produced through the crowd's identification with the wrestler coded most closely to crowd members' ethnic self-image. An exciting match "allows the crowd to participate in a ritualized confrontation between good and evil, a participation made more intense by the possibility of identifying with the characters of the wrestlers" (73). But because "fair and foul play are both available to all wrestlers, whatever their roles" (77), and wrestlers can thus change their moral identifications in the course of the match, the subtext of a battle between self and other outweighs the significance of the ethical text.

Freedman (1983) also reads wrestling as a coproduction of the wrestlers and the working-class audience. Observing that small-town Canadian spectators acknowledge that wrestling is "all phony" but enjoy it nevertheless, he proposes that wrestling's appeal lies in their ability to read wrestling as a critique of the ideology of the work ethic under capitalism. The inefficacy and corruption of authority, the futility and irrelevance of fair play that are central features of the genre dramatize the disjuncture experienced by the spectators between the ideology of liberal capitalism and its practice.

For Webley and Freedman, as for Barthes, the contrivance of wrestling is intelligible as a process of sign production in which the wrestlers create and their audiences collaborate. Other analysts read wrestling instead as a text produced, with a greater or lesser degree of conscious intent, by the authors of the wrestling scripts.[1] Bruce Lincoln (1989) interprets wrestling as a ritual of symbolic inversion, in which individual wrestlers are placed within a classificatory system that in turn determines the outcome of each individual match and of the event as a whole. In line with Webley, he argues that wrestlers are marked not only as "heel" and "babyface," but as more or less ethnically "American." In each set of matches, the intersecting codes of virtue/wickedness and more American/less American are used to construct a dialectic that leads from an initial match in which the less American baby-face wins, through a series of matches in which the Americans win, but are heels, to a resolution in which the more fully American babyface triumphs. Like Freedman, Lincoln reads the middle set of matches as a critique of the Protestant work ethic, but he understands it as a liminal phase. The final match figures as a vindication of the ideology that previous matches critique. The text of wrestling, then, is an inversion ritual, legitimating the dominant order.

Sam Migliore (1993) also asserts the existence of a consciously acted "script" and interprets wrestling as a legitimation of existing power relations. Although he concedes that the anticapitalist subtext that Freedman observes may exist at live events in small arenas, he contends that it is absent from the televised, mass-mediated phenomenon that most spectators see. Their error, Migliore argues, lies in the failure to distinguish between "participa-tory and media constructed rituals" (68). As a media-constructed ritual, wrestling loses the subversive edge it might have in other contexts. Migliore claims, moreover, that wrestling's longer-term narratives serve as mythic signs in the Barthesian sense. By taking the ongoing fortunes of the wrestler Sergeant Slaughter during the winter of 1991 as his unit of analysis, Migliore shows how the sequence of Slaughter's actions (i.e., taking on an Iraqi mana-ger, making anti-American statements in and out of the ring, and reverting to his original role as "heel") produced a metaphoric association between opposition to the Gulf War and betrayal of the United States. Slaughter's subsequent moral reclamation following the war, he argues, functioned as a symbolic repatriation of the war's opponents.

What these analyses have in common is the premise that the meaning of wrestling is to be found in the fact of its falsehood. Its staging may be under-stood to take place at any number of levels (intentionally produced, ongoing narrative strategies; dramatic spectacles of ideal types and grand gestures; and so on), but in each instance theatrical contrivance is taken as a starting point. That the fighting is faked, that there is no "real" contest, is treated as a given.

But in fact, how much of what one sees is choreographed and how much is "real" may not be so obvious. Surely one of the many lessons of the out-come of the "Rodney King" trial is that real violence can be misrecognized as fake. It is possible that although the characters are "fake," the matches are not, or not always. In contrast to all the rest of wrestling's analysts, Donald Nonini and Arlene Teraoka (1992) have argued that wrestling is not rigged, and that the assumption of fakery is merely an instance of bourgeois mis-recognition. They cite a list of the injuries sustained by wrestlers in the ring—

injuries too severe and sustained too frequently, in their view, to be reasonably attributable to accident—as evidence of wrestling's veracity. They insist that the excessive, theatrical gestures that Barthes and the rest read as dramatic convention are really tactics used to fake out opponents and actual responses to physical pain. Likewise, the graduated character of violence in a match (in which harmless, but loud, slaps may follow or be followed by apparently more damaging blows) and disregard for or manipulation of the rules constitute a range of tactics available to the wrestler in order ultimately to pin the opponent.

Like other workers under capitalism, Nonini and Teraoka argue, wrestlers sell their labor power, put their bodies at risk and try to do the minimum necessary to "get the job done" (in this case pinning the opponent). Wrestling recapitulates the labor process under capitalism, and therein, they claim, lies its appeal to the working-class audience. As representatives of the bourgeoisie, analysts and journalists alike refuse to recognize wrestling for what it is, for the same reason they cannot afford to recognize the labor process in all its brutality. The class habitus of the bourgeois analyst precludes not only the taste for the sport, but any understanding of it.

I think there are problems with Nonini and Teraoka's argument, which relies on a facile model of a homogeneous bourgeoisie and does not try to account for the various trappings (costumes, roles, characters) that mark wrestling off from other sports. These authors nonetheless raise an interesting question: Do we, as observers, really know whether anything happens in the ring in addition to those intentional signifying practices treated as theater or scripted performance? And need this question structure our analyses?

In assuming the scriptedness of wrestling, analysts have positioned themselves in terms of who "owns" the meaning of wrestling. Migliore (1993) and Lincoln (1989) suggest that the authorial intentions of whoever writes the "scripts" determine (to a greater or lesser extent) what meaning wrestling is to have. Barthes (1972), Webley (1986), and Freedman (1983) take a more Bakhtinian position, asserting, more or less strongly, that the spectacle of wrestling is a collaborative work of the audience and the wrestlers. For Nonini and Teraoka (1992), however, the wrestlers' gestures have effects-in-the-world independent of what they may be used to signify. For them the "meaning" of wrestling is transparent, its appeal the result of commonsensical desires produced by class relations. Workers like to watch wrestling not because it represents capitalist relations, but because it coexists with these relations yet simultaneously resists certain of their terms. The phenomenon to be explained, then, becomes not the sport, or the audience, but the perversity of the analysts who see wrestling only as faked.

177

At base, however, the spectacle's meaning is not determined by the truth or falsehood of the violence. In Mexico, one sees matches that feature slapstick routines that can only have been choreographed. At other matches, those in the front rows can *smell* the losing wrestler's blood. Clearly the social meaning of the genre can stand independent of the wrestlers' experience in the ring. This being the case, I want to move away from the question of whether it is a contest (and therefore a sport) or a theater piece (and therefore not-a-sport) to a paradigm that is potentially more productive for understanding the significance of *lucha libre* in Mexico: all sport is drama, but professional wrestling is sport in the melodramatic mode.

Thus, it makes sense that the genre has been very popular in Mexico, where melodrama has been central to the constitution of urban popular culture. As Ana Lopez (1995) has recently noted, the historical trajectories of melodrama have differed in North American and Latin American contexts. Whereas in the former "the melodramatic was devalued in favor of realism in the twentieth century through a gendering process . . . [to become] a 'women's' form[, in] Latin America . . . the devaluating of melodrama is explicitly class-based rather than primarily gendered" (260). Such diverse and distinguished intellectuals as Carlos Fuentes, Carlos Monsiváis, Jesús Martín-Barbero (1995), and Michèle Mattelart and Armand Mattelart (1990) have recognized the centrality of the melodramatic mode to the constitution of mass popular audiences in Latin America, whether to celebrate, denigrate, or critique its role.

The melodramatic mode can be characterized by two central features. Originally, the term *melodrama* referred to a nonverbal genre of popular theater in which emotional states were conveyed through conventionalized gestures. Over the course of time, the term was expanded to include partly or primarily verbal performance genres, but in its modern usage, melodrama is performance that presents a polarized worldview in which "moral struggle is made visible, announcing itself as an indisputable force" (Joyrich 1992, 232), through an externalization of internal emotions. Whereas in tragedy the narrative conflict is located within a mind of a single subject, in melodrama it is played out between clearly marked characters.[2] Second, and of particular significance for Latin Americans, according to Jesús Martín-Barbero (1993), what is at play in melodrama is "the drama of recognition: son by father, father by son. What moves the plot along is always the unawareness of identities, the struggle against bewitching spells and false appearances, trying to cut through all that hides and disguises" (225). I would add, however, that the desire to expose the hidden implies a corresponding love of disguise and concealment.

Finally, although the melodramatic text may appear semiotically transparent, it is not necessarily so. As Podalsky (1993) has recently argued for film, and I will show for *lucha libre*, the seeming transparency of melodrama can conceal considerable structural ambiguity.

Lucha Libre: Sport in the Melodramatic Mode

Professional wrestling was brought to Mexico from the United States in the early 1930s, but once it arrived it was enthusiastically adopted by a Mexican public, and its iconography was adapted in ways that Mexicanized the genre.[3] The nationalistic themes that structure the North American version were played down, and new elements of dramaturgy, movement vocabulary, and dress were added.[4] From the point of view of technique, the Mexican version makes use of a wider range of acrobatics and judo-influenced throws than the North American version. There is less hitting, less talking, and more athletics.

In Mexico, as elsewhere, wrestling events pit a team of bad guys against a team of good guys. As in other genres of melodramatic performance, *lucha* depends on gestural hyperbole for its effect. Whereas boxers and martial artists work to cultivate an impassive demeanor, wrestlers are trained to show pain and anger. The good obey the referee and suffer for it. The bad respect no one, gang up on their opponents, and taunt the outraged spectators. Good guys suffer abjection at the hands of the cowardly, guileful bad guys. Then, at the last minute, their passion renewed, they rout their oppressors.

Many of those who write about Mexican *lucha libre* have tended to account for its appeal in terms of fairly straightforward catharsis, in which the spectacle of abjection is redeemed through the triumph of good (Monsiváis 1995; Blanco 1990; Coe 1992). Certainly *lucha* does offer a dose of catharsis to its fans, but that alone does not explain the popularity of the Mexican version of the genre. One problem with interpreting *lucha libre* this way is that it assumes that fans identify with the good guys, and that the good guys usually triumph (at least in the final match). This assumption is problematic for two reasons. First, of the matches I have seen in Mexico, bad triumphs as often as good, including in the final match. Second, the good guys are not universally admired, nor are the bad guys universally despised. On the contrary, the bad guys always have their own cheering sections and their own fan clubs.

Although Freedman's (1983) analysis may help to account for this, it does not fully explain it. He and, to some extent, Barthes (1972) argue that the pleasure for the audience lies not in the triumph of good, but in the representation of the audience members' worldview. I believe this to be the case in Mexico as well. But whereas in rural Canada the point of wrestling is to dramatize the contradictions of liberal capitalism, in Mexico the point is to dramatize the moral and political ambiguities of mid- to late-twentieth-century urban life.

The drama of wrestling, as we have seen, is constituted through the confrontation between the bad guys and the good guys, in Mexico known as *rudos* and *técnicos* or *científicos*, respectively. The term *rudo* has several connotations, one of which involves crudity or excess. In a culture that values formality as a central tenet of honor (especially masculine honor), a *rudo* does not exhibit the self-control of a real *macho*.[5]

The *rudo* (and the *ruda*) displays qualities common to bad guys around the world: sadism, underhandedness, cowardice, betrayal. The *rudo* uses illegal techniques, smuggles in weapons, and tries to leave the ring to avoid injury. *Rudos* in Mexico also display tactics that I have not seen pro wrestlers use in the United States: appealing to official authority in the person of the referee and attempting to suborn members of the opposing team. The *técnico*, on the other hand, uses skill to win. While displaying an appropriate indifference to the referee, he or she conforms to a higher authority and uses illegal tactics only when unreasonably provoked.[6]

There is, however, an ambivalence in the two roles, which leads to a position of "guttural and visceral passion for the *rudos*, and dubious admiration for the *científicos*" (Monsiváis 1995, 126) for many Mexican fans.[7] One of the differences between Mexican and U.S. styles of wrestling is that in Mexico the wrestlers' moral coding is made much more explicit. In the United States, fans know the "heel" or the "babyface" by his or her conduct and demeanor in the ring and in the pre- and postmatch interviews. In Mexico, when competitors enter the ring, they are officially introduced as *rudos* or as *técnicos*. Whereas U.S. television commentators will express horror over the tactics of the "heel," Mexican commentators will debate the advantages and disadvantages of the *técnico* mode and the *rudo* mode. *Rudos*, they say, bring *sabor* (gusto) to *lucha libre*. They are said to fight from passion. In the words of the *ruda* "La Briosa": "The *técnico* trains more, spends more time at the gym. *Rudos* are more free, we let ourselves be driven more by temperament" (quoted in Pacheco 1990, 319).

The term *rudo*, moreover, has another connotation, beyond that of excess. In Mexico City, outside of the context of *lucha libre*, the *rudo* is the streetwise urbanite, from the roughest parts of the city, like Ciudad Nezahualcoyotl or the *barrio bravo* of Tepito, who lives by his wits on the margins of society. In fact, in arenas located in those parts of the city, cheering sections for the *rudos* are often bigger than the cheering sections for the *técnicos* (in contrast to the arenas located in the center or in the calmer outskirts in the state of Mexico). One alternative reading of the two roles, then, is that they represent opposing models of integration into the urban environment.[8] The *técnico* barters technical skill within the rules of constituted authority. The *rudo* manipulates the rules when practical, flouts them when convenient. Just as the underhanded crudeness of the *rudo* can be alternatively read as passion or street smarts, the technical capabilities of the *técnico* may also be read against the grain insofar as the terms *técnico* and *científico* themselves are far from neutral in Mexican political discourse. The word *técnico*, when not applied to wrestlers, is the usual term for partisans of the technocratic wing of the ruling Partido Revolucionario Institucional (PRI). *Científico*, on the other hand, conventionally refers to the late-nineteenth-century positivists associated with Porfirio Díaz, the antinationalist villains (at least until recently) of standard Mexican history texts. Thus the ostensible good guys, the ones who "make it" by following the rules, are linguistically aligned with forces of xenophiliac technocracy.

Concealment and Revelation: The Drama of the Mask

The second important component of melodrama, the centrality of narratives of recognition and revelation, is also an evident preoccupation of *lucha libre*, and one that echoes concerns important to the problematic of Mexican national identity. One of the most important features differentiating *lucha libre* from its Anglophone cousins is the use of masks, not only as a part of the wrestler's costume, but as a crucial dramatic element. Masks have always been important to traditional popular religious and quasi-religious ritual in Mexico, and the symbolism of masks and masking has also figured in the literature of Mexican national identity since the middle of the twentieth century. In Octavio Paz's (1985) classic formulation, Mexican cultural concern with forms and formality constituted a mask used to hide a deep sense of alienation. The Mexican, Paz writes, "whether young or old, *criollo* and *mestizo*, general or laborer or lawyer, seems . . . to be a person who shuts himself away to protect himself. His face is a mask and so is his smile" (30).

The mask, for Paz, is a symbol of alienation, used by "the Mexican" to hide his "true" self, to dissimulate. But others have suggested that Paz does not go far enough in his evocation of the mask as a potent symbol of *lo mexicano*. Claudio Lomnitz-Adler (1992, 242–43) has proposed that the metaphoric masks of formality should instead be understood to have functions analogous to those of actual masks used in ritual. They allow the wearer to embody a role, a capacity important to Mexican constructions of personhood.

In *lucha libre*, the use of actual, physical masks dates from the late 1930s, not long after the introduction of the sport in Mexico. Andrew Coe (1992) attributes the success of masked wrestling less to a conscious nationalist identification with the symbol of the mask than to a crossover between *lucha libre* and comic books. The introduction of wrestling masks in Mexico coincided with a craze for comics featuring masked heroes. One was the Phantom, whose chief characteristic was that he never removed his mask, even at home. According to Coe, "He usually appeared unmasked as a disguise when he was trying to infiltrate some enemy hideout and not tip them off that he was the Phantom" (160). Another was the hero of the comic book treatment of Dumas's *Man in the Iron Mask*, which also featured a character for whom the mask was not removable.[9]

A mask was first used as a novelty in 1934 by an American wrestler, Cyclone Mackay, although it was designed and executed in Mexico by Victor Martinez Sr., shoemaker and inventor of the wrestling mask. By the 1940s, many of the most successful wrestlers wore masks. One of these, Rodolfo Guzmán, known as "El Santo," became the best-known, most-loved wrestler of all time, and star of dozens of wrestling movies. Guzmán started his career as a *rudo*, and took up the mask at the suggestion of his promoter, Jesus Lomelín. Guzmán renamed himself El Santo: El Enmascarado de Plata (The Saint: The Man in the Silver Mask), after Simon Templar, hero of a series of detective novels and movies, and switched to the *técnico* mode. As El Santo, he set the standard for protection of the mask's charisma, never allowing his face to be seen in public until shortly before his death in 1984.[10] Even in death, however, he remained the masked hero. He was waked and buried in full wrestling costume, including his trademark silver lamé mask.

The mask symbolizes not only the persona of the individual wrestler, but the mystique of *lucha libre* itself. It functions in the arena as a concentrated point of dramatic tension. First, it allows the wrestler to subsume his or her own personality and assume a persona more easily and unambiguously than costuming and makeup would allow. Second, it supports an air of mystery about the wrestler. Masked wrestlers' identities are closely guarded secrets. These secrets are often in part about origins, about kinship. Many wrestlers come from wrestling families. In general, the kin connections between wrestlers are known to wrestling's public. This is true for many masked wrestlers as well. Everyone knows, for example, that the five masked "Villanos" are all sons of Ray Mendoza, but no one is supposed to know their names. Young wrestlers often assume their fathers' or uncles'

El Santo, the best-loved *luchador* of all time, suffers a leg lock from Alejandro Cruz while the referee looks on (c. 1948). Photograph from Colección Hermanos Mayo, Archivo General de la Nación, Mexico; used with permission.

costumes, and use names like Hijo del Santo (Son of El Santo) or Dr. O'Borman Jr. But the kin connections behind the masks are not always authentic. A Jr., II, or Hijo de might or might not be a blood relation of the original. As in other forms of melodrama, the real blood tie might be hidden, or a spurious one fabricated.

But perhaps the most important thing about the mask is that it *can* be removed, and the personal, everyday identity of the wrestler revealed. Wrestlers talk about masking as a consciously chosen and serious commitment never to be seen unmasked, to uphold the mask's charisma. But the charisma is fragile, and can be destroyed. Thus part of the pleasure in a wrestling event depends on the possibility and indefinite deferment of the moment of revelation.

Removal of the mask by an opponent constitutes, in the words of José Joaquín Blanco (1990), an attempt to "despoil the most cared for and coveted virginity on earth" (31). A mask can be removed in the arena in one of two ways. It can be forcibly and illegally ripped off (usually by a *rudo*, sometimes by a *técnico* provoked to righteous anger). If this occurs in the course of a match, the expected behavior of the unmasked wrestler is to hide his or her face and begin an elaborate pantomime of shame and outrage until the mask

183

is returned. While it disqualifies the unmasker, it humiliates the unmasked. Second, the mask can be deliberately risked as a bet on the outcome of a match. For the wrestler who loses, the mask is lost for good. With face exposed, the wrestler might retain his or her charisma or lose his or her career.

The Mask and the Public Sphere

These rituals of wrestling are not confined to the arena. On the contrary, they represent social codes that have become recognizable to many Mexicans and have traveled beyond the confines of the ring, the comic book, and the movie screen. Two years after the Mexico City earthquake of 1985, and three years after the death of El Santo, the Asemblea de Barrios (a coalition of groups that first emerged to advocate for those left homeless by the earthquake and later began to organize around issues of housing rights and democratization) presented a man dressed as a wrestler as their new spokesman, "Superbarrio Gomez." He was first intended as a novelty, to add an element of humor to political organizing, but Asemblea activists soon found that there were distinct advantages to keeping him on as their representative. First, they discovered that having to negotiate with a masked man made officials uncomfortable. His presence disoriented them, made them feel awkward, unsure if they were being mocked, unable to assert their authority over the Asemblea representatives. Second, they realized that he was difficult to control and impossible to co-opt, because no one in government knew who he "really" was.

In the same year, another retired wrestler, Ecologista Universal, also moved from *lucha libre* to the *lucha social* when he volunteered himself as a representative of the movement to stop the Laguna Verde nuclear power plant project in Veracruz. Since then, several more "social wrestlers" have entered the public arena on behalf of women, animals, children, and other marginalized groups.

It is reasonable to wonder why this seemingly frivolous gesture so quickly found a legitimate place in Mexican public discourse. The answer lies in two related explanations. First, Superbarrio was conceived as a conscious appropriation of the mystique of the late Santo and the role of hero left vacant by his death. But, in addition, as a wrestler he represented a cultural form long denigrated by the middle class. The deployment of *lucha libre* imagery meant employing a set of cultural tropes that were fun to use and *belonged* to the communities that made up the Asemblea's membership. Second, anonymity provided a weapon against the Mexican government's policy of controlling dissent through co-optation. By donning masks (and perhaps only by donning masks), Superbarrio and his spin-offs were able to represent fairness and the struggle for justice to a jaded public.

The tactics employed by Superbarrio—conscious use of the charisma of the mask and the advantage of anonymity, and the incorporation of humor and theater in political organizing—were subsequently appropriated by Subcomandante Marcos and the EZLN. Whether by intentional reference to wrestling or not, the EZLN distinguish themselves sartorially from other Latin American guerrillas by donning ski masks instead of the more commonplace bandanas. In so doing, they allude to a set of social codes that were played out most explicitly during the government offensive in early 1995. On 9 February of that year, the attorney general's office released a photograph of a man they claimed (rightly or wrongly) to be Marcos himself. Ripping off his mask, they revealed him to be Rafael Sebastian Guillén Vicente, university professor and son of a Tampico furniture dealer. Government officials claimed the photograph's circulation in and of itself as an important government victory. Two days later, the *New York Times* quoted an unnamed official as insisting (rather prematurely) that "the moment that Marcos was identified and his photo was shown and everyone saw who he was, much of his importance as a symbol vanished. . . . Whether he is captured or not is incidental" (Golden 1995, 1).

On the face of it this statement makes very little sense. Although Guillén was clearly not indigenous (a fact that officials used to undermine the EZLN's claim to represent the indigenous Maya of Chiapas), there had never been any pretense to the contrary. His identity was revealed to be what everyone more or less expected. Alma Guillermoprieto (1995) observes that it did, perhaps, temporarily lessen his sex appeal. As a politico-military gesture, however, it made sense if seen as a familiar trope from *lucha libre*.

Marcos responded in kind, echoing an earlier incident involving the wrestler Hijo del Santo (the son of El Santo, and inheritor of his role). In the middle of their divorce, Hijo del Santo's soon-to-be-ex-wife sent photographs of what she claimed to be his unmasked face to the press. Hijo del Santo responded by denying that he was the man in the photographs. Because there was no way to know unless he unmasked himself, her claim was impossible to prove (Rugos 1994).

That was precisely the reaction of Marcos to the same *rudo* ploy. Within days, he relayed a message to the Mexico City press in his familiar epistolary style:

> *P.S. that rapidly applauds this new "success" of the government police:* I heard they've found another "Marcos," and that he's from Tampico. That doesn't sound bad, the port is nice. . . .

P.S. that despite the circumstances does not abandon its narcissism:
So . . . Is this new Subcomandante Marcos good-looking? Because lately
they've been assigning me really ugly ones, and my feminine correspondence
gets ruined.

P.S. that counts time and ammunition: I have 300 bullets, so try to bring
299 soldiers. . . .

[signed] The Sup, rearranging his ski mask with macabre flirtatiousness.
(quoted in Guillermoprieta 1995, 44)

Like the son of El Santo, through simple denial he was able (as Guillermoprieta
notes) to reestablish his revolutionary credentials, his imperiled sex appeal,
and, most important, the charisma of the mask.

Notes

1. Although several critics of wrestling assert that the events are choreographed and
   scripted into medium- and long-term story lines, none attributes such planning to any
   specific agent. If it is just a dramatic performance, it is not clear who is supposed to be
   writing the script.
2. Witness, for example, the ongoing saga of the perennially losing Peruvian national soccer team. For Peruvians, the central dramatic tension of each game is: How will victory
   be torn from our grasp this time? (Eduardo Bryce, personal communication). In
   Mexico, biographical pieces about famous boxers are frequently structured as tragedy,
   recounting the boxer's rise from poverty to his pathetic fall, usually attributed to a
   combination of alcoholism and hubris.
3. According to the Museo de Culturas Populares in Mexico City, seventy million tickets
   are sold by Mexico's 187 arenas every year.
4. Mondak (1989) argues that conservative xenophobia has always been the central
   theme of pro wrestling in the United States, and that its popularity has always peaked
   during periods of strong isolationist sentiment, regardless of its relationship to mass
   mediation. This also appears to be true for Japan, where professional wrestling was introduced in the early 1950s as a televised genre. There the favorite dramas of postwar pro wrestling pitted finally triumphant Japanese against ultimately vanquished
   "Americans" (Thompson 1986).
5. In some contexts, however, the capacity to behave excessively is central to the construction of machismo (see Lancaster 1992; Monsiváis 1981). Although this relationship of wrestling roles to the discourse of machismo is crucial to the moral coding of
   male wrestlers, it is important to keep in mind that *lucha libre* is not a male-only occupation. Women have been involved in *lucha libre* since the late 1940s, and there are
   now well over one hundred *luchadoras* in Mexico.
6. This, at least, is the ideal. In fact, I have seen a number of matches in which *técnicos*
   have openly cheated, without ceasing to be identified as *técnicos* by their fans. The
   only thing that a *técnico* cannot do without altering his or her long-term identification
   is betray his or her partner(s).
7. Translations of Monsiváis (1995), Pacheco (1990), and Blanco (1990) are my own.

8. During the period in which *lucha libre* was introduced, Mexico was undergoing a transition from a predominantly rural to a predominantly urban society. A central concern of many forms of Mexican popular culture was the negotiation of identities and of new modes of behavior implied by this shift. For a related discussion of the use of comic books in facilitating the rural-to-urban transition, see Rubenstein (forthcoming).

9. The crossover between comic books and *lucha libre*, both staples of Mexican mass culture, has gone the other way as well. El Santo (see below) was the subject of a long-running comic (1949–76) by comic industry stalwart Jose G. Cruz; El Santo eventually sued Cruz (unsuccessfully) for unauthorized use of his name and image (Poniatowska 1990).

10. Starting in 1952, and continuing into the 1980s, the Mexican film industry produced hundreds of wonderfully campy movies featuring wrestlers. El Santo was recruited to the film industry in 1958 and went on to act in about a film a year until 1983. Although *lucha libre* was a popular entertainment before El Santo and others crossed over into film, the cinema contributed to its ever-widening audience. And as the movies appropriated the figure of the wrestler, live wrestling in turn appropriated the mystique of the cinema. Many urban Mexicans have never been to a wrestling match, but I have yet to meet anyone in Mexico City who has never seen an El Santo movie.

Works Cited

Barthes, Roland. 1972. *Mythologies*. New York: Hill & Wang.

Blanco, José Joaquín. 1990. No respondo chipote con sangre. In *Un Chavo Bien Helado*. Mexico City: Biblioteca Era.

Coe, Andrew. 1992. La Máscara! La Máscara! *Icarus* 8: 157–70.

Doane, Mary Ann. 1987. *The Desire to Desire: The Woman's Film of the 1940s*. Bloomington: Indiana University Press.

Freedman, Jim. 1983. Will the Sheik Use His Blinding Fireball? The Ideology of Professional Wrestling. In *The Celebration of Society: Perspectives on Contemporary Cultural Performance*, ed. Frank E. Manning. Bowling Green, Ohio: Bowling Green University Press.

Golden, Tim. 1995. Mexico's New Offensive: Erasing Rebel's Mystique. *New York Times*, 11 February.

Guillermoprieto, Alma. 1995. The Unmasking. *New Yorker*, 13 March, 40–47.

Joyrich, Lynne. 1992. All That Television Allows: TV Melodrama Postmodernism and Consumer Culture. In *Private Screenings: Television and the Female Consumer*, ed. Lynn Spigel and Denise Mann. Minneapolis: University of Minnesota Press.

Lancaster, Roger N. 1992. *Life Is Hard: Machismo, Danger and the Intimacy of Power in Nicaragua*. Berkeley: University of California Press.

Lincoln, Bruce. 1989. *Discourse and the Construction of Society: Comparative Studies of Myth, Ritual, and Classification*. New York: Oxford University Press.

Lomnitz-Adler, Claudio. 1992. *Exits from the Labyrinth: Culture and Ideology in the Mexican National Space*. Berkeley: University of California Press.

Lopez, Ana. 1995. Our Welcomed Guests: Telenovelas in Latin America. In *To Be Continued . . . : Soap Operas around the World*, ed. Robert C. Allen. New York: Routledge.

Martín-Barbero, Jesús. 1993. *Communication, Culture, and Hegemony: From Media to Mediations*. Newbury Park, Calif.: Sage.

———. 1995. Memory and Form in Latin American Soap Opera. In *To Be Continued . . . : Soap Operas around the World* ed. Robert C. Allen. New York: Routledge.

Mattelart, Michèle, and Armand Mattelart. 1990. *The Carnival of Images: Brazilian TV Fiction*. South Hadley, Mass.: Bergin & Garvey.

Migliore, Sam. 1993. Professional Wrestling: Moral Commentary through Ritual Metaphor. *Journal of Ritual Studies* 7: 65–84.

Mondak, Jeffery J. 1989. "The Politics of Professional Wrestling." *Journal of Popular Culture* 23, no. 2.

Monsiváis, Carlos. 1981. *Escenas de Pudor y Livianidad*. Mexico City: Editorial Grijalbo.

———. 1995. *Los Rituales del Caos*. Mexico City: Biblioteca Era.

Nonini, Donald M., and Arlene Akiko Teraoka. 1992. Class Struggle in the Squared Circle: Professional Wrestling as Working Class Sport. In *The Politics of Culture and Creativity: A Critique of Civilization. Essays in Honor of Stanley Diamond*, ed. Christine Ward Gailey. Gainesville: University of Florida Press.

Pacheco, Cristina. 1990. *Los Dueños de la Noche*. Mexico City: Editorial Planeta Mexicana.

Paz, Octavio. 1985. *The Labyrinth of Solitude (and the Other Mexico, Return to the Labyrinth of Solitude, Mexico and the United States, The Philanthropic Ogre)*. New York: Grove.

Podalsky, Laura. 1993. Disjointed Frames: Melodrama, Nationalism and Representation in 1940s Mexico. *Studies in Latin American Popular Culture* 12: 57–73.

Poniatowska, Elena. 1990. *Todo Mexico* (vol. 1). Mexico City: Editorial Diana.

Rubenstein, Anne. forthcoming. *Bad Language, Naked Ladies and Other Threats to the Nation: A Political History of Comic Books in Mexico*. Durham, N.C.: Duke University Press.

Rugos, Ralph. 1994. Q: What's the Difference between Superman and Superbarrio? A: Superbarrio Exists! *L.A. Weekly*, 14–20 January.

Thompson, Lee Austin. 1986. Professional Wrestling in Japan: Media and Message. *International Review for the Sociology of Sport* 21: 65–81.

Webley, Irene A. 1986. Professional Wrestling: The World of Roland Barthes Revisited. *Semiotica* 58: 59–81.

Part III ▸ Buying and Selling Nations and Bodies

Field of Soaps:
Rupert v. Kerry as Masculine Melodrama

David Rowe and Jim McKay

Melodrama offers us heroic confrontation, purgation, purification, recogni-
tion. But its recognition is essentially of the integers in combat and the need to
choose sides. It produces panic terror and sympathetic pity, but not in regard to
the same object, and without the higher illumination of their interpenetration.
▸ *Peter Brooks,* The Melodramatic Imagination

Sport is an increasingly valuable commodity in the global media industry. For
instance, in 1980 NBC paid what was then the astonishing sum of $72 mil-
lion for the rights to televise the Summer Olympics. In 1995 the same network expended $715 million on the 2000 Olympics, $793 million on the
2004 Olympics, and $894 million on the 2008 Olympics (all figures in U.S.
dollars unless otherwise noted). These huge sums were committed just for
the U.S. TV rights, with the sites for the 2004 and 2008 games yet to be
decided. It was widely rumored that NBC made this costly deal with the
International Olympic Committee in order to shut out Rupert Murdoch,
whose $1 billion bid for worldwide TV rights to the 2000 Olympics had ear-
lier been rejected. There is no one in the media world who has a greater
commitment to the commercial exploitation of TV sport than Murdoch.
Although his Fox Network ranks only fourth in the United States, behind
ABC, CBS, and NBC, in terms of audiences, it currently has the five-year
telecast rights for football ($2.2 billion) and hockey ($221 million).

Outside the United States, Murdoch controls or is part owner of the TV
rights to British and "Euro" soccer, rugby league, rugby union, West Indies
and Pakistani cricket, and American football via British-based Foxtel (40 percent Murdoch-owned); premier league soccer, boxing, rugby league, rugby
union, cricket, racing, major tennis events, American football, and British
and American basketball via British-based BSkyB (40 percent Murdoch-
owned); American football via German-based Vox (49.9 percent Murdoch-
owned); golf, tennis, Australian rules football, rugby union, motor racing,
and the 1996 and 2000 Olympics via Australian-based Channel Seven (15
percent Murdoch-owned); and Chinese soccer, badminton, Japanese baseball, cricket, World Cup soccer, motorcycling, motor racing, rugby union,
tennis, and table tennis via Hong Kong-based Star TV (64 percent Murdoch-

owned). The extent of Murdoch's global sports reach is probably the major reason why in 1995 he became the first person to top the *Sporting News* list of the one hundred most powerful people in sport for two consecutive years.

There is a deep fascination with the life of the Australian-born media proprietor who became a global media mogul: his inheritance of a provincial newspaper company from his late father, Sir Keith Murdoch; his influence on politicians and governments of various persuasions, both in his country of birth and around the world (most notably on Britain's Thatcher administration); his willingness to take up U.S. citizenship in pursuit of media ownership in that country; and the roller-coaster rise, near demise, and then resurgence of his global News Corporation empire. Irrespective of the biographical lure, the activities of Citizen Murdoch, as he is sometimes known (along with less restrained soubriquets such as "The Dirty Digger"), are of keen interest to analysts of the exercise of media and cultural power. TV sport, as we argue below, is an important site where that power is promoted, extended, and contested.

In this essay, we discuss Murdoch's attempt to gain "pay-TV" access to Australian rugby league (hereafter referred to as *league*). We first sketch the background to what the Australian media dubbed the "League War" between Murdoch and media rival Kerry Packer, and then examine the genres that organized and gave meaning to it. Although we focus on the postmodern intertextual and intergeneric dimensions of media discourses, we concur with Stuart Hall (1985) and others (such as Cowie 1977; Ebert 1992–93; Jackson 1992; Mouzelis 1993; West 1989) that social texts, identities, and practices are always in some way anchored by material processes. By this we mean that signification cannot operate independent of structuring forces (such as of class, gender, race, and ethnicity) even in a cultural environment actively suppressing the "final word" of material determination. The "anchor points" in this case, we suggest, are capital accumulation and "hegemonic masculinity" (Connell 1995). In simultaneously addressing the structural and significatory features of the "Super League" story, we are attempting partially to overcome what Silverstone (1994, 995) views as the disabling separation between "the projects of cultural studies and the sociology of culture: the absence in the first of a contextualisation that both relativises, historicises and thereby fixes the particular; and an absence in the second of the dramatic insights that engagement with the particular, at best, produces."

Our argument first takes the form of briefly elaborated political economies of the Australian media and sport. In the process, we introduce Kerry Packer as a protagonist in the drama of TV sport in Australia. We look at the "sense-making" discourses of the Australian media, sports personnel, legal advocates, and judicial figures in the "enframement" of the League War. We attempt to demonstrate how the conventions of melodrama—and specifically of TV soap opera—were deployed and given a masculine inflection in the mediation of a classic struggle between the "robber barons" of the contemporary Australian "sports/media complex" (Jhally 1989).

Murdoch, Packer, and the Control of the Australian Media

It has often been remarked that ownership and control of the commercial Australian media are the most concentrated in the English-speaking world (Schultz 1993). The newspaper industry, which is highly regionalized, is dominated by two "overseas" companies—Murdoch's News Limited, which controls 60 percent of Australian metropolitan daily newspaper circulation, and New Zealand-based Brierley Investments Limited. (Until December 1996, Canadian Conrad Black was the largest shareholder in the Fairfax company, which owns the two most profitable media properties in the country, the *Sydney Morning Herald* and the *Melbourne Age;* he has since sold his controlling share of Fairfax to "value investor" Ron Brierley.). The magazine industry is dominated by Packer, the major shareholder of Australian Consolidated Press, part of Publishing and Broadcasting Limited (PBL), which is responsible for an extraordinary market share of 60 percent. Another strong force in the magazine market is Murdoch, who, along with Packer, has long coveted (and, until recently, had a stake in) the prime publishing mastheads of Fairfax. Packer is also the most successful TV proprietor through the Nine Network, the other arm of PBL, in which he has a controlling 45 percent share. Murdoch is prevented by federal cross-media ownership and foreign investment rules (under review by a recently re-elected conservative government) from extending his commercial free-to-air TV interests. The belated January 1995 introduction of "pay TV" in Australia saw, in spite of the (then Labour) government's claims about greater diversity of ownership and control of the media, contending forces coalesce around the usual adversaries—Packer and Murdoch, with the former allied to the telecommunications carrier Optus and the latter linked with the publicly controlled Telstra corporation.

The rivalry between Rupert Murdoch and Kerry Packer has long shaped the media and political scenes in Australia. Packer, Australia's richest individual, is not as well-known outside Australia as Murdoch because of the lesser degree of internationalization of his operations. There are, nonetheless, some similarities between their experiences. Packer also inherited a media empire from his father, the late Sir Frank Packer. And like Murdoch, Packer built up the family business with a combination of commercial ruthlessness and political strategy. Unlike Murdoch, however, Packer has a flamboyant public profile as an international polo player and a gambling high roller. Whereas in the United States Murdoch is known as the foreigner who has shaken up the film, TV, book publishing, and newspaper industries, Packer is better known as a spectacular presence in the casinos of Las Vegas. As one recent article states:

> In this casino city in love with schlock monuments, the MGM has a giant yellow lion out the front; Caesar's Palace has fake Italian marbles; the Mirage a man-made waterfall. They might just as well have a huge bust of Kerry Packer.
>
> Australia's richest man is a figure of almost mythic proportions here. Last month, the *Los Angeles Times* declared him to be "the most formidable of the world-class gamblers." In his office at the Las Vegas Hilton, Michael Stirling uses a more colourful expression. "Kerry Packer," he says, "is a whale."
>
> In the gambling world, a "whale" is the highest of the high-rollers; somebody prepared to gamble several million dollars in a single session. (Attwood 1996, 5s)

Packer's capacity to visit Las Vegas casinos and win (apparently $18 million on one occasion in May 1995) and lose (reportedly $13 million in February 1993) vast sums of money is principally derived from a combination of "casino capitalism," government courtship, and tax minimization in the conduct of his business affairs in the Australian media. No small part of his commercial success is attributable to the role that sport has played in the attraction of audiences (and therefore advertisers) to his TV stations.

Australian Sport: From Amateur Hour to Prime Time

Until the 1970s, sport in Australia was voluntarily administered by "old boys" and relied heavily on grassroots support. We have detailed elsewhere how the amateur ethos that was ascendant for much of Australia's sporting history was rapidly supplanted by both corporate and global "turns" during the past two decades (McKay 1991; McKay, Lawrence, Miller, and Rowe 1993; Rowe, Lawrence, Miller, and McKay 1994). All professional (men's) sports are now governed by executive boards that employ specialists in advertising, management, marketing, and public relations, and most amateur and semiprofessional men's and women's sports have also become reliant on corporate support. A key feature of the corporatization and globalization of Australian sport has been an exponential increase in TV coverage. In 1966, some 250 hours of sport were screened by Australian TV networks; by 1986 this figure had jumped to nearly 4,000 hours (admittedly, with an increase in the number of networks from three to five). Cable, satellite, and microwave technologies (broadcast to a small but growing subscriber base) have now supplemented free-to-air sports coverage with twenty-four-hour sports channels.

Televised sport is cheap and popular (especially among young men with high levels of disposable income) and assists commercial networks in meeting the quota of local content set by the Australian Broadcasting Authority. A major reason Packer's Nine Network has topped the national TV ratings for twelve consecutive years is the amount of sport it telecasts. A prime example is its four-hour Saturday afternoon *Wide World of Sports*, which is a clone of the original American program. Nine also telecasts most of the major international events in tennis, golf, and Formula One and Indy car racing. Packer's Sky Channel has for several years carried horse racing to nondomestic sites ("pubs and clubs"), and he has a 5 percent share in Optus Vision (with a 20 percent shareholding option), which telecasts American sports via ESPN. On occasion, it has been expedient for the commercial media proprietors to cooperate rather than compete. For example, in September 1995, Murdoch took a $50 million, 50 percent stake in Packer's Sky Channel, thus avoiding a costly struggle over TV rights and providing Sky with an international outlet through Murdoch's Star TV (Asia). As we will see below, this pragmatic media deal making sits ill with rhetorics of loyalty and tradition in sport.

Two particularly profitable TV sport revenue sources for Packer are Nine's telecasts of the key local sports of cricket and league. In the late 1970s, Packer usurped control of cricket, one of Australia's most popular spectator sports, from the amateur Australian Cricket Board and the International Cricket Conference (Miller 1989). Packer signed individual players to lucrative contracts for his World Series Cricket, which was organized on the basis of lively one-day "packages," as well as on the leisurely five-day format of traditional test matches. Packer spectacularized cricket with innovations such as colored uniforms, night games, white balls, limited overs, and extra cameras (Harriss 1990), ultimately acquiring exclusive broadcast and marketing rights to the game in Australia. Since the early 1990s, Packer's Nine Network has also dominated the broadcasting of games played in the Australian Rugby League (ARL). In 1994, telecasts of an annual best-of-three interstate series between Queensland and New South Wales (NSW) occupied the top three positions in the yearly TV ratings. The third game of the 1991 series had already set an Australian TV program ratings record, with 65 percent of households in Brisbane, the state capital of Queensland, having at least one TV set tuned to the event.

League is, then, a major TV commodity on the eastern seaboard of Australia, but in spite of its breakaway from rugby union in 1907 on the issue of payment of player "expenses" (later wages), it has been slow to become a sophisticated commercial sport. In the late 1980s the American soul singer Tina Turner was used in a campaign intended to broaden the sport's support base and to modernize its image, but well into the 1990s league continued to reveal its semiprofessional, working-class masculinist origins (Headon and Marinos 1996). An attempt to nationalize and then internationalize a still highly parochial game led, in 1995, to the major league competition extending across and beyond the nation—to Perth in the far west, Townsville in the far north, and east to Auckland in New Zealand. It was also planned to take the game south to the population centers of Adelaide and Melbourne and, over time, to develop multilevel competitions across Australasia and the Asia-Pacific. These planned and initiated developments in the game were essentially driven by the expansionist imperatives of commercial TV.

Ironically, as the ARL increased the number of participating clubs, sites for play, and TV audience reach, several current teams, especially in inner Sydney, were in decline due to gentrification, the aging of core support, and the rise of competing, imported sports such as basketball and baseball. Pressure was already mounting from the prospering clubs outside Sydney (such as the Brisbane Broncos and the Canberra Raiders) for a more streamlined premier competition that would prevent lopsided contests between the "unbeatables" and the "unwinnables," and that would ensure that a larger proportion of revenue from TV, sponsorship, and merchandising went to the elite clubs and players. The conditions existed, then, for a radical shake-up in a game of patchy economic health and significant televisual appeal at a time of ferocious competition between pay-TV companies and carriers in their start-up phase in Australia.

League: The Pay-TV Prize

The preceding discussion sketches the context in which Packer's seemingly secure grip on league telecasts was threatened by Murdoch. Although there were rumors in mid-1994 that Murdoch was planning to establish a rival competition, the first overt challenge occurred early in 1995, when Murdoch's

News Limited announced its intention to form a "Super League" in 1996 consisting primarily of club franchises and players drawn from the establishment ARL. In response, the ARL insisted on "loyalty agreements" restraining all twenty clubs from joining Super League. The struggle intensified in February 1995 when an ARL executive revealed, to the surprise of several clubs, that Packer owned the pay-TV rights (through Optus Vision) for the rest of the century. This "revelation" that Packer had locked Murdoch out of the pay-TV market for the most popular televised winter sport in NSW and Queensland spurred News Limited in March to launch a claim in the federal court against the ARL over its loyalty agreements, claiming that the ARL had used economic duress, thus breaching the Trade Practices Act. Shortly afterward, Super League announced that it had signed several star players to well-paying contracts. In April, the ARL launched a countersuit against News Limited, claiming that it had infringed the ARL's intellectual property rights. In June, on the eve of the rugby union World Cup final in South Africa, Murdoch's News Corporation announced that it had paid $550 million for exclusive global TV rights to telecasts of international rugby union matches, including a new Southern Hemisphere "Super Twelve" competition. Packer had also tried to set up his own World Rugby Corporation, but on this occasion Murdoch had prevailed.

A détente of sorts seemed to have occurred between the Packer and Murdoch camps in November, after Nine announced that, if the court permitted, it would televise two Super League games per weekend in 1996, as part of a long-term contract in which Foxtel would telecast five games weekly. This deal followed the earlier agreement on the TV coverage of racing, thereby illustrating the role of economic pragmatism in the symbolic and material contest for supremacy between media moguls. One of the smaller players in the Australian media industry, Kerry Stokes, remarked that "it looks like Rupert Murdoch has decided to play Father Christmas to Kerry Packer." Packer had not informed the ARL of the agreement, somewhat diminishing the "man of the people" versus "enemy of the people" image that he and the ARL had been assiduously cultivating. There was, however, to be another twist to the Rupert and Kerry story—one of the suitors was jilted. A clandestine meeting in London between Murdoch and Packer in late 1995 laid the foundation for a cease-fire, but Murdoch claimed in March 1996 that, after reaching an agreement with Packer, the latter had reneged: "'I came to a settlement with Mr Packer two or three months ago and he welshed on it. Super League would have thrived under it,' Mr Murdoch said" (Fife-Yeomans 1996, 1).

At such points the political economy of sport and media meets the symbolic contestation inscribed in the intense media coverage of the struggle over sport and its representations. The "war of position" between contending interests is represented through narrativized myths of progress, loyalty, and honor. In the preceding discussion we have briefly outlined the historical and economic context wherein league has been caught up in a struggle between the ARL/Optus/Packer and News Corp./Foxtel/Murdoch camps. These are not simply matters for the business pages of broadsheet newspapers. Each camp has been required to seek popular support by enunciating competing, binary rhetorics of "progress" versus "tradition." The various media disciplines, including sports journalism, have translated or interpreted this conflict in popularly digestible terms. In reviewing this media coverage over a period of a little more than a year, we have found it striking that the news media have, above all, deployed melodrama as their principal enframing genre, albeit one that has displayed a highly masculinist character.

Media Sport and Masculine Melodrama

In addition to boardrooms, locker rooms, and courts, the struggle for control of league was played out in the media. Apart from receiving coverage by sports journalists, it quickly became front-page news, the lead item on TV news and current affairs programs, ubiquitous in both editorials and letters to the editor, a topic in feature articles in various sections of magazines and newspapers, and a boon to the advertising industry. A one-hour program was devoted to the events by the publicly owned Australian Broadcasting Corporation's *Four Corners*, arguably the most respected current affairs TV show in the country. These representations exhibited a high level of intertextuality, with codes borrowed from soap opera, melodrama, war, action/adventure, thriller, science fiction, epic, and sport, all with a masculinized inflection.

In their analysis of TV culture, Rose and Friedman (1994, 23) note that sport occupies a contradictory position. On the one hand, watching sport epitomizes the passivity, distraction, and escapism traditionally associated with female patterns of consumption, especially of daytime TV soaps. On the other hand, sport is a "quintessentially masculine genre," and the classical male gaze has tended to be defined as "voyeuristic, linear, and contemplative." Yet whereas the classical male viewer conformed to work, family, and the rhythms of industrial society, the "postindustrial male worker" is interpellated by the "distracted" flow that characterizes contemporary patterns of work and leisure. For Rose and Friedman, "this analytical discourse [of televised sport] is ultimately qualified by the *melodramatic:* the human angle, the personal drama, and the insistence on 'mind over matter' which inform each assessment of the physical play of the game" (26). Thus they argue—with certain qualifications—that men's consumption of televised sport parallels the ways in which women usually have been said to view soaps.

It is not just sporting contests per se that can be read as melodrama. Media coverage of dramatic and spectacular sports-related events (e.g., the O. J. Simpson case, Magic Johnson's "disclosure" that he is HIV-positive and his subsequent retirements and comebacks, the conflict between the management of the San Francisco 49ers and superstar Joe Montana) is replete with characters, narratives, and plots derived from classical melodrama and TV soap opera (Cole and Denny 1994; King 1993; McKay 1993; McKay and Smith 1995; Muller 1995; Rowe 1994). Various scholars have decoded the melodramatic narratives and genres surrounding representations of masculinity in film and TV (Cohan and Hark 1993; Kirkham and Thumin 1993). We argue that the commercial struggle for control over league and pay TV between Murdoch and Packer was represented by the media as an elaborate masculine melodrama interleaved with other masculine-inflected genres and narratives. Interrogation of the media's production of the Super League "text," then, helps inform a greater understanding of the relationships among sport, media, capitalism, and hegemonic masculinity.

Whannel (1993) argues that there are striking homologies between the types of hegemonic masculinity manifested in sporting life and corporate life. The "organization men" in both homosocial institutions conform to Taylorized bodily regimes set by authority figures in displaying loyalty, discipline, combativeness, and a masochistic "no pain, no gain" commitment to performance. Sport plays an important role in the masculine realms of corporate life: men exchange information and make deals on golf courses and in locker rooms; corporations are major sponsors of many individual athletes, teams, and entire sports. Sporting terminology is a ubiquitous feature of everyday conversation in corporate organizations; for instance, managers often depict both their personal and organizational goals by using combative and sporting metaphors (such as "putting runs on the board," "making the hard yards," "leading from the front," "leading the troops," "putting the puck in the net," "slam dunk," "scoring touchdowns") and by expressing admiration for archetypal tough coaches, athletes, or teams (McKay 1997). The exclusion of women from this homosocial corporate world is evident in the number of "power feminism" books that instruct aspiring corporate women on how to become familiar with sporting language, thereby beating the boys at their own game.

Similarly, sport has taken on most of the trappings of corporate culture

(Rowe 1995, 139). It is not only business that has appropriated the language of sport—sport has also seized the connotative linkage between sporting and business competition, with commentators referring routinely to the "business end of the match," when players' corporeal investments begin to "pay dividends." On occasion this connection takes the form of a recognition of the industrialization of sport, such as in the theme for the 1994 conference of the Australian Society of Sports Administrators: "The Business of Sport: Gaining the Competitive Edge." At the same time, the media have hitched sport and business speech in various permutations—by using sports metaphors in the business and political pages and in advertising, and also by deploying business metaphors in sports reports (Rowe 1991). The bringing together of sport and corporatist metaphors produces a mutually enlivening drama that, as we demonstrate below in examining the case of *Murdoch v. Packer*, transmutes easily into a full-fledged narrative of melodramatic excess.

Super League: The Soap

Although media coverage of Super League was scripted according to a variety of genres, melodrama was the main anchoring principle and TV soap opera its formal expression. The Super League "soap," as constructed by the Packer media, the ARL, and more traditionalist journalists, had the following formula. The "bad guys" were Murdoch and his hired corporate guns of Super League. Both were traitors, the former because he gave up his Australian citizenship to become an American and the latter because they had turned their backs on a sacred Australian institution. The "good guys" were Packer and the ARL, who had remained loyal to "the workingman's game" and attempted to repel the rapacious "foreigner" and his treacherous mercenaries. There were also the usual twists and turns in the plot, as the major local hero also became a Judas by apparently selling out to the foreigner, thus leaving the old guard in a very precarious position. As we have seen, the Murdoch-Packer "sellout" of league fell through, leaving the former to protest that he had been, in the manner of melodramatic special pleading, betrayed.

Examples of this soap genre were evident in iconically powerful themes representing sport as the plaything of media proprietors. One striking and much-echoed front-page lead image in the *Sydney Morning Herald* was of Murdoch and Packer, wearing the headbands favored by many league players, facing each other in apparently mortal combat under the headline "Rugby

League Revolution——Packer v. Murdoch." Beneath this clash of titanic leaders were a range of minor stories of struggle and betrayal:

> Everywhere you looked, famous and feted players were disappearing at the hands of one or other of the agents of News Limited. With them moving quickly and often under the cover of darkness, each morning brought new headlines of the lengthening list of defectors, to the screams of the ARL hierarchy and the groans of the ARL/Packer forces who were trying to hold onto them. The News Limited troops kept foraging forward regardless. (Fitzsimons 1995, S–4A)

One essential ingredient that turns personalized "kitchen-sink" melodrama into a more generalizable tragedy is the inversion of order, a world turned upside down in which stable, predictable relationships no longer obtain. The binary structure of tradition and loyalty was, therefore, productive of a series of minidramas as former friends and allies became enemies and rivals. A pervasive theme here was the threat that "corporate greed" allegedly posed to that quintessentially Australian masculine practice of "mateship":

> League men are now calling each other "treacherous," "duplicitous" and bare-faced liars. Life-long friends . . . no longer communicate . . . [a] time of frayed tempers, severed friendships, unanswered phone calls, curt comments and brutal faxes. (Masters 1995b, 71)

> So emotional was the upheaval that it set mates against mates, from boardroom down to the dressing room. Few were untouched. (McGregor 1995, 1)

The abstract conception of friendship was made concrete in such pronouncements through the specific formation of working-class *brother*hood. In question is not merely the testing of old affiliations, but the possible demise of the workingman's game and, by extension, of male working-class solidarity and identity itself. In an interview with John Ribot, a former national player and member of the ARL's policy committee who became CEO of Super League, a journalist asked:

> The *Sydney Morning Herald* this week headlined a John Ribot profile "Is This Man a Traitor or a Visionary?" Right now, your profile stinks. You're perceived as the guy who stole the working-man's game. The pay packet, it sure must be good?

To which Ribot replied:

> [There has been] a lot of turmoil, a lot of blood in the streets . . . everyone's
> carrying on about losing friends. . . . You know, in this whole thing I have not
> lost one friend. If you lose a friend through this, he or she wasn't a friend.
> (Crawley 1995, 34)

This convergence—and, in some cases, sundering—of class and masculine mateship was emphasized by a former coach turned journalist:

> From cloth cap to salary cap could be the working title for a story of 100
> years of rugby league. . . . In Australia, the league for the masses has become
> the code for all classes. . . . The confidence of Murdoch's chief lieutenant,
> Ken Cowley, in the new pro league for the proletariat is such that his Super
> League outfit will run at a loss for Foxtel. Not only are Australia's two rich-
> est men—Rupert Murdoch and Kerry Packer—fighting for control of the
> game, but prominent members of Sydney's professional classes sit on rugby
> league boards. . . . Men in Armani suits with gold Amex cards run the
> game. . . . Rugby league risks losing its "done it hard" ethos, a reflection of
> the war-like territorial nature of the game itself. (Masters 1995a, 64)

This depiction of a world we have lost was a major theme for Masters
and others in the process of popular sense making. According to another
writer, this time an academic and occasional media commentator on sport:

> In the nasty 90s, football club mergers and "Super Leagues" focus the pain
> and danger many people feel in their workplace and their daily life. Change
> today, like the changes wrought by the "dark satanic mills" of the Industrial
> Revolution, and by the invading whites who came in the First Fleet two cen-
> turies ago, influences us all. Initially they wreaked massive human havoc and
> out of them would later arise both rugby league and star Aboriginal foot-
> ballers. (Alomes 1995, 24, 28)

This narrative construction was not confined to news media elaborations of
what, from some vantage points, might have appeared to be rather dour and
routine maneuvers over commercial and industrial laws. The melodramatic
theme was seized upon both by the lawyers for the ARL and, in his strongly
pro-ARL finding, Justice Burchett of the federal court himself. For example,
in the opening address by the ARL counsel, it was asserted:

Our objective in these proceedings is to stop the cleavage, put the league back together again and to have Your Honour condemn without blinking what we regard as the treachery and avarice of News Limited. . . . Loyalty and mateship may have no place in business but until the pursuit of wealth for its own sake infiltrated it in the league, they were passwords both on and off the field. (quoted in Scott 1995, 1)

Burchett picked up on this theme in his colorful 218-page judgment, where he described Super League's "meticulously planned operation" as involving secrecy, suddenness, and deception intended to leave the "ARL defenceless against a virtual takeover by News Limited."

Against this sense of lost (male) organicism, Super League's emphasis on progress, excellence, and globalization emerged as rather less than affectively potent. There is considerable irony in this outcome, given that the ARL had already made much of its business acumen, its national and international development of league, and, most strikingly, its attempts to redefine the masculinism of the game. As various writers have indicated (e.g., Lynch 1993; Yeates 1995), the use of Tina Turner and male pinup calendars in its promotional campaigns and various other attempts to incorporate women and children more fully into league and to move teams out of declining inner-city Sydney neighborhoods formed part of an essential survival strategy for a "workingman's game" experiencing the long-term effects of deindustrialization and social reconstitution. In spite of the much-touted modernism of the ARL, it could not outprogressivize the global media profile of Murdoch. It retreated, therefore, to a populist little Australianism that, improbably, constructed Packer, Australia's richest individual, as a "man of the people."

For this move to work, Murdoch, through various extravagant vectors of intertextuality, was demonized as a dissolute foreigner. He was compared to the "factionalized" ruthless media magnate Citizen Kane, among others. Following the conventions of tragedy and melodrama, notions of succession and patrimony were pivotal. Considerable attention was paid to the fact that both Murdoch and Packer are Australian-born sons of media barons who are, in turn, grooming their own sons as potential managers of their corporations. Lachlan Murdoch and James (formerly known by the diminutive "Jamie") Packer were deeply involved in signing players to both camps. The classic father-son dimension of melodrama was, therefore, given full rein. For instance, an article headlined "Time for the Young Bulls" stated:

The battle between Kerry Packer and Rupert Murdoch over rugby league is just one more clash in a dynastic duel that has been building for nearly

203

75 years. Appropriately, it has also seen the blooding of the two sons, James Packer and Lachlan Murdoch, the new generation who will likely carry the duel into the 21st century. . . . Unlike their fathers [whose own fathers had died suddenly], both have been able to think and plan about the succession. . . . In those circumstances, nothing would be more natural, or inevitable than to blood them in a preliminary head-to-head combat over rugby league. One could not think of a better stoush to show them what lies ahead. (McCrann 1995, 29, 32)

One novel turn in the plot was the surprise decision of Kerry Packer, shortly after the federal court had ruled in his favor in February 1996, to stand down as chairman and to install his son James as chief executive of PBL. Here, the theme of intergenerational succession spiced the Super League intertext. In fact, the story is set to run and run. The court decision, which banned Super League and forced the rebel players back to the ARL, was immediately subject to a Full Bench appeal by News Limited. In October 1996, Rupert Murdoch got the verdict he was looking for. The three-judge Full Bench overturned Burchett's decision, setting aside all orders and freeing players, referees, and administrators to start up Super League in 1997. It was the Packer camp's turn to go back to the courts, with the ARL immediately signaling its intention to seek leave to appeal to the High Court of Australia. While Kerry Packer was conspicuously silent after the federal court judgment, his pay-TV ally, Optus Vision, promised a financial package of Aus$164 million that was designed to allow the ARL to sustain a rival competition with Super League at least until the end of the century. Although there was much media speculation about compromises, capitulations, and defections in favor of Murdoch, a major obstacle to "peace" appeared to be his ego-laden feud with Packer.

Other fictional genres were also deployed in narrativizing events. Super League was framed as an epic, revolutionary event ("51 Days That Shook League" and "7 Days That Shook the Sports World") and a war ("civil war," "marketing war," "propaganda war," "courtroom battle") that was fought by "generals," "lieutenants," "rebels," "patriots," "troops," "defectors," and "soldiers." Some typical headlines were "The Seven-Day War"; "When the Guns Fell Silent . . . the Cold War Began"; "The Split: How Footy War Was Waged"; "ARL Attacks News with Huge Damages Claim"; "News Accused of Blitz Attack on ARL"; "League Plundered by Pillaging Visigoths: QC"; and "Battle for Big League Supremacy." Murdoch and Packer were often portrayed in sporting/physical contexts ("a dynastic duel," "media titans," "media gladiators," "sledgehammer businessmen"). One journalist scripted his story along the lines of a heavyweight-title-fight commentary and introduced Murdoch as follows:

[In this corner] . . . Rampaging Rupert Murdoch, the media magnate out of Adelaide—175 cm tall, and weighing in at some [Aus]$15.5 billion. He has a reach that extends from Los Angeles in the East to Los Angeles in the West, and a right hook that has already pulled in soccer in Britain and the National Football League in America . . . voted the most powerful man in world sport by the influential American magazine *Sports Illustrated*. (Fitzsimons 1995, S-4A)

This boxing metaphor proved particularly popular—another journalist observed, "At various times it seemed Packer then Murdoch had KO'd each other, only to discover neither had a glass jaw" (McGregor 1995, 1). When Murdoch and Packer sought agreement on various issues, many commentators found it difficult to follow the boxing analogy to its logical conclusion— that the Murdoch-Packer bout had, in fact, been "fixed."

Indeed, so preoccupied were many journalists with extracting the maximum connotative value from sports metaphors and similes that they often continued to make a disingenuous distinction between the "reality" of wider society and the artificial world of sport, implying that the latter is a politically innocent realm that becomes corrupted only by "outside" forces. Not only is this representation of the magical space of politics-free sport patently fantastical, it is repudiated in one very obvious respect by much journalistic practice. That is, pro- and anti-Murdoch and Packer positions were in many cases traceable directly to journalists' employers. Print and electronic media coverage from the two camps was so arrantly partisan that even the most naive viewers or readers quickly became aware that, at any one time, they were receiving the Packer or Murdoch Super League News, not neutral reportage of issues and events. The Fairfax Press, a takeover target of both media barons, relished its role of giving "unbiased" coverage by often painting unflattering portraits of both men. Analysis of media coverage of the Super League story is, then, instructive both in showing the reliance of journalists, legal advocates, and the judiciary on imagery derived from various long-standing popular mythologies and in exposing the absurdity of claims by sports and other journalists that sport and "objective" reporting transcend the everyday round of material conflict.

Conclusion

In telling our version of the Super League story, we have outlined its political economic "enframement" and also employed textualist techniques to map out the discursive practices and ideologies that offer up particular meanings to the often confusing patchwork of phenomena that constitutes social life. In particular, we have noted the ways in which social institutions and actors consciously and unconsciously narrativize the world. The range of speaking positions and the significatory dynamism entailed in any witness to events in the social world mean that the final story can never be told. However, we can trace their origins and trajectories as products of institutional processes within the sport, the media, the judicial system, and so on. If it is important to highlight the intertextual and intergeneric dimensions of everyday life, it is also necessary not to succumb to the glassy-eyed, dematerialized pluralism that all too often passes for contemporary critical analysis.

In our case study, virtually all of the images and texts that we analyzed were by, for, and about men—more specifically, white, able-bodied, heterosexual, rich, powerful, aggressive men. Developing an understanding of media coverage of the Super League phenomenon, therefore, requires a broader understanding of the workings of gendered power in the economy of culture and in the cultural economy. A feature of our analysis was the prominence of the elaborate genres of melodrama that were used to anchor these texts. Whether such melodramatic representations of men have the potential to destabilize hegemonic masculinity is questionable—these representations seem to be fairly traditional variations on a theme of "what a [bourgeois] man's gotta do" and as expressed in laments for the good old days of patriarchal Australia, when beer, "footy," and proletarian mateship reigned supreme (McKay and Middlemiss 1995). To be sure, this gender order has been challenged by women and gay men and is being supplanted by new types of hegemonic men, who have class backgrounds different from those of traditional working-class men. Yet these "new men" in the worlds of business and sport were portrayed as having more in common with Gordon Gekko than Ben and Jerry, followers of what Connell (1990, 535) calls "the cult of the ruthless entrepreneur in business." The representations we analyzed had a pronounced degree of ideological closure, reinforcing the notion that both sport and business are almost exclusively men's domains and that real men in both spheres are hard and tough, with the homosocial ethos of masculine mateship frequently seen as threatened by the sociopathic masculinity of buccaneering entrepreneurialism without frontiers.

Whatever assessment we might make of changing masculinity, the Super

League provided the barest glimpse of it. For all the breast-beating about the decline of the working-class man and his game and the rise of the middle-class functionary, the dominant icons were patriarchal—Rupert and Lachlan Murdoch versus Kerry and James Packer and their respective coteries of male lawyers, journalists, and corporate executives. These very much unreconstructed media moguls, inheritors of their fathers' accumulated media capital, were struggling over the spoils of new media technology (pay TV) before handing over the family businesses to their favored sons. Whether Rupert, Kerry, Lachlan, and James are likened to J. R. Ewing, General Patton, or Woody Allen now and in the future, one thing is clear—sport is still above all a man's world, and inherited class advantage and disadvantage still count for much in the conduct of both corporate and semiotic guerrilla warfare.

Coda

Just after Christmas 1996, Kerry Packer helicoptered into a remote bay in New Zealand where Rupert Murdoch was vacationing on his $38 million yacht, *Morning Glory*. In a deal later tidied up in Sydney by their sons, Murdoch awarded Super League's free-to-air TV rights to Packer's Nine Network. The news "shocked" the ARL's Ken Arthurson (popularly known as Arko), who said, "We firmly believed that Nine, Optus and the ARL would march arm-in-arm and be the staunchest of allies." Two days later he resigned. Rupert and Kerry had given the plot another twist.

The narrative continued to unfold throughout 1997. There was an urge to "bury" the second-rank antagonists in order to precipitate a compromise that would result in the unification of the two disastrously unprofitable competitions. The chief executives of the ARL and Super League, the Johns Quayle and Ribot, walked the plank. Ken Cowley, Arko's "shadow," retired as executive chairman of News Limited in April, to be replaced by Rupert's heir apparent, Lachlan. In the middle of the year, the extent of the losses incurred by the combatants in the league and pay-TV wars became (for them, at least) depressingly evident. September was a fateful month. The federal government, after months of agonizing over how to keep two competing media moguls happy without giving the appearance of doing so, abandoned, on pain of a party revolt and popular disapproval, any immediate attempt to change Australia's cross-media and foreign-ownership rules. So Kerry didn't get Fairfax as a "Christmas present," in the now infamous words of son James during an interview on the Packers' own television station. And Rupert didn't get control of the Seven TV network. For now, they had canceled each other out. The Supreme Court upheld the ARL's player loyalty agreement, thereby bringing on the inevitable Super League appeal. The Perth Super League franchise was abandoned on economic grounds. Finally, there was a dream result for the ARL in the grand final of its Optus Cup competition, when the champion Manly Sea Eagles (the most hated team in the league on account of its reputation for bourgeois affluence and arrogance) lost in the last few seconds to the underdog Newcastle Knights (who were participating in their first final and hail from a deindustrializing provincial town commonly referred to as Steel City). Suddenly, all the rhetoric about the "workingman's game," "loyalty," and "tradition" came flooding back, to the manifest advantage of the ARL. Some fans even said that Newcastle had saved the ARL by defeating Manly, Arko's old club, just as the man himself said that they had saved it before by *not* joining Super League. As mass celebrations spilled out over Newcastle and the Hunter Region, questions were asked about the future of the rival Super League franchise—the Hunter Mariners. Meanwhile, behind the scenes, the agents of Rupert and Kerry continued to work for a solution to the monstrous problem they had created in the tussle over sports pay-TV viewers. A compromise was eventually reached: the Mariners were disbanded, the South Queensland Crushers crushed, and the Melbourne Storm "brewed"; a new, combined National Rugby League was formed; the pay and free-to-air TV spoils were shared around; and many clubs were told to merge by 1999 or face extinction. Like all good soap operas, this is one we can tune out for a while and then switch on again without "losing the plot." For this opportunity we can thank the transparent greed, ruthlessness, and hypocrisy of characters straight out of capitalism's central casting.

Works Cited

Alomes, Stephen. 1995. "Murdoch Sends Sport Away with the Pixies." *Sydney Morning Herald*, 18 December, 24, 28.

Attwood, Alan. 1996. "The Highest Roller." *Sydney Morning Herald*, 23 March, 5s.

Brooks, Peter. 1985. *The Melodramatic Imagination.* New York: Columbia University Press.

Cohan, Steven, and Ira Rae Hark, eds. 1993. *Screening the Male: Exploring Masculinities in Hollywood Cinema.* London: Routledge.

Cole, Cheryl, and Harry Denny. 1994. "Visualizing Deviance in Post-Reagan America: Magic Johnson, AIDS, and the Promiscuous World of Professional Sport. *Critical Sociology* 20: 123–47.

Connell, Robert W. 1990. "The State, Gender, and Sexual Politics: Theory and Appraisal." *Theory and Society* 19 (October): 507–44.

———. 1995. *Masculinities.* Sydney: Allen & Unwin.

Cowie, Elizabeth. 1977. "Women, Representation, and the Image." *Screen Education* 23 (summer): 15–23.

Crawley, Steve. 1995. "Ribot Rejects Compromise." *Weekend Australian,* 29–30 April, 34.

Ebert, Tereas L. 1992–93. "Ludic Feminism, the Body, Performance, and Labor: Bringing Materialism Back into Feminist Cultural Studies." *Cultural Critique* 23 (winter): 5–50.

Fife-Yeomans, Janet. 1996. "Packer v. Murdoch: The game hots up." *Australian,* 20 March, 1.

Fitzsimons, Peter. 1995. "Playing for Possession." *Sydney Morning Herald,* 8 April, S–4A.

Hall, Stuart. 1985. "Signification, Representation, Ideology: Althusser and the Post-structuralist Debates." *Critical Studies in Mass Communication* 2 (June): 91–114.

Harriss, Ian. 1990. "Packer, Cricket, and Postmodernism." In *Sport and Leisure: Trends in Australian Popular Culture,* ed. David Rowe and Geoff Lawrence. Sydney: Harcourt Brace Jovanovich.

Headon, David, and Lex Marinos, eds. 1996. *League of a Nation.* Sydney: ABC.

Jackson, Stevi. 1992. "The Amazing Deconstructing Woman." *Trouble and Strife* 25 (winter): 25–31.

Jhally, Sut. 1989. "Cultural Studies and the Sports/Media Complex." In *Media, Sports, and Society,* ed. Lawrence A. Wenner. Newbury Park, Calif.: Sage.

King, Samantha. 1993. "The Politics of the Body and the Body Politic: Magic Johnson and the Ideology of AIDS." *Sociology of Sport Journal* 10 (fall): 270–85.

Kirkham, Pat, and Janet Thumin, eds. 1993. *You Tarzan: Masculinity, Movies, and Men.* London: Lawrence & Wishart.

Lynch, Rob. 1993. "The Cultural Repositioning of Rugby League and Its Men." *ANZALS Leisure Research Series* 1: 105–19.

Masters, Roy. 1995a. "100 Years of League." *Sydney Morning Herald,* 26 August, 64.

———. 1995b. "When the Guns Fell Silent . . . the Cold War Began." *Sydney Morning Herald,* 8 April, 71.

McCrann, Terry. 1995. "Time for the Young Bulls." *Courier-Mail,* 8 April, 29, 32.

McGregor, Adrian. 1995. "The Split: How Footy War Was Waged." *Weekend Australian,* 23–24 September, 1.

McKay, Jim. 1991. *No Pain, No Gain? Sport and Australian Culture.* Sydney: Prentice Hall.

———. 1993. "Marked Men and Wanton Women: The Politics of Naming Sexual Deviance in Sport." *Journal of Men's Studies* 2 (August): 69–87.

———. 1997. *Managing Gender: Affirmative Action and Organizational Power in Australian, Canadian, and New Zealand Sport.* Albany: State University of New York Press.

McKay, Jim, Geoffrey Lawrence, Toby Miller, and David Rowe. 1993. "Globalization, Postmodernism, and Australian Sport." *Sport Science Review* 2: 10–28.

McKay, Jim, and Iain Middlemiss. 1995. "Mate against Mate, State against State: A Case Study of Media Constructions of Hegemonic Masculinity in Australian Sport. *Masculinities* 3 (fall): 38–47.

McKay, Jim, and Philip Smith. 1995. "Exonerating the Hero: Frames and Narratives in Media Coverage of the O. J. Simpson Story." *Media Information Australia* 7 (February): 557–66.

Miller, Toby. 1989. "World Series Sound and Vision." *Meanjin* 48 (spring): 591–96.

Mouzelis, Nicos. 1993. "The Poverty of Sociological Theory." *Sociology* 27 (spring): 675–95.

Muller, Nicole M. 1995. "As the (Sports) World Turns: An Analysis of the Montana-49er Social Drama." *Journal of Sport & Social Issues* 19 (May): 157–79.

Rose, Ava, and James Friedman. 1994. "Television Sport as Mas(s)culine Cult of Distraction." *Screen* 35 (spring): 22–35.

Rowe, David. 1991. "Play on Words." *Media Information Australia* 59 (February): 59–66.

————. 1994. "Accommodating Bodies: Celebrity, Sexuality, and Tragic Magic." *Journal of Sport & Social Issues* 18 (February): 6–26.

————. 1995. *Popular Cultures: Rock Music, Sport, and the Politics of Pleasure.* London: Sage.

Rowe, David, Geoffrey Lawrence, Toby Miller, and Jim McKay. 1994. "Global Sport? Core Concern and Peripheral Vision." *Media, Culture & Society* 16 (October): 661–75.

Schultz, Julianne. 1993. "Queens of the Screen or Princes of Print? The Media and Concentration of Ownership." In *A Sociology of Australian Society: Introductory Readings* (2d ed.), ed. Jake Najman and John Western. Melbourne: Macmillan.

Scott, Jody. 1995. "News Accused of Blitz Attack on ARL." *Australian,* 28 September, 1.

Silverstone, Roger. 1994. "The Power of the Ordinary: On Cultural Studies and the Sociology of Culture." *Sociology* 28 (November): 991–1001.

West, Cornel. 1989. "Black Culture and Postmodernism." In *Remaking History,* ed. Barbara Kruger and Paul Mariani. Seattle: Bay.

Whannel, Garry. 1993. "No Room for Uncertainty: Gridiron Masculinity in *North Dallas Forty*." In *You Tarzan: Masculinity, Movies, and Men,* ed. Pat Kirkham and Janet Thumin. London: Lawrence & Wishart.

Yeates, Helen. 1995. "The League of Men: Masculinity, the Media, and Rugby League Football." *Media Information Australia* 75 (February): 35–45.

Cultural Links: An International Political Economy of Golf Course Landscapes

Bradley S. Klein

The landscape has a textuality that we are just beginning to understand.
▸ *Edward W. Soja*, Postmodern Geographies

What do they know of cricket, who only cricket know?
▸ C. L. R. *James*, Beyond a Boundary

The strength of any social theory is its ability to explain the relationship between the particular and the general. The more apparently mundane the phenomenon, the more important the analytic framework by which we position it critically. Even in the case of something as apparently simple (some might say numbing) as the game of golf, it is possible—and I would argue urgent—that it be situated within a framework that makes some sense of its conspicuous place in high-modern culture. There are few practices that are so paradigmatically Western in their origin and outlook, that so readily promote and articulate modernist class interests, and that along the way occupy so much space.

In this essay, I explore golf course design as one moment in the unfolding of modernity. I take golf courses seriously as aesthetic and cultural landscapes, with all that entails about their status as negotiated spaces mediating realms of territorial place, human cultural activity, and complex market relations transcending immediate regional boundaries.[1] At one level, this is an empirical exercise in the description of a common if radically understudied "working landscape."[2] By this I mean not merely the formal recounting of immediately functional design features—of mounds and contours that steer the ball this way or that—but also of the larger social geography that gives these particular managed spaces their function and identity. The concept of working landscape thus plays on the distinction between *natural* and *managed*—recognizing all along that the difference, while helpful in focusing attention upon certain strategies of human endeavor upon the land, is nonetheless dialectical insofar as no "natural" landscape is entirely removed from human intervention. The difference, rather, lies in that realm where quantity slides into quality—where, in other words, the burden of human planning and architecture establishes that site as fundamentally different from an area that, though affected or influenced by human practices, is not directly restructured according to plan.

By construing golf courses as functional landscapes rather than merely as sites for a game or sporting contest, it is possible to indulge a deeper, more theoretically informed—if here only preliminarily developed—level concerning the transition from modernity to postmodernity. In light of a rapidly proliferating literature in landscape studies, the politics of land planning, and the geography of site selection, we can literally "read" the aesthetic and functional forms of course architecture as a succession of sites upon which culture inscribes itself.[3] That such readings are debatable speaks to the complexity of land use and the essential contestability of leisure in contemporary society; what one developer sees as a golf course and resort complex is viewed by local peasants as an ecologically disastrous intrusion by First World interests upon the Third World. Or in a more subtle vein, such as now being debated in Scotland, the home of golf, a municipally controlled asset like the Old Course at St. Andrews, available to town residents for no fee, can be partially made available through private tour operators for astronomical fees. When the British firm Keith Prowse Hospitality strikes a deal with the St. Andrews Links Trust to buy 7 percent of tee times for $7.5 million over ten years in order to resell them to an ultra-upscale tourist market—at $1,200 for a two-day outing—then something has dramatically altered in the nature of that working landscape.[4] A treasured example of classical, natural linksland golf design—itself an element of national identity—is thereby transformed into a precious commodity that circulates on global exchange markets.

Such a political economy of the golf course can be deployed to explore not only the marketing of the game but also to see how the landforms themselves have been literally shaped and reshaped in terms of their architecture. Does the course emphasize native ground contours, or has it been extensively made over through earth-moving equipment? Are its grasses indigenous, or are they cultivated only through application of extensive agronomic management and heavy use of pesticides? Are the holes designed to maximize native contours and landforms, or are they the products of extensive manipulation by bulldozers? Are the holes themselves intended to harmonize with the site, or are they intended to make a marketing point by pointing attention to some symbolic artifact?

The mapping strategies required to read such sites are part of extra-disciplinary practices by which we can articulate a certain reterritorialization of politics at both the domestic and global levels. Such a focus is significant in restoring to the forefront of political analysis those immediately experi-

212

enced realms of space subject to civic action and mobilization. A politics of land use, zoning, and regulation may well prove more accessible as an object of democratic organization—and thus political contestation—than those realms of international relations, sovereignty, or "the state" normally examined in social and political theory.

The Space of Golf

Every contour has a history. Golf courses first developed on Scottish linksland from the sixteenth century through the late nineteenth. They were then transposed to the English countryside, and from there exported to become the basis of modern, American-inspired styles of manicured parkland. Lately, these have become internationalized in the form of world-class resort facilities and as nodal points of a culture of state building and modernization in a wide variety of postcolonial contexts. The changing face of the golf course can thus be seen in terms of contending agendas regarding public and private land use, the commercialization of leisure, environmental sensitivity, and the tensions between local and global cultural forms of practice. As a central element in the international tourism industry, golf courses are also markers of cultural identity and privilege. The status attached to their place in society extends even down to the selection of turf grasses—whether native varieties or imported hybrids demanding extensive maintenance regimens and massive watering.[5] Each element is a moment in the articulation of certain cultural links that can be read and interpreted as part of an informal global political economy.

Among the issues that prove relevant here are the origins of the private country club, the link between colonialism and golf, how competitive economic pressures within the golf industry manifest themselves in increasingly showy and costly designs, the growing significance of environmental regulation upon course architecture and maintenance, and how modernist course architecture has been challenged by postmodern design. In response to modernism, a number of design strains are identifiable. Interestingly enough, current debates about the political disposition of postmodernity— as a veiled neoconservative extension of pure commodity relations, or as a democratically inspired proliferation of identity politics and substate social movements—are replicated in two divergent tendencies within what I call postmodern golf course design. On the one hand, we find a hyperreal evocation that draws upon classical imagery to suggest, and sometimes to simulate, a pseudospace of tradition; on the other hand, we find a minimalist antimodernism—golf's version of a low-budget return to nature—that seeks

213

radically to simplify the golf experience, and with it, the accompanying landforms.

The golf course thus transcends the confines of its immediate geography. These are not merely attractive playfields. These are products of ingenuity and technology, artistic creations that are available for public use. They are also contested spaces, appropriated for one use and thus unavailable for others. The ecology of courses, their function as protective green spaces or as noxious and toxic fairways, is a legitimate object of public policy making. And of course, they are important commercial enterprises. The industry in the United States alone generates $15 billion in trade annually. Moreover, those who play the game enjoy disproportionately high disposable income, introducing elements of social privilege into issues of land use.

Golf courses thus deserve to be taken seriously as works of art, culture, politics, and economy. Among the nongolfing public, the game suffers an embarrassing reputation, with its players disparaged for their taste in clothes and golf itself dismissed as boring. The vast landscapes upon which the game is played are seen as little more than overmanicured lawns, exclusive playfields reserved for the privileged classes. Golfers themselves, of whom there are twenty-four million in the United States and about forty million worldwide, have always been fascinated by the golf courses they play. But their understanding of "reading a green" has been basically confined to instructional concerns, such as interpreting the slope and speed of a putting surface.[6]

In their natural setting, their landscape contours and plantings, these functional landscapes are the unique products of the interaction between native habitat and human ingenuity.[7] They are landforms that are carefully scripted as products of their culture, technology, and economy. No popular form of recreation enjoys a more aesthetically diverse or complex playing field than golf. The only rule governing dimensions of the golf course is that the space into which the player tries to deliver the ball must be four and one-quarter inches in diameter. For the sake of clarification, note that in course design, the term *hole* usually refers to the large open space stretching between a teeing ground and a putting green that includes the fairway and rough, not merely to the little cup in which the ball winds up on each green. A golf course comprises nine or eighteen such holes in the expanded sense. Each such hole differs from other holes in terms of its distance, width, shape, texture, and placement of hazards according to the character of the particular site, the imagination of the designer, and the willingness of an owner to foot the bill. The resulting look and feel of the course are also dependent upon the care—or neglect—undertaken by maintenance staff. In effect, a golf course is never fixed and secured in its identity. By its very nature, it evolves as an organic work of art.

There are some fifteen thousand golf courses in the United States, some twenty-five thousand throughout the world. Each occupies on average some 110 acres. This means that in the United States, an area comprising 1.65 million acres, or some 2,678 square miles—an area twice the size of Rhode Island, or half the size of Connecticut—is devoted to golf.[8]

Curiously, not a single serious work has been devoted to the place that these landscapes occupy in our culture and aesthetic sensibilities. There are some suggestive works on the art of golf course architecture, most of them dating back to the 1920s, and all of them dealing with the elements of sound design and how these might be practically implemented into an ideal golf course.[9] As both literature and practical guides, such books are invaluable to students of the field seeking to understand what makes a sound golf hole. But none makes any pretense of connecting to a wider world—except for a quirky chapter in a recent publication of a long-lost manuscript in which the author, Dr. Alister MacKenzie, in comparing Bolshevik Russia to the United States of the early 1930s, attributes the Soviet Union's relative cultural impoverishment to its never having taken up golf![10] The charge that golf is inherently a bourgeois sport and so merited banishment from Communist regimes is a prejudice only affirmed since 1989, with golf now enjoying a boom precisely as an element of post-Communist proof that such societies are indeed Westernizing.[11]

From Classical to Postmodern

Golf course architecture is a creative endeavor incorporating three basic elements: terrain, human imagination, and technology. Over time, it is possible to discern several basic styles of design that have resulted. For reasons that will become clear, I will call them classical, modern, and postmodern.[12]

Classical design derives from the origins of the game along the Scottish seacoast. The earliest courses gradually emerged along the receding coastal sand, at the foot of the raised marine platform, or "links." No earth was moved, no plantings made. Players simply stroked the ball from one spot to the next. Eventually, paths of play developed, and then people assumed responsibility for maintaining the clearances that had evolved—thus the origin of the greenkeeper. Sand bunkers were not built, they evolved where local golfers habitually gouged out the turf or where native animals, seeking shelter from the weather, had created sandy hollows.

At a certain point, sometime around the middle of the nineteenth century, the old Scottish links were lengthened and updated for play to accommodate increased traffic—and the enhanced performance of the mass-manufactured gutta-percha golf ball, which replaced the old handmade "featherie" (itself concocted from a boiled-down hatful of duck feathers that were then stuffed into a leather pouch). Still, the basic sites remained very much as they had originally been found. A few wheelbarrows of dirt were hauled from here to there, and some flattening and rolling of surfaces were needed to achieve a rough version of putting greens, but the game's tradition was to utilize available land—all of it, it must be noted, in the public domain—and to run the holes through natural dunes and features.

The classic charm of seaside links is that their look, their texture, and their turf are all inseparable from centuries of evolution and history. The juxtaposition of railways and golf courses, such as at Prestwick in Scotland or Royal Lytham and St. Annes in England, speaks volumes about how the steam engine linked seaside resort towns and major cities. Golf courses, even in resort areas, were invariably located close to town centers, on the seaward side of a residential area, and readily accessible via the predominant mode of popular transportation—walking. To this day, it is a common sight in Scotland, for instance, to see schoolboys trudging their clubs across town to queue up at the starter's shack, where they take their places next to schoolteachers and other working people out for a round of golf. A round takes only two and a half hours to play—compared with five hours on average in the United States and at most Western-style resorts—so there's that much more time in the day to enjoy a round, and at rates that are within easy reach of most households.

The juxtaposition of such courses with historical markers gives many of these courses an antiquated sensibility, evoked, for example, by castle ruins that dot some golf landscapes, such as at Lahinch in Ireland and Cruden Bay in Scotland. And nothing can emulate the historic ambiance of a golf course like St. Andrews, on Scotland's Fife Coast, which derives its power and grace from its location literally in the midst of a medieval university town. To this day, the influence of classical seaside links layouts has been crucial. Even though only 19 percent of Scotland's 425 courses today are properly classified as linksland, their hold on the game's traditions and on subsequent generations of designers and players has been absolutely decisive.[13]

Linksland, meanwhile, was being rapidly exhausted—and at the same time, the game was moving south and inland to England, starting in the second half of the nineteenth century. Golf courses were being located near industrial and residential centers, where the inland clay and loam soils did not offer the same porosity as sand and thus drained more poorly. Golf course design had to be developed properly as a craft so that land not ideally suited for such turf grasses could be specially prepared. Site preparation became a subject of much study. Essays that began appearing before the First World War concerned themselves with preparing meadowland and parkland for golf's demands. Issues of drainage became paramount. Initially surface water was steered into gullies, but it did not take long for subsurface pipe drainage to be added. Sand bunkers were now artificially installed in an attempt to recapture the seaside feel of the classical links. Hundreds of cubic yards of fill had to be moved to build greens and teeing areas.

This early-modern period, particularly the 1920s, was golf design's most innovative era, especially in North America, as a burgeoning middle class, now able to travel out into the countryside thanks to the automobile, took up this pastoral game. Site selection, however, was still based upon the preexisting natural rolls and features of the land. Architects such as A. W. Tillinghast (1874–1942), Donald Ross (1872–1948), Alister MacKenzie (1871–1933), and George Thomas (1873–1932) were often free to choose one plot or the next one down the road as they searched for more suitable land. Horse-drawn scrapers could shave off slices of land and make a few decisive cuts for the sake of visibility. But most of the work was done by hand—much of it by low-wage immigrant laborers. Earth moving was limited to what could be dynamited and carted away.

The era of modern design began with the advent of major earth-moving equipment in the late 1920s and early 1930s. The steam shovel enabled architects to build mounds in a matter of hours rather than days. The introduction of tractors and bulldozers liberated architects from the constraints of the site. This was the beginning of what came to be known as total site preparation: the use of automated equipment to plow down trees, level the earth, and create features entirely by machine. It soon became customary to move hundreds of thousands of cubic yards of dirt.

The modern look of the golf course in North America reached its triumph in the late 1950s and early 1960s, with the smooth, clean look of designers such as Dick Wilson, Robert Trent Jones Sr., George Cobb, Joe Lee, and Joe Finger. They emphasized massive scale and the power game—an appropriate style for an era of unquestioned American hegemony in things cultural and political. Classical design had rewarded shot making, maneuverability, and the ground game. Modern design, by contrast, emphasized high, lengthy shots and "victory through air power." No one typified this confident, broad-shouldered approach better than the self-styled "master builder," Robert Trent Jones Sr.[14] He was to course design what the other "master builder," Robert Moses, was to the vitality of urban existence—a creative

217

destroyer of the highest order.[15] Jones was regularly invited in by the patriarchs of older, established clubs to "modernize" (that was the term) their golf courses for a new era marked by athletic golfers, high-tech steel shafts (replacing wood shafts in 1930), and the frictionless world of the aerial game. Dozens upon dozens of classical layouts were subjected to his treatment of bulldozing, expanding, and widening. Like Haussmann's redesign of Parisian back streets after the Commune, Jones paved the way for a new era of design—typified by a modernist architectural vision.

Modern course design has always been insensitive to established landforms. In large part the problem is simply that so much suitable land has already been used for other purposes before it becomes available to golf course developers. Yet changes in techniques and attitudes have also been decisive. The post–World War II emergence of the professional landscape architect—embodied in the 1946 formation of the American Society of Golf Course Architects—was in many ways a logical extension of the triumph of science and machinery over native landforms. Yet a good case can be made that the advent of formal training in civil engineering or landscape architecture actually weakened the creative and idiosyncratic features that had characterized classical design. In typical Weberian fashion, the professionalization of the craft led to its diminishment as bureaucratic credentials and professional disciplinary boundaries effaced traditional craftsmanship and aesthetic vision.

Such works liberated the game from topographical constraints and heralded an extraordinary shift in course conditioning—the perfectly manicured look by which the golf course became an extension of suburbia. A thorough research effort, undertaken through partnership between the governing body of the amateur game and privately incorporated turf grass suppliers and equipment manufacturers, ultimately led to the replacement of native rye and Bermuda grasses by imported and agronomically sensitive strains of bent grass—which required extensive applications of water, fertilizers, pesticides, and fungicides to remain green and playable.[16]

Along the way, courses lost subtlety and an organic relationship with the land. To cite one of many examples, consider the palatial Georgian railway hotel called Gleneagles in Scotland's Perthshire Hills. Its original two courses—the Kings and Queens—were hand-built just after World War I, with the holes routed through glacially deposited drumlins that gave the courses their naturally crumpled, corduroy look. In the late 1980s, Jack Nicklaus's design group built a third golf course there—but in doing so, they simply bulldozed the drumlins and started over. The result, not surprisingly, is a golf course—replete with paved cart paths—that looks like it was airlifted in and bears no relations to native land forms. Typical, I might add, for Nicklaus, who does most of his design work on computers rather than the old-fashioned way—on the ground.

In the hands of such aggressive modernism the game became a kind of automatic enterprise, which one course designer has likened to a "freeway" style.[17] This characteristic has been intensified with the rapid proliferation of motorized golf carts, which have further removed players from the integrity of the terrain and led to a thoroughly mechanical version of the experience of place.

It is this "high modernist" golf course that has become the standard internationally—to the point where throughout Asia, for instance, native kikuyu and broadleaf grasses that are easily maintained are being eased out in favor of Western-style turf grasses, primarily Bermuda grass and bent grass. In the absence of indigenous agronomic skills to manage such turf, whole armies of superintendents and chemical maintenance programs are being imported—a kind of agronomic *dependencia* on a global scale. Indeed, the whole development of golf in Asia reflects the tensions of neocolonial politics and culture in ways that bear close scrutiny.

Golf follows wherever there is economic growth. The pattern was set a century and a half ago, when the English upper and middle classes imported the game on a large scale from Scotland. In so doing, they also invented the craft of golf course design. It had been easy to set up a links on Scotland's porous, sandy soil. It was quite another to bring golf inland to clay-based parkland and meadows. The art of surface and subsurface drainage and turf preparation was born of the need to allow golf to survive in England. The game was then brought to the United States, where golf took a decisive turn. It was adopted by the upper classes—reflected, for instance, in the founding of the United States Golf Association in 1894 by five of the country's most exclusive blue-blood clubs. For the next half century, the game's politics and economics were controlled by the interests of this exclusionary private sector. Only with the advent of post–World War II consumer culture and leisure pursuits did golf overthrow its private character and move into the public domain—to the point where today 70 percent of all courses are in the public (i.e., daily-fee) domain and host some 75 percent of all rounds played in the United States.[18]

In Asia, the private sector dominates the game. Golf was established by British colonialists. All of the early golf venues—Royal Calcutta, Royal Hong Kong, Kobe Golf Club—were built and enjoyed by the diplomatic, business, and military representatives of the imperial powers. The pattern changed modestly after World War I, when a rising tide of independence gave birth to an indigenous ruling elite, and they, in turn, took up the game, started their own clubs, and created national golf associations. This is when the first Western architect made his mark on the Asian golf scene: Charles Alison of England, who designed Hirono and Kasumigaseki Golf Clubs in Japan. The development of Japanese golf was halted on nationalist grounds during the 1930s, and any hopes for its domestic growth were dashed by the demands of World War II. The game remained a very limited affair until 1957, when Japan's surprise victory in the World Cup competition sparked widespread national interest in the game. The worldwide media coverage of such recognizable figures as Arnold Palmer, Jack Nicklaus, and Gary Player gave added impetus to the game, and the celebrity status of those three golf superstars was confirmed during their much-publicized tour of Japan in 1967. The Australian design team of Peter Thomson and Michael Wolveridge made major inroads on the booming Asian golf market. Soon thereafter came the American celebrity designer Robert Trent Jones Sr., quickly followed by his son, Robert Trent Jones Jr., and a handful of other prominent Western figures trying to establish themselves in the lucrative new market.

What is it about golf that makes it so popular? Part of its appeal has to do with its cultural status. It is one of the truly international manifestations of Western leisure. There is a great cachet value associated with access to the game. It seems to assure the social standing of anyone who plays. It is, in effect, one of the ironic consequences of "modernization." Golf is a symbol of Western culture that designates the participant as having made the transition into a modern "world capitalist system." That is why access to golf courses is so valued among those seeking international validation. Moreover, state bureaucrats, military officials, and aspiring businessmen gain crucial access to Western contacts through their appearance on the golf course and their ongoing contact with representatives of Western economic, political, and military power. As one aspiring Indonesian tradesman acknowledged in a 1993 *Times of Papua New Guinea* report about "Golfmania," "For me, playing golf is part of doing business."[19]

What holds true in Asia is valid for the newly emerging post-Communist states of Eastern Europe as well. Reporting on the growth of golf in the Czech Republic, *Sports Illustrated* cites a straightforward explanation by a newcomer to the game: "'We want to move toward the West,' says Otakar Jurecka, vice chairman of Investioni Banka, the nation's third-largest bank, 'and we know it is not possible without golf.'"[20]

Historically, the pattern of Asian economic development has meant that golf had long been the exclusive preserve of the expatriot community. Thirty years ago it became a game for the corporate elite of the multinational business world. Now an Asian golf boom is being driven by the addition of a new social force, the leisure demands of the emergent upper middle classes from the capital-intensive countries that are subsidizing, and profiting from, regional economic development. In other words, it used to be colonialists who played the game. Then it was the local, postcolonial elites. Now the white-collar vacationers from the leading centers of investment capital are playing the game. They are doing so increasingly on courses designed by American and European professional golf stars who are cashing in on their marquee value through so-called signature designs, one of those peculiar terms of late-modern cultural "branding" by which aspiring celebrity designers cultivate particularly distinctive looks to their designs that are to be associated with them as personal trademarks. The golf course thereby comes to assume less the look of the local land than of the image propagated by a transnational business empire. Befitting the temperament of our day, it is the label, the signifier, that sells, and it is the market that determines quality— to the point now where a commercial real estate venture needs to have a "name" architect to be taken seriously by prospective investors. The phenomenon confirms David Harvey's observation about the invasiveness of contemporary capitalist trade practices that appropriate space: "Much of post-modern production in, for example, the realms of architecture and urban design, is precisely about the selling of place as part and parcel of an ever-deepening commodity culture."[21]

This selling does not take place without generating opposition, however, and at two readily identifiable levels. The first is articulated on a trans-national basis, roughly a countercultural techno-elite that is the functional equivalent of Jacques Attali's "fast nomads" in its opposition to the game of golf.[22] Inspired by Western ideals of cultural mobility, and armed with cellular phones, fax machines, e-mail, and no small scientific expertise, the Tokyo-based Global Anti-Golf Movement (popularly known as GAG'M) has managed to organize support throughout Pacific Asia against the environmental impact of golf course development. Claims of its membership are highly contested, and much of it seems to revolve around the whirlwind activities of a single organizer, Gen Morita. But there is no doubt that his message of golf's destructive impact on ecology and on social values as well as the deleterious work conditions (low pay, sexual harassment of female caddies) has found resonance among certain sectors of Asia and the Pacific where golf development continues apace.[23]

More anchored in organic social relations, and thus tied to a more traditional representation of social and political space, are indigenously based popular movements that arise in opposition to specific projects. One such

221

movement can be found an hour south of Mexico City, in the town of Tepoztlan. There, between four hundred and two thousand of the town's fourteen thousand inhabitants have formed the antigolf Comité de Unidad Tepozteca (CUT) to defeat a proposed $311 million project. Plans call for turning a 462-acre site into 592 luxury homes, a resort hotel, a Jack Nicklaus-designed golf course, a corporate park, and a helicopter pad to serve upscale commuters from Mexico City. With the intended site comprising communal land, a national park, a habitat corridor, and Aztec ruins, local opposition has been so fierce that the project has essentially been put on hold despite prior permitting approval from the local government.[24] In a region where control of land is seen as decisive, and where economic class inequities are growing as the country signs on to international development projects, CUT has been able to draw upon environmental concerns as well as issues of sovereignty to reappropriate land threatened by global designs.

Design Strategies for the Postmodern

The contested nature of such spaces is part of an increasingly frenetic attempt to commercialize golf course development. In terms of design features, this competitive economic culture has led to some significant architectural developments—led by the proliferation of sensational works that, despite their apparent diversity, may broadly be characterized as postmodern.

We find, for one, an aggressive approach to self-promotion of the golf course—as if the primary force in the design is for it to be distinguishable—whether as the teaser for an upscale real estate community, to be photographed for the cover of a golf magazine, or identified from an approaching airplane. What distinguishes these works is that they embody an indifference to local land forms and instead appear to be oriented more toward proliferating their exchange value as cultural markers, as "simulacra," in the parlance of contemporary criticism. So we find the Segovia Club in Japan, with holes designed to emulate the works of classical Spanish painters; or the Bob Cupp Course on Hilton Head Island, South Carolina, with golf holes featuring trapezoids, pyramids, and triangular features whose straight edges are derived exclusively from a computer-assisted design program that spawned them.[25] We find golf holes in the shapes of mermaids, holes that tell tales of classical antiquity, and artificial island greens, replete with their own refrigeration and heating systems, for which deep channels in an environmentally sensitive lake had to be dredged—but at least it looks great on the cover of a magazine. There is also Tour 18, a golf course outside Houston that purports to reproduce on a dead-flat plain some of the "greatest" holes from various golf courses on the PGA Tour. Or we have the "instant heritage" of a course in northern Michigan that honors the classical design work of Donald Ross by reproducing eighteen of his most famous holes—from eighteen different golf courses.

As has been frequently noted, postmodern design is characterized by a multiplication of signifiers that have been severed from any putative connection to "real things."[26] Placelessness, in the sense of James Howard Kunstler's "geography of nowhere," comes to prevail over the subtle relations covering a classical ensemble of materials, forms, and modes of participation.[27] The market is now the tourist, the global traveler rather than the member of a local community. And so the intimate connection between place and social practice is severed in the name of economic circulation.

There is much more to be said about postmodern forms of golf course design than indicated in this brief space. But what is most important here is to suggest the extent to which the language of social theory can pertain to a wide array of practices having to do with the "working landscapes" that occupy our public spaces. Yet Disney World versions of Main Street U.S.A. are not the only means by which to invoke challenges to modernism. There is a more labored effort available, having to do with the reclamation of local experience in a sustained way rather than through frantic gesturing. Let me then end with some examples of how another kind of design is being cultivated that eschews sensationalism and the temptations of the market for a more sustained attempt at meaningful—that is, lived—social practice.

It is sometimes called minimalism, though that term is misleading, given that it requires a maximal site in terms of existing terrain features and soil conditions. Let us just pose the possibility of an experience tied to recapturing rather than repudiating the complex ensemble of place, local materials, natural contour lines, and aesthetic sensibility that distinguishes contemporary experience.

MacKenzie, Thomas, Tillinghast, Charles Blair MacDonald, and H. S. Colt were unique precisely because, as self-taught practitioners, they had acquired their knowledge in the field through a subtle engagement with the land. Rather than plow over the land to start anew, they elicited and sharpened the contours they found on site. There was nothing, strictly speaking, "natural" about their work. The point is that they knew how to make things look as if they had been undisturbed. The acknowledged master of this was MacKenzie, who prior to taking up course design was founder of the British Army's camouflage school and a designer of World War I trenchworks.

A survey of course design today reveals that a number of designs excel precisely because they have worked with rather than against what was already there. In this sense, the idea of refined course architecture is to enhance an established habitat and to complement local cultural traditions. Consider two recent works by architect Pete Dye. At the Indianapolis 500 Motor Speedway in Indianapolis, he has just rebuilt a golf course where some of the holes incorporate sections of the old racetrack wall. One hole is backed up into the grandstand alongside turn number three, and four holes sit on the track infield. Lest there be any mistaking this American Gothic landscape, the incoming holes bring into play or view the following structures: high-voltage power lines, railroad tracks, petroleum storage tanks, a barn, and a motel.

Over in West Virginia, when Jimmy Joe LaRossa hired Dye to turn an abandoned coalfield into a golf course, the owner offered to clear the site of rusted mining equipment. Dye told him not to touch a thing. What one person sees as trash, another sees as the raw material of art. The visual effect of such cultural artifacts is now on display at the Pete Dye Golf Club. A cart path at one point actually leads into an old mine shaft that cuts through a mountain of coal. One green sits under an exposed coal seam. Railroad tracks and loading sheds adorn the back nine, and a number of bridges are historic wooden structures that add a creaky feel to the grounds. Even a sixty-year-old haystack and rusted farm implements have been incorporated into the design. Modern energy is also a theme at a long hole that lines up right into a trio of eight-hundred-foot smokestacks that rise up two miles behind the green. Such touches create a distinct sense of place.

But questions remain as to the point of such an inflated evocation and use of signs. To some extent, the signs are part of the given terrain, and yet there is also the possibility that they can become marketing tools that help promote attention. The difference here from some of the more egregious flauntings of postmodern kitsch and commodification is that at least the materials were there before the golf course, and so they have not been entirely manufactured but in fact highlighted. There remain strong elements of a museum tableau approach here, as if golfers are being invited to view a retrospectively imagined community that has been pieced together with oversized artifacts—some of which are still functioning.

The globalization of culture has a tendency to generate simultaneous extremes. At the same moment international businessmen and tourists are lining up at high-end golf resorts—an ironically mundane version of Appadurai's "global ethnoscape"[28]—we find in the very heartland of the United States a minimalist repudiation that moves the game way back to "nature."

Welcome to the Sand Hills Golf Club, dead center in the grass-covered duneland of central Nebraska. Only a minuscule amount of dirt was moved during the entire construction process. It is as natural a golf course as anyone has ever produced—a real throwback to links-style golf, and on equally firm sandy soil. The only difference from classical linksland is that there's no ocean to be found. Nor, for that matter, is there a single lake or tree on the golf course, or ornamental flower beds, arrows pointing the way around, dress code, cellular phone, real estate sales office, gated community, wrought iron fence, or, for that matter, a clock. What gives the course its power and character are the three central elements of links golf: sand, howling winds, and firm turf. Cattle ranchers have been squeezing a living out of this dry turf for years. Now a vast stretch of treeless scrub on the banks of the Dismal River is home to a heralded golf course. In defiance of the market, or perhaps in a culmination of a longing for identity and authenticity, its remoteness has become its chief attraction.

How to account for the strange allure of Sand Hills? Perhaps there's something to its cultural politics—the fact that guests find it a more appropriate working landscape than the many modernist versions of the game available at more heavily traveled destinations. If we take seriously the debates about land use and public space pointed to in this essay, however, there can be no privileging the experience of such land, as if it represented something pure and "natural." Cultural links assume multiple forms, and they do so simultaneously. What from one perspective looks like the periphery of modernity could well be its leading edge.

Notes

1. Sharon Zukin, *Landscapes of Power: From Detroit to Disney World* (Berkeley: University of California Press, 1991).
2. Tony Hiss, *The Experience of Place* (New York: Vintage, 1991), 103–25.
3. Charles W. Moore, William J. Mitchell, and William Turnbull Jr., *The Poetics of Gardens* (Cambridge: MIT Press, 1991); Karl B. Raitz, ed., *The Theater of Sport* (Baltimore: Johns Hopkins University Press, 1995).
4. "Selling out St. Andrews," *Sports Illustrated*, 4 December 1995, 19.
5. Virginia Scott Jenkins, *The Lawn: A History of an American Obsession* (Washington, D.C.: Smithsonian Institution Press, 1994).
6. Robert Trent Jones Jr., *Golf by Design* (Boston: Little, Brown, 1993).
7. Michael Pollan, *Second Nature: A Gardener's Education* (New York: Atlantic Monthly Press, 1991).
8. Bradley S. Klein, *Rough Meditations* (Chelsea, Mich.: Sleeping Bear, 1997).
9. H. S. Colt and C. H. Alison, *Some Essays on Golf Course Architecture* (New York: Charles Scribner's Sons, 1920); Alister MacKenzie, *Golf Architecture* (London: Simpkin, Marshall, Hamilton, Kent, 1920); Robert Hunter, *The Links* (New York: Charles Scribner's Sons, 1926); George C. Thomas, *Golf Architecture in America: Its*

Strategy and Construction (Los Angeles: Times-Mirror Press, 1927); Charles Blair Macdonald, *Scotland's Gift: Golf* (New York: Charles Scribner's Sons, 1928); Tom Doak, *The Anatomy of a Golf Course: The Art of Golf Architecture* (New York: Lyons & Burford, 1992); Donald Ross, *Golf Has Never Failed Me* (Chelsea, Mich.: Sleeping Bear, 1996).

10. Alister MacKenzie, *The Spirit of St. Andrews* (Chelsea, Mich.: Sleeping Bear, 1995), 261–63.

11. Cindy Hahn, "The Money Game," *Sports Illustrated,* 14 November 1994, 27–28.

12. Klein, *Rough Meditations,* 49–53.

13. Robert Price, *Scotland's Golf Courses* (Aberdeen: Aberdeen University Press, 1989); Geoffrey S. Cornish and Ronald E. Whitten, *The Architects of Golf* (New York: HarperCollins, 1993); Robert L. A. Adams, "Golf," in *The Theater of Sport,* ed. Karl B. Raitz (Baltimore: Johns Hopkins University Press, 1995), 231–69.

14. Bradley S. Klein, "Robert Trent Jones Sr.: Hero of American Golf," *Links Magazine,* April 1995, 60–64.

15. Marshall Berman, *All That Is Solid Melts into Air: The Experience of Modernity* (London: Verso, 1983); James Howard Kunstler, *The Geography of Nowhere* (New York: Oxford University Press, 1991).

16. Jenkins, *The Lawn.* Recent industry developments reducing the reliance upon pesticides and herbicides are documented in Bradley S. Klein, "New Chemical Credo: Less Is Better," *Golfweek,* 23 November 1996, 19, 24.

17. Michael Hurdzan, *Golf Course Architecture* (Chelsea, Mich.: Sleeping Bear, 1996), 15.

18. National Golf Foundation, *Golf Reference and Media Guide, 1995–96 Edition* (Jupiter, Fla.: National Golf Foundation, 1995).

19. Quoted in "Golfmania," *Times of Papua New Guinea,* 1 July 1993, 14.

20. Hahn, "The Money Game."

21. David Harvey, "From Space to Place and Back Again: Reflections on the Condition of Postmodernity," in *Mapping the Futures: Local Cultures, Global Change,* ed. Jon Bird, Barry Curtis, Tim Putnam, and Lisa Tickner (London: Routledge, 1994), 8.

22. Jacques Attali, *Millennium: Winners and Losers in the Coming World Order* (New York: Random House, 1991).

23. Brett Avery, "The Anti-Golf," *Golf Journal,* August 1996, 38–43.

24. Bruce Selcraig, "Mexican Golf War," *Golf Digest,* June 1996, 78–88.

25. Bradley S. Klein, "Cupp's New Angle: Palmetto Hall Design Not Just Plain," *Golfweek,* 6 March 1993, 31.

26. David Harvey, *The Condition of Postmodernity* (Oxford: Basil Blackwell, 1989); Zukin, *Landscapes of Power.*

27. Kunstler, *The Geography of Nowhere.*

28. Arjun Appadurai, *Modernity at Large: Cultural Dimensions of Globalization* (Minneapolis: University of Minnesota Press, 1996).

Talking Trash: Late Capitalism, Black (Re)Productivity, and Professional Basketball

Gitanjali Maharaj

In one of a series of television spots in Nike's NYC-Attack campaign, Peewee Kirkland, a legend of street basketball, offers himself as an example of both the deferment and the fulfillment of the American dream.[1] In 1980, Peewee was drafted by the Chicago Bulls ("every kid's biggest dream"), an offer he turned down in order to continue playing street basketball in New York City. His "life on the streets" soon turned to drug addiction and homelessness ("every kid's worst nightmare"). The TV spot ends with Peewee exhorting today's youth to remember that "the street takes lives," as the Nike logo appears discreetly on the screen. The curious ellipsis in Peewee's monologue, between his "dream" and "nightmare," marks a space rich in the contradictions and paradoxes of African American life in fin de siècle American society, where despite the inroads made by African Americans in professional sport, the entertainment industries, corporations, and academia, the life chances for black people as a whole are bleak and not improving.[2]

Seen from the vantage point of fans and players today, Peewee's rejection of an offer to play in the National Basketball Association (NBA) is incomprehensible. However, if we follow the cues in the Nike advertisement, Peewee's decision to remain on the "street" is continuous with his eventual slide into criminal activity and, presumably, drug addiction.[3] After more than thirty years since the publication of the Moynihan Report for the U.S. Department of Labor, the association of the "street" with black male lawlessness, parental irresponsibility, and emasculation has become a part of American common sense, for both African Americans and white Americans.[4] Indeed, Peewee's own narrative succumbs to the pressures of this paradigm by staging his "fall" as the consequence of his renunciation of the corporatized, disciplined, professional realm of the NBA for a life of hoop hustling and street basketball.

As one of its dubious achievements, the Moynihan Report continued a tradition in U.S. society that has historically constructed the black body as the exemplary site through which anxieties about the (re)production of labor, the nuclear family, and gender have been played out, all in the national interest. Yet the pervasiveness of the Moynihan "thesis" cannot alone account

227

for the appearance of a dichotomous opposition, as it appears in Peewee's narrative and elsewhere, between the "street" and the professional sport arena as sites for black male annihilation and recuperation, respectively. By another route, then, we have returned to that ellipsis separating "nightmare" and "dream" that both sutures Peewee's tale as one of conversion (to corporate, disciplined productivity as product spokesman) and leaves it with an unaccounted-for silence. Why, in 1980, did Peewee Kirkland choose to play street basketball instead of professional basketball?

By asking this silence to speak, we discover that the story of African American men "making it" in the NBA (as anywhere else in post-civil rights integrationist America) must be made accountable to the "rhetorical practices of contemporary U.S. cultural production . . . that incorporate the images of black men in popular representation even as those who live under its categorical sign are increasingly displaced by social, political, and economic practices of exclusion."[5]

The paradox that Nike's NYC-Attack campaign cannot contain is that the same multinational-capitalist economic practices that led to deindustrialization and the immiseration of black urban communities in the post–World War II United States also produced the black basketball star as a commodity and an object of desire for mass consumption; that both the "nightmare" of the urban ghetto and the "dream" of being a celebrity professional athlete are manifestations of the economic and cultural workings of late capitalism. To admit such a paradox is, first, to suggest that basketball's association with black urban bodies is a historical and by no means "natural" one and, second, to raise a question about the function of "visibility" in the public sphere, image industries, and professional sports for a minority group within the context of late-capitalist America. As Wiegman has discussed, an economy of the visible has particular consequences for African American communities, whose "gains" in a post-civil rights society bear a striking resemblance to the "old economy of corporeal enslavement . . . situated instead in the panoply of signs, texts, and images through which the discourse of race functions now to affirm the referential illusion of an organic real."[6] The burden of corporeality and racial marking borne by slaves in modernity continues to situate black bodies always already outside the definitions of citizenship and family and always already under the sign of white paternalism.

Within the race and gender matrix that evolved from and justified a modern slave society in the United States, the "Negro problem" has historically been read as a crisis of black masculinity and black paternity. According to liberals like Daniel Moynihan, the ability of the nation-state to discipline black bodies into a productive workforce has been hindered by the aberrant black familial structure of female-headed households, a structure that emasculates black men and retards their entry into the mainstream of American society. The recurring insistence that black NBA players serve as "role models" to embattled black urban youth is a particular indication of the salience of discourses of race, gender, and the family to our contemporary understanding of professional basketball.[7]

Even Charles Barkley's vociferous refusal to act as surrogate parent to young black fans has done no more than secure the continuing centrality of concerns about the black family, black masculinity, and black economic productivity that subtend the spectatorship and sponsorship of the game. But what does all of this have to do with Peewee Kirkland and his career as a street basketball legend and Nike spokesman? Although it may not be immediately apparent, Peewee's personal story offers a window through which we can see the production of professional basketball as an ideological site for the recuperation of black masculinity and black economic productivity under postindustrial conditions.

Significantly, the Nike advertisement fails to say that when offered a chance to play with the Chicago Bulls in 1980, Peewee decided not to join the NBA because street basketball was a more lucrative occupation.[8] Although Peewee's narrative for Nike participates in the widespread pathologizing of the "street" and black men on the "street" as outside social and economic controls, this is clearly a retrospective reading of events. At the time of his decision in 1980, Peewee believed that he had a greater opportunity for economic advancement on the "street" than in professional basketball.[9] My contention here, however, is that the ostensible opposition between Peewee's participation in the informal economy of pickup games (his "life on the streets")[10] in the late 1970s and early 1980s and his appearance in the corporate world of product endorsements in the late 1990s points to the crucial mechanism underpinning the recent success of the NBA as one of the most lucrative cultural enterprises in the United States: the recuperation of the inner city and of socially abject bodies as commodities and objects of desire.

The dichotomy between the informal and formal economies, between the "street" and the professional sports arena, forms a coupling that relies on ascriptions of difference where the racially marked and gendered body stands in for the inferior term. In the American context of deindustrialization, the rhetorical appearance of the "welfare queen" is a paradigmatic instance of the ideological use made of the association of black female bodies with urban blight and the effects of economic restructuring. Within the dominant imaginary, the "street" is always peopled by either black single mothers or their violent, criminal male offspring; poverty, urban decay, crime, and unemployment are manifestations of individual failure and black social pathology. The postindustrial city has become the emblematic landscape for the operation of narratives about unruly sexualities and economic dependency, and the emblematic subjects of these narratives are the hustler and the welfare queen.[11] In debates about affirmative action, ongoing racial inequality, and the responsibilities of the "welfare state," these two characters are opposed to the black ladies and professional black men whose successes prove that the system really does work. What is denied in the operation of such binary oppositions, however, is the unnaturalness of the designations (i.e., their discursive and material production), and their contingent and mutually reinforcing meanings. For example, the boundary between informal and formal sectors of the economy has its historical roots in a period of ascendant industrialization, when the movement of surplus value had to be regulated and centralized for capital-intensive production. Although the codified boundaries between informal and formal economic activity are not maintained to the same degree in multinational capitalism,[12] the ideological apparatuses separating work from play and gainful employment from unproductive distraction continue to discipline bodies and determine life chances along racial lines. Nike's use of Peewee's story as a "before" and "after" narrative of disciplined, productive employment turns on precisely these ideological codings of space and bodies. Peewee, the hoop hustler, must renounce the "streets" if he is to enter the productive space of professional employment. His is a literal passage from exteriority to interiority, from the "street" world of economic dependency, hyperreproductivity, crime, and drug addiction to the regulated, economically productive, patriarchal, and white world of corporate life.[13]

In dominant narratives, the ghetto (i.e., the "street") is intelligible only as a public zone, without a compensatory private realm where interiority, nuclear families, or patriarchal authority can dwell. Hence, when the hoop hustler is juxtaposed with the NBA sports star in "The Streets," the implication is that African Americans have traveled down a progressive continuum of individual achievement where the ability to "just say no" (to "street" life and "matriarchal" culture) is all that distinguishes those men who have failed from those who have reaped the rewards of success and citizenship. In this context, Peewee's injunction reads as a challenge to African American male youth to get off the "street" and resist the incomplete masculinization, aberrant familial structures, economic unproductivity, and biological hyperreproductivity that have come to signify urban blackness. Yet, for urban black youth, the "street" provides the very site of their interpellation into consumerism and "corporate citizenship."[14] There is an ostensible contradiction here for (black and white) consumer-spectators because they must repudiate the inner city as a site of abjection even as they consume commodified images of its metonymic personifications. The hustler and welfare queen are deplored as socially aberrant, while the inner city becomes the locus of authentic blackness and consumers' acquisitive desire. This contradictory coding of urban blackness accounts for the status of Peewee's narrative as both a public service announcement and an advertisement for Nike products.

Capital, to be sure, experiences none of the contradictions faced by consumers. Indeed, the status of "difference" as the commodity in postmodernity attests to the increasing reliance of capital on precisely such contradictions. That is to say, it is extraordinarily economical (in both senses of the word) for capital to make the postindustrial city productive once again through its symbolic representation as the locus of racial and sexual difference. As Nike's NYC-Attack advertising campaign demonstrates, the material and ideological construction of the urban ghetto as a site of dereliction, drug abuse, and economic dependency is transformed into a commodified image that can produce surplus value. Wiegman has remarked that "such a commodity status is not without irony in the broad historical scope of race in this country, where the literal commodification of the body under enslavement is now simulated in representational circuits."[15] The coordinates "nightmare" and "dream" in Peewee's monologue point to this simultaneous process of abjecting and recuperating ghetto bodies that drives contemporary popular representations of African Americans. In order to make these connections among late capitalism, professional basketball, and black (re)productivity clearer, I will have to take a brief detour through the recent history of the NBA.

The extent of the NBA's current success can be gauged by the fact that few people recall that sports arenas could not attract enough spectators fifteen years ago to cover operating costs. In 1980, the year Peewee turned down a professional draft offer, the league's annual gross revenues were $118 million, with seventeen of the twenty-three teams losing money. Estimates at the time claimed that 75 percent of the league's players were on drugs, and around the league "hotels became known as 'party palaces' with marijuana and wall-to-wall hookers." The NBA had a serious "image" problem, and corporate sponsors were reacting by withdrawing their support. David Stern, who was hired in 1980 to bolster the league's public relations, marketing, and broadcasting and then went on to become commissioner in 1984, recalls that "sponsors were flocking out of the NBA because it was perceived as a bunch of high salaried, drug-sniffing black guys."[16]

What is striking about the administrative responses to the NBA's unprofitability is the overt recognition that the "race problem" had to be managed in order to make the league not only economically viable but also profitable. As Stern has commented, "It was our conviction that if everything else went right, race would not be an abiding issue to NBA fans, at least not as long as it was handled correctly."[17] Two significant points can be drawn from Stern's comments: first, while race was the NBA's problem, the solution had to be economic; and second, profitability for the league could be achieved through a skillful management of perceptions of the black players' productivity. The specific administrative changes Stern introduced to handle this situation were a much-admired drug program, a collective bargaining agreement, and a salary cap.[18] By late 1983, the NBA set an attendance record, and in ten seasons under Stern's leadership the league experienced 1,600 percent growth in annual revenues, ending 1994 at the $3 billion mark, with international monies accounting for $500 million.[19] Currently 170 countries belong to Federation Internationale de Basketball (FIBA), the international basketball association that guarantees overseas broadcasting of NBA games in its member countries.

The dichotomy between the "street" and the professional sports arena that surfaces in Peewee's story is a structuring tension that has defined the relationship between the NBA and its black players throughout Stern's tenure as commissioner. Significantly, the league's efforts to rehabilitate the perception of its black players as "overpaid, drug-sniffing black guys" have not involved simply eradicating "street" elements from the confines of the arena; rather, they have depended on the recuperation of black players as model citizens and productive employees. The controversy surrounding the refusal by Mahmoud Abdul-Rauf (of the Denver Nuggets) to sing the national anthem and pledge allegiance to the American flag before games is the most recent illustration of the league's concern to represent its black players as respectable working Americans.[20]

Rather than being dissolved through management directives, the ties between the "street" and the sports arena are reinforced and subjected to a rationalization process whereby the black sports celebrity is contractually obligated to serve as surrogate parent to the "fatherless" children of the inner city. This expectation is demonstrated in the documentary film *Hoop Dreams* (1994) when Isiah Thomas makes a surprise visit to his Detroit high school alma mater to address the aspiring players of the boys' varsity basketball team. Within the context of the protagonist Arthur Agee's life, Thomas is, briefly, a source of paternal advice for the youngster, whose own father, a chronically unemployed drug addict, abandons the family. This type of surrogacy role is facilitated by the league's careful monitoring of its players' on- and off-court behavior and by the cultivation of ties between the "community" and the players. Stern credits the growth of the NBA to the fact that teams have become "important elements in their communities. Virtually all of our teams have community relations directors, public relations directors, [and] kids' programs—the kinds of things that you expect from good neighbors."[21]

It is ironic that David Stern invokes the idea of neighborliness when speaking of the NBA's community relations programs, which, properly understood, represent a corporate interest in protecting its market shares. When Stern joined the NBA in 1980, inner-city New York neighborhoods were already bearing the scars of economic restructuring, capital flight, and a manufactured fiscal crisis that justified social services cutbacks for the most disadvantaged of the city's population.[22] Language about "good neighbors" in the corporate context of the 1980s is incongruous with the reality of government-subsidized corporate relocations to the suburbs, which left urban neighborhoods severely dislocated and underserviced.[23] The flexibility of capital accumulation under late capitalism has also provided a global economic context of "unlimited growth" for the U.S. image industries, of which the NBA is a significant part. Executives like David Stern, however, see only expanding consumer markets and not an increasing disparity in wealth between African Americans and white Americans, or between North and South. Stern has commented: "I keep thinking in terms of NAFTA and the North American concept. . . . we've expanded to 29 million fans to the north (Canada) and there are 80 million more fans to the south, with Latin America still to come. It seems like a sensible thing to think about."[24] As Melvin Oliver and Thomas Shapiro have forcefully demonstrated, however, continuing racial inequality in the United States is maintained through a tripartite system of institutionalized racism that "fosters the accumulation of private wealth for many whites [as] it denies it to blacks, thus forging an intimate connection between white wealth accumulation and black poverty."[25] A further paradox, then, in Peewee's public service advertisement for Nike is how it repudiates black socioeconomic marginality while embracing black consumerism as a way to enter the socioeconomic mainstream. I have already alluded to one of the contradictions for white consumption of black urban authenticity. Here, the tautology in Nike's hailing of the black consumer is the suggestion that an economically marginal and systematically impoverished community can participate in its own recovery into the center of American economic (and, by extension, political, civil, and social) life through consumption. In effect, black consumers are being told, "You will be making money by spending money. You will enter the productive economic mainstream by being marginal to it." Ultimately, however, this message produces a version of bootstrap social theory that accounts for growing black impoverishment by adding the inability to consume properly to the list of black social pathologies.[26]

Nike's interest in producing the NYC-Attack advertising campaign came at a time in 1994 when the spectatorship and consumption of the game were undergoing a change. Advertisers, corporate sponsors, and the NBA were becoming aware of growing disaffection among fans who felt that the game had "lost touch with its roots."[27] Exponentially increasing players' salaries, a series of bench-clearing brawls during the 1994 NBA Championships, and low-scoring games had begun to generate spectator-consumer hostility. The scenario in 1994 bore an uncanny resemblance to the circumstances in 1980, when David Stern was hired to rehabilitate the league's "image problem." The charge of unprofessionalism was again linked to a perception that black players were not earning their high salaries. The NBA's response in the following season was to implement a series of rule changes that were designed to increase scoring, shift play from defense to offense, and reduce the "rough play" that had provoked on-court fights among players. Rod Thorn, vice president of operations for the NBA, justified the rule changes by commenting, "We had gradually gone back to where we were sixteen or seventeen years ago, with guys riding people up the floor."[28] Whereas the league's actions reflect an anxiety about maintaining the boundary between the professional arena and the "street," Nike's NYC-Attack campaign was an attempt to counteract consumer alienation by returning to the "roots" of the game. It should not go without saying that the "roots" of basketball are understood to be in the corner courts of inner cities in the postindustrial United States, and not in West Springfield, Massachusetts, where the game originated in the nineteenth century.[29] It was on an expedition to the inner city of New York that Nike found the "submerged" history of Peewee Kirkland and his legendary status in street basketball.

The NYC-Attack advertising campaign represents a departure from Nike's previous advertising in two ways: first, it was designed to disassociate the athletic sportswear and sneaker manufacturer from the NBA in the minds of consumers; and second, it was the first city-specific campaign produced for Nike. NYC-Attack, as the name implies, was a media assault developed specifically for New York City. The television spots, print advertising, billboard art, and animated movie trailer designed for NYC-Attack were not shown outside the boundaries of the city.[30] Nike's interest in downplaying the affiliation with the NBA at a time when negative publicity surrounded the league directed the campaign producers to seek out images of the game's enduring authenticity. In order to escape the stench of commercialization and professionalization that began to permeate the arenas of professional basketball in 1994, Nike retreated to the "purity" of the game's "roots" as an urban community practice. In light of my earlier discussion about the dichotomous relationship between the professional sports arena and the "street" as formal and informal economic sectors, Nike's flight to the inner city to protect its corporate productivity is more than simply ironic; rather, Nike's NYC-Attack campaign enacts the economic and cultural logic of capitalism, which produces "trash" and recuperates it as a sign of difference and a site of desire.

In developing the NYC-Attack campaign, the advertising executives at Wieden and Kennedy had to work within a small budget and short production schedule, conditions that influenced the creative path they eventually chose. Armed with simple video cameras and sound-recording equipment, the creative team engaged in the kind of fieldwork one would expect from sociologists, anthropologists, ethnographers, and cultural studies scholars interested in studying black urban cultural practices: they conducted interviews, collected footage, and compiled a series of oral histories about street basketball and people's local involvement with the game. These interviews provided the raw material out of which the NYC-Attack campaign was produced.

The nineteen television spots follow two distinct formats. In the first type ("That's It-2," "Color," "Joe Regular," "Helicopter"), no editing cuts are used. Instead, a voice-over narrative is superimposed on grainy footage of congested city streets and traffic, a wall covered with graffiti, or the intricate weave of a chain-link fence surrounding a city basketball court; this footage, played back in slow motion, was filmed by a stationary camera. The ambiance of these advertisements is reminiscent of Martin Scorsese's depictions of New York City in the 1970s films *Mean Streets* and *Taxi Driver.*

In the second type of spot, the camera movement mimics the flow and pacing of the narration. In "Trash Talk," the camera bobs and weaves around Peewee as he boasts: "Hey man, you can't guard me. I got so many moves, last game I shook myself"; in "Jock Strap," the camera follows Master Rob across the court in slow motion, eventually settling on the ground so that he is filmed from below, crotch in the center of the frame, when he says: "I was at half-court, and I just let [the ball] go. And it went all bottom, and the crowd ran back in, jumped on the court, and ripped my shirt off, ripped my shorts off. I was standing out there with a jock strap and a pair of Nikes." In a variation of this second type ("Sittin on the Rim," "Quarter," "Young vs. Old"), the background scene consists of medium shots of young black men playing on a street basketball court, dunking and flying in the air, the backboard and netless hoop jerking back and forth. A close-up of the narrator is digitally superimposed on this backdrop and serves as a visual and aural window into the scene.

Displaying a documentary realist aesthetic, albeit a heavily stylized one, NYC-Attack used the interview sequences and grainy footage of the city to construct an organic connection between the game of basketball and black male urban culture. The many fond reminiscences about rivalries between players, legendary styles and plays, and trash talking (the artful put-down) provided a context in which black male socialization could be appropriately recoded for consumption by disaffected fans. This time, black males visible on the "street" provided a glimpse of better times, a golden age in basketball before contracts, deals, and salaries took over the game. In contrast to the commercialized realm of the NBA, the courts of the derelict city were depicted in NYC-Attack as uncorrupted spaces of play and communal activity. In "Rucker," Peewee reminisces about the paragon of all New York City street basketball spaces, the Holcombe Rucker Basketball Courts on West 155th Street in Harlem: "At Rucker, it wasn't about money. It was heart, hustle, and soul. It wasn't about fame. Had nothing to do with gold. It was all about your reputation. Until you get to Rucker, no matter what you did in your life, don't mean nothing. But when you get to Rucker, that's the arena. The arena of goodwill."

Nike's recoding of the black male body as a site of play and pleasure in NYC-Attack, however, relies on the very same set of assumptions that stigmatize the urban black body as economically unproductive and biologically hyperreproductive. In both instances, the black body is the organic real, an essential entity unrestrained by the fetters of modernity. Nike's depiction of Rucker as outside the circuits of capital accumulation, however, simultaneously identifies the street basketball court as the very site of interpellation for black consumption of Nike products. Furthermore, the suggestion that street basketball is pure, in contrast to the commercialization of professional basketball, is a disavowal of the institutionalized channels connecting the "street" and the arena, and informal and formal economic activity (Nike's ABCD program being one important example). The curious ellipsis in "The Streets" between "nightmare" and "dream," with which I began, marks then the anxious reiteration of the boundary between the sports arena and the "street" as productive and unproductive sites, respectively, while that boundary is being transgressed by corporate interests. Whereas the reiteration of the boundary attests to its discursive instability, the coding here of blackness as pleasure, play, and authenticity effectively fetishizes black bodies as commodities to serve capital's expanding consumer needs. Robyn Wiegman's critique of the heightened commodity status of blackness in the wake of Afrocentric political demands addresses this "visual culture predicated on the commodification of those very identities minoritized by the discourses and social organization of enlightened democracy."[31]

In this essay I have tried to draw together questions of consumption and productivity as they relate to the context of professional basketball to address the paradoxical representation of African Americans as both image industry celebrities and social parasites. By focusing on the NYC-Attack advertising campaign and its symbiotic relationship with the NBA, I have attempted to draw to the surface the contradictory narratives about black masculinity and black (re)productivity that undergird the spectatorship and sponsorship of the game and serve to construct professional basketball as an important ideological site in the late-capitalist United States. The relationship between the informal sporting practices of the "street" and the multi-million-dollar industries of the NBA and athletic-wear advertising attests to the material and symbolic means through which surplus value is created in late capitalism. Significantly, the postwar construction of African Americans as consumers rather than producers coincides with the unprecedented focus of attention on black participation—as simultaneously desirable and deviant—in the material, representational, and political economic matrices of U.S. public culture. What I have tried to suggest here is that by attending simply to consumption practices as a site of black popular resistance, cultural critics must be mindful not to reproduce the very disciplinary apparatus that has kept African Americans lagging behind white Americans in their pursuit of the American "dream." Even in Nike's ode to Rucker as a "goodwill" space uncorrupted by "money or gold," the mask of the United States as a meritocratic or egalitarian society slips to reveal the far less charitable doctrine dictating the possible futures available to African Americans. As Peewee concludes in "Rucker," "Either you did it or you got it done to you." This ominous appraisal of life on the "streets" would also seem to describe the conditions under which Peewee receives his redemption from the winged goddess in the form of a product endorsement.

Notes

I would like to acknowledge the invaluable help of Seamus Culligan, campaign director of NYC-Attack at Wieden and Kennedy, who provided me with all the NYC-Attack campaign materials and generously answered my questions about the campaign's development.

This essay owes its genesis to Robin D. G. Kelley's observations about basketball and the postindustrial city in "Playing for Keeps: African American Youth in the Postindustrial City," in *The House That Race Built: Black Americans/U.S. Terrain*, ed. Wahneema Lubiano (New York: Random House, 1997); I have greatly benefited from my conversations with Robin Kelley about basketball and other topics. Special thanks are due to Ephen Glenn Colter, Philip Brian Harper, and Toby Miller for their engaged and critical readings of this essay.

1. "The Streets," NYC-Attack television spot, Nike, 1995. The NYC-Attack campaign, which ran in 1995, consisted of nineteen television spots and one animated film trailer. The TV advertisements focused on former and current legends of street basketball: the Goat, the Pearl, the Destroyer, Jackie Jackson, Master Rob, the Future, and Herman Knowings. Peewee Kirkland received the greatest attention in the campaign, appearing in five of the nineteen spots: "Trash Talk," "Stickman," "Backboard," "Rucker," and "The Streets."

2. Melvin L. Oliver and Thomas M. Shapiro, *Black Wealth, White Wealth: A New Perspective on Racial Inequality* (New York: Routledge, 1995).

3. I use scare quotes when referring to the "street" in order to draw attention to the discursive production of the "street" as more than simply a physical location. The quotes are intended to disrupt the naturalized reading of the "street" as the antithesis of good U.S. civic life and other normative forms of "publicity." See Bruce Robbins's introduction to *The Phantom Public Sphere*, ed. Bruce Robbins (Minneapolis: University of Minnesota Press, 1993); and Michael Warner, "The Mass Public and the Mass Subject," in *Habermas and the Public Sphere*, ed. Craig Calhoun (Cambridge: MIT Press, 1992), for a discussion of the "public" and "publicity." For an extended and specific discussion of race and "publicity," see Robyn Wiegman, *American Anatomies* (Durham, N.C.: Duke University Press, 1995). As background to these discussions about the "public sphere," see Hannah Arendt, *The Human Condition* (Chicago: University of Chicago Press, 1958), chap. 2.

4. Daniel P. Moynihan, *The Negro Family: The Case for National Action* (Washington, D.C.: U.S. Department of Labor, Office of Policy Planning and Research, 1965).

5. Wiegman, *American Anatomies*, 144.

6. Ibid., 41.

7. See Gail Bederman, *Manliness and Civilization* (Chicago: University of Chicago Press, 1995), for a discussion of race and gender discourses in the context of interracial professional boxing in the nineteenth century.

8. My knowledge of Peewee's economic calculation of the relative dividends offered by the NBA compared with a street basketball career comes from personal communication with Seamus Culligan (10 November 1995), campaign director for NYC-Attack. Culligan interviewed Peewee Kirkland (along with other legends of New York City street basketball) during the preproduction phase of the NYC-Attack campaign.

9. Pete Axthelm, in *The City Game: From the Garden to the Playgrounds* (New York: Penguin, 1982), offers a robust description of the interplay between professional basketball and the street basketball culture that has sustained it. Written at the cusp of the ideological transformation of basketball into a specifically black urban practice, Axthelm's ode to basketball as a quintessentially urban game presciently marks the tensions around race that would come to the fore in the NBA during the 1980s. Axthelm documents the street basketball players' bitterness about quota systems, which limited the number of black players on professional teams, and rule changes, like the NCAA's "no dunk" rule, intended to impede both the advancement of black players and the appearance of "street" styles in the sport. The "no dunk" rule was introduced by the NCAA during Lew Alcindor's (Kareem Abdul-Jabbar) career at

UCLA. While the book is an unabashed celebration of the "Knick phenomenon," it does contain extensive (and reverential) descriptions of the world of street basketball and pickup games. The legendary plays of Herman "Helicopter" Knowings and Earl Manigault are described. Knowings's legendary encounter with Willis Reed was featured in an NYC-Attack spot called "Helicopter." See Axthelm's chapter "The Fallen Idol: The Harlem Tragedy of Earl Manigault" for a narrative precursor to Nike's "The Streets" television spot about Peewee Kirkland.

10. The following films offer exemplary depictions of hustling and the informal economy of pickup games: *The Hustler* (1961), *The Color of Money* (1986), and *White Men Can't Jump* (1992). For an anthropological account of hustling and "welfare dependency" in a northern black urban community that refutes the Moynihan Report point by point, see Bettylou Valentine, *Hustling and Other Hard Work: Lifestyles in the Ghetto* (New York: Free Press, 1978).

11. My understanding of how the term *welfare queen* functions as an ideological weapon is as the embodiment of economic unproductivity and reproductive excess. This black female excess is predicated on and simultaneously produces and sustains black male emasculation and economic immaturity. Hence, whenever *welfare queen* is put to ideological use, both black femininity and black masculinity are being delimited in a national political economic frame. I am trying here to flesh out the implied but unnamed figure of the hustler as the partner to the welfare queen.

12. Philip Harding and Richard Jenkins, *Myth of the Hidden Economy: Towards a New Understanding of Informal Economic Activity* (Milton Keynes, U.K.: Open University Press, 1989).

13. See Wiegman, *American Anatomies*, chaps. 1 and 2, for a discussion of race and citizenship in relation to notions of interiority, exteriority, and the decorporealized public sphere.

14. My thanks to Toby Miller for this point. The notion of "corporate citizenship" links consumption to good civic life by projecting an image of corporations as civil societies unto themselves, heralding a return to middle-American values, albeit inflected by the transaction of money. Corporate citizenship through consumption has been the underlying ethos behind Nike's emergence as the leader in sales of basketball apparel and shoes. Using its multimillion-dollar marketing budget, Nike established the Academic Betterment and Career Development (ABCD) program, ostensibly as an academic program to prepare high school basketball players for the rigors of college life. Through his association with Nike, the young black athlete supposedly learns how to value intellectual achievements, to act responsibly, and to plan for a future after his basketball career is over. In actuality, the ABCD program, which includes the annual Nike All-American camp, works as a funneling device to identify the most talented inner-city black high school athletes, make them available to college basketball recruiters, and guarantee the players' (and college coaches') lifetime association with the Nike trademark. See Darcy Frey's *Last Shot: City Streets, Basketball Dreams* (Boston: Houghton Mifflin, 1994) for a description of the ABCD program and other systematic processes that mine the inner cities for young black basketball talent.

15. Wiegman, *American Anatomies*, 117.

16. Quoted in Roland Lazenby, "Stern Goes Global," *Lindy's Pro Basketball*, October 1994, 8.

17. Quoted in ibid.

18. The salary cap does not extend to management positions. Counting on the owners' fears that he would become baseball's commissioner instead, Stern brokered for himself a $27.5 million, five-year contract, including a $10 million bonus.

19. Players receive 53 percent of certain league revenues, but nothing on the sale of T-shirts and other memorabilia, where overseas money is generated.

239

20. It remains unclear why the NBA threatened suspension in March 1996 when Abdul-Rauf's compromise of waiting in the locker room during the playing of the national anthem had been accepted (by management and teammates) since the start of the season in September 1995. Clearly, however, the notion of "respectability" remains high on Stern's agenda: he has also battled with states and provinces to prevent legalized gambling from "staining the integrity of the game" (see Lazenby, "Stern Goes Global," 8). When an injury in March forced Abdul-Rauf off the starting lineup, sports commentators called the situation "resolved," thus highlighting the connection between visibility and respectability.

21. Quoted in ibid., 11.

22. Sharoll Zukin, *Landscapes of Power: From Detroit to Disney* (Berkeley: University of California Press, 1991); Peter Marcuse, "On the Ideology of Urban Fiscal Crisis and Its Uses," *International Journal of Urban and Regional Research* 5 (summer 1981): 332–55; Marshall Berman, *All That Is Solid Melts into Air: The Experience of Modernity* (New York: Viking, 1982).

23. Oliver and Shapiro, *Black Wealth: White Wealth*, 15.

24. Quoted in Lazenby, "Stern Goes Global," 11.

25. Oliver and Shapiro, *Black Wealth, White Wealth*, 5.

26. My thanks to Alondra R. Nelson for drawing my attention to the notion that the black poor are also stigmatized as irresponsible consumers. Oliver and Shapiro make a similar point when discussing the "economic detour" experienced by African Americans, which forced them into the role of consumers because they were prevented from participating in the U.S. economy as producers; ibid., (47).

27. Seamus Culligan, personal communication, 10 November 1995.

28. Quoted in Clifton Brown, "Can't You Hear the Whistles Blowin'?" *New York Times*, 30 October 1994, sec. 8, 1. The new rules beginning in the 1994–95 season included an increase in fines from $100 to $500 for each technical foul, the automatic suspension of any player who leaves the bench during an altercation and a fine of up to $20,000, automatic ejection of any player with two flagrant fouls, and several rules specifically designed to deter "aggressive defense." For a complete list of the new rules, see Clifton Brown, "NBA 94–95: By the Way There's No Taunting Either," *New York Times*, 30 October 1994, sec. 8, 9. Given the NBA's concern about the incursion of the "street" into the arena, it is instructive to compare professional basketball with the ritualized spectacle of white-on-white violence that takes place regularly in professional ice hockey (and often in the very same venues where professional basketball is played). See Richard Gruneau and David Whitson, *Hockey Night in Canada: Sport, Identities, and Cultural Politics* (Toronto: Garamond, 1993), for a discussion of the fetishization of violence in ice hockey. My thanks to Toby Miller for this point and reference.

29. Pete Axthelm, *The City Game*, ix.

30. The success of NYC-Attack prompted Nike to commission Wieden and Kennedy to produce a city-specific campaign for Los Angeles. According to Seamus Culligan, the campaigns differed significantly in the type of basketball ethos represented: whereas style, showboating, and performance are valorized by New York City basketball culture (to the extent that the score doesn't always indicate who the winner is), in Los Angeles winning and "making it" (to the NBA) are the players' primary goals. Other city-specific campaigns, according to Culligan, are on the horizon.

31. Wiegman, *American Anatomies*, 49.

Part IV ▸ Signifying Sport

Head Fake:
Mentorship and Mobility in *Hoop Dreams*

Bruce Robbins

Toward the end of the documentary *Hoop Dreams* (1994), Coach Pingatore of St. Joseph's pronounces judgment on William Gates's high school basketball career, which has just ended. He tells the camera that William has had "a good career, not a great career." Because Coach Pingatore is something like the film's villain—its most visible representative of the systematic exploitation of young black athletes, and its most enthusiastic spokesman for a win-at-all-costs, write-off-your-family philosophy that William explicitly repudiates at the end—it is tempting to take his statement as a neat inversion of the film's moral. Thus we would read the film as a self-critical version of the narrative of upward mobility: a cautionary tale against the American dream and its costs, especially its costs to the family. In short, the film would be saying that life is about trying to be good—morally good, good to your family—rather than trying to be great: athletically but amorally great, great in the eyes of the coach and the fans.[1]

Now this is a moral I find myself not liking as much as I think I am supposed to. For one thing, it reduces a situation that's very specific in race and class terms to the familiar dilemma of "work versus family," a dilemma that can and will be taken as universal, the same for rich and poor, white and black.[2] It makes all public action and achievement seem conceivable only at the expense of private, genuine family life. Like the cliché that "power corrupts," it points to something real, but its realism is partial and deeply conservative. And on the part of people who don't share the protagonists' situation, it is a somewhat self-serving moral. It's hard to escape the idea that people who've already climbed the ladder should not be the ones to piously kick it away, or even to applaud when those below decide to climb down off it.

Of course, one might argue that the real problem with this moral is, on the contrary, that the film doesn't make it stick. From the beginning right down to the final news of William's and Arthur's offscreen successes, the film remains intensely if not fully invested in the pleasures of vicarious accomplishment that it pretends to disapprove of.[3] And these pleasures, the pleasures of the upward mobility story, clearly have everything to do with the film's becoming (according to *Nightline*) one of the most successful documentaries ever made. At the same time, you could also say that by choosing to give its materials the shape of a narrative of achievement, however vexed and complicated, the film misses an opportunity, politically speaking, to "do" the real issues of the inner city with some seriousness. Thus the reasons for the film's popular success would have to include evading the real issues and offering up an upward mobility story instead, even an upward mobility story disguised as a morality tale.

From this point of view, the "moral" reading would be correct in trying to take William and Arthur out of the game; the problem would be that this is the same game that the film itself, also an underdog, continues to play and to win at. My own view is that the game must go on.

The upward mobility of the film and the upward mobility of its protagonists can indeed be paralleled, as many viewers have noticed, but they can be paralleled in such a way as to cast a somewhat more favorable light on both. If you take this parallel seriously, then the success story of the filmmakers might be seen as an impure but analytically compelling rationale for the success story of the characters. The logic would go as follows: (1) You couldn't get anyone to look at a film about the inner city that did not find some way of narrativizing its issues, that is, embodying them in a temporal structure of desire. (2) Any documentary that audiences would actually want to watch, however real, complex, and improving its subject matter, would therefore have to find some means of giving pleasure. (3) In an imperfect world, the giving and taking of pleasure is always tainted by the powers that be, always to some degree expresses and sustains existing authorities, existing models of subjectivity and social order. Conclusion: in the imperfect world we inhabit, the lonely hour of "the real issues" never comes. The real issues must always rest on, pass through, be distorted by pleasure and power. And this is just as true for William Gates and Arthur Agee as for the makers of *Hoop Dreams*. In an imperfect world, upward mobility does not happen without your winning some endorsement, sponsorship, support, or merely acceptance from above, from the same power or order that has kept you down. Thus it does not happen without extreme moral ambiguity. But this would be a conclusive argument against it only in a perfect, perfectly immobile, unambiguous world.

In the larger study of upward mobility narratives to which I hope this essay will belong, I've found myself thinking in particular about a set of figures who bear some structural resemblance to Coach Pingatore: mentors, counselors, benefactors, fairy godmothers, gatekeepers, surrogate parents, or what Jerry Watts calls "facilitators."[4] All of them represent, among other things, the powers that be, and for that reason all of them are capable of offering decisive help of some sort to the striving, discontented, upwardly mobile protagonist. But *why* should they do so? What are their motives? Rather than simply altruistic, they are more likely to be self-interested in devious, sublimated, and unconventionally or indefinitely erotic ways: older women interested in younger men, older men interested in younger men.[5] And, most important, what sort of fissure or contradiction do their mixed, uncertain motives open up in the powers that be? These questions guarantee that all such figures also tend to be ethically ambiguous in the extreme, like Hannibal Lecter in *Silence of the Lambs* and Vautrin in Balzac's *Le Père Goriot*. They are so ambiguous because they, rather than the often somewhat blank or bland protagonists, embody the full social and ethical complexity of the protagonists' attempt at upward mobility.

The mentor or surrogate parent figures are the major means, that is, by which these upward mobility narratives address their major problem, the problem that Hortense Spillers neatly outlines in her "post-date" to Harold Cruse's *Crisis of the Negro Intellectual*: "Although we can boast today a considerably larger black middle class and upper-middle class, with its avenues into the professions, including elective office, some corporate affiliation, virtually *all* of the NBA, and the NFL, and a fast break into the nation's multi-million dollar 'image' industries, the news concerning the African American life-world generally is quite grim."[6] Against the indecent background of six hundred thousand black people in prison—the population of a decent-sized city—what is the value of a success story (whether that of William Gates and Arthur Agee, or that of black studies programs and departments), however much that story is qualified? What is the value of a story in which some representative of that population escapes, or even fails to escape but in such a noble way as to encourage rather than discourage others?

According to Pierre Bourdieu, there is *no* value in such a narrative, because there is no ambiguity in the people or institutions who preside over and mediate it. As everyone doubtless knows, Bourdieu's chosen theme is "reproduction," in other words, "the stability of the basic field of relations."[7] His view of the stable field is very close to the popular belief, realistic and conservative, that "nothing ever really changes." Upward mobility within a given field is not impossible for Bourdieu. Indeed, he notes the possibility that, as in *Hoop Dreams*, the role of mediator in someone's rise out of the lower classes might be played by institutions of education. Yet that role is not a genuinely mediating one. The school does not intercede between power and the protagonist, try to work on the latter's behalf, try to reconcile them, or even occupy an intermediate position. It is a branch of power: faithful, transparent, and unerringly effective.

Consider, for example, Bourdieu's model of the "oblate" in *Homo Academicus*. Originally an oblate was "a child from a poor family entrusted to a religious foundation to be trained for the priesthood."[8] For Bourdieu, the term refers to children without social capital whose upward mobility depends entirely on the educational institution to which they are entrusted, and who respond to it with unconditional loyalty. "They offer to the academic institution which they have chosen because it chose them, and vice versa, a support which, being so totally conditioned, has something total, absolute, and unconditional about it."[9] According to this model, upward mobility means selling yourself, that is, selling out, within the total, absolute, and unconditional terms of all-powerful institutions.

Perhaps coincidentally, the critique of this position by Craig Calhoun in *Critical Social Theory* takes up the example of basketball. "Bourdieu's account of the habitus," Calhoun writes, includes "tacit knowledge, even embodied in modes of action that agents are unable to bring to linguistic consciousness, like basketball players able to perform hook shots better than describe them."[10] As Calhoun points out, the concept of the habitus as rich but inarticulate knowledge or skill does not allow for correct and successful calculations on the part of those who possess it. Such knowledge or skill might involve, he says, implicitly continuing the racialized example of the basketball player, "a more complex strategy—achieving success in one field which seems relatively open while minimizing investment in another—say school—which seems closed, while half-consciously or even unconsciously engaging in strategies for achieving a sense of personal autonomy or perhaps escaping the ghetto and gaining a better standard of living."[11]

This is a possibility that *Hoop Dreams*, like Bourdieu, tries to deny, but (I would argue) should *not* deny. I don't say this in order to make the predictable move of asserting an optimistic, very American autonomy of the self as against Bourdieu's very French, very pessimistic assertion of absolute, systematic, immobile "field." On the contrary. If Bourdieu's (very French) mistake is to take away the double ambiguity of the institutions that fill the mediator or surrogate parent slot, thereby making them both too absolutely powerful and too unquestionably unjust, the solution is not simply to assert (the very American position) a larger role for individual skill, initiative, and autonomy. The point is to restore a necessary centrality and ambiguity to the mediator or surrogate parent slot, and to the mixed blessings it offers to the protagonist's talent.

Here I can only give a very rapid and schematic version of a longer argument. In the context of other upward mobility stories, where skill or more generally merit is a relatively smaller element and where the responsibility of the mediator is correspondingly larger, it seems to me that *Hoop Dreams* puts too much of a burden for success on the skill or merit of Arthur and William. And it does so, despite its own attention to that burden, by pushing a subtle moral line that, as I have suggested, backs the claims of the family against those of the coach. To me one of the most moving aspects of *Hoop Dreams* is the almost unbearable psychological weight that William and Arthur seemed to be carrying because, precisely, all the responsibility for their own rise, and so many of the hopes of their families, rested on their own individual skill and achievement.

Yet this is especially true because—in a kind of undermining of its own moral from within—the film shows that the line between mediator and family is not after all very clear. One thing wrong with the moral reading, which opposes the choice of being good in the family to being great for the coach, is that it's the families—or at least their male members—that so visibly want the kids to be great. As William's voice-over tells us at the very end, this is about the dreams of the older generation more than those of the young one, and about getting out from under them. Of his brother Curtis, William says, "I always felt that Curtis should not be living his dream through me." At another point he says, "Everybody I know is my coach."

When William's team loses its last game in his senior year, which means they won't go downstate for the championship, it's at least partly because his family has gotten him to the game twenty minutes late, which meant he was benched for part of the game as punishment. Curtis says this was "bad coaching." Despite its opinion of Coach Pingatore, it is not clear that the film agrees, either about this or about coaching in general. What is clear is that bad coaching can also be what you get from the family. The real family can no longer be opposed to the world of coaches, the world of the surrogate family, as moral refuge is opposed to social battlefield, as place of origin is opposed to destination. Unfortunately, the family must still be defined by its lack of that semimagical power that upward mobility narratives accord to coaches or surrogate family, the power to bring that destination closer.

I'm not arguing that Bourdieu doesn't recognize individual skill as a legitimate means of upward mobility; I'm arguing that he doesn't recognize the ambiguity of the mentor/benefactor role, an ambiguity that has, and *should* have, more responsibility than the individual in the narrative task of making room for the individual's mobility. In spite of its moralizing (which tells us all to give up on the surrogate family and return to the real family), I think *Hoop Dreams* is better than Bourdieu in this respect: less populist and less cynical at the same time. Like Bourdieu, the film is tempted simply to blame the people and institutions that fill the mentor/benefactor function. But unlike Bourdieu, it in fact exposes meaningful change in that function. It suggests, specifically, that (at least compared with other upward mobility narratives) it's a combined *expansion* and *weakening* in the mentor/benefactor role that puts such agonizing pressure on the merits of the protagonists.[12]

The film's major figure for this shift in the mentor/benefactor function is television. Television is referred to in the film again and again, beginning with the early shots of William and Arthur raptly watching coverage of the Bulls and the Pistons. Comparison is thus invited between TV and the school, which clearly cannot command the same level of attention. In a sense, the entire film expatiates on the cliché that television has now displaced school as the primary agent by which American children get socialized. And thus television also displaces school in upward mobility narratives, in the film's understanding of power and of the ambiguous mentor/benefactor role.

The filmmakers don't step out from behind the camera, but they do show us "real" coaches—real in the specific sense that, because they coach the best college teams, teams that make it to national TV, those of us who watch televised basketball will have seen them there.[13] The known-ness of these "real" or television-mediated coaches obviously functions in the film as a sort of "objective" standard of merit, a way to judge how good William and Arthur *really* are, and thus also how good the filmmakers themselves really are. (It would of course have been much easier to do the film in reverse, as it were: to start with someone already famous and piece together the necessarily much scantier evidence of how he got there. The filmmakers could not have known in advance how good these two fourteen-year-olds were going to become.) The powerful "reality" of these TV supercoaches validates the parallel between the filmmakers themselves and the ordinary coaches and talent scouts they film, the impossibility of separating the talent of the kids from *their* talent in spotting the kids and sticking with them. If the documentary genre is the guarantor not of truth so much as of *merit*—which the fiction film, unlike documentary, could of course arrange to manifest at will—it is TV that offers validation to the merit of aspiring documentary.

As a representation of democratically accessible power, television is both alluringly available and stingy in its actual benefactions. Perhaps the defining moment in this new version of ambiguous mentorship is the sequence when, very early in the film, Isiah Thomas appears suddenly and miraculously incarnate in the gymnasium of St. Joseph's High School. In effect, he descends from the television, where the film has already shown him, into the world from which he himself has arisen, and thus validates the reality of the path between the two, the ladder of mobility. Yet he remains a symbol of that path rather than an active agent helping anyone along it. Like television itself, he is part of a deception, and there is little solace in the fact that no one tries to hide this deception. It's how the game is played. Arthur finds himself, at fourteen, going one-on-one with Isiah. Smiling, hamming for the audience, Isiah nevertheless throws a good head fake. Arthur goes for the fake, and while he's up off his feet, the camera follows Isiah around him for the easy layup. Arthur's mobility is upward, but only transiently so.

This is the head fake of what has been called the "winner-take-all society," a society in which (to quote Michael Lind) "the top performers tend to monopolize pay and prestige, leaving little in the way of either gain or glory for the vast numbers of also-rans—the equivalent of a third world in the professions, with a few wealthy oligarchs and a miserable majority."[14] Still, it would be a mistake to group television with Bourdieu's unambiguous and all-powerful institutions. In the unspoken competition with television that animates the documentary (ending when *Hoop Dreams* beats and joins its rival), it's not always clear which side we should root for.

The film's self-effacing style and the filmmakers' decision never to put themselves in front of the camera mark among other things a withdrawal of the filmmakers themselves from the mentor/benefactor slot.[15] It's as if they, and the white audiences watching the film, did not belong to the white world that supports everything we see in the film. Making themselves invisible thus means making themselves seem powerless, powerless to interfere and also powerless to help (though of course they did both, and not just by paying the electric bill when the lights were turned off). Yet the power and responsibility to do something should not and cannot be left entirely to the protagonists.

One paradoxical consequence of the invisibility of the observers is that the film has trouble representing the full measure of its subjects' real achievements on the basketball court. In order for the film to show how good Arthur and William really are in this team sport, it would have required the extra technical resources permitting coverage of the court from multiple angles simultaneously. By strenuous editing, it could thus have revealed the particular work of the guard, which is largely invisible to a single camera: the art of leadership, tempo, passing, the instant interpretation of nine other players in complex motion. It would have required an obtrusive style closer to that of television, with its stop action, its ostentatious replays and drawing-board shots, its willingness to interrupt the flow and offer an open display of the commentators. Instead, the film is forced to let William's missed free throws, for example, stand as the icon of failure in a purely individual test of merit. If the truer or fuller appreciation of artistry on the court needs a display of the observer, then there's an argument to be made that TV's unreality effects are in a sense preferable to the high seriousness of documentary realism.[16] Extending this observation, we get the principle that a foregrounded, meddlesome mediator, however unpleasant to contemplate, offers a truer picture of the conditions in which the striving protagonist is forced to operate.

In addition, we might speculate that concern with winning or losing, which of course plays a huge if incalculable role in sports spectatorship, is undercut or at least somewhat decentered by a very different identification: the spectator's still more mysterious investment in how the game of television is played. Of necessity, the spectator of televised sport identifies both with a favored player or team and with the ubiquitous mediatory apparatus of television itself. Composed of both the famous and the anonymous, combining active, self-conscious intervention with the spectator's own enforced passivity and distance vis-à-vis the athlete's efforts, TV would seem to offer lessons about upward mobility that are analytically distinct from those of the sports it represents: lessons about team membership, individual and collective achievement, "free agency," "success." How can the spectator's identification with the mediatory apparatus not affect her or his imaginative positioning in narratives of upward mobility? Yet without further investigation, we cannot assume that this effect is undesirable.

In conclusion, let me offer a final instance, from outside the arena of sport, of mediation that is obnoxious and/or dangerous but also inescapable. In *The Crisis of the Negro Intellectual*, Harold Cruse uses the term *paternalism* to describe the surrogate-familial obstacle faced by African American intellectuals trying to escape from the weight of the white left.[17] In a white-dominated society, even the white left starts off with far greater access to power. Hence, despite its putative good intentions and its manifest weakness relative to the powers that be, it can be thought of as paternalist and assimilated to the category I've been discussing: the ambiguous mediator or benefactor, the shadowy gatekeeper who might either open or block the gateway to power.

Yet there is no moving up, whether individually or collectively (Cruse is interested in both), without some mediation by holders of power. A Bourdieu-like denunciation of the mediatory role demands in effect that the protagonist sustain a lonely and perhaps impossible heroism. As Cruse himself notes, at least intermittently, to ask African American intellectuals to achieve an absolute separatist or nationalist purity is to lead them into self-contradiction and failure. That's why it's so interesting to take Watts's concept of the "facilitator," outlined in his reaction to Harold Cruse, as an implicit revision of Cruse's "paternalism." This is how Watts redescribes, for example, the Communist Party, which Cruse attacks for its manipulation of Afro-American intellectuals and its neglect of the needs of Harlem: "Regardless of form, the social marginality facilitator has ultimately one purpose: to increase, protect, and nurture the individual's artistic and intellectual 'space.' For instance, Richard Wright used his membership in the Communist Party U.S.A. as a social marginality facilitator."[18] On the next page, Watts joins in the critique of paternalism without noting how, in the language I just quoted, it's something very like the displaced paternal and maternal warmth of the family (protecting and nurturing without asking any questions, as it were) that gets recoded, positively, as a "social marginality facilitator." The chill abstraction of those three words can't conceal a functional parallel: the facilitator is a sort of surrogate family.

The right way to think about such surrogates is to restore and explore their ambiguity, and their burden. They must be seen as central to the narrative of upward mobility because they mediate and represent power, in all its ugliness and in all its potential for self-contradiction, and because it is only that power that can take some of the lethal responsibility away from the pure, unprotected merit of the upwardly mobile protagonists. The accomplishment of *Hoop Dreams* is not after all to show that we don't know which way is up. Its accomplishment is to show that a moral critique of the mentor/benefactor's power, including the power to set a standard, can mean taking away upward mobility itself, whether individual or collective. In a perverse but entirely logical way, Bourdieu's "reproduction" belongs to what my colleague Michael Warner calls "repro culture." Like the moral reading of *Hoop Dreams*, it backs the natural, heterosexual family against the artificially engineered, ethically and sexually ambiguous mobilities of the surrogate family, the world of leering coaches who are all less altruistic than they seem. On behalf of those necessary if always disturbing ambiguities, the upward mobility story of *Hoop Dreams* needs to be defended against the film itself.

Notes

This essay was originally presented as part of a panel discussion titled "Bourdieu and Race" at the American Studies Association in November 1995. My thanks to Kenneth Warren for the invitation and helpful conversation.

1. This is precisely the moral that Charles Barkley draws in his introduction to Ben Joravsky's book *Hoop Dreams: A True Story of Hardship and Triumph* (New York: HarperPerennial, 1995). Barkley begins by wishing that "kids, especially black kids, didn't dream so much about playing in the NBA" (9). And he concludes: "What's so uplifting about the story of the Gates and Agee families is that almost all the

characters, despite their disappointments and setbacks, never lose track of what really matters in life. It doesn't matter how many points you score, or rebounds you grab, or games you win. In the end what will matter is the kind of father, son, brother, husband, and neighbor you are. . . . That is something the Agees and Gates understand, and if anything makes them special, it's that" (10).

2. Note that while filming, the filmmakers were clearly obliged to spend more time away from their families than their subjects were from theirs.

3. One essay that articulates this case is Jillian Sandell, "Out of the Ghetto and into the Marketplace: *Hoop Dreams* and the Commodification of Marginality," *Socialist Review*, 95, no. 2 (1995): 57–82.

4. Jerry Gafio Watts, *Heroism and the Black Intellectual: Ralph Ellison, Politics, and Afro-American Intellectual Life* (Chapel Hill: University of North Carolina Press, 1994), 16.

5. These are displaced from, but still share a great deal with, the more straightforward narratives of, say, younger women and their male employers, that is, erotic bondability aiming toward or at least evoking the paradigm of eventual biological reproduction.

6. Hortense Spillers, "*The Crisis of the Negro Intellectual:* A Post-Date," *boundary 2*, 21 (fall 1994): 69.

7. Craig Calhoun, *Critical Social Theory: Culture, History, and the Challenge of Difference* (Oxford: Basil Blackwell, 1995), 143.

8. Pierre Bourdieu, *Homo Academicus*, trans. Peter Collier (Stanford, Calif.: Stanford University Press, 1988): "Those whom I call 'oblates,' and who, consigned from childhood to the school institution (they are often children of the lower or middle classes or sons of teachers) are totally dedicated to it" (xxiv). See translator's note, 291 n. 31.

9. Ibid., 100–101.

10. Calhoun, *Critical Social Theory*, 149.

11. Ibid., 129–30.

12. *Hoop Dreams* is actually much more nuanced and interesting on coaching than the moral reading makes it seem. It entertains the idea that after all the protagonist can make it only by sacrificing something to the coach. The key to Curtis Gates's lack of success, we are told, is that, though highly talented, he was "uncoachable." The film also has much to say—though one wishes it had been more—about the positive figures of Luther Bedford, Arthur's coach at Marshall, and Earl Smith, the scout who discovers them both.

13. In this sense, universities themselves depend on television for their funding and even perhaps their legitimacy.

14. Michael Lind, "Why the Rich Get Richer," *New York Times Book Review*, 24 September 1995, 15. Lind reviews Robert H. Frank and Philip J. Cook, *The Winner-Take-All Society* (New York: Free Press, 1995).

15. The film, too, had its mentors, as *Nightline* pointed out. The film critics Siskel and Ebert did something they had never done: they previewed and reviewed it even though as yet it had no distributor and no opening date.

16. For all its imposing, seriousness-guaranteeing length, the film in fact goes by very quickly. To disperse the responsibility for its protagonists' meritorious achievement, the film would have to slow down.

17. Harold Cruse, *The Crisis of the Negro Intellectual* (New York: Quill, 1984 [1967]).

18. Watts, *Heroism and the Black Intellectual*, 16.

Back-Page Bylines:
Newspapers, Women, and Sport

An Interview with Liz Kahn, Mary Jollimore, and Wanda Jamrozik

Amanda Smith

Liz Kahn is a freelancer in London who writes for the *Daily Telegraph,* the *Guardian,* and the *Mail on Sunday.* She started writing about sport in the 1960s. Mary Jollimore is a producer for the Canadian Broadcasting Corporation's *Newsworld Sports* and a former columnist with the *Toronto Globe and Mail.* She began her career in 1979. Wanda Jamrozik joined the sports desk of the *Australian* at the beginning of 1995. All three women worked as beat reporters and feature writers before they took to the back pages.

The following is a transcript from an Australian radio program, *The Sports Factor.* The program, presented by Amanda Smith and produced by Michael Shirrefs, is broadcast weekly on the Australian Broadcasting Corporation's Radio National and Radio Australia networks. *The Sports Factor* seeks to debate and discuss issues and events in sport in a wide social and cultural context.

Across time zones and in studios in London, Washington, Sydney, and Melbourne, the discussion began with how and why three women got into writing sport. The interview was broadcast on 2 September 1995. Wanda Jamrozik died in January 1996, at the age of thirty-five. This article is a remembrance of her passion and her bloody-mindedness. Australia lost an intelligent and provocative sports journalist with her death.

AMANDA SMITH: How did each of you get to be sports journalists, and why did you choose sport as your subject?

LIZ KAHN: I was sports mad when I was a youngster. I think as a journalist I fell into sport because a friend of my brother's was a sportswriter and I just thought it was quite a normal thing to do. My first assignment was going to Wimbledon and being told how to sit on a court and report tennis and then put over the copy. I never realized that there was anything odd about reporting sport until I got into it.

MARY JOLLIMORE: For me I suppose it had something to do with the fact that I knew how to keep score in tennis. One day about fifteen years ago when I was

working at UPI [United Press International], the wire service in Toronto, the
sports reporter was sick. I was general news reporter, and the sports editor asked
if there was anybody to fill in who could recognize Björn Borg or John McEnroe
and knew how to keep score. I fitted the qualifications so I got the assignment,
and that's how it really started.

WANDA JAMROZIK: I actually wasn't at all keen on sport as a youngster. I was
part of that thing in Australia that says if you can read, you can't be into sport—
there's a big traditional divide between the jocks and the people who wear spectacles. I'd always sided with the people in spectacles, but gradually over the last
five or six years I just found that more and more I was reading newspapers from
the back to the front, and eventually I decided if I was reading the back first,
I may as well be writing there as well.

AS: Has the increasing number of women entering the field changed the scope
or the parameters of sports journalism?

WJ: I think so. I tend to think in a way what we're seeing is a gentrification of
sports coverage. There's been an awareness that newspapers around the world
are facing shrinking readerships and so are trying to work out ways they can get
across to different parts of a market. One of the tricks that they've come up
with, if you like, is to explore the possibilities of writing about sport in a reasonably intelligent way, which was not something that was traditionally part of the
sportswriter's beat. And interestingly enough I think it's women who have been
able to capitalize on the opportunity there is for writing in a different way.

MJ: I certainly prefer to write about issues rather than what happened at last
night's match. I still have to do that, but I find it kind of boring. Last year I went
to the men's World Basketball Championships and I think I covered forty basketball games in twelve weeks. I wasn't able to see the difference between one
team and the next by about game twenty-five. But if you look for the features
behind the games, it's a way of keeping yourself interested, and that's what I
like about what I do now as a columnist.

    I like nothing better than to go and find a woman athlete that no one's
heard of, who's trying to make the Olympics, and sit and talk to her for an hour.
I much prefer that than talking to some $5 million-a-year basketball player
who's a prima donna and doesn't like talking to the media in the first place.

AS: Well, Liz Kahn, are women less fascinated by the "scores-and-groin-injuries"
aspect of sport than men?

LK: I think . . . some are and some aren't. I mean some do straightforward reporting. I think women generally have a wider perspective. I think women are

more interested in the emotional makeup of a person, they're more interested in their motivation, they're more interested perhaps in the psychological aspect of the sport than a man is, and that probably comes out in their writing. I think it does vary according to the sports writer.

In Britain we're perhaps more limited than in Australia or in America. We have a tabloid press and the tabloid press is interested in big names and big stories. So it's very difficult to go and find somebody who's done absolutely nothing, as Mary suggests, unless she's extremely good-looking. I mean the tabloid paper that I write for . . . is quite likely to say, "Is she good-looking?"

AS: And how do you deal with that?

LK: You have to just say yes or no. I used to kick against it and object, but if you want to work, then you've got to go along with it, which is sad. But I came to the conclusion in covering sport where people wanted to know about the good-looking athletes, that if that got people through the gate watching the event, then they'd see everybody. And I tended to look at it that way because it was probably more comfortable to look at it that way.

AS: Now something that interests me about the way sports reporting has tradi-tionally worked is that it tends to be written from the inside, by blokes who've either been players or worked hard at getting close to players. By contrast, do women sports writers tend to stand on the outside and look in, and therefore write more critically or analytically than their male colleagues?

WJ: Yes, I'd say that's pretty right. And that "scores-and-groin-injuries" aspect you referred to, that is pretty much the insider's view. It does tend to be what athletes talk about to one another. They are talking about how they pulled up after the last match, or whether that ankle is still giving them trouble, and so on. I don't find that terribly interesting. I do feel outside that. And I also think in the course of going out and reporting on sport that my male colleagues often don't leave me in any doubt that I'm outside as well.

But there's certainly advantages. Sport is very elastic if you aren't com-pletely submerged in the fine detail. You can write very emotionally, you can write very technically or analytically; you can seize on characters, you can seize on conflict. It's a very open field if you're able to see it. So in a sense I'm glad that I'll never be able to actually stand in the urinal next to Jonah Lomu after a rugby game. While that might be a big thrill, I think I'm probably better off watching the game, thinking about what's gone on there, looking at how other people have reacted to it and just choosing from lots of different ways of cover-ing it.

AS: But does that mean that you face the criticism that you're not qualified to write about men's sports, about football or baseball or whatever, because you haven't played these sports?

MJ: One of the big things that keeps getting tossed back in the face of women sports journalists in North America, in particular where American football is considered the be-all and end-all of sports, is this constant reminder to women that we have never played American football, therefore how can we dare to aspire to cover it? Or how can we do it justice? And first of all that makes the assumption that women have never played football. I used to toss a football around when I was a kid; I never played organized football, but there are young women nowadays who do.

Further, the response that most women have developed over the years to throw back to those men who say that is, "Every newspaper has a person who writes the obituaries, and they haven't died or experienced death in order to write obituaries."

The fact that I never played professional football doesn't actually set me apart from most of my colleagues in the press box. Most of them haven't played professional football either. I don't know any sportswriter in America—a writer—who's played a professional sport. Most of the ex-athletes are talking heads on TV, they're the commentators, they're the so-called expert analysts.

I think also that being a woman you're not part of the pack journalism that goes on in sports coverage. It also means that you're not in awe of these athletes. And let's face it, it's a huge travesty for anyone to think that covering games requires a lot of intelligence—it doesn't. Nine-year-olds know how to play base-ball. Young kids know the rules of football. It's not rocket science, you know.

AS: Liz Kahn, does that mean you're treated differently by athletes or coaches or officials when you're covering a story? And I mean that either positively or negatively.

LK: I think it does, yes. I've always been put down, from the time I started. And I think the problem about that is that if sportswriters, your colleagues, tend to put you down, then the athletes get hold of that and they also sometimes try to do the same thing.

I gained entry for women into the locker room at the open golf champion-ship a couple of years ago, and that was merely because there are times when you do need to go in for a story. And I was in there one day and Jack Nicklaus came in, and he knows me quite well, and he says to me, "What are you doing in here?" So I looked at him and I said, "I'm a golf writer, Jack, and I'm doing my job." He said, "I don't care what you are, you're a woman." And I have to say he does that sort of thing in front of other people so that they can hear Jack Nicklaus putting a woman down and then all join in and do the same thing.

I've probably been thrown out of more places than most people have walked into, trying to do my job. I wasn't allowed in the Royal and Ancient Clubhouse when all the other golf writers were. The first time there was an open championship there I went in and there was an attendant on the door and he said, "I'm sorry madam, you can't come in here." So I said, "Well, all my colleagues are in here and my badge says I can come in here." And he says, "No madam, no women allowed in here. Not even the Queen."

And I was unceremoniously chucked out, and I was bodily evicted later from a locker room. This has gone on and on and you do get the message that you're different, and you do cover sport differently because of it.

On the other hand, I think that you can get some athletes to open up in a different way from a male journalist, and you do go more for the jugular sometimes because you don't play that sport as they do, and you're able to get more information out of them perhaps. You ask more questions than a man would, so there are advantages as well.

WJ: This business of male sports journalists being much more on the inside: you get on the inside for a price.

The price is that you don't betray the trust of those friends of yours who happen to be the athletes. But it seems to me that the closer into a sport you get, the more you're foreclosing on the things that you might write about. Because if you do write something that upsets someone in there, and what you've said has been a privileged piece of information that you've obtained by being on the inside, you'll never be allowed in again. The "insider trading" was certainly striking to me when I first started covering sport; it seemed to me much greater than in other areas that I'd worked as a journalist.

And you get phenomenal things in sport, like the traveling media circus that follows the professional tennis around—a group of mostly men, fifty or sixty of them who spend months on end on the road with the athletes that they cover. And there's a tremendous number of protocols that go on in that situation, and an awful lot of paying of your dues. People were absolutely up-front in saying to me that if I wanted to get access to some of these athletes, well I'd have to show that I could be trusted, that is, that I wouldn't write anything that would upset them. So that's a bit of a selling of your soul that's going on there. I don't know necessarily whether it's a price that's worth paying.

AS: Well, Mary Jollimore, do you try and keep that distance also to be able to be critical or analytical?

257

MJ: I think it's more difficult to avoid doing that if you're a beat reporter, and that's why I would never really want to be a beat reporter, because I do think there's a certain compromising of your principles. And I do agree most definitely that women get told things that men don't get told. I've been told by male athletes that they cried after certain things happened. They wouldn't tell that to a male sportswriter, they simply wouldn't. You get much different answers.

Sometimes you get treated with more respect because you're a woman. I've had professional athletes, male athletes, call me ma'am and rise from their chairs when I came into a room. At first I thought they were leaving, but they were just being polite! The really young ones—because I'm in my mid-thirties—some of them treat you like you're a mother almost.

But there is a certain testing when you're first covering a team, or when you're new to a certain sport. They'll challenge you. You have to prove that you know the rules, you have to prove that you're serious, you have to prove that you're professional about your job. You have to prove that you didn't get into this because you're looking to sleep with athletes or socialize with them.

It's been told to me by other male writers that once the players found out I was married and had been happily married for a long time, then they understood that I wasn't in this for sex. But always in the back of their minds they think you're a groupie because there are groupies all around the place in sport in North America.

AS: Liz Kahn, have you had similar experiences to those Mary describes?

LK: Yes, I have. I started when I was very young and obviously, as Mary says, people think you're just out for sex and that's it. I was certainly propositioned a lot of times, and you learn how to handle it, and you have to be professional about what you're doing. But there were times when if I just talked to a man, then the gossip would go around that I'd been to bed with him. And if I wrote a story about him, the same thing. This was in a very different era—I'd never heard of sexual harassment either. When I first started, the women's movement had hardly started up, and I think I probably had to find out the hard way how to go about it. I had to make a lot of compromises.

It wasn't until I went and covered the women's professional golf tour in America that I had independent, achieving women to identify with. That was a great relief for me, because I saw that it was all right to be doing what I was doing, here with these women doing what they were doing. And that really opened a lot of doors for me personally.

AS: Do any of you feel that you have a responsibility to write about or promote women's sport?

WJ: I'm much more interested, I have to admit, in covering male sports than female sports, and I actually quite like knocking around with the men. It's almost an aesthetic thing, where I enjoy the added power and crunch in a lot of male physical contact sports. It takes my breath away. Or when you see top-level tennis and you just see how Andre Agassi can send a ball back across the net. It's beyond anything that I could ever imagine being able to do. And when I see the women, I think, God, can't they speed it up a bit?

MJ: But Wanda, have you ever stood on the other side of a net when Martina Navratilova fired a serve?

WJ: No, of course I haven't stood on the other side of a net. But she's not serving at two hundred and twenty Ks though, is she?

MJ: No, but for a woman she's serving pretty damn fast.

WJ: Dead right, for a woman.

LK: I think it's a very dangerous trap to fall into, to compare men's sport to women's sport. You're pandering to all the sports editors' views of their readers if you say, "Well I prefer what men do to what women do in the same field."

MJ: This reminds me that early on in a woman sportswriter's career, she wants to cover the sports that are going to get prominence in the sports section, and not be pigeonholed. Fifteen, twenty years ago, when I was starting out, I resisted that too, because you don't want people to think that you're just there to write the fluff pieces, or the players' wives' stories, and that sort of thing. And that's why I got into covering professional ice hockey, the NHL and all those sorts of sports, because I wanted to be treated equally with my male counterparts.

But three years ago when the *Globe and Mail* asked me to write a column, they wanted me to write about issues, including women and sport. They had done a focus group which showed that they were giving lousy coverage to women in sport. I took it on because I felt it was a responsibility—if I didn't do it, I wondered who else would. The novelty of making sure my byline was on the main page of the sports section wore off for me a long time ago. I'd rather do something that's interesting and this is to me why I do it.

AS: For you is that about writing "pioneer stories," you know, the first woman to break a barrier in sport, or is it about trying to normalize women as athletes?

MJ: What I try to do is not so much the pioneer thing. I try to write about the things no one's heard about. And that's not too difficult because women athletes, and the whole range of issues that affect women in sport, have been ignored for

259

so long. For example, to write about stupid policies that keep women out of sport. I still don't understand why the International Olympic Committee doesn't have an equal number of events for women at the Olympics as they do for men. And why there wasn't a marathon for women at the Olympics until 1984. Obviously this old boys' club known as the IOC thought women were just too darn delicate to run that far. It's never difficult to find something to write about.

WJ: But it's also a question of interest. I came to sportswriting out of my own sports interests, which were cricket and football. Those are what I knew the most about. Plus they're the sports that are the most central in the culture here. They're the arenas in which the most occurs, not just in terms of what happens on the field, but the other aspects—the politics and so on. So I'm very reluctant about this responsibility-to-women thing. I think we should all be free to write about whatever the hell we want to write about and none of us should feel obligated by gender or age or whatever to feel that we have to concentrate in certain areas.

AS: Female athletes often have to face having their sexuality, and authenticity as women, questioned. You've talked about having to prove that you're not groupies, but do you also have your sexuality questioned?

MJ: I think there are two issues that will never go away, no matter how much progress is made in terms of women's sports becoming more mainstream or more popular with fans or whatever. One is that the prize money will probably never be totally equal, and two is that a female athlete's sexual preference will continue to be a nagging issue. Because of the whole idea that women who are muscular want to look like men.

For me as a journalist, this issue came up a couple of years ago when I was on a radio program in Winnipeg in Canada, with three other women sports journalists. A caller phoned in—a male caller who wanted to know how many of the four of us were lesbians. Unfortunately he was immediately cut off, the host wouldn't let us answer the question. I wanted to put it to the caller that if there were four male sports journalists on the program, would he have called and even dared to ask them what their sexual preference was? But this guy seemed to think it was a relevant question for us. And it was really frightening to me that this fellow—who sounded like he was in his twenties—could think that way. But I know a lot of women athletes who get asked that all the time. Or it's simply assumed that they're lesbians.

AS: So how much have things changed for you and for women writing sport in the time that you've been involved?

MJ: I think it's a lot easier now than it was in the 1970s when I started. I give a lot of credit to the women who came before me. There's a woman in Toronto who covered the Toronto Blue Jays baseball team as her beat for six seasons. She traveled with the team each day during the season and covered their games on a regular basis. She's the type of woman to let most stuff roll off her back when it occurred, but she also knew exactly what to say in order to deal with it.

There was a time in a locker room when a player jumped up on a training table and was naked and dancing in front of her, to try to get her attention or rile her. And she looked over at him and said, "My, that looks like a penis only smaller."

So the guy knew that this woman was not to be messed with: she had a sense of humor, she showed that she was willing to just let this go off without it bothering her, she took it in her stride and she was able to do that beat for six years.

I've never had anything quite that blatant happen to me in the locker room. But it's much easier now, and I think that as a new generation of athletes come into the men's professional sports—Tiger Woods replaces Jack Nicklaus—they're going to understand that this is not a profession entirely for men and that women should be welcome. The younger hockey players now, for example, they have sisters who play hockey. They understand that sports is an area that women compete in and write about, and they're a little bit more open to the idea of women sports reporters than perhaps the hockey players were ten, fifteen, twenty years ago.

I think it will only improve, and as the number of women sports reporters increases—there aren't that many in Canada, I can only think of maybe twenty in the whole country, there are far more in the United States—but as more women get into it and don't allow themselves to be pigeonholed as women writers writing about the players' wives' hairdos or whatever, and make their presence known, things will have to improve.

Sports Trademarks and Somatic Politics:
Locating the Law in a Critical Cultural Studies

Rosemary J. Coombe

The relationship between law and cultural practice is both productive and diacritical. The legal status of cultural texts, the ability to exercise power over meaning, and the denials of ambiguity that law effects—as well as the resistances such denial engenders—are central to contemporary fields of cultural politics. I will draw upon a limited area of juridical discourse—laws of trademark—and a range of cultural activities—examples of cultural politics engaging sports trademarks in the United States—to make my case. Legal regimes, I suggest, provide spaces of governance and accountability, as well as means and mediums for transgression and social transformation. The instances examined here exemplify the significance of intellectual property laws in a wider field of contemporary cultural politics that we might deem a politics of publicity.

Intellectual property laws and their interpretation compel our interest because of their power to achieve particular political effects—legitimating practices of cultural authority that attempt to limit the play of intertextuality in public spheres increasingly dominated by industrial-commercial forms of publicity. Such laws provide generative conditions and prohibitive boundaries for hegemonic articulations. To the extent that specific legal infrastructures create particular forms of signifying power, they also enable, provoke, or invite particular forms of resistance or alternative appropriations. Often, as we shall see, these are aw(e)fully appropriate to the forms of legally regulated signification to which they may be seen as forms of response. Drawing exclusively upon examples of trademarks in the field of athletics further focuses the inquiry. An emphasis upon the commodity/sign in sports arenas provokes new perspectives upon regimes of corporeal specularity—dominant representations of commodified, racialized, and politicized bodies and struggles to redefine the parameters of the body politic they legitimate.

Olympics and Monumental Bodies

Walking down the street in Toronto one day in 1987, pedestrians were surprised to see a message flashing across an electronic billboard—"Lesbians fly

Air Canada." It was gone the next morning. This broadcast was abruptly ter-
minated because the government threatened a gay rights group with an injunction to prevent the organization from using the publicly owned airline's
name.[1]

The tactics of appropriation involved in hegemonic articulations simultaneously invoke and transform fields of power and representation. Bodies
politic are signified by symbols that are legally protected. The polysemic
power of the nation, the seductive power of the commodity form, and the
instrumental power of the state are legally bestowed powers that also shape
the expressive activities that seek to challenge the contours of the body
politic configured through such signs. Public propensities to remark upon
(and put one's own mark upon) dominant forms of signifying power are apparent in the case of "official marks"—signs held by public authorities in the
name of the public interest.[2] These are often key symbols in national and
international cultural lexicons with which subaltern groups seek affirmative
association.

Governments bestow the most extensive signifying powers upon authorities that control the signs of the nation, the state, and transnational
institutional icons.[3] For example, in the United States, there is a group of
"national" symbols (ranging from Smokey the Bear to Little League and the
Future Farmers of America) that the federal government protects from unauthorized use (under the same provisions that once penalized desecration
of the flag).[4] Rarely, however, are the "public authorities" in control of these
marks elected political bodies. More often, government agencies and nonprofit corporations are given the discretion and discriminatory power to determine their own definitions of the public interest. The signs they hold
often identify key institutions of local, national, and transnational authority.[5]
The visible and monumental power of these institutions invites others to appropriate their signs in a "politics of direct address"—acts of publicity seeking recognition, inclusion, and representation that take the form of struggles
over key symbols and their connotative fields of reference.[6] Not surprisingly,
subaltern groups have a tendency to mobilize in identifications with signs
that promise new forms of legitimacy in the public sphere.

Those who hold the intellectual property rights in such signifiers, however, may attempt to control both the sign's circulation and its meanings.[7]
By creating monopolies in fields of representation, the law inserts signifiers
into systems of political economy that "reduce symbolic ambivalence in order
to ground the rational circulation of values and their play of exchange."[8]
Texts are denied their indeterminacy and polysemy by laws that protect

their exchange value. "Owners" of mass-media signifiers may well permit the social production of significance when it mints meanings with potential market value, but they may also prohibit the material circulation of connotations that contest the valences they have propagated. Indeed, most trademark holders have an economic interest in so doing. Unless they "police" their marks, they are in danger of losing them through legal doctrines that deprive holders of their exclusive rights if marks lose their distinction and become part of the general vocabulary.

In the case of official marks, however, public authorities are statutorily endowed with exclusive rights to control particular signifiers without any legal requirement that they monitor their use or risk of loss.[9] This absolute power to prohibit the use of certain symbols is often legitimated by public order and safety concerns. Dangerous confusion is avoided by univocally fixing the referent for a sign like the red cross, for instance, and restricting its use to a single organization. Consumer confusion provides another rationalization; it is improper and misleading to suggest government endorsement of one's goods or services. The powers over signification bestowed by such statutes, however, go far beyond those necessary to avoid such harms. Having adopted the sign, authorities are enabled with the singular capacity to dictate the sign's "official" meanings. They may threaten, enjoin, and prosecute those who give the signifier unsanctioned connotations. Such discretionary power to prohibit alternative usages often manifests ideological interests and reveals particular prejudices about the proper character of the social body.

If official signifiers seldom feature prominently on elite political agendas (a refusal by the U.S. Senate in 1993 to renew the design patent for the United Daughters of the Confederacy being a rare exception), socially they figure as cultural targets and as resources in struggles for political legitimation. In 1981, for example, a nonprofit group called San Francisco Arts and Athletics (the Athletics Group) organized a promotional event to create a more positive image of the gay community. T-shirts, buttons, and bumper stickers financed the Gay Olympics. The U.S. Olympic Committee (the Committee) brought suit to stop the games and to preclude the group from making use of the term *Olympic*. The Committee had exclusive rights to use the word *Olympic* under the Amateur Sports Act and successfully enjoined the Athletics Group's use of the term in court appeals culminating in the U.S. Supreme Court's 1987 decision upholding the Committee's exclusive and absolute rights to the word *Olympic*.[10]

Olympic, of course, is a term with a long history of connoting human excellence and achievement. It is recognized transnationally as a humanist symbol and one with which the dispossessed have traditionally sought to identify in aspirations for social affirmation and as a medium for public education. The Committee itself acknowledged the significance of the symbol in achieving social recognition; it had authorized groups of the disabled to hold "Olympic" games to encourage their greater social incorporation. As one dissenting judge at the court of appeals remarked, "It seems that the Committee is using its control over the term Olympic to promote the very image of homosexuals that the [Athletics Group] seeks to combat: handicapped, juniors, police, Explorers, even *dogs* are allowed to carry the Olympic torch, but homosexuals are not."[11] Indeed, the Committee's own counsel was a member of a local Olympic Club—an exclusive, segregated, all-male social club with a history of discrimination against gays and minorities.

Cultural studies has alerted us to practices in which signifiers circulate in social fields and become inflected with new meanings. This dispute, however, serves as a cautionary reminder that the domains of discourse in which symbols figure as sites for identification may shape and limit their availability for new articulations. If counterhegemonic tactics endeavor to put signifiers into fields of symbolic exchange, such practitioners are at a disadvantage when they come up against proprietors interested in maintaining the signifier's market value. When connotations of Olympic as a festival celebrating human excellence and bodily energy (implicitly linked to a nonreproductive sexuality) encountered the Olympic signifier's status as a commodity, the sign's exclusionary values were carefully contained to ensure the maximum flow of merchandising royalties.

Visible, recognized, and pervasively objectified, the Olympic signifier denotes legitimacy and prestige; its connotations are legally managed through structures of prohibition. As an official sign of power and value, it is both uniquely attractive to those who seek political recognition and particularly important to those who seek to preserve contemporary hegemonies. Like other monumental signs, it attracts efforts of appropriation and rearticulation by those who wish to inscribe their own authorial signature on the people, the nation, the state—the body politic. Such acts of subaltern recoding seem to engage the signifiers of power in a fashion appropriate to their mode of signification. This at least is what I shall attempt to elaborate in the following discussions of trademarked stereotypes, trademark rumors, and postindustrial publicity relations.

Redskins and Specularized Alterity

As citizens and consumers, commodified signifiers mark our identities and our social boundaries.[12] Not surprisingly, these also attract the energies of those who would alter such parameters—to highlight and to challenge the implicit inclusions and exclusions that social distinctions invariably effect. Scholars concerned with contemporary public spheres (and, to a lesser degree, academics and activists who seek to articulate the characteristics of contemporary civil society) rightly suggest that we attend to the quotidian cultural politics that engages commodity/signs.[13] Michael Warner makes perhaps the most global claim for the significance of trademarks in public spheres—as characteristic media forms that interrelate collectivities and imagined national communities, he suggests, they provide a common discourse that binds the subject to the nation and its markets. As he points out, "We have brandnames all over us."[14] Some of "us" and "our" ancestors, however, are, in fact, brand names: Cherokee®, Oneida®, Pontiac®, Winnebago®, Crazy Horse™, Aunt Jemima®, and Uncle Ben®. Some of "us" may have national trademarks all over our bodies, others of "us" have bodies, nations, and ancestors that are all over the commercial landscape as trademarks.

Cultural histories of imperialism remind us that the emergence of consumer societies involved the commodified objectification of colonized others and the domestication of social alterity in daily practices of consumption that bound citizen/consumers in imagined communities of belonging.[15] The visual cultures of mass markets are often saturated with signs of social difference; histories of imperialism and colonialism, territorial annexation, and political disenfranchisement are socially inscribed across commercial landscapes. When these icons assume the form of marks used in trade—black mammies, Indian princesses, Mexican bandits, Hawaiian hula dancers, for instance, they may be legally claimed as private properties by those who assert them as marks of their own distinction in commerce.

Trademarks are signifiers that distinguish the goods of one manufacturer, retailer, or service provider from those of others. These may be logos, brand names, characteristic advertising images, or other forms that condense and convey meaning in commerce. The ubiquity of trademarks in national social arenas and their currency both as culture and as private property creates generative conditions for struggles over significance; they are simultaneously shared in a commons of signification and jealously guarded in exclusive estates. Their status as trademarks, however, makes them simultaneously appropriate, available, and vulnerable to the claims of those they (mis)represent.

Contesting claims that stereotypical images of themselves be considered primarily the marketing vehicles of others, Native peoples come up against commercial indifference, corporate animosity, and public ridicule. The movement to end the use of Native American team names, logos, and mascots in the world of professional sport has been particularly protracted. The

Washington Redskins, Atlanta Braves, Cleveland Indians, Chicago Black-hawks, Kansas City Chiefs, and Florida State University Seminoles are nominations that bind fans across ethnic and generational lines. They are also legally protected trademarks that, along with accompanying logos and mascots, provide steady streams of income. Neither economics nor emotion, however, fully accounts for the cultural power of such symbols or the almost willful refusal by team owners and fans to entertain Native peoples' concerns. The financial interests and social sentiments expressed in this controversy are, as I argue in more detail elsewhere, epiphenomena of a deeper convergence of historical, psychosocial, and legal forces.[16]

The most common basis for antagonism is the conviction that the names, logos, mascots, paraphernalia, and related fan activities represent racist stereotypes of Native American cultures. Historic depictions of Indians as bloodthirsty, warlike savages are reproduced and perpetuated in these rituals. Terms like *redskins* recall a historical period in which there was a bounty upon red skins, a genocidal referent that we would tolerate with respect to no other peoples.[17] Critics of those who oppose the use of these marks make contradictory but telling arguments. Many claim to be sensitive to Native American concerns but simply do not find the team names demeaning. Others argue that the use of these names pays a form of tribute to Native Americans by alluding to their bravery and fighting spirit.[18] In athletic competition, aggressiveness, dedication, courage, and pride are prized attributes, and Indians are recognized to embody them. Ted Turner, owner of the Atlanta team, claims that "Braves" "is a compliment. Braves are warriors."[19] Ironically, many who assert that these signifiers are tributes to Native American people simultaneously argue that they don't really refer and were never meant to refer to any particular people; their public meanings have entirely to do with the teams and their time-honored traditions.

There is a paradoxical sense in which all of these contradictory assertions are true—in which the use of Native American names and images is both insulting and complimentary, in which the names and images make reference to Indians but refer to no people in particular, and have more symbolically to do with American audiences than with oppressed nations. To comprehend how this might be the case, however, we need to consider the peculiar role of Indians in American colonial discourse. White views of Indians have been inextricably bound up with an evaluation of their own society and culture and reflect Euro-American ambivalence toward modernity.[20] Not surprisingly, the figure of the (imaginary) Indian is internally contradictory:

267

Encompassing . . . contrasting modes of performance, the Plains warriors performed complex and contradictory roles of enemies and American heroes, of local specimens and national symbols. With or without their permission, Indians participate in the often violent struggle over what and who is or is not American. In the symbolic economy of Wild West violence especially, American Indians are richly polysemic. . . . Indians could signify reckless defiance in the face of oppression and tyranny [as they did for Anglo-Americans cross-dressing at the Boston Tea Party]. . . . disenfranchised of a continent, American Indians could also signify holders of legitimate entitlement to either repatriation or revenge. From the time of Plymouth, the Indian appeared in the bad conscience of white mythology as a symbol of savage retribution.[21]

Such a dramatic field of connotation is particularly apt for the arena of competitive national sport, not least because it reiterates central tropes of American colonialism—the American frontier as a contested space, testing and consolidating a pioneering male spirit perpetually threatened by races and cultures beyond it.[22]

Homi Bhabha's consideration of the stereotype as a major discursive strategy of colonial discourse helps us to comprehend the effectivity of the trademark and the type of truth it encompasses. The stereotype of the Indian figures as an object of both derision and desire; it is both disparaged and admired. The question of whether Indian trademarks are positive or negative representations thus ceases to be salient. Instead of subjecting stereotypes to judgments of political normativity, Bhabha suggests that we explore them in terms of the "processes of subjectification" (identities and identifications) they make possible and plausible.[23]

If colonial discourse fixes otherness in an ideological discourse, it does so in a fashion that demands a continuous and anxious repetition. The force of ambivalence is what gives the colonial stereotype its currency and longevity.[24] Perhaps this is at the heart of the trademark's cultural value—"Indian" trademarks, more obviously than other commodified stereotypes, resonate with an extensive history of national mythmaking in which both the Indian's noble resistance and his ultimate defeat on expanding frontiers are repeatedly imagined and reenacted. Such trademarks may operate more powerfully than others in the political aesthetics of spectator positioning that forge "American" allegiances.

To the extent that sports spectacles embody collective social memory, their performative corporeality demands consideration.[25] Sports trademarks do not stand as abstract icons in the public sphere, but focus a kinetic interpellation of spectator/fans that links bodies in the production of "esprit de corps"—what we might call "team spirit."[26] Discussing the performative dimensions of homosocial bonding in sports, Milind Wakankar notes:

> At the core of such collective activity is the establishment of the link between the male body and the mass through physio-psycho-sociological assemblages of series of actions . . . for the effective interpellation of the subject. The proximity of so many uniformed, uni-forming, bodies-in-unison initiates a kind of silent communion. . . . Since every action mimes another, collective mimesis sustains the possibility of collective regeneration. As Bourdieu explains, "collective bodily practice," by "symbolizing the social, contribute to somatizing it and . . . by the bodily and collective mimesis of a social orchestration, aim at reinforcing that orchestration."[27]

Stereotypical trademarks seem to serve as totemic forms that mark and galvanize bodies in public rituals of homosocial bonding. Not only do fans inscribe these marks on their bodies by donning licensed goods, they engage in corporeal appropriations of alterity—imitations of and intimations with imaginary indigenes. Surrounding and animating these trademarks are rituals such as the infamous "tomahawk chop," the "war whoop," the smoking of "peace pipes," the beating of "tom-toms," the wearing of "war paint" and warbonnets while on the "warpath," the assumption of an alleged Indian ferocity in songs, dances, and even the ritual planting of flaming spears.[28] In addition to clothing, fans can cater to their bodily needs with coffee mugs, bath towels, and even toilet paper adorned with trademarked caricatures.

This is certainly not the first instance in U.S. history in which living peoples have been metaphorically erased through appropriations of their alleged alterity in the forging of other identities. Indeed, there seems substantial evidence of such activity in both working-class popular and elite literary culture. Eric Lott's work on antebellum blackface minstrelsy points to the contradictory impulses at work in stereotypicality and the dominant racial subjectivities it enables. Significantly, he also explores bodily caricature in popular cultural practice. Lott denies that the meanings of popular culture are ever simply reflective of relations of political domination. The blackface mask "is less a repetition of power relations than a signifier for them—a distorted mirror, reflecting displacements and condensations and discontinuities."[29]

Lott explores the simultaneously transgressive and oppressive dimensions of racial cross-dressing that made possible the "formation of a self-consciously white working class" and contributed to ideologies of working-class manhood.[30] Combining fear and fascination with degraded others in a mimicry of potent masculinity, feelings of racial superiority were indulged while class insecurities were assuaged, class resentments voiced, ethnic conflicts mediated, and a class identity articulated.[31] Among other things, blackface acts elevated the "black Irish" (and, later, Jews) to the status of white Americans: it was "an 'Americanizing' ritual of whitening through parodic distance."[32] Again, this space of cultural cross-dressing is a largely masculine ideological field.

In these Americanizing rituals, however, black peoples themselves are absent. From the very beginning of discussions and accounts of the form, the fact of white impersonation appears to have been forgotten. The performers became "those amusing darkies" or "the negroes" even in the most serious discussions of blackface and its meaning, as if the originals were in some way lost.[33] Behaviors that simultaneously involve amnesia and impersonation—erasure and enactment—are not socially unusual. They mark a relation between surrogacy and effigy central to the creation of circum-Atlantic identities. Roach argues that "public enactments of forgetting" or "dramas of sacrificial substitution" in spectacles of cultural surrogation were crucial to the self-inventions of modern "cultures."[34] The surrogated double is often alien to the culture that stages it; signs of the socially marginal may provide the cultural idioms through which communities assert identity.[35] What is socially peripheral may well be symbolically central.

As Roach eloquently phrases it, "The relentless search for the purity of origins is a voyage not of discovery, but of erasure."[36] What are erased, of course, are the mixtures, blends, and hybridities in the histories of a people, and the contemporary social life of those others whose cultural forms are appropriated in the displacement of memory into more amenable representations.[37] The violence instrumental to the creation of America is forgotten, as is the actual life of indigenous peoples, whose return is nonetheless staged by the performative occupation of their caricatured bodies. Their difference is appropriated, as it were, in effigy: "A general phenomena of collective memory . . . [t]he effigy is a contrivance that enables the processes regulating performance—kinesthetic imagination, vortices of behavior, and displaced transmission—to produce memory through surrogation."[38] As a noun the effigy is a pictured likeness or crudely fabricated image, but as a verb, "it means to evoke an absence, to body something forth, especially something from a distant past."[39] In sports arenas I suggest that we see

> more elusive but more powerful effigies fashioned from flesh. Such effigies are made by performances. They consist of a set of actions that hold open a place in memory into which many different people may step according to

circumstances and occasions. . . . performed effigies—those fabricated from human bodies and the associations they evoke—provide communities with a method of perpetuating themselves through specially nominated mediums or surrogates.[40]

Blackface minstrelsy "functioned as a dominant cultural figuration of black people that covered up the people themselves" and held them captive to representations constructed by others.[41] It took years to loosen the grip of such stereotypes on the popular imagination. Today, indigenous peoples in North America are similarly disguised, dissimulated, and disempowered by representations that have less to do with their culture than with mediated white responses to it, refracted through racist impositions. The enactment of Indianness in athletic arenas, held constant by the totemic power of the trademark form, functions, I suggest, as a contemporary form of whiteface minstrelsy.[42] Hence the special disturbance Native peoples voice when African Americans don "Indian" regalia in the contexts of sports events and the hostility expressed at the hypocrisy of another historically oppressed and stereotyped minority engaged in such behavior. This disturbance registers an implicit recognition that not only is the black caricaturing the "Indian" in such moments, he is asserting his "whiteness" in so doing.

Just as blackface minstrelsy had disastrous consequences for black social representation, Native Americans have suffered a lack of representation of living peoples by virtue of the very ubiquity of the stereotypes of vanishing, conquered, or comic Indians that pervade popular culture. An extended period of Native American political powerlessness and exclusion from the public sphere has enabled stereotypes to become ingrained in American memory. Today, many Native Americans feel that their presence as stereotypical images is stronger and more visible than the conditions of their lives, their poverty, and their political struggles. Legally, Native Americans are again disenfranchised by virtue of this history of powerlessness and representation, because laws of trademark privilege dominant public meanings in the allocation of rights. Here, critics of Native peoples' complaints about trademarks unconsciously articulate the law's logic when they assert that whatever a mark might originally have represented, it no longer has this meaning. Nicknames, mascots, and rituals are not racist, they suggest, because through their very longevity they have acquired a distinctive meaning apart from whatever Indian origins they might have had—they are now primarily and most meaningfully aspects of the traditions of the teams they distinguish. So, for example, John Cooke asserts that the word *Redskins* simply means football in Washington, D.C., and the NFL commissioner quite plausibly states that "fans don't identify, for example, Redskins with Native Americans."[43]

The legal doctrine of secondary meaning supports these claims. To the extent that a descriptive term has come by extensive use as a mark in commerce to be associated with a particular manufacturer, retailer, or service provider, it will be recognized as a signifier to which that entity has exclusive rights, by virtue of the fact that the public now associates the term with its wares. For Native peoples, however, these new meanings and their public recognition are products of (and an ongoing source of) injustices they have historically suffered. Many Native American names, for example, are more prominent due to their mass reproduction as trademarks than are their original referents. People hear Winnebago used to refer to vehicles more often than they do to refer to a people; they are more likely to know Oneida as a silverware than as a tribal group in Wisconsin, and to recognize Pontiac as a brand of car, not as a statesman of historical repute.

To tell Native Americans that these terms no longer refer to them is not to make a mistake of fact, but simply to reiterate this injury. It is yet another of the many ways in which Native Americans are reminded of their symbolic status as invisible, vanquished, and vanishing peoples, whose images serve primarily as effigies in national culture. Victims of the frontier and symbols of its loss in the nation's imaginary, they have figured as a meaningful absence for so long that their contemporary presence struggles to find visibility and voice. Commercial imitations of their embodied alterity mark their continuing colonization in mass-mediated culture, precluding full political engagement in the public sphere.

We know, however, that "in the objectification of the scopic drive there is always the threatened return of the look."[44] If the powers bestowed by trademark laws serve primarily to protect the entrenched privileges of those who hold proprietary rights in these stereotypes, the economic and symbolic power of the trademark ironically also provides sites for emergent forms of counterpublicity. The very public recognition that makes a trademark so valuable provides public opportunities to effect forms of *detournement* that American Indian media activists and their supporters have ingeniously exploited. The annual nature of sports spectacles affords regular occasions for counterpublicity, as do the accomplishments of teams that bring them to media center stage. At such times, the nicknames, mascots, and other marks of team distinction are pervasive, and anything relating to these teams is news and thus likely to attract national media coverage. Ironically, then, Native Americans may receive more public attention and media respect (as well as new hostilities) for their grievances and problems at precisely the moments when these stereotypes are most prominent. As Vernon Bellecourt of the National Coalition Against Racism in Sports and Media ruefully acknowledges, unlike so many other Native American issues, "a story about the offensiveness of the name of a football team will get coverage from coast to coast."[45] On occasion, protesters have mimicked the forms of corporeal specularity endemic to sports arenas to make their point. Cross-dressing as "pilgrims" and "Quakers" at sports events for media consumption, Indian activists have appropriated their opponents' practices of embodying alterity in their tactics of counterpublicity. The real challenge for Native activists may be to use the media attention that accrues goodwill for the trademark to dispel old stereotypes and to educate the public about a wider range of Indian social concerns.[46]

A quarter century of protest has failed to erase racist stereotypes in professional sports arenas (although reforms at the levels of primary, high school, and college athletics have been effected, state legislatures have shown support, and media sympathy for the issue has grown). Legal grounds are increasingly proffered for challenging the intellectual property rights in such images—including trademark expungement proceedings, defamation suits, passing-off litigation, publicity rights claims, and state civil rights actions—the most ambitious of these being the effort to seek cancellation of federal registration for the "Redskins" trademark.[47] Legal challenges to the use of these marks have thus far failed to induce any professional teams to change their names, but they too serve to keep the issue of racism toward Native Americans in the national spotlight.[48] They also create negative publicity for team owners, a form of pressure that might ultimately yield other dividends for Indian peoples. To be effective, however, pressure upon trademark holders who exploit embodied alterity need not necessarily be so direct, as the following discussion will illustrate.

Trademark Rumors and Corporeal Vulnerability

FILA® brand sportswear became popular among inner-city youth, who used the expensive goods to mark local hierarchies. Once aware of the products' popularity among minority youth, the manufacturer targeted this market with a new jean carrying the trademark TAG. Among gang members, a kill is called a tag. Accusations circulated that the corporation was deliberately promoting violence.[49]

Rumors of corporate promotion of violence through the deployment of trademarks allude to an anxious ambivalence at the heart of consumer cultures;

273

they may also constitute a unique form of cultural politics. The nature of corporate power, I will suggest, is both acknowledged and (temporarily) arrested in the rumors that people spread about the meanings of corporate trademarks.[50] Indirectly commenting upon corporately disseminated and mass-mediated "culture" in so-called postindustrial societies and registering an anxiety about corporate anonymity, they provoke corporate publicity efforts and may compel companies to assume higher profiles and new social obligations.

As production moves offshore and industrial landscapes become further removed from the "imaginary space of postmodernity," the power of corporations becomes increasingly dematerialized.[51] Corporate presence in the public sphere is reduced to publicity relations and the ubiquitous presence of brand names, company logos, and advertising lingo—different manifestations of the corporate trademark. Rumors, Bhabha suggests, "weave their stories around the disjunctive 'present' or the 'not-there' of discourse."[52] In the disembodied presence of the corporation and the "not-there" of production, trademark rumors assume new significance.

In the distribution of (often functionally indistinguishable) mass-market goods, trademarks have become an increasingly important site for capital investment. In the late twentieth century, the focus of commodity fetishism shifts from products to the sign values that can be made to imbue products with significance. Value lies increasingly in intangibles—well-known brand names, advertising auras, captivating slogans. Distinctive signifiers may be the most valuable assets a company owns.[53]

Trademarks legally mark a unique source of origin for mass-produced goods, but it is very difficult for consumers to trace them back to any singular location, given the complexities of corporate ownership and licensing arrangements. The brand name or logo marks an imaginary moment of contact or manufacture—in its mass-media circulation it conjures up a mysterious source of origin while it magically garners goodwill for its invisible owner.

The most famous marks receive the greatest legal protection. Through legal doctrines that permit companies to preclude the "dilution" of the positive valences of their marks, corporations with large market shares are enabled to immunize themselves against oppositional cultural strategies. Attempts to contain tactical appropriations of corporate marks of power are not, however, always successful. Clearly this is the case in instances involving rumor. Elusive and transitive, anonymous and without origin, rumors belong to no one but are possessed by all. Without identifiable source, they circulate without accountability, making them available for insurgency. Their transitivity also makes them tactically powerful as a subaltern means of communication.[54]

> Its intersubjective, communal adhesiveness lies in its enunciative aspect. Its performative power of circulation results in the contagious spreading, . . . the iterative action of rumour, its *circulation* and *contagion*, links it with panic— as one of the *affects* of insurgency. . . . uncertainty and panic is generated when an old and familiar symbol develops an unfamiliar social significance as sign through a transformation of the temporality of its representation.[55]

In rumors, Bhabha suggests, everyday and commonplace forms are transformed in archaic, awesome, and terrifying figurations; the circulation of cultural codes is disturbed by new and awful valences.[56]

> In the habitus of death and the daemonic, reverberates a form of memory that survives the sign. . . . And then suddenly from the space of the *not-there*, emerges the remembered historical agency "manifestly directed towards the memory of truth which lies in the order of symbols" . . . by which marginalized or insurgent subjects create a collective agency.[57]

Demonic others figure in many consumer rumors, and the devil seems to assume the image of evil most compelling in the spheres in which it circulates. Ku Klux Klan rumors, for instance, circulate among African Americans in postindustrial enclaves; targeting corporate powers by focusing upon their trademarks, they register historical legacies of hostility, anger, and distrust of white authorities.[58] Let me repeat one such rumor before exploring the import of such interventions in contemporary public spheres.

A line of sportswear was introduced into inner-city communities in the mid-1980s under the name Troop. As I have suggested elsewhere, the marketing campaign for the goods capitalized upon an incipient male military aesthetic among black youth.[59] Reports on community radio stations alerted consumers that the Troop trademark was owned by the Ku Klux Klan, which was deploying the mark to create public perception of an inner-city militia as a means to legitimate and fund the Klan's own paramilitary operations.[60] Troop Sport, however, was a New York firm owned by Korean and American entrepreneurs with production operations based in Asia. No Klan affiliations could be established. This errant rumor captured the public imagination.[61]

> A Chicago variation of the rumor has rap singer L.L. Cool J. ripping off a Troop jacket on the Oprah show and accusing the firm of hating blacks. The singer has never appeared on the talk show. . . . In Memphis, the rumor was that the letters in Troop stood for: To Rule Over Our Oppressed People. And in Atlanta some believed that the words "Thank you nigger for making us

275

rich" were emblazoned inside the tread of Troop's tennis shoes. . . . Troop's [black] marketing director . . . [claims] that he has gone to great lengths to disprove the alleged Klan connection. "I went to Montgomery, Alabama to a store and cut open five pairs to prove it wasn't like that."[62]

To counter the rumor, the company affirmed its allegiance to civil rights and a $200,000 public relations effort enlisted the aid of Operation Push, the NAACP, as well as black musicians and athletes. Black students were awarded scholarships, alliances were forged with black fraternities, and anti-Klan posters were distributed. Soon after, the company filed for bankruptcy. Whatever the primary cause of its business misfortunes, the injury the rumors did to the company's reputation cannot be denied.

Black response to the Troop marketing strategy—the Ku Klux Klan rumor—although false, served to connote historical truths about black male subordination. The Troop marketing strategy stirred something in the political unconscious of black Americans that surfaced in the form of a fantastic recognition of black social identity. British Knights running shoes and Reebok shoes have also been visited with accusations and beliefs about Klan affiliation (in the Reebok case, support of South African apartheid was an accompanying theme). Like Troop, Reebok publicly disclaimed the Klan affiliation and went to great lengths to repair the company's image, sending representatives out on the road to speak with African American community groups, employing black athletes to speak on its behalf, and declaring its political commitments to human rights and "a responsible corporate America."[63]

Although academic folklorists have little to say about the significance of trademarks in "mercantile legends," the following speculation by Gary Alan Fine seems apposite:

> The social-psychological rationale of these attitudes seems based on the separation of the public from the means of production and distribution. . . . separating people from the means of production under capitalism will result in alienation; this alienation provides a psychological climate in which bogey legends can flourish.[64]

Companies at the center of such rumors are usually well-known (or at least their trademarks are) and deal almost exclusively in consumer products. The management and production operations of such corporations are more anonymous: "These rumors symbolically mirror the ambivalence between knowledge of the product and ignorance of the individuals who direct the creation and marketing of these products."[65]

In conditions of postmodernity, I speculate, demonic others are used to indict systems of consumer capitalism in which the symbols that convey commodities are abstracted from the sources of their production and alienated from social constellations of meaning. Fetishes of evil are apprehended and attached to the fetishism of the commodity/sign.[66] Trademark rumors cannot, however, be reduced to any absolute alienation. This ignores the rich social significance of their symbolic content. Such rumors seem to articulate a local awareness of historical and contemporary subject positionings in the political economy of capital accumulation. Rumors attach to specific goods with specific advertising strategies that assume particular local meanings in the context of such histories. Contemporary Ku Klux Klan rumors, for instance, continue a tradition of inner-city urban folklore that focuses upon the imperiled black body and its markings by and for the purposes of others.[67] They serve both as reminders of black bodily experience and as acts of collective self-recognition in black communities.

It is perhaps neither incidental nor accidental that so many of these rumors focus upon sportswear and sporting goods, given the significance of athletics as a potential field of upward mobility for black youth and as the domain from which so many symbols of status aspirations are drawn. I have explored the Troop rumor in more detail elsewhere as evidence of an anxiety about white enmity consequent upon the experience of having local black Signif(y)ing practices appropriated and projected back upon the community by anonymous forces of white capital.[68] The Knights and Reebok rumors also register anxieties in the black public sphere. Certainly the rage for athletic footwear in the 1980s concerned many in black communities. Some black leaders accused athletic-wear companies of stoking confrontational violence by inspiring lust for their goods. In 1990, for example, the Reverend Jesse Jackson urged black consumers to boycott products manufactured by Nike because the company had shown so little corporate responsibility toward the black community.[69]

Although one of the world's largest athletic footwear manufacturers, Reebok had a vision of American corporate responsibility at the time that did not seem to include the provision of any manufacturing jobs in the African American communities that constituted so great a share of its market. Like other corporations, it had adopted strategies of flexible capital accumulation, shifting the place(s) of its production operations to take advantage of low-wage labor and legislative regimes that impose the least onerous regulatory constraints upon its operations. The effects of global capitalist restructuring have been particularly grave for African Americans, whose neighborhoods have been left economically devastated by its attendant spatial transformations.[70]

Like Troop and other athletic-wear companies, Reebok located its manufacturing operations in China and Southeast Asia.[71] Reebok typified a pattern of disinvestment in black communities that grew throughout the 1980s—providing only low-wage service-level jobs without benefits or security, and only to those youth able to commute to the company's retail outlets. Reebok's shoes might retail for $50 to $150, but they might be produced (largely by women and children) in minimal-wage sweatshop conditions, under subcontracting arrangements, and in export-processing zones to increase profit margins. These conditions of production—or, indeed, any places of manufacture for the consumer goods with which African Americans mark status distinctions—have no visible presence in black communities. This makes rumors of demonic production and distribution more compelling than they might be if African Americans had any role in the goods' manufacture.[72]

These rumors focus on the racial body and its surveillance and susceptibility in the United States. They remark a suppressed subaltern truth by pointing to the bodily vulnerability of those whom American industry has controlled, contained, and ultimately discarded as redundant in contemporary economic conditions. Rumor, then, may be seen as a form of resistance—one of the few "weapons of the weak" in a society where culture is commodified and controlled from indeterminate sources.[73] The "folk idioms of late-twentieth-century life" are resources with which marginalized consumers contest "ubiquitous billboards, glossy advertisements, coupons, and television commercials."[74] Moreover, rumors spread in a fashion that mimics the mode in which the trademark itself makes its way into the public sphere. The nature of signifying power shapes the form of the appropriations it engenders.

If the mass media provide a surplus of anonymous, fleeting signifiers characterized by a dearth of meaning and an excess of fascination, they also seem to invite tactics of counterpublicity with similar characteristics. Traveling anonymously, without clear meaning, authority, or direction, rumors colonize the media in much the same way the trademark does. Such forms of counterpublicity reproduce patterns of commercial speech. The anonymous signs of mass-mediated corporate capital provoke anonymous others to mimic the mass circulation of commodity/signs with any means of mass reproduction accessible—graffiti, billboard defacement, sandwich boards, T-shirts, bumper stickers, talk shows, and hot lines are typical media used to repeat rumors—seizing the authority of the mass media to legitimate African American knowledge of their perceived bodily excess and real corporeal vulnerability.[75]

Such subaltern forms of counterpublicity inevitably provoke corporate response; anonymous appropriations compel corporate actors to assume greater public presence. They may provoke some companies to make more political commitments—Troop Sport and Reebok were pushed into overt political engagement and greater solidarity with African American communities and concerns. Corporate authorities often seek black authorities to validate their own benign intentions and, in so doing, publicly affirm the specificities of their consumer base (which may involve the provision of education and employment opportunities, as well as more obvious incidents of spin doctoring).

Such rumors may be seen as political in their significance, if not in their intent. As Bhabha remarks, "What articulates these sites of cultural difference and social antagonism, in the absence of the validity of interpretation, is a discourse of panic that suggests that psychic affect and social fantasy are potent forms of political identity and agency for guerilla warfare."[76] The massive investments manufacturers make to counter the influence of rumors also suggest that they are not ineffective interventions in the public sphere.[77]

The Celebrity and the Sweated Body

Trademark rumors are an indirect and subaltern means of calling corporations into account by posing a threat to the exchange value of the commodity/sign. If such rumors indirectly challenge dominant regimes of commodity fetishism, more direct oppositions to the political economy of the commodity/sign are emergent. Whereas manufacturers have been dragged into the public sphere only reluctantly by the proliferation of rumors, others with economic interests in maintaining the value of their trademarks have been more directly challenged. For years, laws protecting publicity rights have enabled the famous to capitalize upon their celebrity and to license the use of their names and likenesses in commerce.[78] Certainly many professional athletes now recognize that endorsement contracts and product merchandising arrangements afford a longer term of predictable revenue than the salaries they are likely to command as players. The commodified names and images of the famous increasingly serve as trademarks in consumer markets. These postmodern authors are only now being called into account for the global production practices upon which the value of their trademarks is consolidated.

The economic value of the commodity/sign has long been realized upon the backs of Third World women, but only recently has this phenomenon emerged as a political issue in North American public spheres. The great numbers of sports and entertainment figures who "lend" their names to lines of sportswear and athletic equipment provide a unique opportunity to effect a form of articulatory praxis that connects the economic value of the commodity/sign achieved through the marketing of fame to the economic exploitation of those who produce the goods to which it is attached. The recent controversies attaching to the labor conditions of goods bearing Kathie Lee Gifford's name suggest that new tactics for interrogating commodity fetishism are emergent. The law recognizes rights of commercial exploitation of personality only to the extent that the public associates the name, image, likeness, or other attribute with a particular individual. The celebrity is effectively capitalizing upon public recognition (as in the law of trademark proper, she is deemed to own the meanings that the public bestows upon her image as proprietary value). Only to the extent that such recognition is positive, however, are corporations likely to extend endorsement privileges, and such public figures may also be under contractual obligation to monitor their behavior (and their press) so as not to tarnish their public image. Precisely because the trademark in such instances *is* the persona of a prominent individual, a singular target of cultural authority is available for alternative assertion and associations.

Few were impressed when Gifford, who made $5 million for her Walmart "sportswear" line in 1995 alone, claimed that she was simply unaware that the clothing was produced by underage girls in Honduran sweatshops (and, it soon appeared, in New York City). When at first she appeared unconcerned with the girls who worked in these conditions (engaging in an angry tirade against the labor activist who "outed" her and threatening to sue him),[79] public opinion was not entirely sympathetic. Having consolidated her fame propounding Christian virtues, traditional family values, and a devotion to child welfare, charges of hypocrisy were inevitable. As one television commentator put it, "They hit her slam bang right where she lives."[80] A caller to a national talk show declared, "Kathie Lee is responsible. That's how she makes her money, on the name Kathie Lee. . . . when you're making money on your name, you're responsible for what's sold under that name."[81]

Not unsurprisingly, Gifford realized (with the assistance of Howard Rubenstein Associates) that the ongoing marketing value of her persona would be better served by a more overt show of concern for those whose labor commanded thirty-one cents an hour in the production of goods bearing her smiling face and her dedication to children's charities. Her decision to "do the right thing" and take up the cause of workers in the garment industry may be greeted with some cynicism, but there is no denying the political boost that this gave to labor activists in North America and abroad. As one editorial suggested: "Like it or not, Gifford's association with the sweatshops will probably do more to target outrage than a lifetime's worth of published investigative reports about the abuses."[82]

"Here's the difference between Kathie Lee and normal shit," says Jim Dwyer, the *Daily News* columnist who broke the sweatshop story that sent Frank [Gifford] scurrying to West 38th Street with crisp bills the next morning. "Last year, I did a column on kids working in a sweatshop in Sunset Park, Brooklyn. They were working 80 hours a week, no minimum wage, no over-time, terrible conditions. It got no attention at all. Zip. Zero. Now we have Kathie Lee. It's five weeks later, and $40,000 in fines and $20,000 in back wages have been paid by the owners, and there's a national forum about the issue. . . . All because of one celebrity, who is famous for *what?*"[83]

Gifford testified before congressional human rights subcommittees, helped to ensure participation at a fashion industry forum organized by Secretary of Labor Robert Reich, pressed other celebrities into assuming responsibility for the conditions under which their clothing lines are produced, and built public support for greater numbers of inspectors to monitor factory conditions. Such activities suggest hidden political possibilities for a renewed social realism in the hyperreality of celebrity. With the cooperation of her husband, a former football hero and still a player in professional sports circles, Gifford was uniquely situated to publicize and put pressure upon those who benefit from the legal protection of celebrity, and to extend more concrete protections to others. There is no guarantee that celebrities like Michael Jordan—who pitches Nike products produced by children in conditions that are alleged to involve forced labor, coerced overtime, and physical abuse—will do any more than shrug their shoulders and hope that "Nike will do the right thing, whatever that might be."[84] On the other hand, every public assertion of lack of concern has a price in terms of the merchandising value of the celebrity persona, even in the eyes of the corporations that exploit its publicity value. It is too early to tell what the ultimate consequences of these articulatory practices will be, but the legal protection of the celebrity form has provided a new site for rendering authorities accountable, publicizing the neocolonial conditions that underlie postmodern authorship, and exposing the lie of a "postindustrial" society.

Conclusion

Practices of authorial power and appropriation, authorized meanings and alternative renderings, owners' interests and others' needs cannot be addressed simply in terms of dichotomies such as domination and resistance. Romantic celebrations of insurrectionary alterity—too popular in cultural studies—cannot capture the dangerous nuances of cultural appropriation in circumstances where the very resources with which people express alterity are the properties of others. Acts of transgression, though multiply motivated, are also shaped by the juridical fields of power in which they intervene. Law provides means and forums for both legitimating and contesting dominant meanings and the social hierarchies they support.

Law is not simply an institutional forum or legitimating discourse to which social groups turn to have preexisting differences recognized; rather, more crucially, it is a central locus for the control and dissemination of those signifying forms with which social meanings are made and remade. The signifying forms around which political action mobilizes and with which social rearticulations are accomplished are attractive and compelling precisely because of the qualities of the powers legally bestowed upon them. Such mobilizations and new articulations may have political consequences when they "provoke a crisis within the process of signification and discursive address."[85]

The law creates spaces in which hegemonic struggles are enacted as well as signs and symbols whose connotations are ever at risk. Legal strategies and legal institutions may lend authority to certain interpretations while denying status to others. The recodings, reworkings, and reactivations of commodified texts celebrated in many variants of cultural studies are possible only given the contingent fixations enabled by the law's proprietary guarantees. Had intellectual property laws not protected such texts in the first instance, they would not have acquired the posterity that makes them such ideal candidates for parodic and polemic redeployments. Law's productive power as well as its sanctions and prohibitions, then, must be kept in mind.

The constitutive power of law is not simply the provision of instruments and forums through which social groups may seek to have their differences legitimated or their needs addressed (although it may be experienced in this fashion). Law also generates many of the signs and symbols—the signifying forms—with which difference is constituted and given meaning. It provides those unstable signifiers whose meanings may be historically transformed by those who wish to inscribe their own authorial signature on the people, the nation, the state—the official social text. It invites and shapes activities that legitimate, resist, and potentially rework the meanings that accrue to these forms in public spheres. Such processes of institutionalization and intervention are both ongoing and unstable, effecting unanticipated disruptions and destabilizations.

Social struggles focusing upon trademarks serve to illustrate the importance of the commodity/sign in contemporary public spheres—its modalities of signification and significance—bespeaking their allure as visual symbols of power, their capacity to interpellate subaltern subjects, and their service as sites for transgressive articulations. They enable us to see how trademarks figure in the making of imagined communities—bodies politic—and in the making and remaking of minority subjects, the racialized bodies of contemporary body politics. They remind us of the creative activities of those marginal to centers of symbolic authority who are marked by a relationship to signs they do not author but often alter in their struggles for recognition and voice. They may also attest to an emergent receptivity to articulatory practices that reconnect the postmodern, the postindustrial, and the postcolonial with the practices of bodily exploitation they avoid and obscure. Contemporary means of publicity, may, ironically, provide both new inclinations and new capacities to challenge the very commodity fetishism that gives them their force.

Notes

1. This story circulates in Toronto, and I first heard it from sociologist Mariana Valverde in the form presented here. I later learned from a friend of one of the organizers that the sign had been conceptualized as part of a citywide progressive art exhibit by Public, a nonprofit arts organization. Before it was broadcast, lawyers advised the group of its potential liability and the likelihood of injunction. A decision was made not to convey the message, but the story circulates as if the event had taken place—an apocryphal rumor that bespeaks a truth about gay and lesbian citizenship in Canada. Given the significance I attribute to rumor, it seems an especially apt anecdote.

2. An early version of this discussion of official signifiers was first published in Rosemary J. Coombe, "Tactics of Appropriation and the Politics of Recognition in Late Modern Democracies," *Political Theory* 21 (1993): 411–33. A more elaborated discussion, which is not limited to domains of sport, is found in Rosemary J. Coombe, *The Cultural Life of Intellectual Properties: Authorship, Appropriation, and the Law* (Durham, N.C.: Duke University Press, 1998), 130–65.

3. Whereas the use of other trademarks may be enjoined only when such a use is confusing to the consumer or depreciates the trademark holder's goodwill, public authorities have unlimited power to prevent (or charge exorbitant royalties for) the use of their registered marks in any and all circumstances.

4. In Canada, "no penalty is provided in the statute for the adoption and use of any such marks and s.107 of the Criminal Code, therefore, becomes applicable." Harold G. Fox, *The Canadian Law of Trademarks and Unfair Competition* (Toronto: Carswell, 1972).

5. In Canada there are more than three thousand of these signs. Listed under s.9 of the Trade Marks Act R.S.C. 1985, c.T-13, are sixteen categories of prohibited marks, including a category that includes "any . . . mark . . . adopted and used by any public authority in Canada as an official mark for wares and services, in respect of which, the Registrar . . . has given public notice of its adoption and use." The number of marks so claimed increased from five- to tenfold (i.e., 500 to 1,000 percent) from 1980 to 1985 alone. In the United States, there are probably millions of such marks, given the greater number of state jurisdictions and operative public authorities. It is impossible to know precisely, because the costs of doing searches are so exorbitant as to preclude a complete compilation. In early editions of his treatise *Trademarks and Unfair Competition* (e.g., vol. 2, 2d ed. [New York: Clark Boardman Callaghan, 1984 and 1990 supp.], 869–72), J. Thomas McCarthy includes a list of many *federally* protected names, characters, and designs, but specifies that the list is neither complete nor exhaustive.

6. See Kirsty McClure, "The Subject of Rights," in *Dimensions of Radical Democracy: Pluralism, Citizenship, Community*, ed. Chantal Mouffe (London: Verso, 1992), 108–27.

7. For a more extensive discussion of this point, see Rosemary J. Coombe, "Objects of Property and Subjects of Politics: Intellectual Property Laws and Democratic Dialogue," *Texas Law Review* 69 (1991): 1853–80.

8. Jean Baudrillard, *For a Critique of the Political Economy of the Sign* (St. Louis: Telos, 1981), 146–47.

9. In Canada, for example, "Section 9 supports public order and as such places the Crown and public authorities in a position of virtual invulnerability. An official mark is virtually unexpungeable." Roger Hughes, *Hughes on Trademarks* (Toronto: Butterworths, 1992), 453.

10. 36 U.S.C. §371–396 (1988). In particular, Section 110 of the act, set forth in 36 U.S.C. §380 (1988), provides that "the [USOC] shall have the exclusive right to use . . . the words, 'Olympic,' 'Olympian,'" and the like, subject only to lawful uses of these words established prior to 1950. Moreover, it was determined that there were no defenses available to anyone who used the term without authorization. *San Francisco Arts & Athletics, Inc. v. United States Olympic Committee*, 107 S.Ct. 2971 (1987).

11. *International Olympic Committee v. San Francisco Arts & Athletics*, 789 F.2d 1319 at 1323 (per Kozinski, J.).

12. See the historical discussion of U.S. trademark law in Rosemary J. Coombe, "Embodied Trademarks: Mimesis and Alterity on American Commercial Frontiers," *Cultural Anthropology* 11 (1996): 202–24, where I discuss instances in which the boundaries of national frontiers are negotiated in commercial idiom.

13. For examples, see Nicholas Garnham, "The Mass Media, Cultural Identity, and the Public Sphere in the Modern World," *Public Culture* 5 (1993): 251–65; Dana Polan, "The Public's Fear: Or, Media as Monster in Habermas, Negt, and Kluge," in *The Phantom Public Sphere*, ed. Bruce Robbins (Minneapolis: University of Minnesota Press, 1993), 33–41; Michael Warner, "The Mass Public and the Mass Subject," in *The Phantom Public Sphere*, ed. Bruce Robbins (Minneapolis: University of Minnesota Press, 1993), 234–56. I use the term *commodity/sign* to reflect the fact that the trademark is both a commodity with an exchange value in its own right and a sign that condenses the relationships among a signifier, a signified, and a referent (linking, for example, a logo, a lifestyle, and a product).

14. Warner, "The Mass Public and the Mass Subject," 243.

15. See Anne McClintock, *Imperial Leather: Gender, Race, and Sexuality in the Colonial Contest* (London: Routledge, 1995). For discussions of images of alterity in advertising with respect to consumer goods, see Raymond William Stedman, *Shadows of the*

Indian: Stereotypes in American Culture (Norman: University of Oklahoma Press, 1982); Piterse Van Nederveen, *White on Black: Images of Africa and Blacks in Western Popular Culture* (New Haven, Conn.: Yale University Press, 1992); William O'Barr, *Culture and the Ad: Exploring the World of Otherness in the World of Advertising* (Boulder, Colo.: Westview, 1994).

16. This discussion is drawn from Coombe, *The Cultural Life of Intellectual Properties*, 166–207.

17. Mark Shuman, "Native Voice," *Denver Post*, 28 January 1996, citing Tim Giago. See also Tim Giago, "Indian-Named Mascots Like Those in World Series Assault Self-Esteem," *Buffalo News*, 26 October 1995, 3.

18. See, for example, Joe P. Hutchinson, "Nuances of a Nickname," *Arizona Republic*, 5 November 1995, C5.

19. Quoted in Dan Burkhart, "Turner Won't Change Braves' Name, But Wouldn't Mind Stopping the Chop," *Atlanta Journal*, 3 December 1991, at F8.

20. See Roy Harvey Pearce, *Savagism and Civilization: A Study of the Indian and the American Mind* (Berkeley: University of California Press, 1988 [1953]); Deborah Root, *Cannibal Culture: Art, Appropriation, and the Commodification of Difference* (Boulder, Colo.: Westview, 1996); Richard Slotkin, *Regeneration through Violence: The Mythology of the American Frontier* (Middletown, Conn.: Wesleyan University Press, 1973).

21. Joseph Roach, *Cities of the Dead: Circum-Atlantic Performance* (New York: Columbia University Press, 1996), 205.

22. Such others are often represented as Indians, even when they are encountered in Cuba or Vietnam. See Richard Drinnon, *Facing West: The Metaphysics of Indian-Hating and Empire Building* (Berkeley: University of California Press, 1980).

23. Homi K. Bhabha, *The Location of Culture* (London: Routledge, 1994), 67.

24. Ibid., 66.

25. "Kinesthetic imagination is a faculty of memory [that] . . . inhabits the realm of the virtual. . . . its truth is the truth of stimulation, of fantasy (although its social effects may be tangible indeed)." Roach, *Cities of the Dead*, 27.

26. Pierre Bourdieu, "Programme for a Sociology of Sport," in *In Other Words: Essays Towards a Reflexive Sociology* (Stanford, Calif.: Stanford University Press, 1990), 167.

27. Milind Wakankar, "Body, Crowd, Identity: Genealogy of a Hindu Nationalist Ascetics," *Social Text* 14, no. 4 (1995): 59, citing Bourdieu, "Programme for a Sociology of Sport," 167.

28. This is a composite of the many ritualized behaviors that accompany games played by teams with "Indian" names (by both fans and fans of opposing teams). No single event would encompass all of these, and some of these performances are specific to particular teams.

29. Eric Lott, *Love and Theft: Blackface Minstrelsy and the American Working Class* (New York: Oxford University Press, 1993), 8.

30. Ibid.

31. Ibid., 68–69.

32. Ibid., 96. See also Michael Rogin, "Blackface, White Noise: The Jewish Jazz Singer Finds His Voice," *Critical Inquiry* 12 (1992): 426.

33. Lott, *Love and Theft*, 98.

34. Roach, *Cities of the Dead*, 3.

35. According to Peter Stallybrass and Allon White, in such constructions of subjectivity we see "a psychological dependence upon precisely those Others which are being rigorously opposed and excluded at the social level." Peter Stallybrass and Allon White, *The Politics and Poetics of Transgression* (Ithaca, N.Y.: Cornell University Press, 1986), 5.

36. Roach, *Cities of the Dead*, 6.

37. Ibid., 6–7.
38. Ibid., 36.
39. Ibid.
40. Ibid.
41. Lott, *Love and Theft*, 99.
42. There is a long history in North America of cultural cross-dressing, of which the Boston Tea Party, with its howling "Indians" and "blacks," is perhaps the most famous example. Masked bands of "Indians" were part of nineteenth-century charivaris in which contemporary social mores and behaviors were commented upon. There are also many instances of whites representing themselves as Indian sages, translating Indianness for white audiences while fulfilling stereotypical anticipations of authentic Indianness (and getting far more attention in the public sphere than actual Native activists struggling for their people's political rights and economic survival). New Age shamanism and some ecofeminisms provide recent examples.
43. Quoted in Bruce Kelber, "Scalping the Redskins," *Hamline Law Review* 17 (1994): 548.
44. Bhabha, *The Location of Culture*, 81.
45. Quoted in Doug Grow, "The Way to Redskins Owner's Heart Is through His Wallet," *Star Tribune*, 11 September 1992, 3B.
46. Many Native activists recognize the publicity potential thus afforded. For example, Ed Choate, assistant sports editor of the *Times-Picayune* and a Mississippi Choctaw, asserted that more care had been taken in professional sports to represent birds correctly than to avoid racial caricatures of Indians. However, he used the forum provided by the World Series to address issues of Native American poverty, high school dropout rates, suicide, the health of the elderly, and cultural extinction. See Ed Choate, "Mascots Not the Biggest Issue," *Times-Picayune*, 29 October 1995, C3.
47. If successful, the action would end the exclusive rights that the Washington team has in this appellation. This will not, however, preclude others from using the term, but will only prevent the team's ability to enforce its rights against others (and thus diminish licensing revenues). It is assumed that the loss of these rights would devalue the trademark so dramatically that the team would voluntarily abandon it.
48. Because nearly all stadium construction requires public funding or the posting of bonds, state legislatures are in a position to deny funds and make such bonds difficult to obtain by prohibiting discrimination against Native Americans, the use of disparaging images, and mockery of Native American symbols. State civil rights powers also create opportunities to control such imagery with respect to public schools and other publicly funded institutions.
49. This rumor was reported to me by an anthropology graduate student at the annual meeting of the Society for Cultural Anthropology in 1994.
50. This argument is developed at greater length in Rosemary J. Coombe, "The Demonic Space of the 'Not There': Trademark Rumors in the Postindustrial Imaginary," in *Culture, Power, Place: Critical Exploration in Anthropology*, ed. James Ferguson and Akhil Gupta (Durham, N.C.: Duke University Press, 1997), 249–74. Here, I evoke only those examples that deal with sportswear.
51. The term *postindustrial* should be approached with great caution. I use the term here to refer to a *perception* of industrial production's disappearance and some of the cultural manifestations of this structure of feeling. For good discussions of these issues, see Grant Kester, "Out of Sight Is Out of Mind: The Imaginary Space of Postindustrial Culture," *Social Text* 35 (1993): 72–92; Neil Lazarus, "Doubting the New World Order: Marxism, Realism, and the Claims of Postmodernist Social Theory," *Differences* 3, no. 3 (1991): 94–138.

52. Bhabha, *The Location of Culture,* 200.

53. For discussions of the multimillion-dollar trademark, see Thomas Drescher, "Article and Report: The Transformation and Evolution of Trademarks—From Signals to Symbols to Myth," *Trademark Reporter* 82 (1992): 301–40; Richard Barnet and John Cavanagh, *Global Dreams: Imperial Corporations and the New World Order* (New York: Simon & Schuster, 1994). Failure to police the use of marks creates the legal risk of losing exclusive rights over them. Once trademarks fall into the public domain, they cease to have exchange value: a nonexclusive license is worth very little on the market, and revenue streams are diminished if they don't entirely dry up.

54. Gayatri C. Spivak, "Subaltern Studies: Deconstructing Historiography," in *Selected Subaltern Studies,* ed. Ranajit Guha and Gayatri C. Spivak (New York: Oxford University Press, 1988), 23.

55. Bhabha, *The Location of Culture,* 200-202.

56. Ibid.

57. Ibid., 199–200.

58. In her compelling book *I Heard It through the Grapevine: Rumor in African-American Culture* (Berkeley: University of California Press, 1993), Pauline Turner discusses the central role of the KKK in African American subcultures and their demonic reputation.

59. See Coombe, "Tactics of Appropriation."

60. I am grateful to Kathleen Pirrie Adams for her insights into this issue.

61. Spivak, "Subaltern Studies," 23.

62. "Klan Rumor Helped Ruin Sport Clothing Firm," *San Francisco Chronicle,* 22 July 1989.

63. Turner, *I Heard It through the Grapevine,* 130–31.

64. Gary Alan Fine, "The Goliath Effect: Corporate Dominance and Mercantile Legends," *Journal of American Folklore* 98 (1985): 80.

65. Gary Alan Fine, "Among Those Dark Satanic Mills: Rumors of Kooks, Cults and Corporations," *Southern Folklore* 47 (1990): 144. Despite references to the "post-industrial state," Fine does not suggest any reason people in a postindustrial society would be any more suspicious of corporate power than those of an industrial age.

66. See Coombe, "Tactics of Appropriation"; Coombe, "The Demonic Space."

67. Apologists for slavery in the eighteenth and nineteenth centuries often claimed that Africans had been visited with an ancient, if not biblical, "curse" that "marked" them for slavery. See the discussion in Diane Roberts, *The Myth of Aunt Jemima: Representing Race and Region* (New York: Routledge, 1994).

68. See Coombe, "The Demonic Space."

69. "Although African-American consumers purchase 30 percent of all Nike shoes, blacks had no Nike executive positions, no subcontracting arrangements, and no seats on the company's board of directors; moreover, the footwear giant did not advertise with black-owned media outlets. With the possible exception of such celebrity spokesmen as film director Spike Lee and basketball superstar Michael Jordan, both of whom received large sums in exchange for product endorsements, Nike simply was not sharing its profits with blacks." Turner, *I Heard It through the Grapevine,* 173.

70. Michael Dawson, "A Black Counterpublic? Economic Earthquakes, Racial Agendas and Black Politics," *Public Culture* 7 (1994): 209.

71. See the discussion in Barnet and Cavanagh, *Global Dreams.*

72. For further discussion of the role of the trademark in the configuration of African and African American identities in inner-city contexts, and of the conflicted politics of the black public sphere in conditions of economic globalization, see Rosemary J. Coombe and Paul Stoller, "X Marks the Spot: The Ambiguities of African Trading in the Politics

of the Black Public Sphere," in *The Black Public Sphere*, ed. Black Public Sphere Collective (Chicago: University of Chicago Press, 1995), 249–85.

73. For further discussion, see Fine, "The Goliath Effect"; Turner, *I Heard It through the Grapevine*.

74. Turner, *I Heard It through the Grapevine*, 178.

75. Many rumors contain accounts of their own verification in the media (for example, "It must be true, a friend of mine heard it on *Oprah*"). For an account of the way in which rumors are validated by further rumors of national media accounts, see Turner, *I Heard It through the Grapevine*, 84.

76. Bhabha, *The Location of Culture*, 203.

77. Cited in Turner, *I Heard It through the Grapevine*, 166.

78. For a longer discussion of publicity rights and the politics of allocating exclusive rights in celebrity images, see Rosemary J. Coombe, "Author/izing the Celebrity: Publicity Rights, Postmodern Politics, and Unauthorized Genders," in *The Construction of Authorship: Textual Appropriations in Law and Literature*, ed. Martha Woodmansee and Peter Jaszi (Durham, N.C.: Duke University Press, 1994), 101–31.

79. Charles Kernaghan, head of the New York-based National Labor Committee, has also exposed U.S. government-sponsored exploitation in Haiti and mobilized consumers to put pressure on the Gap to improve working conditions for Latin American workers.

80. Susan Rook, *Talk Back Live*, Cable News Network, Inc., 4 June 1996, Transcript 415.

81. Ibid.

82. "Editorial," *San Francisco Chronicle*, 11 June 1996, a22.

83. Cited in Barbara Lippert, "How Does She Do It?" *New York Magazine*, 22 July 1996, 34–39.

84. Quoted in Caroline Brewer, "Disney, Others Profit by Exploiting Child Labor," *Bergin Record*, 18 June 1996, N11, in a discussion of labor conditions in Southeast Asia, where many sporting goods manufacturers have their products made.

85. Homi K. Bhabha, "DissemiNation: Time, Narrative, and the Margins of the Modern Nation," in *Nation and Narration*, ed. Homi K. Bhabha (London: Routledge, 1990), 297.

Contributors

Rosemary J. Coombe is associate professor of law at the University of Toronto. She writes on the local and global politics of intellectual property protections and the social life of commodified signs in transnational contexts. She is the author of *The Cultural Life of Intellectual Properties: Authorship, Appropriation, and the Law.*

Grant Farred, an avid fan of West Indian cricket, is editor of *Rethinking C. L. R. James* and author of *Midfielder's Moment: Politics, Literature, and Culture in Contemporary South Africa* (forthcoming).

Qadri Ismail teaches postcolonial studies in the Department of English at the University of Minnesota. He has coedited a collection of essays, *Unmaking the Nation: The Politics of Identity and History in Modern Sri Lanka.* He wishes he had the opportunity to watch more cricket.

May Joseph is assistant professor in performance studies at New York University. She is the author of *Nomadic Identities: The Performance of Citizenship* (Minnesota, 1999) and coeditor (with Jennifer Natalya Fink) of *Performing Hybridity* (Minnesota, 1999). She is on the editorial boards of *Cultural Studies* and the *Journal of Sport & Social Issues* and has been a guest editor of *Women and Performance.*

Bradley S. Klein is assistant professor of government at Clark University in Massachusetts. He is also the architecture editor for *Golfweek.* His publications include *Strategic Studies and World Order,* numerous essays on international relations and modernity, and a collection of his golf essays, *Rough Meditations.*

Heather Levi is a doctoral student in anthropology at New York University. She has recently returned from fieldwork with professional wrestlers in Mexico City, where she learned (among other things) to both give and receive a flying crossbody from the third rope. Her articles have appeared in *Social Text* and *Sexualities.*

Gitanjali Maharaj is completing a doctorate in the American studies program at New York University, with a focus on postcolonial theory. Her current work is in the area of organizational transformation and change management, and her articles have been published in *Social Text, Current Writing,* and *Diva: Quarterly Journal of South Asian Women.* She resides in Cape Town, South Africa, and works for a public interest organization devoted to social justice and sustainable democracy.

Randy Martin is professor and chair of the Department of Social Science at Pratt Institute. He is author of *Performance as Political Act: The Embodied Self; Socialist Ensembles: Theater and State in Cuba and Nicaragua* (Minnesota, 1994); and *Critical Moves: Dance Studies in Theory and Politics.*

Jim McKay is associate professor in the Department of Anthropology and Sociology at the University of Queensland. He is the editor of the *International Review for the Sociology of Sport.* His most recent books are *No Pain, No Gain? Sport and Australian Culture; Managing Gender: Affirmative Action and Organizational Power in Australian, Canadian, and New Zealand Sport;* and (with Michael Messner and Donald Sabo) *Men, Masculinities, and Sport.*

Toby Miller is associate professor of cinema studies at New York University. He is the author of *The Well-Tempered Self: Citizenship, Culture, and the Postmodern Subject; Contemporary Australian Television; The Avengers; Technologies of Truth: Cultural Citizenship and the Popular Media* (Minnesota, 1998); and *Popular Culture and Everyday Life.* He is coeditor of *Social Text,* editor of the *Journal of Sport & Social Issues,* and coeditor of the Sport and Culture book series for the University of Minnesota Press.

Michael Real is professor and director of the School of Communication at San Diego State University. His books include *Exploring Media Culture, Super Media,* and *Mass-Mediated Culture.* His articles have appeared in dozens of scholarly and popular publications. He holds a Ph.D. from the University of Illinois and has directed a variety of local, national, and international research and production projects. His work is focused on media, culture, and social responsibility.

Bruce Robbins teaches English and comparative literature at Rutgers University. He is the author of *Secular Vocations: Intellectuals, Professionalism, Culture* and *The Servant's Hand: English Fiction from Below,* and the editor of *Intellectuals: Aesthetics, Politics, Academics* (Minnesota, 1990), *The Phantom Public Sphere* (Minnesota, 1993), and (with Pheng Cheah) *Cosmopolitics:*

Thinking and Feeling beyond the Nation (Minnesota, 1998). He is a former coeditor of *Social Text*.

David Rowe is associate professor in the Department of Leisure and Tourism Studies at the University of Newcastle, Australia. He has published many articles in international academic journals such as *Cultural Studies, Media, Culture & Society*, the *Sociology of Sport Journal*, and the *Journal of Sport & Social Issues*, and is a frequent commentator in print and electronic media. The author of *Popular Cultures: Rock Music, Sport, and the Politics of Pleasure*, he has edited three books (with Geoffrey Lawrence): *Power Play: Essays in the Sociology of Australian Sport, Sport and Leisure: Trends in Australian Popular Culture*, and *Tourism, Leisure, Sport: Critical Perspectives*. He also contributed to Stuart Cunningham and Toby Miller's book *Contemporary Australian Television*. His latest book is *Sport, Culture, and the Media: The Unruly Trinity*.

Amanda Smith is the presenter of *The Sports Factor* on Australian radio, a program broadcast weekly on the Australian Broadcasting Corporation's Radio National network. *The Sports Factor*, established by Smith at the beginning of 1995, seeks to debate and discuss events and issues in sport in a wide social and cultural context.

Jon Stratton is associate professor of cultural studies at Curtin University of Technology, Perth, Western Australia. He has published widely in the area of cultural studies, his most recent book being *The Desirable Body: Cultural Fetishism and the Erotics of Consumption*.

Permissions

The University of Minnesota Press gratefully acknowledges permission to reprint the following essays in this volume.

"The Nation in White: Cricket in a Postapartheid South Africa," by Grant Farred, was originally published under the same title in *Social Text* 50 (spring 1997), 9–32. Copyright 1997, Duke University Press; reprinted with permission.

"Batting against the Break: On Cricket, Nationalism, and the Swashbuckling Sri Lankans," by Qadri Ismail, was originally published under the same title in *Social Text* 50 (spring 1997), 33–56. Copyright 1997, Duke University Press; reprinted with permission.

"The Composite Body: Hip-Hop Aerobics and the Multicultural Nation," by Randy Martin, was originally published in *Journal of Sport & Social Issues* 21, no. 2 (May 1997), 120–33. Copyright 1997; reprinted by permission of Sage Publications, Inc.

"On Mexican Pro Wrestling: Sport as Melodrama," by Heather Levi, was originally published as "Sport and Melodrama: The Case of Mexican Professional Wrestling," by Heather Levi, in *Social Text* 50 (spring 1997), 57–68. Copyright 1997, Duke University Press; reprinted with permission.

"Field of Soaps: *Rupert v. Kerry* as Masculine Melodrama," by David Rowe and Jim McKay, was originally published under the same title in *Social Text* 50 (spring 1997), 69–86. Copyright 1997, Duke University Press; reprinted with permission.

"Talking Trash: Late Capitalism, Black (Re)Productivity, and Professional Basketball," by Gitanjali Maharaj, was originally published under the same title in *Social Text* 50 (spring 1997), 97–110. Copyright 1997, Duke University Press; reprinted with permission.

"Head Fake: Mentorship and Mobility in *Hoop Dreams*," by Bruce Robbins, was originally published under the same title in *Social Text* 50 (spring 1997), 111–20. Copyright 1997, Duke University Press; reprinted with permission.

"Back-Page Bylines: Newspapers, Women, and Sport. An Interview with Liz Kahn, Mary Jollimore, and Wanda Jamrozik," by Amanda Smith, was originally